Forward

I believe the greatest need of the church is intimacy "one thing" that is necessary. It's important to spend time live in His victory, and it's not easy in our distracted culture first. The enemy's first question, "Did God really say?", is the one that he's still attacking our culture with today. While we need fresh experience with God, we must have it built on the eternal foundation He has laid in His word. The greatest blessing God can release to us is Himself. I pray that you will encounter Him afresh as you journey through these readings. I hope you experience as much joy in reading them as I did in writing them!

To Dom & Karly with much love!

Tom

One Thing

"The Lord answered and said to her, 'Martha, Martha, you are worried about so many things; but only a few things are necessary, really only one, for Mary has chosen the good part, which shall not be taken from her."
Luke 10:41-42

Mary chose the good part. She was "listening to the Lord's words, seated at His feet." (Luke 10:39) She was enjoying the Lord, being refreshed by His presence and changed by His words.

Jesus said this was the one necessary choice. All the rest of life will flow out of this vital relationship if we will just make it our priority. "Necessary means something you cannot do without."

Martha hadn't made that choice. She loved the Lord but she was "distracted with all her preparations." (Luke 10:40) Jesus implied that she was living the bad part; serving Jesus without enjoying Jesus. Giving and giving and giving without receiving from His Word and presence. Distracted from the glorious One by our busy lives that are supposed to be in service to Him.

Have you ever fallen into this trap? Life gets busy. Priorities get mixed up and pretty soon the urgent rather than the important starts dominating our lives. We stop really living and find ourselves barely surviving.

We usually, like Martha, find someone else to blame. "Lord, do You not care that my sister has left me to do all the serving alone? Then tell her to help me." (Luke 10:40) What's she really saying? "Lord, don't you see that I'm burnt out – do something! It's Mary's fault! It's the church's fault or my spouse's fault or my boss' fault"...the list goes on.

Jesus is gentle but firm: "What Mary has, she has chosen – she has chosen and she has chosen correctly. I'm not going to take away her joy because you're miserable. Martha, you too can have what Mary has. Choose to fellowship with Me. Let your service be fueled by My Presence." (my paraphrase)

Jesus said, "Come to Me you who are weary and heavy laden and I will give you rest." (Matthew 11:28) Do this one thing and continue to do it and everything else in your life will take its proper place.

January 1

Intimacy with God

"Then the eyes of both of them were opened, and they knew that they were naked; and they sewed fig leaves together and made themselves loin coverings. They heard the sound of the Lord God walking in the garden in the cool of the day, and the man and his wife hid themselves from the presence of the Lord God among the trees of the garden. Then the Lord God called to the man, and said to him, 'Where are you?'" Genesis 3:7-9

You and I were created for intimacy with God. After the fall God came to the garden to walk with Adam and Eve and they were hiding from His presence. The fact that walking with Him was a habit is evident by the reason they were hiding: "They heard the sound of the Lord walking..." How did they know it was the Lord and not an animal or the wind? I think it was the time of day He regularly came, and He never missed this appointment. You'd think that their sin would have caused the Lord to stay away, but He came as He always did as if to say, "I haven't left the place of intimacy, you have."

He asked, "Where are you?" not to get information, but to bring this first couple to a place of confession. This is the first question God asked in the Bible and I believe that He is still asking it today: "Where are you?" People today are hiding from God and from one another and it is leading to emptiness and depression because we were made for intimacy. Some of us hide in our work, others in bitterness, still others in alcohol, entertainment, or pornography, yet God is still asking, "where are you?"

Genesis 3:21 says, "The Lord God made garments of skin for Adam and his wife, and clothed them." The killing of an innocent animal to make a skin is the first physical death in the Bible and it points to the need for a sacrifice to make atonement. Jesus was the Lamb of God who was sacrificed for the sins of the world. All that was required for Adam and Eve to have God clothe them was to take off the fig leaves they had sewn to hide themselves, and put on the skin that God had made. Today God calls us to lay down whatever front we're hiding behind; whether it be pride, religious behavior, or our own self-righteousness, and confess our faith in His sacrifice. He Himself then clothes us with the righteousness of Christ so that we can be forgiven and restored to His Presence. He's still asking, "where are you?" today because He still longs to walk with each of us in the place of restored intimacy.

January 2

Walking with God

"Enoch walked with God; and he was not, for God took him." Genesis 5:24

You were made to walk with God. Before the fall God would meet with Adam and Eve in the cool of the day to walk together in a place of intimacy. After they fell, He gave a promise and a picture of what He was going to do in Jesus Christ to restore the place of intimacy, but it doesn't seem like anyone until Enoch really got a hold of what God was after. Enoch walked with God. It doesn't say he did any great thing, or that he built any huge monument, or that he held any important position; the Bible just says that he walked with God. This is the heart of what God wants from you and me.

We owned a Siberian husky named Kayla who was very hard to walk with. I'd get out of the house and be jerked forward because Kayla couldn't wait to go as fast as possible, but was restrained by the leash that would practically choke her. To take the strain off, I would start to run with her and we'd go along for awhile like that until she found something interesting along the way and then stop, so suddenly it would cause another jerk on her neck as I ran past her because I couldn't stop as fast as she did. I'd wait patiently for a while and then have to pull hard, once again almost choking her, to get her to leave the thing she was enamored with. I just wanted her to walk by me, but that rarely happened.

I think this is a good picture of God and us. As young believers we are often filled with our own ideas and zeal so we run ahead of God. We get self-righteous because others aren't doing as much as we are, or being as "holy" as we think we are, and the whole time the Lord is trying to pull us back to the place of intimacy where He is the center of attention, and not us. Or we get enamored by something along life's way and we get stuck. It could be a sin, our work, sports, shopping, or even a hobby that so dominates our thoughts and attention that God is put aside. The Lord begins by pulling gently and then has to tug harder, because we aren't responding.

My favorite part of our walk was when we got in the country and Kayla could run free because there was no danger. I loved to see her run uninhibited and then gladly run to me when I called her. This is the freedom God wants for each of us.

The Lord doesn't want to have to continually discipline us to keep us safe; He wants us to draw near willingly and learn to simply walk with Him.

January 3

The Longing of God's Heart

"How often I have longed to gather your children together, as a hen gathers her chicks under her wings, but you were not willing." Luke 13:34

Parents and all those in authority are used to taking care of everyone else, so it's often hard to allow someone else to take care of us, even God. Why were the Jews unwilling to allow God to intimately care for them as He longed to do? I think it was because it meant they would have to humble themselves and admit they were really just vulnerable little chicks who needed to be taken care of.

We pride ourselves in America on our ability to be independent. The books on success encourage us to tell ourselves we are strong and can do anything we set our mind to do. But the truth is that we are not strong in ourselves, and we aren't mother hens who are able to take care of everyone else. We too, are only little chicks, who need to be gathered under the wings of God.

Isn't it awesome that the all sufficient One has a longing at all? He has a longing we can meet by simply acknowledging that we are not as important as we thought, we aren't as smart as we appear, and we are not as invincible as we would want everyone else to believe. We are in fact, like little chicks who need to be gathered under the wings of our Savior to simply be held and protected by Him. Could there be a more intimate picture than a chick being hidden in the secret place of its mother's wings? God longs to have you and me that close to Him.

I love this truth even though I easily forget it. I often pray something like this, "Lord, here I am, your little chick. Go ahead and meet the longing of Your heart by holding me. Go ahead and do what you've been waiting to do, pour out your grace upon me." David prayed along these lines in Psalm 61:4: "I long to dwell in your tent forever and take refuge in the shelter of your wings." Is it any wonder he is remembered as the man after God's own heart, when His longing to dwell under God's wing was matched by God's longing to gather him to that place of intimate care?

Maybe you've been weary taking care of everyone else and today you need to let God take care of you. Why don't you pray right now and ask Him?

January 4

Bored

"All things are wearisome... That which has been done is that which will be done. So, there is nothing new under the sun. Is there anything of which one might say, 'See this, it is new?'" Ecclesiastes 1:8-10

King Solomon was in the same state that many Americans are in today. He was bored. He had money, position, and time to do everything and anything he wanted, so he tried it all and still found himself bored. He sought after pleasure through laughter, alcohol, and sex. He sought satisfaction through work, education and the accumulation of wealth. (See Ecclesiastes 2) After all of his pursuits he said, "All that my eyes desired I did not refuse them.... Thus I considered all my activities which my hands had done and the labor which I had exerted and behold all was vanity and striving after wind and there was no profit under the sun." (Ecclesiastes 2:10)

Under the sun. That's the key. If all you live for is that which is under the sun, your life will be mediocre at best. You may have an existence, but you won't really live. You may accumulate a lot of stuff, and have lots of toys, but eventually they will bore you. For instance, I don't think many Americans are caught up in gambling today because they want to get rich. I think it's because they are bored with life under the sun, and gambling gives them a little excitement.

There's a better way. Seek for the One who is over the sun. Jesus said, "Behold, I make all things new." (Revelation 21:5) When a person truly lives for God a new purpose guides their activities; a new excitement comes into even the mundane duties of life. "Whatever you do, work at it with all your heart, as working for the Lord, not for men, since you know that you will receive an inheritance from the Lord as a reward." (Colossians 3:23-24) All of a sudden housework becomes holy. You're not just cleaning for your family, you're cleaning for Jesus. Work becomes more challenging because you're not just trying to please the boss, who only checks once in a while, you're trying to please the real Boss, who is watching all of the time. Life is exciting over the sun.

Are you bored? Stir yourself to seek the One who makes all things new.

January 5

The Heart of God

"But while he was still a long way off, his father saw him and was filled with compassion for him; he ran to his son, threw his arms around him and kissed him." Luke 15:20

Hopefully we have all heard the truth many times: "God loves you." But what does that really mean? Jesus tells a story in Luke chapter 15 to explain God's emotions for sinful human beings.

A son leaves home demanding that he get his share of the inheritance. He spends it all quickly, carelessly, and sinfully, and when he runs out of money he works for a farmer, but is paid so little that he longs for the food the pigs are eating. At this point he decides that he will go home, admit his sins, acknowledge that he is no longer a part of the family, and ask to become a hired man.

The hired man in that culture worked for a slave's wages but didn't stay in the house. The prodigal's feeling was that his father might be willing to provide for him, but that he would not want to be close to him, or to even have him around.

Do you ever think that's how God feels about you? He may meet your needs because He is good. He may forgive your sins because Jesus died for them and legally He has to. But the bottom line is that He doesn't really like you, or desire you because of the person you've been. I think a lot of us can feel this way in our hearts even though our minds may be able to give all the right answers. Perhaps we don't really know God's heart for us.

As the prodigal starts home, he may have been rehearsing to himself all of his sins and wondering what kind of a reception he would receive. Would it be avoidance; the lights are all shut off, the door is locked and no one answers no matter how many times he knocks? Or would it be guilt; "Do you have any idea what you have put your mother and I through..." with a rehashing of all his sins after all their generosity! Or would it be cold business? "This is the amount you took when you left. Yes, you can have a job, but you will pay back everything that you owe."

Jesus explained how God really feels when any of us sincerely repent and ask His forgiveness: "He was filled with compassion, and ran and embraced him, and kissed him." No avoidance, no guilt trip, no coldness. God rejoices over you and me, and His heart desires intimacy, not performance.

Missing True Intimacy

"He answered and said to his father, 'Look! For so many years I have been serving you and I have never neglected a command of yours; and yet you have never given me a young goat, so that I might celebrate with my friends....' And he said to him, 'Son, you have always been with me, and all that is mine is yours.'" Luke 15:29,31

You can go to church, keep the ten commandments, and have everyone think you're a good person, yet miss true intimacy with God. The older brother in the story of the prodigal son represents the Pharisees who were also listening to him and grumbling to themselves, "This man receives sinners and eats with them." (Luke 15:2) The name Pharisee means, "separate one." These guys kept all of God's laws outwardly, went to synagogue all the time, and presumed that they were pleasing to God because of their performance. The older brother was angry that the father had received back the prodigal because he felt that his younger brother didn't deserve forgiveness and the party his father threw for him.

In the text quoted above Jesus tells of how the older brother had served the father and kept all of his commandments. The brother then complained that nothing had been done to reward him for all of his performance. He was living more like a slave than a son and was waiting for the father to pay him. The father says, "you have always been with me, and all that is mine is yours." You can't work for what is already yours. If he wanted to have a party all he needed to do was ask. That is how grace works.

Galatians 4 tells us that Jesus was born under the law so that he might "redeem those under the law, that we might receive the full rights of sons." It goes on to say that the Father has sent His Spirit into our hearts so that you and I are "no longer a slave, but a son; and if a son, then an heir through God." (Galatians 4:4-7) We could never have become God's children by the law of performance because His holiness demands a perfection we could never obtain. So He sent His own Son who lived perfectly under the law and then died as a sacrifice for all of us who have broken the law. We become His children by receiving His grace.

Sometimes we lose track of grace when we've been in the church awhile. We can begin to think that we are worthy of the place we have in Christ because of all of our service. It is important that we keep the "amazing" in grace, remembering that He came to save and love undeserving people just like us.

January 7

Delighting in God

"Delight yourself in the Lord..." Psalm 37:4

A few years ago I had a life changing experience while preparing for church early one Sunday morning. The text on this particular morning was from Hebrews 12: "...let us run with perseverance the race marked out for us, fixing our eyes on Jesus..." and I was praying through the message and planning the altar call.

I was going to tell a story about a father who was coaching his kindergarten son how to win the "all class race" which was taking place that day. His son was very fast, but also easily distracted. The dad knew it didn't matter how fast he was; if he didn't run straight, he wouldn't win. So he made a strategy: "Son, when the race starts I will be directly across from you at the finish line. Don't worry about who is running next to you, or bother watching your own progress; just focus on me, and run straight into my arms."

The question I was going to ask our people was: "What's at the end of your race?" What are you really living for? Is it money? Pleasing people? Your retirement? etc... As I was thinking how powerful this was going to be, a question jumped into my mind which I knew was from the Lord. "What's at the end of your race?" I knew instantly it wasn't what I thought it was.

The answer came quickly as well as the consequences of my wrong priorities. "Jesus" was not at my finish line; it was something subtly different called, "influence for Jesus." It was plain to me that I had become a worker for God, before I was a lover of God, and equally clear what the costs were of my wrong priorities:

1. I wasn't delighting in God, because my reward was no longer Him, but in how many people I was influencing for Him.
2. I had lost my delight in people. I could no longer enjoy people because I always needed them to do something. People were becoming projects that I had to work on instead of people that I could just enjoy.

The final sentence I heard whispered in my spirit was, "I'm calling you to be My bride, not My PR man."

A bride represents the Bridegroom in a different way than a promoter does. She knows Him intimately, and has even taken on some of His fragrance. Yes, she can answer all the basic questions, but that is not her joy. Her joy is to be with Him, and her influence is spontaneous, not forced. This is what Jesus wants from us.

What's at your finish line?

January 8

The Secret of the Lord

"The secret of the Lord is for those who fear Him, and He will make them know His covenant." Psalm 25:14

The margin of my Bible has "intimacy" as an alternate translation of "secret." I believe that a certain measure of the fear of the Lord is necessary for anyone to come to Christ. Proverbs says, "The fear of the Lord is the beginning of wisdom." (Proverbs 9:10) Then, a revelation of God's love for us in our weakness and immaturity is necessary to grow us up in our faith. (Ephesians 3:17-19) But I think that to walk close to God's presence another level of the fear of the Lord is required.

It says in Isaiah 11:3 that Jesus delighted in the fear of the Lord. He experienced the secret promised by Psalm 25:14, enjoying the continual intimate friendship of His Father. He didn't fear man, He didn't fear death, He didn't fear storms, He didn't fear lack of supplies – He only feared God and cared only about obeying what the Father was saying. (John 5:19)

Maybe the idea of the fear of the Lord seems heavy to you. I think it was just the opposite for Jesus which was why He was able to say, "My yoke is easy and My burden is light." (Matthew 11:30) He only had to please the Father to be a complete success. Paul said something similar to this: "Therefore we also have as our ambition, whether at home or absent (from the body), to be pleasing to Him. For we must all appear before the judgment seat of Christ, so that each one may be recompensed for his deeds in the body, according to what he has done, whether good or bad. Therefore, knowing the fear of the Lord..." (2Corinthians 5:9-11a)

Only one ambition! What a simple life, what an easy yoke, what a light burden. May God pour out the Spirit of the fear of the Lord on each of us and make it our delight for His glory.

January 9

Private Devotion

"Woe to you, scribes and Pharisees, hypocrites! For you clean the outside of the cup and of the dish, but inside they are full of robbery and self indulgence. You blind Pharisee, first clean the inside of the cup and of the dish, so that the outside of it may become clean also." Matthew 23:25-26

Many years ago I went on an extended fast with the purpose of obtaining more of the power of God and the gifts of the Spirit. One day near the middle of the fast I was crying out to God for those things, and He spoke a clear word to my mind. I believe it was God because it was so different from what I was praying, and clearly not the result of my natural thought processes. Here was the thought: "I never want your public anointing to be greater than your private devotion."

With that thought came an immediate realization that my current public anointing was already greater than my private devotion which meant that I was in a dangerous place as a minister. Here I was praying for more public anointing, which would have made the imbalance even greater, while God was wanting to do something more foundational inside of me. Needless to say, the focus of my fast changed from that moment on. It's not that I didn't still want the power, I just knew the road to it must include a greater devotion that could sustain the greater ministry.

The Pharisees were concerned about the outward. They measured God's favor by their outward blessings and continually sought to put forward the best possible image of themselves. They were more concerned about how they appeared before others than about how they actually were before God. Jesus told them to stop focusing on the outward and to start cleaning up the private, inward parts. He assured them that if they would do this, the outward would take care of itself.

Don't worry about being a Christian example to others. Concern yourself with actually being a Christian before God. Having to appear to be anything other than you are in public is a massive burden and almost impossible to keep up. No wonder Jesus' burden was so light; He never worked on appearing. He made sure things were right before the Father, He kept a strong private devotion, and then just lived it out all day.

January 10

Redefining Success

"The friend who attends the Bridegroom waits and listens for him, and is full of joy when he hears the Bridegroom's voice. That joy is mine, and it is now complete. He must become greater; I must become less." John 3:29-30

I am redefining success on the basketball court. It used to be all about winning or losing which meant leaving the game either excited, discouraged, frustrated, or depressed, depending on the final score and how I played. My new definition is that just getting exercise is a "win," but it's a difficult transition because I've labored under the old mindset for a long time. I have to remind myself each game of my new way of looking at it. "It doesn't matter that I missed that shot or that we are losing by 10; I'm playing, sweating, and running – I need nothing else to enjoy the game."

The text quoted above is John the Baptist's response to disciples who came to him with the news that his ministry was decreasing while someone else's was getting bigger. "Rabbi, that man who was with you on the other side of the Jordan...well, he is baptizing, and everyone is going to him." What they were really saying was something like this: "Do something! We've got to get the crowds back here because we've always baptized more people than anyone else. Let's get some posters up, let's interview the man on the street and find out why so many are going elsewhere. Why not have a party with free pizza?"

Americans love results. Bigger is always better. Work hard and if it's not producing, work harder. Results rule. John had a different definition of success in life: intimacy with God. He informed his disciples that his joy was not in the ministry, so it really didn't matter whether it was getting bigger or smaller. His joy was in hearing the Bridegroom's voice and in being His friend.

To be a friend of God and to respond to Him with joyful obedience when He speaks is the greatest thing you and I can do. It's not about production, it's about the relationship. The Westminster Confession states, "The chief end of man is to glorify God and to enjoy Him forever." Remember to enjoy God today and you already have the win.

January 11

An Audience with the King

"O Lord, You have searched me and known me. You know when I sit down and when I rise up. You understand my thoughts from afar. You scrutinize my path and my lying down, and are intimately acquainted with all my ways.... How precious are Your thoughts to me, O God! How vast is the sum of them! If I should count them, they would outnumber the sand."
Psalm 139:1-3; 17-18

In 2010, then President, Barack Obama, came to Madison and while he was here made a surprise visit to La Follette High School. When the football coach called the team together, the president addressed running back Jaylen Plummer by name and said he knew that he had scored three touchdowns in a game played the Friday before. Plummer's response when interviewed by the Wisconsin State Journal about the meeting was, "amazing, ... the president knows my name."

What an experience! A regular high school student having such a personal meeting with the most powerful man in the world. Our president is the CEO of the world's largest economy and the commander-in-chief of the world's largest military. There's no one who comes close to wielding that much power. For him to take the time to stop at a regular football practice and then to show knowledge of such a specific event - truly amazing.

Now consider with me for a moment what it means that God wants to have a personal relationship with you. There have been many presidents and there will be more in the future if Jesus doesn't come back soon, but there is only one God. There is no one like Him; He is the beginning and the end. He isn't just the president of one country, He's the King of all kings. He's not just the CEO of the world's economy, He owns everything and provides for His children out of His boundless riches. If it doesn't exist, He can create it. He needs no military because the word out of His mouth can slay all the armies of this world in a moment. (Revelation 19:15)

No doubt President Obama was briefed on La Follette's football game on the way to the surprise visit. He had just learned about the three touchdowns and would probably forget about them an hour after the meeting. God doesn't need a briefing on you. He knows your name and everything about you. The only thing He forgets is your sins when you bring them to the cross. I hope we never lose the amazement that the King of the whole universe wants to be our friend.

January 12

Quieting Your Soul

"O Lord, my heart is not proud, nor my eyes haughty; nor do I involve myself in great matters, or in things too difficult for me. Surely I have composed and quieted my soul; like a weaned child rests against his mother, my soul is like a weaned child within me." Psalm 131:1-2

David learned how to quiet his soul. Infants immediately seek for milk when near their mother's breast and have to be weaned away from the habit. After a child has been weaned, they will rest quietly on their mother's lap without frantically searching for food. Similarly, we naturally worry about that which we cannot control and have to be weaned from this tendency, so that we can find our rest in God. How do we quiet our noisy souls within us?

1. Accept with humility the limits to human understanding. Although we can learn things about God, there are heights and depths to who He is and the way He does things that are beyond our capacity to figure out. David had surrendered those areas and recognized that it was only his pride that kept him from trusting God when he didn't know the answer to all the "whys" of this life.

2. Recognize that God is the center, not you. "Be still and know that I am God. I will be exalted in all the earth..." (Psalm 46:10) Astronomers have recently discovered that there are billions more stars than they originally thought. The earth is a small place in a small galaxy that is a small part of the universe. The greatness of the heavens should help us to grasp both the enormity of God and the smallness of us. When we become large in our own eyes, anxiety easily creeps in. Our strength doesn't come from our activity, but in our quietness and confidence in God. (Isaiah 30:15)

3. Trust God's love for you and in His willingness to save you. Weaned children rest content because they have eaten solid food. It is not enough to stifle our need for control, we must actively feed on God's love and salvation. We are safe in His care. Although we can't control anything, He can, and He will exercise loving and wise oversight to our lives if we will only trust Him. Peter says it this way, "Cast all your anxiety on Him, because He cares for you." (1Peter 5:7)

January 13

The Greatest Reward

"Let not a wise man boast of his wisdom, and let not the mighty man boast of his might, let not a rich man boast of his riches; but let him who boasts boast of this, that he understands and knows Me, that I am the Lord who exercises loving-kindness, justice and righteousness on earth; for I delight in these things..." Jeremiah 9:23-24

The greatest benefit of being a Christian is not something God does for us, but God Himself. Therefore the greatest reward for praying, serving, or sacrificing is not an answered prayer or a changed circumstance, but an increased revelation of who He is. Think about it: our future is only as good as God is. It wouldn't matter where we went if the One who was there was not filled with beauty, love, and righteousness. If God wasn't perfect in every way then our future would be unstable and unpredictable. It's not His promises, but His character behind His promises that is our ultimate guarantee.

It is a shallow Christianity that is just trying to get what God offers in salvation without seeking the God behind the offer. Who is this that has promised all of heaven to those who come to Him in faith? Who is this who has died for us and calls us to be His bride? Who is this who has made us to be the very children of God, sons and daughters, who no longer are to live in shame, fear, and guilt but in the security of the beloved?

Do you enjoy God? I hope so. If not, you're missing something very important. Instead of trying to make your life work just so, or trying to make your dreams come true, seek to make God Himself your delight. Everything else will fall into place if you aim for the greatest reward. As David wrote, "Delight yourself in the Lord and He will give you the desires of your heart." (Psalm 37:4)

January 14

Seeing Your Brother

"But when this son of yours who has squandered your property... We had to celebrate and be glad, because this brother of yours was dead and is alive again." Luke 15:30,32

You were not just made for a relationship with God; you were made for a relationship with your brothers and sisters in Christ. The older brother had stopped seeing the prodigal as his brother – he only saw him as his father's son: "this son of yours..."

When the prodigal left, his father's heart broke, not just because of what he was losing, but because of what his oldest son was losing. The father had heard these sons laugh together, seen them compete with each other, and watched them defend each other their whole lives. He probably dreamed of them being life-long friends who would enjoy seeing their children grow up together and enjoy the bonds of family. The family was broken up when the prodigal left, and it was a great loss for everyone. Our sin doesn't just separate us from communion with God, it hurts the whole family.

When the wayward son returned, the father was overjoyed because the family could be whole again, but the older brother didn't see it that way. When he refused to join the party, the father went outside to reason with him: "This is your brother who had died to all that is good and beautiful. He is back; we can be a family again. Please embrace him and let us rejoice together." (My paraphrase)

The father was ready to make him a son, but his oldest was not ready or willing to see the prodigal as his brother again. His life was smaller because of it.

How about you? Has the Father come to you and asked you to give a brother, sister, friend, parent, or child another chance? Let's die to our right to be angry or wounded; let's forgive and start seeing value in the broken people around us that God is trying to redeem. Let's go into the feast and rejoice in God's love together, for the sake of our Father, and for the sake of our own brothers and sisters.

January 15

The Disabled List

"Strengthen your feeble arms and weak knees. Make straight paths for your feet, so that the lame may not be disabled but healed." Hebrews 12:12-13

The author of Hebrews is writing about how to respond to hardships in life. All hardship, he says, is part of God's discipline or training, to grow us up. (Hebrews 12:7) Yet the very hardship that was designed by God for our healing can end up hurting us if we respond in the wrong way. We need to strengthen ourselves and stay on the straight path in these trying times, or we are in danger of ending up on the disabled list.

What makes us weak in hardship are the lies of the enemy. A few verses earlier we are warned to not be discouraged by discipline, or to take it as a sign of God's rejection. God loves us and His discipline is actually a sign of His acceptance. (Hebrews 12:4-5)

A great danger in 21st century America is the belief that God's chief end for us is to be happy right now, so anything difficult must be prayed away or rebuked as being from the devil. God wants us to be healthy, not just happy, and sometimes that means He allows things in our lives that we wouldn't choose for ourselves. Even if the devil initiated the difficulties because he hates us, God will use them for our good if we'll trust Him. (2Corinthians 12:7-9; Revelation 2:10)

Because of this, James tells us we should rejoice when we face various trials because God's end is that we would become complete in Him, lacking nothing. All we have to do is allow patience (our patience with God) to finish its work. (James 1:2-4)

Are you in a time of difficulty? It is easy to be offended and wander away from God. Strengthen yourself right now by embracing the truth. God loves you and this present difficulty is only going to make you better if you just hang in there. Choose to trust in God's love and rejoice in His wisdom even when you can't figure out how something so hard can work for your good. (Romans 8:28)

January 16

Drinking the Spirit

"If anyone is thirsty, let him come to Me and drink. He who believes in Me, as the Scripture said, 'From his innermost being will flow rivers of living water.'" But this He spoke of the Spirit..." John 7:37-39

The words Bilbo spoke in *The Lord of the Rings* came to me several years ago: "I am like too little butter scraped over too much bread." Running, ministering, doing... all on fumes. I'd been like a cell phone that is beeping to tell you it's low on power. I told myself it needed to be charged but maybe I could make one more call before I lost power? Recharging takes time and sometimes we feel like we don't have any to spare.

How about you? Do you need a drink from the fountain of living water? Have you learned how to survive even while you've got signs everywhere that there is nothing in the tank?

Jesus invites you and me to come to Him for a fresh drink of the Holy Spirit. How do we drink of the Spirit?

1. Recognize that there is a difference between actually drinking of the Spirit and only believing in drinking, reading about drinking, or talking about drinking. (If any of these constituted drinking of the Spirit, I would be continually renewed.)

2. To drink I must own my need to drink and bring that thirst to Christ Himself. Oftentimes we bring our thirst to the empty pleasures of this world that turn out to be cisterns that are leaking. (Jeremiah 2:13) We get a small emotional renewal up front but in the end we become even more weary.

3. To drink I must believe in the abundant grace of God and that He has created me for intimacy. He died so that sin could not keep me from Him, and He lives to help me drink of His Spirit who He knows I need.

4. To drink I must make time. Bilbo got away. The cell phone must be plugged in for a while and be unavailable to carry around for a time.

But what about all the people who "need" me? If you take serious time for renewal you may touch fewer people, but God will be able to touch more. And in the end, people really need God, not you, anyway.

January 17

The Mysterious Bride

"The kingdom of heaven is like a king who prepared a wedding banquet for his son." Matthew 22:2

In this parable a king (God the Father) is having a wedding feast for his son (Jesus), and his people (the human race) are invited to attend. The first invited (the Jewish race) reject the invitation which leads to their judgment (Matthew 22:7), yet this leads to others being invited (the Gentiles), both good and bad, but even then, "many are called, but few are chosen." (Matthew 22:14)

What is unclear is who the son is marrying. In Matthew 25 Jesus tells another parable about a coming wedding feast and this time the people being described are in the wedding party. There are ten bridesmaids who are waiting with the bride (who is not mentioned in the parable) for the bridegroom's party to come and take them to the wedding feast. If it was an honor to be invited by the king to a wedding feast for his son, it is a greater honor to be in the wedding party. But we are still left with the question: Who exactly is Jesus marrying?

Finally we have a definitive answer in Ephesians 5:31-32: "For this reason a man shall leave his father and mother and shall be joined to his wife, and the two shall become one flesh. This mystery is great; but I am speaking with reference to Christ and the church." You and I aren't just invited to the wedding; we aren't just part of the bridal party; we are called to be the bride! Our invitation is actually a proposal from God. No wonder John wrote, "Blessed are those who are invited to the wedding supper of the Lamb." (Revelation 19:9)

Yet when Paul writes the words, "...and the two...," he is saying that Jesus is one – the Bridegroom, and the church is the other one – the bride. You and I aren't called to be brides, but to be part of the bride. No wonder Jesus prayed that the Father would make us one! (John 17:21) Individually we are sons and daughters, but we are only the bride together. One bride – there isn't a young bride and an old bride; there isn't a black bride, a Latino bride, and a white bride; there isn't a male bride and a female bride; there isn't a rich bride and a poor bride; and there aren't Catholic, Methodist, Lutheran, Baptist, and Charismatic brides. There is only one bride which is why pleasing God must involve us letting go of our prejudices, and learning to love and accept one another in Christ.

Jesus is calling, inviting, knocking, and yes, even proposing to you. Will you refuse the One who gave His life for you, or will you respond by giving Him all of your heart?

January 18

John's Secret

"One of them, the disciple whom Jesus loved, was reclining next to him. Simon Peter motioned to this disciple and said, 'Ask Him which one He means.' Leaning back against Jesus, he asked Him, 'Lord, who is it?'" John 13:23-24

Chris Gore, one of the leaders at Bethel in Redding, CA, has a little booklet called, "John's Secret," where he contrasts the foundation of John's faith with the foundation of Peter's faith. Peter was mostly concerned with how much he loved Jesus, while John's focus was how much Jesus loved him.

At the last supper Peter declared that "even though all may fall away, yet I will not." (Mark 14:29) He was sure of his love for Jesus but ended up denying Christ three times and didn't believe even when he saw the empty tomb.

Peter was sure of his love for Jesus, but John was sure of Jesus' love for him. All through his gospel, John, the great apostle and prophet, chooses to refer to himself only as, "the disciple Jesus loved." John was the only disciple that remained at the foot of the cross, and when he saw the empty tomb, he believed. (John 20:8)

The faith and relationship Peter worked so hard for came very naturally to John. We see Peter deferring to John's relationship in the text above when Jesus had revealed that someone would betray Him. And in John 21 after Peter is told by Jesus how he was going to die, his only response was, "Lord, and what about this man (John)?" Jesus' answer to him strikes right at the heart of Peter's competitive, striving spirit. "If I want him to remain until I come, what is that to you? You follow Me." (John 21:21-22)

I've taken John's secret to heart. I've gotten into the habit of reminding myself that Jesus loves me. When I wake up, usually the first thing I say is, "Jesus, You love me. I am Your beloved, favored, child." This may sound simplistic but it has had a profound effect on my relationship with God. Maybe you should try it, Beloved?

January 19

The Tree of Eternal Life

"God knows that when you eat of it your eyes will be opened, and you will be like God..." Genesis 3:5

After the enemy questioned the Word of God by asking Eve, "Did God really say that," he questioned the character of God. In the text above it's as if he's saying, "God is holding out on you and doesn't have your best interests in mind." Once Eve took this bait, she could justify taking matters into her own hands to accomplish what was "best" for her. Instead of trusting God, she became suspicious of Him, and disaster followed. Is anything different today?

The irony of the attack quoted above is that God was offering Adam and Eve something only He possessed, but it could only be found in the other tree, the tree of life. We find out in Genesis 3:22 that this tree would more appropriately be called the tree of eternal life because whoever ate its fruit would "live forever." Adam and Eve were being offered, in the fruit of this tree, the very life of God who "alone possesses immortality." (1Timothy 6:16)

Today God is offering eternal life again through another tree; the cross. His purpose is not to restore us to the state of Adam and Eve before they fell, but to give us the eternal life they never embraced. "For God so loved the world that He gave His only begotten Son that whoever believes in Him will not perish but have eternal life." (John 3:16)

What will happen to those who don't come to the cross and eat of the life only Jesus can give? They will outlive their bodies and face judgment (Hebrews 9:27), and then be cast into hell to pay for their sins against humanity. (Revelation 20:11-15) After that they will be destroyed in hell (Matthew 10:28), be consumed by its fire (Hebrews 10:27), and perish like the beasts (2Peter 2:12) when they experience the second death of the lake of fire. (Revelation 20:15)

Let's trust God's heart for us and receive the eternal life He died for us to have!

January 20

Staying Free from Idolatry

"Dear children, guard yourselves from idols." 1John 5:21

I received a phone call while I was pastoring in Minnesota from a third grader.

"Pastor Tom, this is Taylor, and I need to talk to you."

In all my years of ministry, I had never been called by a little kid and had rarely heard such urgency in anyone's voice. Then his mom came on the phone to set up a time when she could bring Taylor in for a meeting. What could this possibly be about, I wondered. Has he been abused? Is he having nightmares? Why couldn't it wait until Sunday, or why couldn't he just talk to his parents about it?

The next day, Taylor and his mom arrived at the appointed time and he opened his heart to me. "I love a video game more than I love Jesus," was what he finally got off his chest. "It's what I think about in the morning when I wake up and it's what I think about when I go to bed. I used to think about Jesus, but now it's this game. What should I do?"

I knew I needed to be careful. His tender conscience could easily have been convinced that all video games are wrong and that he should never play one again. It also would have been easy to minimize an experience he was having, where the Holy Spirit was making him aware that nothing should be more important than God. I ended up saying something like this:

"Taylor, there's nothing wrong with playing video games; God wants little boys to have fun and excitement. But it's also important to keep God first, and to not have idols. Why don't we ask God to forgive you for putting this game before Him, and then you take a time of fasting from the game. After that, you could try playing it again, and we'll see if God doesn't break the hold it's having on you now."

He thought that was great and we had a time of prayer where he poured out his young heart to Jesus and asked His forgiveness.

The Apostle John tells us to guard ourselves from idols. An idol is anything you regularly look to as a source of comfort and motivation that's not God; something that takes God's place. It can be a person, an addiction, money, work, looks, education, television, and yes, it could even be a video game. We need to guard ourselves from even good things that become too central in our lives.

If and when we discover idols in our hearts, we can ask Jesus for forgiveness and help, just like Taylor did.

January 21

Waiting on God

"Humble yourselves, therefore, under God's mighty hand, that He may lift you up in due time, casting all your anxiety upon Him because He cares for you. Be self-controlled and alert. Your enemy the devil prowls around like a roaring lion looking for someone to devour. Resist him, standing firm in the faith... And the God of all grace, who called you to His eternal glory in Christ, after you have suffered a little while, will Himself restore you and make you strong, firm and steadfast." 1Peter 5:6-10

The language of the New Testament has two different words for time. One of them, "chronos," corresponds to our word for time in definition, but the second, "kairos," has no one English word to define it. "Kairos" is translated in a number of ways: "the right time;" "the proper time;" "an opportune time;" or as it is in the text above, "in due time." All of these have the same basic meaning: "in God's time."

God has His own time for things. He does plan to lift us up, answer us, promote us, provide for us, and heal us in His time, but there is a time of testing that often comes before which requires us to wait on God. The text above gives us important clues of how to wait.

1. Wait on God with humility. "Under God's mighty hand" references God's power. His face is who He is; His hand refers to His ability to act. God is able to do what you need Him to do. To wait humbly we must cast our anxiety about our situation on Him and leave it there. Let go, and let God!

2. Wait on God with confidence. God cares for us. He loves us even when in our minds we question why He doesn't remove the present suffering. It's at this point of waiting that the enemy roars in our ears with accusations against God to undermine our faith. Remember: the loudest voice in your head is often not the truest one.

3. Wait on God with perseverance. When we are suffering there is a great temptation to give up on God and take matters into our own hands. If we persevere, God Himself will use the waiting period before the kairos to make us "strong, firm, and steadfast." "Let us not become weary in doing good, for at the proper time (kairos) we will reap a harvest if we do not give up." (Galatians 6:9)

January 22

A New Beginning

"Before I was afflicted I went astray, but now I keep Your Word."
Psalm 119:67

We had a house cat when we lived in Minnesota named Sugar, and one day Sugar wanted to go outside. The problem was that it was freezing cold and we were in the middle of a snow storm. She put up her paws against the glass patio door in our dining room and meowed at the top of her lungs. I explained to her that she didn't really want to go outside; she wouldn't like it. But she wasn't listening and was driving me crazy with her persistent meowing.

There were so many things she could enjoy if she would just get away from that door. She could watch TV with the kids who were home from school. She could sit on Beth's lap and allow Beth to gently pet her for hours. She could go down in the basement and eat some more or go up to the bedroom and sleep on Beth's bed. She had options, but she wasn't interested in any of them. She wanted to go outside.

Finally I said, "Alright, you asked for this." I opened the door and she shot out. I then closed the door and after about five seconds she wanted back in. Now she was pawing the other side of the glass door and meowing at the top of her lungs to get back in.

I want to assure you that it was always my plan to let her back in – she was a house cat after all and belonged in the house with us. But she wasn't coming back in that easily. Before a new beginning was offered, I wanted her to get a taste of life out in the winter storm. If she wasn't fully convinced, I reasoned, once I let her back in she would quickly forget about how cold and windy it was and think she wanted to go out there again.

When she finally came back in she had obviously learned her lesson because there were no more episodes of her wanting to go where she wasn't allowed.

Sugar's story is often our story with God. We get bored doing the right thing all the time and think we want to investigate the "dark side," or what the Bible calls sin. Instead of enjoying all of God's legitimate blessings we crave something that is off limits and become convinced that we will be happier if we have it. God then becomes "mean" in our eyes because He won't let us have what we want. We pout. We whine. And then finally He allows an opportunity for us to have what we want.

If we won't listen to His word, He hopes we'll listen to our lives. Life doesn't work when we disobey God. Even when we disobey and stray far from Him, He waits for our return, "longing to show us mercy." (Isaiah 30:18)

January 23

Horse Talk

"In repentance and rest is your salvation, in quietness and trust is your strength, but you would have none of it... yet the Lord longs to be gracious to you; He waits to show you compassion." Isaiah 30:15,18

A few years ago my wife and I went with our missionaries to a horse farm where horses are used to teach spiritual truths. Our director asked all of us to be quiet while we observed her with a horse who was unfamiliar with her. She asked us to imagine her as God, and the horse as us, and encouraged us to listen to what the Holy Spirit might teach through the experience.

She was in the middle of a circular pen set up in the arena and had a headset microphone on that allowed us to hear everything she was saying without her having to raise her voice. The horse was then let in with her and she began speaking softly to him, but he was having none of it. He began running around in circles ignoring her, but she kept speaking and never took her eyes off of him.

Once in a while the horse would kick or change direction or even speed up to let her know he resented being locked up in this small space with her. She just kept speaking tenderly and waited for him to tire out. Finally it happened.

All at once the horse stopped, went right to her, and bowed his head, letting her touch him. She told us this was an act of surrender. Now when she spoke and walked around the horse followed her wherever she went.

Here are a few reflections:

1. The circular pen was something artificial that she created for the purpose of establishing a relationship with the horse. Our circumstances are like the pen. God allows us to feel penned in only for the reason that we might come to Him, surrender, and establish a stronger relationship. Even though the horse ignored the director, she never took her eyes off of him and never stopped speaking to him. God's eye is on us even when we resent our circumstances and kick and snort to communicate our unhappiness with Him.

2. Horses were created to be ridden in the beautiful outdoors, not stuck in a pen. God wants to have an intimate relationship with us where we become one with Him. The sooner we embrace this purpose by surrendering to Him, the sooner the adventure of "riding" with Him will begin.

January 24

Heaven's Laugh

"Sarah said, 'God has brought me laughter, and everyone who hears about this will laugh with me.' And she added, 'Who would have said to Abraham that Sarah would nurse children? Yet I have borne him a son in his old age.'" Genesis 21:6-7

The joy Sarah experienced when she had Isaac (Isaac means "laughter") would be shared by others when she told them the story. She was barren, Abraham was too old, and she had given up on having children long ago. People would laugh for joy because this child was tangible evidence of three things:

1. God is alive. Because of the circumstances, this was clearly a miracle that only a living God could do.
2. God is good. Life can be harsh and frustrating, but this child was a desire fulfilled that gave Sarah, and anyone who would hear about it, a taste of how good God is.
3. God is gracious. Sarah had tried to have a child her own way through Hagar, and then laughed cynically when she heard God's promise of her having a child. (Genesis 18:12) When she was asked why she had laughed, she lied because she was afraid. Yet God did the miracle anyway! God does wonderful things, not because of our great faith, but in spite of our imperfect faith.

What does this have to do with us? Everything. "Now you, brothers, like Isaac, are children of promise." (Galatians 4:28) The God who owed us nothing but death, gave us eternal life. The one who was heading to hell is now on the path to heaven. The life that was degenerating in isolation is now regenerating through adoption into God's own family, by the Spirit of life.

We are the miracles that should bring heaven's laugh into this dark, cynical world. God loves us and Jesus died for us! Don't forget to laugh today at how wonderful these simple truths are.

January 25

A Place at the Table

"Behold, I stand at the door and knock; if anyone hears My voice and opens the door, I will come in and eat with him and he with Me."
Revelation 3:20

Jesus isn't inviting us to a one-time experience, but to an ongoing relationship. Amazingly, we're not the only ones who eat when we come to His table. Jesus also eats with us. The longing of His heart for fellowship with us is satisfied when we open our hearts and take our place at the feast He has prepared.

In 2Samuel 9 we have the story of Mephibosheth. He was king Saul's grandson and Jonathan's son. David sought him out because he wanted to show kindness to one of Jonathan's descendants in order to honor the covenant of friendship he had made with him.

When Mephibosheth was brought before David, he was afraid for his life because it was customary for a new king to wipe out all the descendants of the king he replaced. (2Samuel 19:28) But mercy, not judgment, was in David's heart. He gave Mephibosheth all the property that Saul had previously owned, making him a wealthy man, but he wanted to do something more than just give him property. David wanted to have an ongoing relationship with him so he gave him a place at his dinner table as if he was one of his own sons. (2Samuel 9:11)

Redemption doesn't just give us immediate access to the wealth of heaven, it gives us a place at the King's table. However, just because there was always a place set for Mephibosheth doesn't mean he always came to meals, just like God doesn't force us to take the place He's made for us to have fellowship with Jesus.

The church in Laodicea had said in its heart, "I need nothing." They were living as Christians apart from intimacy with Christ and had become spiritually "wretched, miserable, poor, blind, and naked." (Revelation 3:17) Jesus was pursuing their fellowship and was ready to restore spiritual riches, eye salve and garments of white to remove their shame, but they had to respond to His knocking.

He was inviting them to a meal, but not just one meal; the invitation was to start taking their place at the table for all the meals. Physically we need to eat regularly and this is a picture of our ongoing need of daily fellowship with our Savior.

Jesus is still knocking today, have you taken your place at His table?

January 26

The Best Wine

"You have saved the best wine for last." John 2:10

I am convinced that God has saved the best of His Spirit for those who are older. I'm not an expert on wine, but I know that the older it is, the more valuable it becomes.

Paul said we are renewed in our spirits "day by day" and that we are being transformed "from glory to glory." (See 2Corinthians 3-4) The picture here is of ever increasing glory as we grow older in the Lord.

Think about it: The temptations that were so strong in youth no longer grip us when we age, and the youthful pride we often had in our own strength no longer deceives us. As we age, we become better positioned to lose our life for Jesus so that we can find our life in Jesus.

It's not that the Holy Spirit (wine is compared to the Holy Spirit in a number of places in the New Testament) gets better over time, but simply that less of His outpouring is wasted because of the wisdom gained by walking with God for many years. But only if we grow older in the right way.

There will always be a temptation of getting stuck in the past. In Luke 6:39 Jesus says, "But no one who drinks the old wine seems to want the new wine. 'The old is good enough,' they say." This warning is about how our past experiences with the Holy Spirit can prevent us from entering into the fresh thing the Spirit wants to do.

Solomon warns us to not "long for the good old days." (Ecclesiastes 7:10) God says in Isaiah, "Do not dwell on the past; it is nothing compared to what I am going to do. For I am about to do something new. See, I have already begun! Do you not perceive it?" (Isaiah 43:18-19) Dwelling on the past, even the glorious past, will keep us from perceiving the new thing God is doing.

It seems that if we believe our best spiritual days are behind us, then they are. But just think about some of the past giants of faith: Moses was 80 when he led the people of God out of Egypt, Daniel was well into his eighties when he was delivered from the lion's den, and Anna was 84 when she prophesied about Jesus. (Luke 2:37) God is searching for people to show Himself strong through (2Chronicles 16:9) no matter what their age. So why not you? Why not us?

January 27

Hephzibah!

"No longer will they call you Deserted, or name your land Desolate. But you will be called Hephzibah (My delight is in her), and your land Beulah (married); for the LORD will take delight in you, and your land will be married. As a young man marries a young woman, so will your Builder marry you; as a bridegroom rejoices over his bride, so will your God rejoice over you." Isaiah 62:4-5

I often tell people who want to see a modern day miracle that they need look no farther than Kansas City where there has been a prayer meeting going on continually, 24/7, for over twenty years. Mike Bickle has led and organized thousands of young people who have been seeking God for revival in America and in the world for almost two decades. Amazing! There are 84 back-to-back two-hour shifts where one team replaces another – they call it the International House of Prayer or just IHOP. (Google "IHOP Prayer room" to live stream the prayer meeting going on right now!)

We took a group to the One Thing conference they hosted for years, and at one of them, I heard Mike Bickle tell a dream he had that paved the way for this historic prayer meeting. In this dream he was preaching to a large group of young people at the convention center, but the entire message was only one word: Hephzibah.

He shouted over the group from the center of the stage: "Hephzibah!" Then he went to the right and once again shouted: "Hephzibah!" And then to the left hand side of the stage: "Hephzibah!" When he woke up he was determined to find where this vaguely familiar word was in the Scriptures. He was stunned to find that the two verses quoted above were right before his life verses (Isaiah 62:6-7) about the need for unceasing prayer to accomplish all of God's purposes. Then the Lord spoke to him: "They will never go night and day without knowing that My delight is in them."

The power to serve God continually comes from an identity that is secure in the truth that we are God's delight. As long as we are questioning God's delight in us, or feel we aren't good enough to be delighted in, or don't feel we perform well enough for God to delight in us – we are going to struggle. The Father has a one word sermon He wants to speak to our hearts: "Hephzibah!"

January 28

The Price of Free Oil

"The foolish ones said to the wise, 'Give us some of your oil; our lamps are going out.' 'No,' they replied, 'there may not be enough for both us and you. Instead, go to those who sell oil and buy some for yourselves.'" Matthew 25:8-9

Intimacy with God is a gift given to every believer in Jesus Christ. Jesus died and rose again, not just so that we could go to heaven one day, but so that we could experience Him right now.

Imagine for a moment a gas station that is giving away free gas. The only price you pay is the effort to get to that gas station and the time spent waiting while your tank is filled up. In God's economy there is an abundance of the precious oil of intimacy, and it's all free through Jesus, but we must make the effort to get to His station and be patient while He fills us up.

We can't get this oil from one another. You can't give me your relationship with God and I can't give you mine. All we can do is tell each other where the station is and how to get the free oil. Each of us has to go there ourselves.

When we go through trials, when we experience injustice, when we need something that only God can give, and when Jesus comes again, we will wish we had taken time to become intimate with God. When you're in the middle of the crisis there's not time to develop an intimacy that you don't already have.

So don't wait! Set a time and a place every day. Read God's word and purpose to pray back to Him whatever He speaks. Journal those things He gives you and treat them as valued seeds that must be protected and watered. Develop a habit of waiting on God every day.

What starts as only a desire for intimacy must move to a plan for discipline. God's reward will be an eventual delight in your quiet time that will make meeting with Him a highlight you look forward to each day. Desire, discipline, and then delight. Let your desire fuel a renewed effort at discipline. Stay at your discipline and pray for more and more delight.

Begin now to build a secret store of oil that no one else can see except you and God. As it grows, enjoy the assurance that you and God can face anything together and that you will be ready when Jesus splits the sky to come for us.

January 29

Becoming the Real You

"Therefore if anyone is in Christ, he is a new creature; the old things have passed away; behold, new things have come." 2Corinthians 5:17

Modern psychology helps people understand why they do what they do by looking into their past. The premise is that you and I are products of our past. If we can identify where we have been hurt, rejected, or abused in the past, we can better understand why we react the way we do today.

While this can be helpful, especially if identified hurts are forgiven, Jesus comes to a human being in the opposite way - from our future. When you give your life to Jesus Christ you are no longer a product of what has been (that is all washed away by His precious blood) but of what He is making you by His grace. He has predestined you to "become conformed to the image of His Son." (Romans 8:29)

In Christ we are a new creature. The old is passing away. Don't dwell on the old in you, or you will remain trapped by it. Dwell on what He is doing by His grace, and the power of the old will lose its grip. When you dwell on the old in other people you tend to trap them with labels. "That's just how he is." If you look beyond people's faults and find Jesus and what He is doing, it inspires them to rise.

A missionary in India was discouraged because many of his converts to Christianity were still clinging to some of their old habits. He prayed about this on a walk and the Lord directed his attention to a tree that had lost almost all of its leaves, but there were several dead leaves still clinging to the branches. The Lord whispered to him something like this:

"There are two ways of getting the rest of the leaves off. One way would be for you to climb up there and cut each one off individually. That would be a lot of work. The other would be for you to wait until spring, when the new life will come through the same shoots and push the old leaves out naturally. Don't worry about their old habits. Get them focusing on their new life in Christ and they will eventually find themselves completely free."

Focus on what you are becoming, and thank God you're not trapped by who you once were. You're becoming the real you!

January 30

Resting in Christ

"The Lord is my shepherd, I shall not want. He makes me lie down in green pastures..." Psalm 23:1-2

Before our good Shepherd leads us in paths of righteousness, or feeds us in the presence of our enemies, or anoints our heads to do great things for Him, He makes us rest our identity in Him.

Phillip Keller, in his book *A Shepherd looks at Psalm 23* writes: "In every animal society there is established an order of dominance or status within the group. In a pen full of chickens it is referred to as the 'pecking order;' with cattle it is called the 'horning order;' and among sheep we speak of the 'butting order.'

"Generally an arrogant, cunning and domineering old ewe will be the boss of any bunch of sheep. She maintains her position of prestige by butting and driving other ewes or lambs away from the best grazing or favorite bed grounds. Succeeding her in precise order the other sheep all establish and maintain their exact position in the flock by using the same tactics of butting and thrusting at those below and around them.... Because of this rivalry, tension, competition for status, and self-assertion, there is friction in a flock. The sheep cannot lie down and rest in contentment. They must always stand up and defend their rights and contest the challenge of any intruder."

The only time they can rest, Keller goes on to tell us, is when they are in the presence of the shepherd. When he is nearby there is no butting order. Each sheep is special, not because of a place it holds in relation to other sheep, but because the shepherd knows its name. Each sheep has the place the shepherd gives it, not the one it has earned for itself.

Have you noticed that human beings, left to themselves, create a butting order? No one can rest or they might lose their place. Someone said that we "spend money we don't have, on things we don't need, to impress people we don't like." It's all part of the butting order.

The Lord wants you and I to come out of the butting order and learn to live in His Presence. Jesus said, "Come to Me, all who are weary and heavy-laden, and I will give you rest." (Matthew 11:28)

January 31

Letting Go of the Past

"Do not call to mind the former things, or ponder things of the past. Behold, I will do something new, Now it will spring forth; will you be aware of it? I will make a roadway in the wilderness, rivers in the desert." Isaiah 43:18-19

It is hard to go forward when you're stuck in the past. When we allow old wounds to embitter our spirit, it's hard to love new people. When we allow yesterday's failures to weigh on our minds, it's hard to face today's challenges. God wants to free us from our past, so that we will recognize the new things He wants to do in and through us.

Have you been really hurt by someone? Forgive them. "Yeah, but they're not even sorry." Or, "They've said they're sorry, but that doesn't make everything alright." No, only you can make everything alright again by forgiving them. If they don't deserve forgiveness, then remember that you didn't deserve forgiveness from Jesus either. He gave you a new beginning and expects you to do the same for others.

If you choose not to forgive, you are the one who will suffer. You will also hurt the ones you live and work with. Hebrews 12:15 says, "See to it that no one comes short of the grace of God; that no root of bitterness springing up causes trouble, and by it, many be defiled." When we let hatred get into our hearts toward one person it will come out toward others.

"Do not call to mind the former things..." Let go of it. Pray that God will have His way in them and do your part by forgiving them of every word, deed, and thought they've had against you. If you don't, then you will miss the new thing that God wants to do.

He wants to make rivers flow in the desert. Impossible! Not with God. He can do anything in and through you, if you will only believe. Christians should be redemptive. We must deal in truth and therefore recognize things for what they are. Yet at the same time we must see that part of the whole truth includes our God's ability to move mountains. No situation is too difficult. No disease is beyond healing. No relationship is beyond repairing. No soul is beyond saving.

February 1

Stilling Your Soul

"My heart is not proud, oh Lord, my eyes are not haughty; I do not concern myself with great matters, or things too wonderful for me. But I have stilled and quieted my soul; like a weaned child with its mother; like a weaned child is my soul within me. Oh Israel, put your hope in the Lord both now and forevermore." Psalm 131

David learned how to talk to himself. When his soul was apathetic he would command his soul: "Bless the Lord oh my soul, and all that is within me, bless his holy name." (Psalm 103:1) When he was slipping into depression he would tell himself to remember God and God's future for him: "Why are you downcast, oh my soul; why so disturbed within me? Put your hope in God, for I will yet praise him, my Savior and my God." (Psalm 43:5) In today's reading he is being tempted to slip into confusion and anxiety over questions that are outside of his control. His response? "I have stilled and quieted my soul..."

Notice that he didn't ask God to still and quiet his soul, he said, "I have stilled and quieted my soul". Christianity becomes very difficult when we try to control God's part, or when we expect Him to do our part. You and I have control over our souls. We can let them run free, wherever they take us, or we can exercise our wills, like David did, and tell our souls what to do. Sometimes we simply need to preach the gospel to ourselves.

How do you do that? Your heart is full of worry and anxiety over all of life's troubles and circumstances, so you decide to have a talk with your soul. "Stop worrying, Soul, and start trusting God. Jesus loves you and died for you. He's not going to let you down if you turn to Him. He has come through in the past, and He is going to get you through this time, so stop your whining and start praising God." It is amazing how our emotions will follow when we decide to trust God instead of giving in to all of our doubts and fears.

"Be still, and know that I am God. I will be exalted..." (Psalm 46:10) Do you need to take a moment right now to be still, to cease striving, to stop manipulating, and just remember that He is God?

February 2

Living in Grace

"The Lord longs to be gracious to you, and therefore He waits on high to have compassion on you." Isaiah 30:18

Have you ever heard one thing, when the person speaking meant to communicate something completely different? Oftentimes we jump to negative conclusions because we are suspicious of the motives of others, or because we feel so bad about ourselves that we assume the worst. It is easy to do this with God. If our filter is the law, and we feel God's motive is judgment, we will take any communication from Him as negative. This puts a weight of guilt on us leading us to live without the joy, peace, and the sense of expectancy that He wants us to live in. We know we're saved by grace; now He wants us to learn how to live in grace.

A few years ago I lost some tickets to a play Alice and I were excited about going to. I had been careful with them all week long and kept them in a place where I didn't think they could get misplaced but on the day of the event, somehow they were gone. After looking everywhere I was feeling frustrated and embarrassed for losing them. We contacted the ticket office and left a message on a recorder but as we arrived, I was fully expecting to have to pay again to see the performance. Instead, I was greeted by an elderly couple at the ticket table who were filled with mercy. Yes, they had received the message, and no, we didn't have to pay again. "We all lose something once in awhile," said the man who sensed my pain and wanted to make it easy for me to accept the tickets they had made for us.

This is what God is like. He's not thinking about the stupid thing we did and the judgment He's going to bring because of it. He longs to be gracious to us and is waiting for us to look up and receive His compassion. He wants us to let go of past regrets; He wants us to succeed; He wants us to go forward; and He wants us to grow in our confidence in Him. "Let us draw near with confidence to the throne of grace, so that we may receive mercy and find grace to help in time of need." (Hebrews 4:16)

February 3

Living a Life of Love

"Be imitators of God, therefore, as dearly loved children and live a life of love, just as Christ loved us and gave Himself up for us as a fragrant offering and sacrifice to God." Ephesians 5:1

There is a famous quote that encourages us to "love like you've never been hurt." After we've been hurt, offended, betrayed, slandered, and overlooked it's hard to get back up and love again. Yet without being able to receive and give love, life has little meaning. So how do we live a life of love?

First, receive God's love. You and I love the most generously when we feel loved first. People may or may not love you; some people are so broken that they couldn't love you if they tried. But God's love is full, free, and unwavering. "As dearly loved children... live a life of love." It is as we grow in receiving His love and delight in us, even in our brokenness, that we are able to extend love to others even when they're broken. Did you know that you are dearly loved? Believe it, receive it, embrace it, and then confess it. The enemy will try to keep us feeling condemned, so that we have nothing but condemnation for others. Don't let him do it!

Then forgive those who have hurt you as part of your love for God. Jesus gave Himself up for us while we were hurting Him and it was received by the Father as a fragrant offering. We give the same pleasing fragrance to God when we choose to forgive others for His sake. Jesus didn't ask Peter how much he loved the sheep; He asked, "Peter, do you love Me?" Do you love Jesus today? Then He has something He wants you to do to prove it; forgive those who have hurt you. Learn to live a life of love in practical ways. Notice the people around you; ask them questions and care about their answers; do what you can to lighten their burden and pray for them. Simple, yet profound.

February 4

Wholehearted Love

"You shall love the Lord your God with all your heart, and with all your soul, and with all your mind, and with all your strength." Mark 12:39

Jesus told the experts of the law that this was the greatest commandment: to love God with everything in you. I don't believe we can obey this command apart from the filling of the Holy Spirit. You can choose to worship God and you can choose to obey God and you can choose to say "no" to temptation; but you and I can't choose to love God wholeheartedly; we need help. Here's why: I can choose to worship, but I can't make myself enjoy it, which is what is required if I'm going to be wholehearted. I can choose to obey, but I can't force myself to be excited about it; and if I'm not impassioned, it's not wholehearted. When a man is cheering for his favorite team to win, all of his emotions are invested because he wants them to win with all his heart. If it's somebody else's team and he's asked to cheer for them, he might do it as a favor, but his heart isn't really in it. You can't make your heart be into something; that's God's part.

"The love of God has been poured out within our hearts through the Holy Spirit who was given to us." (Romans 5:5) True love begins with God, not with us. When the Holy Spirit is filling us He is able to tap our deep passions and desires and turn them toward God. It takes God to love God. We can choose to obey God and do what is right but Jesus is worthy of more than that! He is worthy of us being passionate about our obedience and wholehearted in whatever we are doing because we're doing it for Him and with Him. For this we need to ask and keep asking to be filled with the Spirit. (Luke 11:13) We are His temple and we only operate rightly when we're filled with Him.

Sometimes the problem is that our hearts have been damaged, or hurt so badly that we can't do anything wholeheartedly any more. Jesus is anointed with the Spirit to mend broken hearts so they can regain the ability to love. (Isaiah 61:1) Once again, we can't heal ourselves, but we can recognize our need and earnestly ask for His healing power to restore us. Ask Him to heal you so you can love yourself and others again; that's good. But a greater prayer is that He would heal your heart completely so that you can give Jesus the kind of love He is worthy of.

February 5

Gentle Warriors

"He trains my hands for battle, so that my arms can bend a bow of bronze. You have also given me the shield of Your salvation, and Your right hand upholds me; and Your gentleness makes me great." Psalm 18:34-35

To become great in heaven's eyes requires us to receive God's gentleness before anything else. His mercy toward us in forgiveness, and His gentle dealings to draw us to Himself win our hearts so that we will do anything for Him. We live in a harsh world and frequently treat ourselves with great harshness. The devil's work is often easy as he only has to put the hammer in our hands, and we will beat ourselves up with shame and regret. On top of this our form of religion can also be harsh, demanding, and judgmental, but none of this is from Jesus.

"Come to Me, you who are weary and heavy laden, and I will give you rest." (Matthew 11:28) Jesus invites us to come and find how tender His love is and how great His ability is to remove our heavy burdens. Have you experienced His gentleness? Paul says that our gentleness toward others should be a result of us living in God's presence. He writes in Philippians: "Let your gentleness be evident to all. The Lord is near." (Philippians 4:5)

God wants us to develop a gentle spirit toward people, but a warrior's spirit toward the spiritual darkness around us. Jesus was tender toward the weak and broken, and tough toward the Pharisees and demons. David was a worshiper who danced before God but also a warrior who cut off Goliath's head. The same God who gently deals with David also trains his hands for war; He wants to do the same in us.

The church is called to be a healthy family and an obedient army. Knowing the love of God makes us healthy, and knowing the fear of God produces in us a spirit of instant obedience. Those whom God uses in the days to come will be growing in both revelations and will be known by both the church and the world as His gentle warriors.

February 6

Diamonds in the Rough

Psalm 16:3 "As for the saints of the earth, they are the majestic ones in whom is all my delight."

David didn't just forgive God's people, and he didn't just tolerate the saints; he delighted in them. How can we do the same? I think the key is seeing them the way God sees them: Diamonds in the rough.

In Exodus 28:17 God commanded Moses to make an ephod with four rows of three precious stones each. The stones represented the twelve tribes of Israel and the priest was to remember that this was how God felt about His people by wearing this ephod over his heart whenever he came into God's presence. Four rows – three in each row – ruby, topaz, emerald; turquoise, sapphire, diamond; jacinth, agate, amethyst; beryl, onyx, jasper – the saints are God's jewels.

A frequent accusation against believers and an argument against the truth of Christianity is hypocrisy. When an unbeliever sees a so-called Christian fall short of their expectation, they say out loud or think to themselves, "I thought you were supposed to be a Christian! Hypocrite!"

But the authentic Christian doesn't claim to be a perfect diamond, but a diamond in the rough. "We have this treasure in earthen vessels," says the apostle Paul, "so that the surpassing greatness of the power will be of God and not from ourselves." (2Corinthians 4:7) We have a sin nature; we have a struggle going on inside of us, but we also have a new nature and are part of a new creation.

Our responsibility toward one another is to look past the rough and start seeing and speaking to the diamond. Christians often focus on the wrong thing and get paralyzed by sin and shame, their own, and that of their brothers and sisters. Can we look past the rough? Peter exhorts us, "Above all, keep fervent in your love for one another because love covers a multitude of sins." (1Peter 4:8) Don't you want others to love you like that? We can't excuse sin but after confession, we dare not dwell on it, or we will miss what God is seeing.

His delight is in the saints; let's learn to delight in them too.

February 7

Guilt Detectors

"But Martha was distracted with all her preparations; and she came up to Him and said, 'Lord, do You not care that my sister has left me to do all the serving alone? Then tell her to help me.'... Mary has chosen the good part and it will not be taken from her." Luke 10:40-42"

Carbon monoxide is known as a "silent killer." It is a colorless, tasteless, and odorless gas that can kill you without you even realizing what is happening. Because of this many homes now have detectors that sound an alarm if the air you breathe has become contaminated with too much of this gas.

We need a similar spiritual detector for guilt. We were created to live in response to God's grace in a place where our relationship with Him is the priority. When guilt begins to infect us we lose track of the main event, as Martha did, and end up with the "bad part." As carbon monoxide kills us slowly physically, guilt based living slowly kills us spiritually. It takes the "want to" of grace and turns it into the "have to" of man-made religion. Christ died to "cleanse your conscience from dead works to serve the living God." (Hebrews 9:14) He wants to expose guilt based living so that He can cleanse us and empower us to live by His grace.

Here are three detectors of guilt based living:

1. I'm serving God but no longer enjoying God. God doesn't take us from the place of delighting in Him, but we can easily lose it. Martha allowed her serving to be so central that she was distracted from fellowship with the Lord.

2. I'm serving God but no longer enjoying people. Martha felt it was her duty to fix Mary. When you're trying to fix people you are no longer able to enjoy them.

3. I feel like it is my responsibility to meet the expectations of those around me. If you can't say "no" to those who ask for help then I fear that you can never really say "yes" to them. You have become a slave to guilt, and any need will get you moving. God wants more for us!

Mary chose the good part and Jesus is inviting us to choose it as well. No more guilt; only His grace. Have you made that choice?

February 8

Coming to the Table

"Behold, I stand at the door and knock; if anyone hears My voice and opens the door, I will come in to him and will dine with him, and he with Me." Revelation 3:20

I want you to think about a housewife who loves her husband and knows her husband loves her but feels emotionally disconnected. Her husband works hard, long hours and is usually exhausted when he gets home. Even when they do get a chance to be alone together, there's so much family business to discuss that they rarely get beyond the mundane. They still have sex, so it's not like there's an unmet physical need; she's just looking for a renewal of intimacy that transcends living together. She longs for first love again.

So she plans a night for just the two of them, and her husband agrees to come home at six for "something special." She arranges babysitting for the kids, makes his favorite meal, puts on her best dress, gets the lighting and the music just right, and then... comes the phone call. He can't make it – something's come up and he's sorry. She packs the food up in the refrigerator, blows out the candles, turns off the music and can't help being disappointed. Something has been lost and that particular moment will never be regained. All he had to do was come home and take his place at the table. She had done all the work to make it happen, but he missed the appointment.

The church at Laodicea had stopped coming to the table. They were saved and had correct doctrine but they had decided in their hearts that they now had all they needed from God. (Revelation 3:17) Jesus had set the table with everything they liked and needed; eye salve, garments of white, gold refined by fire. They were all ready for Him to serve, but they had stopped keeping their appointments.

But it's not just about their loss. Jesus Himself says that He wants to dine with them. Why does He want to be with us so much? I don't know, but I do know that I don't want to disappoint Him.

February 9

Staying in the Right Spirit

"'Lord, do you want us to command fire to come down from heaven and consume them?' But He (Jesus) turned and rebuked them (James and John), and said, 'You do not know what kind of spirit you are of; for the Son of Man did not come to destroy men's lives, but to save them." Luke 9:54-56

James and John were very familiar with the message of grace that Jesus brought. He had said on a number of occasions that He did not come to judge, but to save. (See John 3:17 & John 12:47) Jews of that time had established a tradition of traveling around Samaria because they considered Samaritans to be heretics and didn't want to be defiled by them.

Yet Jesus had asked James and John to make arrangements in Samaria for a place to stay on their way to Jerusalem. They went in a spirit of grace most likely, but when they were rejected; when they felt judgment from others; they shifted to a retaliatory spirit. They had even convinced themselves that this was probably what God wanted them to do until Jesus rebuked them and said they were in the wrong spirit. When we feel judged it's easy to respond in judgment toward others.

I was sitting in the sauna at a health club chatting with a man about a number of things including the remodeling being done on the men's and women's bathrooms. Because male workers were doing the remodeling, the women's bathroom had to be the men's bathroom for a while which meant the usual men's bathroom was now the women's bathroom. There were signs clearly letting everyone know about the change.

This man left the sauna before me but when I came out a few minutes later I saw him going into the women's bathroom. It was too late to give a warning. A few minutes later he came bursting out of the door and announced to all in hearing range, "it's hard to break old habits." He wasn't trying to go in the women's bathroom, he had just reverted back to his usual pattern without even thinking about it.

It's not enough to show mercy once in a while. We need to stay in the right spirit all the time to reveal God's love to a fallen world.

February 10

Our Need for One Another

"Two are better than one, because they have a good return for their work; if one falls down, his friend can help him up. But pity the man who falls and has no one to help him up." Ecclesiastes 4:9-10

There's an African proverb that states, "If you want to go fast, go alone; if you want to go far, go together." The above text is the Bible's way of stating this same truth. You may go fast for awhile, but if you're unwilling to do the work of friendship, eventually you will fall and won't be able to get back up because God created us to need Him, and to need each other.

A few years ago a friend was telling me about his cousin who along with his wife adopted three children from Russia. They couldn't have any children of their own so decided to bring these children into their home. Well, it turned out to be much harder than either of them thought it would be and it led them to the point of despair many times.

The husband told my friend something like this, "We both said 'I'm done,' many times through the years, but as God arranged it, we were never saying it at the same time. When one of us was ready to give up, it just happened that the other one somehow had found encouragement, so we kept going." He said, "I don't know what would have happened if we had both been in the place of despair at the same time."

It's funny that the way we get really close to people is by walking with them through their low times and by letting them walk with us through our low times. "A friend," the Proverb says, "loves at all times." (Proverbs 17:17) We can't even know how good of a friend we are, or how good of friends we have until we've seen them, or they've seen us, at our worst. "All times," means good and bad.

Have you been hurt or betrayed by a friend or by a church? Are you living in isolation because you don't feel like the work of living in community is worth it? I want to encourage you to reconsider because God wants us to walk with Him and with His other children. It's His plan and no other will work.

February 11

Embracing the Wilderness

"Therefore, behold, I will allure her, bring her into the wilderness and speak tenderly to her... In that day you will call Me 'husband' and no longer call Me 'master'." Hosea 2:14; 16

The wilderness seasons of life are difficult. You feel alone, unappreciated, and frustrated. This is Joseph serving in prison; Moses taking care of a few sheep for years; David being chased around a desert – why would a God who loves me lead me into the wilderness?

First, so you will experience His tenderness. As long as God is just a concept to us we will not understand what our lives are about. God doesn't lead us to the wilderness to punish or scold us; He wants us to know who He really is. We naturally assume God loves productive and impressive people (because that's who people love), but all that is stripped away in the wilderness. God's love for us transcends what we do or how we appear. God loves you. He made you and He redeemed you, first and foremost, so you could have a relationship with Him.

Second, so He can change our identity, or how we think about ourselves. "In that day..." In what day? In the day where we experience the tenderness of God in the wilderness; then our motivation will change. Instead of performing for a master, we will be like a beloved bride to her husband. God will become our delight not our duty; our Protector, Provider, and Friend; not just the One we are accountable to.

So how do we respond when God allures us to the wilderness? Usually we fight it by blaming people or blaming God, or we get discouraged and want to give up. All that our wrong responses do is prolong our time in a place we don't want to be. Let's embrace God's purpose in the wilderness. Let's press into Him and bring our loneliness, anger, and frustration to the cross. Let's pick up our Bibles and ask Him to speak to our hearts.

One day very soon we will come out of this season changed by the tenderness of God. It will be said of you: "Who is this coming out of the wilderness leaning on her Beloved?" (Song of Songs 8:5)

February 12

For Men Only - How to Love Your Wife

"Each individual among you also is to love his own wife even as himself, and the wife must see to it that she respects her husband." Ephesians 5:33

When a wife treats her husband with disrespect his automatic response is to treat her in an unloving way. But instead of withholding love until she "deserves it," God commands husbands to love their wives regardless of what you feel the score is. Practically, how does one love his wife?

1. By listening to her and respecting how she feels. The first evidence of real love from God's point of view is "love is patient..." (1Corinthians 13:4) Men tend to withdraw when they are under stress, but women tend to talk it out. If she feels like you aren't listening to her it gives the message that she's not important to you. If she expresses frustration with you by saying, "you never..." or "you always..." it is not time to defend yourself because in your mind her accusation isn't true. Men, we need to go deeper and recognize that it is true that she feels that way right now, and that her feelings need to be validated. Here's the question our wives want us to ask, "Do you want me to just listen, or do you want a solution?"

2. By talking to her. She needs to hear your feelings and not just a list of what you accomplished. God's main reason for marriage was that spouses would not "be alone." Consider that there is no greater loneliness than to be married and feel alone; at least single people have hope of finding someone to share life with. When you won't open up to your wife she feels desperately alone with nowhere to turn. God gave you to her so she wouldn't feel that way.

3. By reconciling with her. Be willing to say these words: "I'm sorry, will you forgive me?" Pride hides and ultimately divides; humility is willing to do the honorable thing even if it means death to self. Ephesians 5:25 says, "Husbands love your wives, just as Christ loved the church and gave Himself up for her..." Jesus died before anyone had responded to Him. Men of honor initiate reconciliation even when they don't "feel" like it because it is what is best for their marriage and family.

February 13

For Women Only - How to Respect Your Husband

"Each individual among you also is to love his own wife even as himself, and the wife must see to it that she respects her husband." Ephesians 5:33

When a husband treats his wife in an unloving way, her automatic response is to treat him without respect. But instead of withholding respect until he "deserves it," God commands wives to respect their husbands regardless of what they feel the score is. Practically, how does one respect her husband?

1. Respect his dreams. Men are risk takers which means that they will make mistakes. Mistakes aren't failures but they make men feel like one. Instead of reminding your husband of his mistakes, encourage him to get back up and dream again. Every mistake is an opportunity from God to grow in character. Believe in your man. Men like to win and they hate to fail, so if you make them feel like they can't win in your marriage, they will stop trying.

2. Respect his needs. Men are fairly simple and have two main needs: 1) Space. Women often relax by venting how they feel while men relax by withdrawing. It's not that he won't talk, he just doesn't want to talk right now. It's not because he's mad, it's because he is stressed, so he needs room. 2) Sex. For whatever reason a man's sex drive is usually stronger than a woman's in his 20's and 30's so he will want to make love more often than she will. If you are going to be the exclusive woman in his life (which you deserve to be – and that includes him refraining from all pornography), then you sometimes need to be willing even when there hasn't been a highly romantic lead up to it. There is something called, "maintenance sex."

3. Respect his position. God has made men responsible for the home which is not a right for a husband to claim, but a responsibility he needs to accept. Men often abdicate their place if a woman wants to take it or if he thinks she can do it better than he can. He needs your encouragement to step up even if he isn't as spiritual as you may be. Do this as an honoring wife; not sounding like his mother.

February 14

Love's Laboratory

"Therefore, as God's chosen people, holy and dearly loved, clothe yourselves with compassion, kindness, humility, gentleness and patience. Bear with each other and forgive one another if any of you has a grievance against someone. Forgive as the Lord forgave you. And over all these virtues put on love, which binds them all together in perfect unity."
Colossians 3:12-14

Maybe you've seen the bumper sticker, "Life is the school, love is the lesson." If life is the school then I propose that marriage is the laboratory in the school. Marriage is where a man and a woman freely lock themselves into this small room with vows to one another, and then give God permission to lock the door from the other side by their vows to Him. God's purpose is that we stay in there until we don't want to ever get out because we've learned how to love.

God knows that if we can learn how to really love one person with all their flaws, we will be able to love anyone. How can we learn to love God's way in our marriages?

1. Focus on how you're loving your spouse, not on how they're loving you. There is no command requiring us to make sure we're being treated in a certain way. When we focus on how our spouse is treating us, we're set up for grievances.

2. Put on love every day. Being in Christ, dearly loved, holy and chosen, doesn't guarantee we will live in love; it only makes it possible. A few verses earlier, we are called to put off the old man and put on the new. (Colossians 3:9) Both outfits are in a Christian's closet. If we don't choose to put on love every day, we are capable of living just as selfishly as those who have no interest in pleasing God.

3. Return to the source when love runs dry. One of the most shocking things we find out in the laboratory of marriage is how unloving we can be. Don't freak out when you don't feel you love your spouse anymore; get a refill. You can be fully assured that Jesus loves your spouse as much as ever and is able to soften and empower your heart again.

After God locks the laboratory door, He walks through it and will be the center of our marriages, if we will only let Him. And a cord of three strands is really hard to break!

February 15

Defining the Relationship

"Now large crowds were going along with Him; and He turned and said to them, 'If anyone comes to Me, and does not hate his own father and mother and wife and children and brothers and sisters, yes, and even his own life, he cannot be My disciple.'" Luke 14:25-26

After a couple has been going out for a while one of the parties, usually the woman, wants to have a DTR (Define the Relationship) talk. What is this? Are we just friends? Are we officially boyfriend and girlfriend? Is this possibly heading toward marriage? This makes the man, or the woman, look at the relationship honestly, and causes them to come to a crossroads where a decision must be made that will affect the future of the relationship.

In the passage above Jesus is asking for a DTR response from the crowds that are following Him. In the book, *Not a Fan*, Kyle Idleman comments on this passage:

> *"Jesus uses such dramatic language here, because in this culture if you were to become a follower of Jesus without having your family's blessing, you would have been thought of as hating your family. A decision to follow Jesus would have been interpreted as turning your back on your family and walking away from them." (pg 57)*

> *Idleman continues: "In Luke 14 Jesus defines the relationship by making it clear that if we follow Him, we follow Him and Him alone. He won't share us – not with money; not with a career, not even with your family. Maybe you read a passage like this and it seems that God is being a little possessive and jealous. But understand this – when Jesus explains that He will not share your affection or devotion, He isn't just saying how He wants to be loved by you; He is making it clear how He loves you.*

Where are you with Jesus? Is He not only first in your life but the center, the one and only, that true devotion requires? We need to define the relationship to move forward in God.

February 16

Patience with People

"Be patient, brethren, until the coming of the Lord. The farmer waits for the precious produce of the soil, being patient about it, until it gets the early and late rains. You too be patient; strengthen your hearts, for the coming of the Lord is near. Do not complain, brethren, against one another, so that you yourselves may not be judged; behold, the Judge is standing right at the door." James 5:7-9

Did you know that God is a patient Farmer? He sends His Word as seed and then patiently waits for it to do its work in and through us. We are the ones who are impatient and it gets us into all kinds of trouble. Oftentimes we value results over process, so we judge ourselves and others too quickly. What may be right on course in God's eyes, isn't far enough along for us, so we begin striving in a way that hinders our growth.

Do you ever take time to celebrate what God has already done in you? We may not be where we want to be, but we're not where we once were either! This should be a cause for rejoicing and also a reason for patience. "I am confident of this very thing, that He who began a good work in you will complete it until the day of Christ Jesus." (Philippians 1:6) When we see what's happening in us as primarily God's grace, not our works, we can enjoy the process more. And it's only when we see ourselves as being in process, not as a final product, that we can extend the same grace to others.

Complaining about other people, especially other Christians, can easily become a habit, and it's destructive. When we judge others, we don't realize that the measure we're using gets used on us by God. (Matthew 7:1-4) If you feel like you're being forced to walk on eggshells in your walk with God, it's probably because you're making those around you walk on eggshells. Listen to the words of Jesus, "Blessed are the merciful for they shall obtain mercy." (Matthew 5:7) This does not just mean mercy in the life to come, but mercy right now.

Make mercy toward others your new habit. Life is hard enough already, let's soften it for everyone around us, including ourselves, and enjoy more of God's grace each and every day.

February 17

A Personal Relationship

"You search the Scriptures because you think that in them you have eternal life; it is these that testify about Me; and you are unwilling to come to Me so that you may have life." John 5:39

I believe many things about my wife, Alice. Some are just facts, like her birthday, her place of birth, her parents' names, and her general history which anyone who is interested could easily learn. Other things require more personal involvement like knowing her character and her heart's desires. My current beliefs about her are numerous, but my relationship isn't with my beliefs about Alice; it's with her. She's a person. Because of this reality, my beliefs are always growing and deepening as we walk together.

But what if I no longer lived with my wife? Wouldn't my belief system become static? I would still believe things, but they wouldn't deepen or grow because of a lack of present experience with her. In the text above, Jesus is rebuking the Pharisees because their relationship isn't with God Himself; it's only with their beliefs about Him.

There is a great danger in evangelical Christianity today of making our beliefs about God an idol that takes the place of an actual relationship with Christ. How can I tell if I'm in danger of this idol? Here are four symptoms:

1. We become unteachable. We no longer believe what we read in the Bible; we only read what we already believe.
2. We become divisive with Christians that don't believe exactly what we believe about God and Christ. We're experts and everyone else needs to listen to us to get it right.
3. We become suspicious of any fresh moving of the Holy Spirit that doesn't fit into our box of who we think God is and how He should act.
4. We find ourselves bored with worship because our hearts actually love what we believe about God more than we love God Himself.

The Scriptures are not an end in themselves; they direct us into a personal relationship with the God who loves us and died for us. We all know "in part" and even the part we think we know is only a seed of all that is true about the transcendent, majestic, unchanging, and uncreated God of the universe. Getting to know Him is the greatest adventure of our lives and will last for all eternity!

February 18

The Song in the Night

"At night His song is with me... I say to God my Rock, 'Why have You forgotten me? Why must I go about mourning, oppressed by the enemy?'"
Psalm 42:8-9

It is one thing to love and praise God when everything is going good; it is another thing to love and praise Him when it feels like darkness is crushing you.

In this dark night of the soul, we can't see God's purpose or understand His goodness, yet it is most important that we learn to sing at this time – I'm calling it the song in the night. Why is this song so important?

1. It forces us to focus on who God is instead of what He does for us. Satan's accusation against Job was that he was using God and didn't really love him. (See Job 1:9-11) Do we really love God or are we only using Him because we love ourselves? The song in the night purifies our worship.

2. It forces us to either go deeper in our faith. "Deep calls to deep in the roar of your waterfalls, all Your waves and breakers have swept over me." (Psalm 42:7) Trees planted by water have shallow roots. Trees in a hostile environment either have roots that go very deep, or the tree dies before maturity. Listen to how deep the roots of the Psalmist have gone in this time of difficulty: "As the deer pants for the streams of water, so my soul pants for You, O God. My soul thirsts for God, for the living God." (Psalm 42:1-2) Instead of turning away from God, His pain brought him to a new place of thirst for God Himself.

3. We are no longer dependent on the faith of others. Darkness isolates us and raises questions about God's goodness. Do I really believe or have I only been part of a social group who wants to believe in a personal God so they can be protected from life's hard realities? God allows this time so that we can experience Him ourselves instead of on the coattails of others.

Does it feel like darkness is suffocating you? This could be your faith's greatest hour. It's time for you to take up the song in the night.

February 19

The Proposal

"I am dark but lovely." Song of Songs 1:5

I love to officiate weddings because engagement is such a beautiful picture of what is happening on planet earth right now. Jesus says: "Behold, I stand at the door and knock, if anyone hears My voice and opens the door, I will come into him and we will sup together." (Revelation 3:20) Jesus' knock is His proposal to the human race today.

When Paul gives the original marriage text of a man leaving his father and his mother to be joined to his wife, and the two becoming one he gives this explanation, "This is a mystery, but I speak of the relationship of Christ and the church." (Ephesians 5:32) Every earthly wedding is pointing to another wedding; the wedding feast of the Lamb. Right now, everyone who has said "yes" to Jesus is engaged to Him and called to be part of that eternal partnership.

The reason I preach the gospel at weddings is that many people who don't regularly come to a church assume God's not interested in them, and nothing could be farther from the truth. They don't feel like they're "the type" of person Jesus loves because of sin they've committed or shame they're carrying or because they haven't been to church lately. On a mission trip, I gave the example of a $20 bill to demonstrate our value before God. First I held up a crisp $20 bill and asked how much it was worth. Then I stepped on it leaving a footprint. "Now how much is it worth?" I asked. Then I crumbled it up in my fist and threw it away. When I found where it had gone, I picked it up, unwrinkled it, and asked for a third time, "How much is it worth now?"

When people betray us, abuse us, or belittle us, it's easy to feel we have less value. When we sin against others and against God and experience the shame and regret of having done things we can't take back, we naturally feel devalued. But before God we're like that $20 bill. Nothing we've done, or had done to us makes God love us less.

We are dark, but lovely to Him. You are the one He desires and He is knocking. He's knocking through pain, through beauty, through sin you can't conquer on your own... even through weddings, church services, and weekly devotionals! But no one gets engaged just by someone asking; we need to say "yes." We need to open the door by saying from our heart, "Jesus, come in, love me, wash me, and make me who You want me to be."

February 20

Gems Around Us

"Be patient, then, brothers and sisters, until the Lord's coming. See how the farmer waits for the land to yield its valuable crop, patiently waiting for the autumn and spring rains. You too, be patient and stand firm, because the Lord's coming is near. Don't grumble against one another, brothers and sisters, or you will be judged. The Judge is standing at the door!" James 5:7-9

God is patient with His people. Just because a corn crop isn't ready to be harvested doesn't mean the farmer isn't pleased with its progress and growth. God is pleased with our process even though we're not finished, so we need to be patient with ourselves and with those around us.

During worship one Sunday when I was about to preach on the above verses, a man in our congregation had a vision and gave permission to share it: "I saw beautiful gems. Many, many beautiful gems. They represented the beauty of God's Kingdom. They were all around us. Then I saw the significance of when we complain and grumble. When we do this, we cover and slather our eyes with mud and we stick our faces in the mud, both of which cause us to have an inability to see the beauty of God's kingdom around us."

Everything God creates is beautiful, but I think we are His gems. The breast piece the high priest had to wear in the Old Covenant had twelve precious gems on it representing the twelve tribes of Israel. (Exodus 28:21) God wanted the priest to know that His people are His gems.

Maybe you have been hurt by people or by the church, so how you see others is tainted by your wound. Why not forgive? Why not consider how you have hurt others and have needed their forgiveness? We all need a new beginning so we have to be willing to give others a new beginning too.

The truth is that, even though you're flawed, you are God's gem, but the only way you'll believe it is to grant that all those around you are also His gems. Father, remove the mud of accusation from our eyes, so we can see one another the way You do.

February 21

The Engine of Grace

"I do not nullify the grace of God; for if righteousness comes through the Law, then Christ died needlessly. You foolish Galatians, who has bewitched you, before whose eyes Jesus Christ was publicly portrayed as crucified? This is the only thing I want to find out from you: did you receive the Spirit by the works of the Law, or by hearing with faith? Are you so foolish? Having begun by the Spirit, are you now being perfected by the flesh?"
Galatians 2:20-3:3

The story is told of the man who first heard about the Model T and decided to have a look. He was impressed with the shiny chrome and the leather seats so he paid the asking price, hooked it up to his horse, and started pulling it home. What the man didn't realize was that the Model T came with its own engine.

The Christian life is not difficult; it's impossible. Oh, you may be able to polish up the outside a little through mere will power and even impress people, but genuine from the heart Christianity is impossible with man. When Peter asked Jesus who could be saved, he answered frankly: "With men it is impossible, but not with God; for all things are possible with God." (Mark 10:27)

Thankfully God designed the Christian life to come with its own engine; His powerful grace. The Galatian Christians knew that they were saved by grace through faith, but then they started living as though it was by works. They were in danger of nullifying the engine of God's grace by hooking all the demands of Christianity up to their own ability to keep the law. The joy and peace that comes when we share Christ's light burden and easy yoke (because He does most of the pulling) were quickly disappearing, and their religion was becoming hard, dull, and void of the miraculous power of God.

Paul questions them in verse five, "Does He then, who provides you with the Spirit and works miracles among you do it by the works of the Law, or by hearing with faith?" Whenever our Christianity becomes man centered we are left with what man is able to do, and that's not much.

Whenever I fall into the trap the Galatians were falling into I remember the man with the Model T. It sure is easier to sit down and let the engine do the work!

February 22

Cleansed from Dead Works

"How much more will the blood of Christ, who through the eternal Spirit offered Himself without blemish to God, cleanse your conscience from dead works to serve the living God?" Hebrews 9:14

What an amazing verse showing a glimpse of the Trinity working together in our redemption. Christ, who shed His blood for us, offers Himself through the Holy Spirit to God the Father who accepts His sacrifice on our behalf. The result is that we are cleansed of dead works. What are dead works? I think they may look like good works, but are from a wrong motive so they are dead in God's sight even though they may be considered right in man's. Hebrews 10:2 says that the power of Christ's sacrifice is that we no longer need to feel guilty for our sins. It's why His sacrifice is superior to the Old Testament sacrifices that could never remove the feeling of guilt but only added to the consciousness of sins.

It is easy as a Christian to live in guilt instead of grace. We feel guilty or condemned so we let that motivate us to do the right thing or, "to do our duty," regardless of how we feel. We hope that by performing the act that guilt demands we will be relieved of guilt's hold on us. The problem is that when we are done performing that act we will only feel guilty again for not performing another. Guilt is an insatiable taskmaster that makes you miserable and everyone around you miserable.

God has another solution for our guilt; He wants us to bring it to Him. If it is legitimate guilt because of sin, He wants us to ask forgiveness so that He can cleanse us, not by our performance, but by Christ's performance for us on the cross. (1John 1:9) If it is illegitimate guilt, or condemnation, He wants to expose its source so we can take a stand against the accuser. "Submit yourselves then to God. Resist the devil, and he will flee from you." (James 4:7) If Satan can't keep us from Christ, He will try to make us unfruitful in Christ.

God loves us and He has died for us, so that we will have a life-giving and guilt free relationship with Him. "What can wash away my sin? Nothing but the blood of Jesus!"

February 23

Honest to God

"My dove in the clefts of the rock, in the hiding places on the mountainside, show me your face, let me hear your voice; for your voice is sweet, and your face is lovely." Song of Songs 2:14

God wants to hear your voice. Not an echo of somebody else, not a voice that has been lost in religious tradition, He wants to hear the real you. David said in Psalm 51:6, "Behold, You desire truth in the innermost being." God values honesty above all else. He wants to see your face, not a religious mask that you may think He wants to see. With God honesty is where the action is. When sin is real to us, then confession is real, forgiveness is real, His Presence is real, and the hope He alone gives is real. If something is wrong ask the Holy Spirit to show you what is going on in your heart.

When we are less than honest as Christians, we may still appear religious, but our hearts go lukewarm. I think the reason why "the hiding places," are mentioned is that we can easily play Christian when we are around others, but it's not as easy when we're alone. Psalm 51 records David's prayer of repentance after his sin with Bathsheba and Uriah. No doubt David had played the part of "man of God" all the way through and no one would have known if God hadn't spoken to Nathan the prophet about what David had done. When Nathan said to David, "You are the man!" (2Samuel 12:7), David's heart was pierced and he once again became honest in his innermost being.

When we are being real with God He delights in our fellowship, our worship, our work and even in our fun. It may be painful up front, but honesty always brings us closer to God. You don't have to put your best foot forward because He knows what the other one looks like anyway. And guess what? He still loves and likes you.

February 24

Are You In Christ?

"Test yourselves to see if you are in the faith; examine yourselves! Or do you not recognize this about yourselves, that Jesus Christ is in you - unless indeed you fail the test?" 2Corinthians 13:5

Are you in Christ and is Christ in you – for real? Christianity is not about being nice or about having a certain set of beliefs or rules. It is about the very life of God being inside of us igniting a lifestyle of faith, devotion, and love. How could someone fail the test the apostle Paul encourages us to take? I think there are two ways to fail:

1. You were never really converted to Christ in the first place. Jesus said, "Unless you are converted and become like children, you will not enter the kingdom of heaven." (Matthew 18:3) Faith takes us beyond our logic and reasoning, so to be saved you and I must embrace what Christ has done for us on the cross and trust our eternity to Him in childlike belief. When we respond to God's drawing in that way, the Holy Spirit will bear witness in our spirit that we are the children of God. (Romans 8:16) It's not that you will never have a doubt in your mind, but there will be a knowing deep inside that God has saved you by His grace.

2. You were once saved but you have backslidden. All of us have ups and downs so I thank God that we don't go in and out of grace because of our weakness and immaturity. However, the seed of salvation can be choked out by the fear of man, the inordinate desire for other things, the worries of this life, and the deceitfulness of riches. (See Mark 4:16-19) Can it be so choked out that the life of God that was once there is completely removed? I don't know, but there are enough warnings about it that if you don't need new life, you certainly need the life you had before resurrected. Repent and ask the Spirit to renew His work in you with childlike faith.

I think it is important to take this test from time to time in light of the fact that Jesus said that "many" would presume to be saved that won't enter into heaven. (Matthew 7:21) But I also think that continually taking the test can lead to the paralysis of analysis. Check presumption, but don't let the enemy get in and rob you of legitimate faith by accusing thoughts that undermine your confidence in God's goodness toward us in Christ.

February 25

God's Care for Detail

"Are not five sparrows sold for two cents? And yet not one of them is forgotten before God. Indeed, the very hairs of your head are all numbered. Do not fear; you are of more value than many sparrows." Luke 12:6-7

"His eye is on the sparrow and I know He watches me." The truth of this song goes to another level when you experience God's providential care first hand.

We were in Minneapolis one weekend because I was speaking at a friend's church on Sunday morning. Our daughters joined us from Winona on Saturday night but were sleeping at a friend's dorm. Late Saturday night I received a call while in bed: "Dad, the car died. I got it into a parking space but it won't do anything when I turn the key." "That's fine, Honey, we'll deal with it tomorrow." How we would get it fixed on a Sunday afternoon in a strange city was beyond me and I needed to sleep, so I just told the Lord I was trusting Him.

We finally got to the stranded car at about 2:00 pm. I got it out of the parking spot and into a large parking lot where it promptly died again. A guy in the parking lot gave me directions to an AutoZone nearby, so I jumped the car again, and headed toward it while the rest of the family followed in our van. Just as I turned the final corner toward AutoZone the car died again. After navigating it over to the curb, I noticed that we were right in front of an auto repair place so I tried the door and it was open! I peeped my head in where a grizzly looking man told me that the shop was closed. He told me he had only stopped by the shop to pick up some tools for a friend; Sunday was his day off. When I told him our predicament he agreed to look at the car.

For a total of $70 he ended up putting in a new battery and an alternator. AutoZone is only a parts store and would not have been able to help us if we didn't have a mechanic who could put the parts in. We were on our way within an hour!

Maybe there are large things that God hasn't come through on yet, but don't let that mystery keep you from experiencing the little ways that He cares for us every day.

February 26

Trusting God in the Storm

"Moses answered the people, "Do not be afraid. Stand firm and you will see the deliverance the Lord will bring you today. The Egyptians you see today you will never see again. The Lord will fight for you; you need only to be still." Exodus 14:13-14

The Israelites were being squeezed between the Egyptian army and the Red Sea and there didn't seem to be any way out. In their humanness they began to speak out of their fear instead of their faith. "Was it because there were no graves in Egypt that you brought us to the desert to die? What have you done to us by bringing us out of Egypt?" (Exodus 14:11) They had seen God's power in the past, but they hadn't really learned to trust His heart so when the storm came they operated in fear instead of faith. Have you been there? Are you tempted to go there right now? Moses gives them three instructions of how to trust God in the storm that are as applicable today as they were back then.

1. "Do not be afraid." You and I don't have to be afraid. God knows what's going on and He has everything under control. He loves us and He won't abandon us when we need Him the most.

2. "Stand firm." This is the time to hold on to God. Peter says the devil goes about like a roaring lion looking for someone to devour so Christians need to "resist him, standing firm in the faith." (1Peter 5:8-9) Our enemy makes a lot of noise and preys on our fears. It's time to recognize who is behind the voice of fear and stand against him in Jesus Name.

3. "Be still." When you're afraid it is easy to speak wrong things and do wrong things that only make the situation worse. "Cease striving and know that I am God; I will be exalted among the nations." (Psalm 46:10) Stop the train of anxious thoughts; quiet your heart, and let Him fill you with a fresh sense of His Presence. He is exalted in our storms when we trust Him.

If the Israelites hadn't been squeezed they never would have seen the miracle of the Red Sea opening. I believe God has a miracle for whatever seemingly impossible situation you're facing right now. Don't be afraid; stand firm, and be still. You are not alone. God is fighting for you!

February 27

Do You Really Want to Be Changed?

"When Jesus saw him lying there, and knew that he had already been a long time in that condition, He said to him, 'Do you wish to get well?'" John 5:6

Why did Jesus ask this question when it seems the answer would be obvious? This man had been sick for 38 years! His life was confined to laying on a pallet waiting for a miracle that he didn't really think would ever happen. We can imagine that he has told others that he wants to be better. He's probably recounted many times all the things he would do if he was better, but now it's real. Do you really want to get better?

Jesus pierces through our religious responses. We know the things to say and especially the things Christians are supposed to say. God doesn't listen to our words as much as He does to our hearts. John the Baptist rebuked the Pharisees telling them that they weren't the children of Abraham just because they said they were. They had to mean it enough to "bear fruit in keeping with repentance." It's not about appearance, but reality. Jesus said to the Pharisees and Scribes, "This people honors Me with their lips, but their heart is far away from Me." (Matthew 15:7) Where is your heart? Have you been mouthing words to God while your heart has been somewhere else?

Maybe you've been stuck in sin or in self pity and have asked the Lord to deliver you out of it. Do you really mean it or are you just saying it? When you and I get serious with God, He gets serious with us. When Jesus saw that this man was sincere He told him to do something, "Get up, pick up your pallet and walk." As he obeyed the power of God came into him and that which had remained the same for 38 years was changed.

Can God change you? He can; but you have to mean it enough to listen to His voice and then obey what He tells you to do.

February 28

Experiencing the I Am

"God said to Moses, 'I am who I am.' And He said 'Say this to the people of Israel, I am has sent me to you.' " Exodus 3:14

To experience God's presence we have to live in the present. He is not the "I was," so if we live in the past, dwelling on yesterday's regrets, we will not find Him there. He is not the "I will be," so if we live in the future worrying about how things are going to turn out, we will not find Him there. He has given us promises for the past and for the future, so we can give both to Him. Then we can experience His embrace in the present. He shed His blood so that our past could be clean of sin, shame, and guilt. He has assured us of the Father's love and care for even the details of our lives, so we don't have to worry about our future. Will we trust Him and enter into His presence right now?

God has revealed Himself as the great "I am." He is right now. His embrace is for right now. His acceptance is for right now. His peace is for right now. Jesus wants to have His life revealed in us, not at some future time, but right now.

In the words of the late Henri Nouwen, "The real enemies of our life are the 'oughts' and the 'ifs.' They pull us backward into the unalterable past and forward into the unpredictable future. But real life takes place in the here and the now. God is a God of the present. God is always in the moment, be that moment hard or easy, joyful or painful... Jesus came to wipe away the burden of the past and the worries for the future. He wants us to discover God right where we are, here and now."

March 1

Faith Inspired by Joy

"The kingdom of heaven is like a treasure hidden in the field, which a man found and hid again; and from joy over it he goes and sells all that he has and buys that field." Matthew 13:44

How's your joy? Strong faith is inspired by joy which is why Nehemiah said "the joy of the Lord is your strength." (8:10) According to this passage in Matthew our joy is related to how much of the hidden treasure we have seen. I did a youth retreat a few years ago and heard a 16 year old girl testify about an experience she had with the Lord during one of the altar times. It was revealed to her that she was in rebellion against her mom, so she repented before the Lord and asked for His forgiveness. Then she said a joy came into her heart that she hadn't felt in a long time. This young lady beamed not just that night, but the rest of the weekend. She had a glimpse of the treasure of forgiveness and intimacy with Christ and was now filled with the joy of His presence.

Sometimes we're in this field called church going through the motions and we assume that that's all there is. Wrong! There is a hidden treasure that requires a heart that will truly seek God and not just do the duty of religion. One young man who was radically touched by the Lord at the retreat told us the next evening that he had led someone to the Lord that afternoon. He just couldn't contain what God had done, so he found someone to share it with and they wanted Jesus too. No wonder David said, "Restore to me the joy of Your salvation; then I will teach transgressors your ways and sinners will be converted to You." (Psalm 51:12)

Has your faith become tired? Why not take a moment right now and ask God to restore your joy?

March 2

The God of Hope

"This I recall to my mind, therefore I have hope, the Lord's mercies never cease, for His compassions never fail, they are new every morning; great is Your faithfulness." Lamentations 3:21-23

The nation of Judah was in the midst of the worst trial of its history when Jeremiah penned these words. If he relied on outward circumstances he would have been tempted to despair, but instead he recalled to his mind the character of God. He preached to himself, "God is still love and He loves me; He is still merciful and wants to show me new mercies every single day; God is still faithful and has not abandoned me even when He's not doing what I want Him to do as fast as I want Him to do it." These truths, Jeremiah said, were his reason for hope.

What's happening in your life today? In the nations there is fear of terrorism, recession, global warming, and a disillusionment with government and man's ability to solve big problems. The secret to hope is getting our eyes off of people and circumstances, and putting them on the God who promises to be with us and to work "all things together for good for those who love Him and are called according to His purpose." (Romans 8:28) All things are not good, but when given to God, they can be worked for good and actually serve as aids to our growth.

We have hope because nothing can hurt us without God's permission, and we know that if we trust God, we will always outlast our problems. God wants us to overflow with hope so that others will trust Him as well. "May the God of hope fill you with all joy and peace as you trust in Him, so that you may overflow with hope by the power of the Holy Spirit." (Romans 15:13)

March 3

Where are Your Eyes?

"But when he saw the wind, he was afraid and, beginning to sink, cried out, 'Lord, save me!' Immediately Jesus reached out his hand and caught him. 'You of little faith,' he said, 'why did you doubt?' And when they climbed into the boat, the wind died down." Matthew 14:30-32

God wants us to walk in faith. We might think that when Jesus told Peter to come out of the boat and walk on water that He would keep the water still to make it as easy as possible, but that's not how He works. Peter got out and the wind got stronger leaving Peter a choice to either keep his eyes on Jesus or to look at the waves and give in to the fear of self preservation. Clearly the wind was under the Lord's control because as soon as they got to the boat the wind stopped and the waves calmed. The test was then over, Peter got rebuked for his lack of faith, but he was no worse for the wear for going through it. It wasn't really about life or death as Peter might have thought; it was just a test.

How does God see our present difficulties? He could easily solve every problem we have right now, but He's trying to build our faith. The wind is blowing and seemingly calling for our attention, but we must keep our eyes on the Lord to stay walking on top of our circumstances instead of under them. As Paul says, "We walk by faith and not by sight." (2Corinthians 5:7)

Where will we focus our eyes? Joshua could have looked at God's promise and presence or at the giants they would face in the land. Gideon could have looked at the odds of his army of 300 defeating the Midianite army of 135,000, or he could look at the One who sent him and gave him a promise. David could have looked at Goliath or at the One who made Goliath look like a little school yard bully that needed to be taught a lesson.

A verse we should all have memorized is 2Timothy 1:7: "For God did not give us a spirit of fear, but a spirit of power, of love, and of self discipline."

March 4

A Mission for Meekness

"Come to me you are weary and heavy-laden, and I will give you rest. Take My yoke upon you and learn from Me, for I am gentle and humble (meek and lowly) in heart, and you will find rest for your souls. For My yoke is easy and My burden is light." Matthew 11:28-30

I read a devotional book that used this scripture immediately after I had read Psalm 37:11: "But the meek will inherit the land and enjoy great peace." I started to get excited and have been on a mission to learn meekness ever since. Here are a few insights I have gleaned in my meditations and study:

1. Meekness is not weakness. The Greek word translated, "gentle," or in some versions, "meek," was also used to describe horses that they trained for war. When they became "meek," they were able to be ridden effectively and safely. Power under control.

2. The differences between a proud heart and a meek heart:
   a. Pride takes now (or tries to) while the meek allow God to give in His time. The meek inherit.
   b. Pride seeks to control while the meek yield to God's control.
   c. Pride lives under the anxious, heavy burden of being its own savior while the meek enjoy peace because they aren't trying to do God's part.

3. Jesus promises an experience of rest for all who will come to Him at any time for anything. However, His promise for a life of rest is tied to us taking His yoke upon us and learning from Him how to become meek of heart. When He washed the disciples' feet He was teaching them about meekness. He said that they would be blessed if they actually put into practice what He was modeling for them. "If you know these things, you are blessed if you do them." (John 13:17)

We live in a culture that often celebrates selfish ambition, self promotion, and pride. If you embrace the mission of Jesus to teach your heart meekness, you will be going against the culture, but you will also find rest for your soul.

March 5

Experiencing Joy

"The kingdom of heaven is like a treasure hidden in the field, which a man found and hid again; and from joy over it he goes and sells all that he has and buys that field." Matthew 13:44

I am convinced that joy is the key to advancing the kingdom of God. If you find joy in something you automatically want to share it. After the Packers won the Superbowl no one had to command Packer fans to share the news with their friends. When we have great joy in something, sharing flows naturally from it. As John said about writing his first epistle, "These things we write so that our joy may be made complete." (1John 1:3) Sharing is actually part of completing the joy we have experienced.

So how do we experience joy? It's all about finding a treasure that is hidden in a field. The treasure is God's love, forgiveness and salvation that can all be experienced by coming to Jesus Christ. Paul calls this relationship with God through Christ, God's "indescribable gift." (2Corinthians 9:15) Into this gift we find that God has generously poured every blessing we could ever desire. This gift of intimacy with God will keep being unwrapped for all eternity by those who value it. (See Ephesians 3:11)

I think the "field" in this parable represents the church, so to experience God's treasure sometimes we have to get past what's wrong in whatever congregation we attend. We may feel the church is outdated, or that we don't like the music, or we may be bothered by the preacher or the people around us in some way.

Someone said that if you find a perfect church don't go there, you'll ruin it. Sometimes we have to get past the humanity we find in the church to find the Divine, but be assured that if Jesus is being preached, and the Word of God is being honored, God is there, even if He seems to be hidden from time to time. Be faithful; there's a treasure of surpassing value that God wants to reveal to each of us that will bring increasing joy to our ordinary lives.

March 6

Seeking God

"You will seek Me and find Me when you search for Me with all your heart." Jeremiah 29:13

God tells us that if we will seek for Him with all our heart we'll find Him, but there is a problem with this. Sin has so corrupted us that we are unable to wholeheartedly seek God without God's help. "No one is righteous, no, not one... no one understands, no one seeks God." (Romans 3:10-11)

It's sad, but even though we are able to be wholehearted about football or shopping or even our version of religion or church, it is not in us to wholeheartedly seek God without the Holy Spirit first inviting and freeing us to do so. When He reveals our sin, we are able to wholeheartedly ask for forgiveness; when He shows us our emptiness, we are able to wholeheartedly ask for His fullness; and when He shows us the depth of our need, we are able to wholeheartedly ask for His help; but when left to ourselves we are apathetic toward God. Even when the Holy Spirit is helping us discern our dependence, we are able to harden our hearts instead of seeking God. (Hebrews 3:15) We do have a role to play.

The Scripture quoted above from Jeremiah is in the context of the Jewish captivity in Babylon. Is it any wonder that right before the verse quoted above, God assures them of His purpose for them, "For I know the plans that I have for you, declares the Lord, plans for welfare and not for calamity to give you a future and a hope." (Jeremiah 29:11) The judgment they were going through was not because God didn't love them, or because He was mean and didn't want them to have prosperous lives. It was because they weren't listening without these extreme measures. Even then, they had a choice, and so do we today. If everything is stripped from us we can either be offended with God, or allow our desperate situation to help us to be wholehearted in our seeking of Him.

Jesus died on a cross so that we could find forgiveness, help in time of need, a sure promise for the future, and a living relationship with God right now. So let's respond quickly to the Spirit's promptings and make this relationship our greatest priority while trusting God's goodness for everything else.

March 7

The Scandal of the Gospel

"The kingdom of heaven is like a treasure hidden in the field, which a man found and hid; and from joy over it he goes and sells all that he has, and buys that field." Matthew 13:44

What is going on in this parable? It was common in that day to bury treasures because banks weren't reliable and nothing was safe in houses because of the frequent plundering of wars.   As this man was walking along it is possible that erosion had exposed some piece of the treasure that led him to dig and discover what was there. The present owner was not aware of what was buried in his property because he offered to sell the field for a price that didn't include the treasure's value.

The joy the buyer felt when he went and sold everything he had was from the deal he knew he was getting. What he was paying for the field was nothing compared to the value of the treasure hidden in the field, so he couldn't wait for the transaction to be done. Anyone who heard the story later would feel bad for the owner who didn't get much in return for such a great value.

What does this have to do with the kingdom of God? Those who understand what they are receiving in return for what they're giving up will be filled with joy because of the scandalous deal they're getting. I can imagine an angel coming to Gabriel after the gospel plan became clear:

"Sir, I'm here on behalf of many of the angels that are having trouble grasping this new plan. Let me get this straight, human beings who have rebelled against God and abused each other day after day are being offered complete forgiveness, are being adopted as sons and daughters, and are being made kings and priests forever? Those who deserve hell are being given heaven? Is this fair? And what is God getting in return? Their weak faith, wavering love, and often empty promises of obedience? Many of us don't feel this is right, sir."

"It's not about fair," I can imagine Gabriel replying. "It's about God's love and generosity. This is how He wanted it and we are to serve these heirs of salvation no matter how scandalous it may seem to you and me."

March 8

Speaking from what God has Spoken

"For He Himself has said, 'I will never desert you, nor will I ever forsake you,' so that we confidently say, 'The Lord is my helper, I will not be afraid. What will man do to me?'" Hebrews 13:5b-6

God wants you to know that He will never desert you or forsake you. People will come and go, even those who love us the most can't be there all the time, but God is always with us. One of His covenant names is Jehovah Shammah, which means, "The Lord who is present." Psalm 46:1 says: "God is our refuge and strength, a very present help in trouble."

Do you believe this? If you do then take the second step of faith and speak it with confidence. It is important that we speak what we believe. To overcome our fears, we need to believe in our hearts God is with us, and confidently say with our mouths that He is our helper.

Romans 10:10 gives the importance of believing first in our hearts, but then also speaking with our mouths. "For with the heart a person believes, resulting in righteousness, and with the mouth he confesses, resulting in salvation. Jesus gives the same principle of faith in Mark 11:23: "Truly I say to you, whoever says to this mountain, 'Be taken up and cast into the sea,' and does not doubt in his heart, but believes that what he says is going to happen, it will be granted him."

Some have used this verse to teach "name it and claim it," which has led to many abuses and caused many to throw out the baby (the importance of confession) with the bath water. But look closer at this verse and you will see that it's not about confession first, but about believing in the heart first, and then speaking from the place of faith.

The only way you can ever believe with your heart is if God Himself has spoken to you first. Romans 10:17 says that "faith comes by hearing and hearing by the word (rhema) of Christ." A rhema (the Greek for "word" used in this verse) is a specific word from God for a specific situation. After God has spoken into our hearts (about a specific mountain we are facing), we complete our faith by speaking with our mouths what God has said about our circumstances. That's when mountains move!

March 9

No Fear

"For you did not receive a spirit that makes you a slave again to fear, but you received the Spirit of sonship. And by Him we cry, 'Abba, Father.'"
Romans 8:15

God doesn't want us to be afraid. Fear is a slave driver that steals joy, peace, and love from us each day and reduces the potential of our lives. Fear of sickness; fear of financial lack; fear of rejection; fear of the future; fear of getting old; etc, God wants to free us from the oppressive power of fear.

According to our text, the Holy Spirit was given so that we would have confidence that God is our Daddy (Abba) and that He will help us whenever we cry out to Him. While studying Genesis I've noticed that the biggest issue all of the Patriarchs faced was fear. God came to each one of them at different times with the exact same message: "Do not be afraid."

Abraham had just freed Lot from his captors but knew that the defeated armies would seek revenge on him. He was afraid. The Lord then spoke to him, "Do not be afraid, I am your shield." (Genesis 15:1) Not just "a" shield; but "your" shield.

Isaac kept having wells stolen from him that were needed for survival. He finally dug a well that seemed safe, yet he was still afraid. God came and spoke, "Do not be afraid. I will bless you." (Genesis 26:24) God wanted Isaac to have something more than present provision; He wanted him to be free from living in the fear of future lack.

Jacob was old and was afraid he couldn't make the long trip to Egypt required by his circumstances. Once again, God spoke and said, "Do not be afraid... I will be with you." (Genesis 46:3-4) He didn't just want to get Jacob from point A to point B; God wanted Jacob to enjoy the trip without any fears. He wants the same for us.

He is our Defender, Provider, and Guide. No fear!

March 10

Who's in Charge?

"So I say, live by the Spirit, and you will not gratify the desires of the sinful nature. For the sinful nature desires what is contrary to the Spirit."
Galatians 5:16-17

The last time I was in Honduras we worked with a family who was temporarily taking care of a two year old named Angel. Angel couldn't talk yet, but he had no trouble communicating what he wanted to the three older girls in this family who watched over him. There was rarely a big scene over Angel because all he had to do was threaten displeasure and his desires would be instantly met. He ate what he wanted when he wanted it, and slept only when he was in the mood.

I started calling him, "Little Napoleon", because he was a tyrant over these three girls. One image I clearly remember was Angel listening to music with an ear piece while walking around in circles (nothing on but his diaper) while one of the girls held the CD player and frantically tried to stay up with him so the ear piece wouldn't come out.

There's a "little Napoleon" that lives in you and me called the sin nature. It has endless desires and wants to be catered to constantly. It wants to be immediately gratified and complains if there is ever a delay in meeting its needs. The sin nature finds reading the Bible, praying, fasting, or going to church boring, and much prefers the instant thrill of the media industry. It doesn't forgive, but rather uses anger and pouting to get its own way. If the sin nature is denied its way in one thing, it immediately seeks to find comfort in any number of other ways without thought of what's right and wrong, or of how it might affect those around. It doesn't like to serve, but lives to be served.

Parents need to decide early that they are in charge, and not their two year old. Have you given notice to your sin nature that it will not run your life? It will submit if you count yourself dead to its power through your identification with Christ's death and then live by the Spirit through identifying with Christ's resurrection. (Romans 6:1-14)

March 11

Me First

"And He said to another, 'Follow Me.' But he said, 'Lord, permit me first to go and bury my father.' But He said to him, 'Allow the dead to bury their own dead; but as for you, go and proclaim everywhere the kingdom of God.' Another also said, 'I will follow You, Lord; but first permit me to say goodbye to those at home.' But Jesus said to him, 'No one, after putting his hand to the plow and looking back, is fit for the kingdom of God.'" Luke 9:59-62

Is there anything wrong with burying your father or saying goodbye to those at home? Of course not. Then why did Jesus say what He said to these seemingly sincere people? One uses the phrase, "permit me first," and the other says, "first permit me," yet both preface their requests by calling Jesus, "Lord." They call Him, "Lord," but want to set their own terms in following Him.

Jesus is calling you and me to put the kingdom of God first, not ourselves, and not our families. If these two had left everything for the kingdom, it's very possible Jesus would have given them the assignment of going home first, like He did to the demoniac who was delivered in the chapter before. (Luke 8:39) But Jesus telling you to go home is very different from you telling Jesus that you're going home before following Him.

I think that family is one of the main idols of the evangelical church in America today. People run their lives around their children, their grandchildren, or their extended family, and just assume that God's okay with that. Listen to the words of Jesus, "He who loves father or mother more than Me is not worthy of Me; and he who loves son or daughter more than Me is not worthy of Me." (Matthew 10:37) If family is first you won't even be able to serve them in a right way because they are in the middle instead of Jesus. This is unhealthy and will end up leading the family you love subtly away from Jesus instead of to Him.

Jesus gave everything for us and He's asking us to give everything back to Him. When we do, there is a freedom from self that brings a great rest into our lives. Let's set our hands to the plow called the kingdom of God and trust God with everything else, including our families.

March 12

Increase Our Faith

"The apostles said to the Lord, 'Increase our faith!'" ... "So you too, when you do all the things which are commanded you, say, 'We are unworthy servants; we have done only that which we ought to have done.'" Luke 17:5; 10

In response to His disciples' request for increased faith, Jesus told about a servant who shouldn't think he deserves anything special for all his work. What does this have to do with faith?

If you approach God as a servant who is looking for pay you will limit grace in your life because grace isn't given on those terms. Serve God and keep His commandments because you love Him, but don't allow a spirit of entitlement to get on you because of your sacrifice or great devotion. After you've obeyed God completely, remind yourself, "I am an unworthy (undeserving) servant. God owes me nothing."

In obedience, we must think of ourselves as servants, but in prayer we must take our position as beloved children. (1John 3:1) A master gives a servant wages based on the servant's performance, but a father gives his children gifts based only on his love and available resources. Jesus said to us, "If you being evil know how to give good gifts to your children, how much more will the heavenly Father give good things to those who ask Him." (Matthew 7:11) In Luke's gospel He says the Father gives "the Holy Spirit to those who ask Him." (Luke 11:13) The Father gives good gifts, natural and spiritual, not to those who are good, but to those who ask as His children.

Jesus said to pray as children of God, saying, "our Father." We are adopted children who come to God through the blood of Christ with only the claim that we are loved, and we are His.

One of my favorite Dennis the Menace cartoons shows Dennis and his friend, Joey, eating a plate of cookies. Joey asks: "I wonder what we did that Mrs. Wilson made us a plate of cookies?" Dennis explains: "Joey, Mrs. Wilson doesn't make us cookies because we're good; Mrs. Wilson makes us cookies because Mrs. Wilson is good!"

The gospel is not about our performance, but about God's generosity. To have increasing faith, we need to think of ourselves as both unworthy servants, and God's favored children.

March 13

Easier and Harder

"If anyone would come after me, let him deny himself and take up his cross and follow me... whoever loses his life for My sake and the gospels will find it." Mark 8:34-35

In his classic book, Mere Christianity, C.S. Lewis compares being good through the power of the natural self to paying taxes. Conscience and culture make demands as to what "good and acceptable" behavior is, so we submit to them with the hope that after we have met those demands there will be time left over to do what we want to do. We pay taxes because it's our duty, but we mostly think about the money we'll have left over to spend however we want to.

"The Christian way," he maintains, "is different: harder, and easier. Christ says, 'Give Me all. I don't want so much of your time and so much of your money and so much of your work: I want you. I have not come to torment your natural self, but to kill it. No half-measures are any good. I don't want to cut off a branch here and a branch there, I want to have the whole tree down. Hand over the whole natural self, all the desires which you think innocent as well as the ones you think wicked – the whole outfit. I will give you a new self instead. In fact, I will give you Myself: My own will shall become yours.'

"Both harder and easier than what we are all trying to do. You have noticed, I expect, that Christ Himself sometimes describes the Christian way as very hard, sometimes as very easy. He says, 'Take up your cross' – in other words, it is like going to be beaten to death in a concentration camp. Next minute He says, 'My yoke is easy and My burden light.' He means both. And one can see why both are true."

We don't have to try to change the old self; it must die. As we embrace this death, we are absolutely free to live in the resurrection life Jesus abundantly provides through the Spirit.

March 14

Taking the Trash Out

"But thanks be to God, who always leads us in triumph in Christ, and manifests through us the sweet aroma of the knowledge of Him in every place." 2Corinthians 2:14

Alice and I once returned to our home to a horrible smell. Something was rotting in our trash can so we quickly tied up the bag and moved it to the outside garbage bin in our garage. The smell was so bad that I was already looking forward to Monday morning when I would take it to the curb and the trash man would take it off our property forever.

A Christian's life is supposed to smell like faith, hope, and love; "the sweet aroma of the knowledge of Him," but sometimes it smells like something else. In our trash cupboard there is one bin for trash and one for recyclables. There are at least three bins in the Christian life that need to be quickly tied up and given to God or a bad smell starts coming from our lives.

1. The sin bin – When the Holy Spirit makes it clear to us that we have sinned against God or people we need to quickly and fully confess and repent. If we justify ourselves it doesn't go away, it starts smelling like condemnation. The Holy Spirit exposes our sin because it comes between us and God and wants only for us to confess it so we will have confidence again. (1 John 1:9)

2. The trouble bin – Part of living on this planet is that we face various types of troubles every single day. If we don't get them to God right away our lives start smelling like anxiety and eventually fear. God allows troubles because He wants us to trust Him and to get to know Him through His intimate care of us.

3. The disappointment bin – When we are disappointed with God or people we become vulnerable so we must give our disappointments quickly to God. When we don't, they turn into discouragement and if we let discouragement go long enough, it becomes depression.

You know, there's an interesting thing about our trash man – he will only take the things that are at the curb. He never comes into my garage looking for the garbage. If it's not at the curb, it doesn't get picked up. It's time to let go and let God!

March 15

Worldview

"I have been crucified with Christ; and it is no longer I who live, but Christ lives in me; and the life which I now live in the flesh I live by faith in the Son of God, who loved me and gave Himself up for me." Galatians 2:20

William Temple (1881-1944) was a philosopher, professor at Oxford, and ultimately the archbishop of Canterbury. His great concern was that Christians would embrace a world view that puts man in the center instead of God. Here is an excerpt from his writings:

"The least popular part of traditional Christianity is Original Sin. I was doing it before I could speak, as has everyone else. I am not 'guilty' on this account because I could not help it. But I am in a state, from birth, in which I shall bring disaster on myself and everyone else unless I escape it. Education may make my self-centeredness less disastrous by widening my horizons. But this is like climbing a tower which widens the horizons of my vision while leaving me still the center of reference. The only way to deliver me from my self-centeredness is by winning my entire heart's devotion, the total allegiance of my will to God, and this can only be done by the Divine love of God disclosed by Christ in His life and death.

In making the world, God brought into existence vast numbers of things, like electrons which always have to obey His law for them and do so. But He made creatures – men and women – who could disobey His law for them and often do so. He did this in order that among His creatures there might be some who answer His love with theirs by offering to Him a free obedience.

This involved a risk in that they would naturally take the self-centered outlook on life, and then, increasingly become hardened in that selfishness. This is what has happened. To win them out of this, He came on earth and lived out the Divine love in human life and death. He is increasingly drawing us to Himself by the love thus shown, but this task of drawing all people to Himself will not be complete until the end of history." (Devotional Classics; page 224-226)

March 16

What About Us?

"Then Peter said to Him, 'Behold, we have left everything and followed You; what then will there be for us?'" Matthew 19:27

Peter wanted to know what was in it for him. He paid a price to follow Christ and like any man, he wanted to know practically what the return would be. Jesus said in reply, "Truly I say to you, there is no one who has left house or brothers or sisters or mother or father or children or farms, for My sake and for the gospel's sake, but that he will receive a hundred times as much now in the present age, houses and brothers and sisters and mothers and children and farms, along with persecutions; and in the age to come, eternal life." (Mark 10:29-30)

Jesus explained to him how grace works. He had already made it clear that they couldn't earn eternal life by telling them in response to their question, "Who then can be saved?" that it was impossible with man. Peter and the other disciples aren't going to be paid back for their sacrifice, as if God could be in their debt. Yet God is generous, and He is pleased when people go "all in" for Jesus and the gospel.

Jesus says something like this to Peter (my paraphrase): "Your life in this world will be 100 times better for following Me. God will multiply your relationships – you will have family everywhere you go. Everything that is Mine (which is everything) will be available to you – I will open houses and lands for your use. However, there will also be trouble for you in this world. Don't take persecution as rejection from God, it will simply be part of your life in this present time. In the world to come, you will have eternal life with God and all the trouble of this life will be removed."

Grace is amazing. We don't follow Jesus to earn anything but because we love Him. God doesn't bless us because he owes us anything but because He loves us and because He is unbelievably generous. He made us His favored sons and daughters in Christ, so He can pour His grace in and through us. Just walk with Jesus today and know that the favor of God rests on you.

March 17

Maintaining a Soft Heart

"How blessed is the man who always fears the Lord, but he who hardens his heart falls into trouble." Proverbs 28:14

One definition of the fear of the Lord can be inferred by its opposite. If hardening your heart is how you express not fearing the Lord; then the true fear of the Lord must involve maintaining a soft, responsive heart. So how do we do this?

First by repentance. To stay soft we must be good at repenting. Joel 2:13 says, "Rend your heart and not your garments. Return to the Lord your God, for He is gracious and compassionate, slow to anger and abounding in love, and He relents from sending calamity." God doesn't want us to fall into trouble, so He wants us to really repent (our hearts) and not just appear to repent (our garments). A great definition for repentance is given in the verse before our text: "He who conceals his sin does not prosper, but whoever confesses and renounces them finds mercy." (Proverbs 28:13)

Secondly by prompt obedience. Hebrews 3:7-8 says, "Today if you hear His voice, do not harden your hearts as you did in the rebellion during the time of testing in the desert." Every time God speaks to us we have the potential of becoming softer or harder. Purpose to obey Him no matter what, small or big, if He will make it clear to you that it is Him speaking. There are many voices speaking today: our own anxieties, demonic influences, false religious expectations; but also the sweet Spirit of God. Test what you are hearing and if it is the voice leading you toward "righteousness, peace, and joy" (Romans 14:17), obey without hesitation and reap the benefits of having a tender heart before God.

March 18

Resisting Temptation

"If you think you are standing firm, be careful that you don't fall! No temptation has seized you except what is common to man. And God is faithful; He will not let you be tempted beyond what you can bear. But when you are tempted, He will also provide a way out so that you can stand up under it." 1Corinthians 10:12-13

Part of the enemy's strategy in getting us to give into temptation is seizing us and making us feel there is no choice except to sin. When God asked Adam what he had done the reply was, "The woman You gave me..." Basically, "it wasn't my fault! It was the woman's fault; in fact, it was kind of Your fault since You gave me the woman." Then God asked Eve what she had done and she also shifted the blame: "The serpent deceived me and I ate."

Our excuses are irrelevant to God and do not lead us into freedom but only into greater bondage. No matter what the circumstances were around our sin, Scripture tells us that God provided a "way out" if we had only looked for it and prayed about it. Proverbs tells us that whoever hides his sin (puts the blame somewhere else) will not prosper, but whoever "confesses and forsakes" it will obtain mercy. (Proverbs 28:13) Own your sin; confess it, confess that you didn't look or pray for the way out, and then forsake it.

But how much better it is to resist temptation and not fall into sin. God's main strategy for us to keep from sinning is to flee that which is tempting us. The idea that we can handle being close to sin without falling into it is a deception because we are all weaker than we think we are. In fact, "if you think you are standing firm be careful that you don't fall!"

Adam and Eve were given a whole garden to enjoy, yet Eve chose to stand right next to the one tree that was forbidden. Not smart. When I was a young believer I had developed a fixation for a certain young woman in our home town. As I was reading Proverbs the warning came, "Don't look into her eyes." (Proverbs 6:25) So from then on I made it a point to not look her in the eyes when I was around her, but I would still find myself driving by her house hoping that she was outside. Later I read another Proverb that said, "Don't even go near her house." (Proverbs 5:8) I was stunned. God's strategy was not "get close and try to be strong," but simply stay far away.

What is the area of your greatest weakness? Why not enjoy the rest of the garden and stay far away from that tree!

Understanding Authority

"All authority comes from God so the one who resists authority is resisting God." Romans 13:1 "We have been seated with Christ in heavenly places." Ephesians 2:6

I fear that most American Christians don't understand how God feels about positional authority. We tend to honor those who we feel are honorable while withholding honor from those we don't think deserve it.

All authority has been instituted by God and therefore should be unconditionally honored. It doesn't matter whether your dad is an alcoholic; if you learn to honor his position, God's blessing for those who honor their parents will rest on you. David, the man after God's own heart, refused to raise his hand "against the Lord's anointed." (1Samuel 24:6) Saul was demon oppressed at the time, so the anointing was not on the man, but on the position he held. (Notice, honoring authority does not mean remaining in a place of abuse as David fled when Saul started throwing spears at him.)

If we only honor authority that we feel is worthy, we will never take the place God has given us unless we feel worthy to take it. How often does that happen? The gospel isn't about us being good enough, it's about God's grace and about a position He wants us to take in Christ. You have been made a child of God (Galatians 4:6), a priest of God (Revelation 1:6), and have been given the "the gift of righteousness," so that you can "reign in life through the One, Jesus Christ." (Romans 5:17)

We need to understand and honor positional authority, so we can honor the position God has given us in Christ. The late Reinhart Bonkhe didn't begin to walk in the miraculous power of God until one day when God said, "My word in your mouth is just as powerful as My word in My mouth." Africa was never the same as unprecedented miracles led to millions of recorded salvations.

I believe God and the world are waiting for each of us to take our position in Christ!

March 20

Don't Get Offended

"Now when John, while imprisoned, heard of the works of Christ he sent word by his disciples and said to Him, 'Are You the Expected One, or shall we look for someone else?' Jesus answered and said to them, 'Go and report to John what you hear and see: the blind receive sight and the lame walk, the lepers are cleansed and the deaf hear, the dead are raised up, and the poor have the gospel preached to them. And blessed is he who does not take offense at Me.'" Matthew 11:2-6

John had obeyed God. He was leading a revival with the spirit of Elijah on him and people were repenting and being forgiven of their sins. The only thing left was for the leadership to repent, so the whole nation could return to God. With that in mind, he confronted Herod Antipas about his wrong relationship with Herodias. Instead of repenting and being part of the revival, Antipas had John thrown in prison. This was not what John had prayed would happen nor what he had expected; he was disappointed.

It was in that place, in prison, alone, disappointed, that the man of God began to question everything. His predecessor, Elijah, went through a similar experience and also found himself alone expressing his disappointment to God. (See 1Kings 19) If these two great heroes of faith were tested in this way, it shouldn't surprise us that dealing with disappointment is also part of our journey.

We all have desires and expectations that we want God to meet. When He doesn't follow our plan in our time we experience disappointment which can easily turn into an offense against God. What John needed was the same thing Elijah needed; a fresh word from God. How intimate that Jesus would take time to give His friend in prison a specific word. He quoted Isaiah 61, a familiar Messianic Scripture, assuring John that He indeed was the Expected One. John had heard right and had done just what God had wanted him to do, but was now faced with his biggest test – disappointment. Jesus gave him the path to freedom: "Blessed is he who does not take offense with Me."

Let's make sure we don't get offended when God's plan is different than ours. If you're sitting in disappointment today and need a fresh word from heaven, why not ask right now?

Kingdom Abundance

"For whoever has, to him more shall be given, and he will have an abundance..." Matthew 13:12

To walk in the kingdom of God we have to change our thinking from lack to abundance and it's not easy. The disciples thought Jesus was referencing bread when he started teaching about the leaven of the Pharisees and Sadducees. They immediately became afraid because they had forgotten to bring the left over bread with them. Jesus was frustrated by their assumption that He was concerned about the lack of bread.

"'Why do you discuss the fact that you have no bread? Do you not yet see or understand? Do you have a hardened heart? Having eyes, do you not see? Having ears, do you not hear? And do you not remember? When I broke the five loaves for the five thousand, how many basketfuls of pieces did you pick up?' 'Twelve,' they replied. 'When I broke the seven loaves for the four thousand, how many basketfuls of pieces did you pick up?' They answered, 'seven.' He said to them, 'Do you still not understand?'" (Mark 8:19-21)

They were supposed to change their thinking. God fully resources those who are giving their lives for Him. Did you notice that He didn't even ask them about how many were fed, but only about the leftovers. God has more than enough. There is an abundance in the kingdom which is why we reign in this life "through the abundance of grace" (Romans 5:17), and why Jesus said He came to give "life abundantly." (John 10:10) Not just enough for us, but leftovers for others.

If we don't embrace the abundance of the kingdom, we will end up living in the fear of self preservation. When we do this, the kingdom can't spread. We must give our lives away with abandon knowing that God will take care of us. In the words of Jesus: "The hour has come for the Son of Man to be glorified. Truly, truly I say to you, unless a grain of wheat falls into the earth and dies, it remains alone; but if it dies, it bears much fruit." (John 12:23-24)

March 22

The Sign of Jonah

"No sign will be given except the sign of Jonah. For as Jonah was three days and three nights in the belly of a huge fish, so the Son of Man will be three days and three nights in the heart of the earth. The men of Nineveh will stand up at the judgment with this generation and condemn it; for they repented at the preaching of Jonah, and now One greater than Jonah is here." Matthew 12:39-41

Jonah is a unique book in the Old Testament. Not only does it foreshadow Christ's resurrection; it also foreshadows the preaching of redemption to God's enemies. The idea of transforming nations that Jesus introduced in the kingdom of God was not practiced in the Old Testament. Leaders, in that time, were appointed by God to restrain evil by staying separate from their enemies, or, if necessary, by engaging them in war.

So we can imagine Jonah's shock when God tells him to preach to Israel's arch enemy, Nineveh. Prophets spoke to Judah and Israel, not Assyria! (Nineveh was the capital of Assyria) Whenever other nations were mentioned by God to a prophet, it was a message about them, never to them.

"Why would God have me go to the land of my enemy and tell them He was going to destroy them in forty days?" Jonah must have pondered. There was only one answer he could come up with. God didn't want to destroy them (or He just would have done it), He wanted to save them. When Nineveh repented, Jonah prayed this to God: "O Lord, is this not what I said when I was still at home? That is why I was so quick to flee to Tarshish. I knew that you are a gracious and compassionate God, slow to anger and abounding in love, a God who relents from sending calamity." (Jonah 4:2)

Mercy, not judgment, was on God's mind, but it wasn't on Jonah's. God gave Jonah a second chance after his rebellion, but Jonah didn't want to give that same chance to others.

Today God has given us His grace and forgiveness in Christ and wants us to extend that same message to others. I hope we do better than Jonah!

Choosing Well

"Few things are necessary, really only one, and Mary has chosen the good part." Luke 10:42

A recent quote I heard has really struck me, "It is almost impossible to overestimate the unimportance of most things." Think about this for a moment. All talk about food and drink is really unimportant. All talk of sports is really unimportant. All talk of weather, past, present, and future is mostly unimportant. All speculation of how the rich and famous live is meaningless and most talk of others is to no valuable end either. It's amazing how much we are able to talk without really saying anything important.

"Small talk," is what we call it. It is purposely unimportant because it breaks the ice in relationships without causing controversy. I get that, but I hope our lives are aiming at something more valuable, or we may end up as empty as most conversations.

Mary was seated at the Lord's feet listening to His Word. There is nothing more valuable than a life focused on a relationship with God. Proverbs 1:32-33 says, "...the complacency of fools will destroy them; but whoever listens to Me will live in safety and be at ease, without fear of harm." This is the good part.

Martha became distracted by her serving and ended up with the bad part; working for Jesus but no longer listening to Him; around Him, but not personally experiencing Him. Jesus is helping her to leave a distracted lifestyle by telling her that what Mary has, she has chosen. It's as if He's saying, "Martha, you are not a victim of your circumstances. You too can choose the good part."

King David made this choice in the midst of his adventurous and busy life. "One thing have I desired and that will I seek after; that I may dwell in the house of the Lord (the Presence of God) all the days of my life, to gaze upon the beauty of the Lord and to seek Him in His temple." (Psalm 27:4)

If something other than Him is the aim of our life, we're on a tangent. Why not make a better choice today?

March 24

The Ground Under Your Feet

"Blessed are the merciful for they shall obtain mercy." Matthew 5:8

I was in an informal conversation with a young pastor recently when he said, "I really struggle giving grace to church people who are not fully committed even though they know better."

I asked if he minded me using the word "mercy" where he had used the word "grace," and he told me to go ahead. "So here's what you're basically saying," I responded. "You struggle to give mercy to those you feel don't deserve it." He understood where I was going. If someone "deserves" mercy it isn't really mercy, it's justice.

Jesus made it clear that our attitude toward others determines the ground under our own feet. If we choose to judge others than the same measure we use will be applied to us. (Matthew 7:1-4) But if we choose to be merciful toward the faults of others, we will find a wide place of mercy under our own feet as well. The merciful obtain mercy.

In Micah 6:8 God laid out clear instructions of how to please Him: "Do justly, love mercy, and walk humbly with your God." Our natural tendency is to give mercy to ourselves, love justice for others, and to walk in self-righteousness, independent of God.

We need grace to do justly instead of making excuses for ourselves. We need grace to not only give mercy, but to love showing mercy to others. And we need grace to simply walk humbly with God. No wonder Jesus said that the key was not us, but Him in us. Apart from Him we can do nothing, but in Him we will bring forth much fruit. (John 15:5)

March 25

The Rudder

"My house shall be a house of prayer." Luke 19:46

In the spring of 2009 the woman leading our weekly prayer meeting requested prayer because the burden of leading was heavy on her. She was in charge because she was a known intercessor and I knew I wasn't. Early one morning while praying for her, I received an impression of a large ship with a small rudder. A sentence came into my mind, "Lead the church from the prayer meeting." With this thought came an immediate understanding of three things:

1. I had been trying to lead the church from Sunday mornings to that point.
2. Because of this I was leading the church politically (human effort) instead of spiritually (trusting God).
3. The large ship represented the church and the small, unseen rudder; the prayer meeting. God was asking me to take my place as the leader of the prayer meeting.

From that time until this I have tried to lead our prayer meetings. From that time we tell all who come to our membership classes that we consider the prayer meeting our most important gathering of the week.

If you've ever been to a Tuesday night you know it's not very impressive. Yet it's the prayer meeting that gives me confidence God is in all the other ministries at church, including Sunday mornings.

Jesus said: "My house shall be a house of prayer." Until we've prayed, we should do nothing. Once we've prayed, we should only go forward as God directs. This is true of a church, but it's also true for individuals. We are the house God lives in today. (2Corinthians 6:16)

So what's the rudder in your life? What is the underlying motivation for all you do? Is it money? Fun? Selfish ambition? Family? Responsibility? The same Jesus who turned the tables over in the temple knocks on our door today asking for our permission to enter. He is still filled with zeal to make us a house of prayer but has chosen to wait for us to make prayer a priority in our lives.

"Behold, I stand at the door and knock; if anyone hears My voice and opens the door, I will come in to him and will dine with him, and he with Me." (Revelation 3:20)

March 26

A Song in the Night

"Deep calls to deep in the roar of Your waterfalls; all your waves and breakers have swept over me. By day the Lord directs His love, at night His song is with me." Psalm 42:7-8

The Psalmist is in a time of mourning and desperation that has invited him to go deeper in God. God's breakers have swept over him and they have broken him down to where all he has left is a thirst for God Himself. (Psalm 42:2) Have you ever been here? Are you there right now? God has a song He wants you to embrace; a song in the night.

David was in the wilderness being chased by Saul even though he had done nothing wrong. He had been anointed by Samuel and had an early victory over Goliath, but now an army was seeking to kill him and he was on the run with his men, hiding in caves. (Psalm 27:3) At this time David heard God say to his heart, "Seek My face." (Psalm 27:8) In the midst of David's great need for His hand (power to deliver), God invited David deeper, to seek His face (who He is). May our response be similar to David's: "Your face, oh God, I will seek." (Psalm 27:8)

Three things happen to us when we embrace the song in the night:

1. Our joy becomes centered in God alone. Habakkuk says that when famine strikes and all external blessings are cut off, he will rejoice in God because God alone is his Savior, Strength, and Guide through life's most difficult times. (Habakkuk 3:17-19)

2. Our identity changes. Hosea declares that experiencing God's tenderness in the wilderness will lead to us calling God our husband instead of our master. (Hosea 2:14-16) It's in the frustration and despair of the wilderness that God calls us deeper and changes us. David says it this way: "Your gentleness makes me great." (Psalm 18:35)

3. We prepare the way for our own deliverance. David says the rising waters will not reach him because God has surrounded him with "songs of deliverance." (Psalm 32:7) Paul and Silas sang this song in jail and it led to an earthquake that freed all of the prisoners (Acts 16). Is it midnight in your life? Lift your eyes higher, seek His face, and sing His song.

Desire, Discipline, and Delight

"If anyone is thirsty, let him come to Me and drink. He who believes in Me, as the Scripture said, 'From his innermost being will flow rivers of living water.'" John 7:37-38

Desire without discipline will lead to defeat. All Christians have a desire for Jesus, but many don't add discipline to their desire so when they are thirsty they go to wrong places. Some go to addictions, others to entertainment, some to human relationships, and others to work, but only Jesus Himself can satisfy the deep thirst of our souls. When we don't take time to be in His presence reading His word, praying, worshipping and connecting with other believers we are ignoring the means by which He pours out His Spirit on us, and this leaves us in spiritual defeat. Many believers have the testimony Paul describes in Romans 7:19, "The good that I want, I do not do, but I practice the very evil that I do not want." Instead of rivers flowing, many believers feel discouraged because of repeated failure.

Discipline without delight will lead only to us doing our duty. If Jesus becomes one more "have to" on our list, our relationship with Him will only be one more burden required of us. It is possible to read the Bible, pray, and go to church without ever drinking from Jesus. It is possible to have a Christianity defined but what "I" do for God instead of what God is doing in me. Trust me, I've lived this way and all it does is produce spiritual pride which results in hardness of heart. Discipline will always start out as a "have to," but if we refuse to make it an end in itself, discipline will eventually give way to delight as our spiritual taste buds come alive to God's presence and word.

No one is impressed by the discipline of a teenage boy who remembers to eat three times a day. Eating is his delight, not his duty. When we reach delight we stop noticing our discipline because it just becomes part of who we are!

March 28

Four Marks of a Godly Life

"For the grace of God has appeared that offers salvation to all people. It teaches us to say "No" to ungodliness and worldly passions, and to live self-controlled, upright and godly lives in this present age, while we wait for the blessed hope-the appearing of the glory of our great God and Savior, Jesus Christ, who gave Himself for us to redeem us from all wickedness and to purify for Himself a people that are his very own, eager to do what is good." Titus 2:11-14

More than clever, gifted, or successful, I want to be godly. We live in such a secular society that many people may not even know what that means. Here are four marks of a godly life from the text above:

1. The godly live close to God. Jesus loves us and gave Himself for us so we could be forgiven and live close to God, in fact, in union with God every day. The godly don't endure God; they make Him their greatest delight. (Psalm 37:4)

2. The godly say "No" to all that is in them that would take them away from God. We have a sin nature that must be put off or died to every day. The sin nature is at war with the Spirit but the Spirit gives us power to overcome it. (Galatians 5:16-17)

3. The godly are eager to do good. Jesus went about doing good and healing all who were oppressed. (Acts 10:38) The truly godly aren't known for what they're against, but for the good works they do. (Ephesians 2:10; Matthew 5:16) Their willingness to serve those in need gives people a taste of the goodness of God in this present age.

4. The godly know the best is yet to come. Every problem will not be solved this side of heaven, and every pain will not be removed, but a better day is coming. Jesus will appear one day to take His bride and we will then be with Him forever. This is the living hope which burns in the godly and gives them strength for the journey. They are convinced that "our light and momentary troubles are achieving for us an eternal glory that far outweighs them all." (2Corinthians 4:17)

Stored Wrath: A Look into Hell

"But because of your stubbornness and your unrepentant heart, you are storing up wrath against yourself for the day of God's wrath when His righteous judgment will be revealed." Romans 2:5

God wants us to contemplate hell now, so we don't end up there. We are told to behold both His kindness and His severity (Romans 11:22) as a protection from us ever having to experience His severity. In His mercy toward us, Jesus spoke more about hell than heaven, not as a threat to His enemies, but as a warning to His friends. Jesus doesn't want any of us to go to hell.

As we take a look into hell from this text, we can see three things:

1. God doesn't send anyone to hell; we send ourselves there. "You are storing up wrath against yourself." Jesus died so we could be forgiven; He's already tasted death for us. (Hebrews 2:9) No one needs to go to hell when God's expressed will for all of us is to be saved. (2Peter 3:9) If we end up in hell, we will have only ourselves to blame.

2. God's anger and wrath against sin is being "stored" now, but will be poured out then. We all outlive our bodies and will face the day of judgment. (Hebrews 9:27) Those who have rejected Christ's love and payment for their sins will make their own payment in the lake of fire. (Revelation 20:15)

3. God's judgment will be righteous. Those who have not received eternal life will eventually be destroyed in the lake of fire, body and soul. (Matthew 10:28) They died physically once, received back their bodies before final judgment (Revelation 20:13), and then will physically die again in the lake of fire which is called the second death. They will eventually perish in hell (John 3:16) but not before they pay, by conscious torment, for every sin they committed against humanity. (Luke 12:47-48) They will ultimately be consumed by eternal fire and will eventually be remembered no more. (Matthew 3:12; Hebrews 10:27; Psalm 37:38)

C.S. Lewis said in *The Great Divorce*, "Some would rather rule in hell than serve in heaven. And to those who reject Christ's rule He will say: 'Your will be done.'"

March 30

Resurrection Righteousness

"But now a righteousness from God, apart from law, has been made known, to which the Law and the prophets testify. This righteousness from God comes through faith in Jesus Christ to all who believe." Romans 3:21-22

The historical event of the resurrection has established a heavenly reality for all who are willing to believe. God is offering the gift of right standing (righteousness) with Him, when we trust Christ.

When we owe a speeding ticket, we are not in right standing with the law until it is paid. If we don't pay our electric bill, we are no longer in right standing with the electric company until we remit the amount owed. If someone makes a payment on my behalf, I gain right standing even though I wasn't the one who settled the account. This is the gospel. God has paid for my sins, so right standing is available to me.

What must I be willing to believe to access this heavenly reality?

1. That I am guilty before a holy God and am unable to make things right on my own. Isaiah says that even our righteous acts are as filthy rags in God's sight. (Isaiah 64:6) We may feel righteous by comparison to others, but God doesn't compare us with other people. He views us through His own perfection.

2. That God made payment for my guilt by dying for my sins. The cross is the greatest display of God's holiness, and of God's love. God's justice demanded payment for sin while God's love provided that payment on my behalf.

3. That I must make it personal by receiving the gift of righteousness. The gospel will not affect me until I believe it. All who reject, or ignore Christ, will one day find themselves accountable to God for all their sins. But the only sin that condemns us is an unwillingness to accept the Spirit's invitation to believe in Jesus. (See John 16:7-9)

Those who do believe can join in the ancient hymn with great joy, "My hope is built on nothing less, than Jesus' blood and righteousness. I dare not trust the sweetest frame but wholly lean on Jesus' Name. On Christ the solid rock I stand; all other ground is sinking sand. All other ground is sinking sand."

Entering the Promised Land

"Have I not commanded you? Be strong and courageous! Do not tremble or be dismayed, for the Lord your God is with you wherever you go." Joshua 1:9

I was talking with a business man recently who was going through a time of tremendous fear and despair. He was so gripped that he questioned whether he could do his job anymore. In the midst of our conversation he said, "I'm right at the Jordan River." What he didn't know was that I was working on a message from Joshua 1, where the Jordan River is between Israel and the promised land. To be "at the Jordan River" is to be at a place where a decision has to be made: Do I go forward in faith, or do I retreat in fear?

In nine short verses God tells Joshua to be "strong and courageous" three times. Why is this? I believe it's because we have a role in whether we go into the promised land or not. God will defeat the giants and take down the walls that oppose us; but He won't do it apart from us agreeing with His purpose and power working in us. (Ephesians 3:20)

The previous group that was at the Jordan River didn't make it into the promised land because of fear. Twelve spies had gone out and brought back two narratives of what was happening:

One narrative, given by ten of the spies, went something like this: "We are in big trouble. There are giants in this land that make us look like grasshoppers. There are impenetrable walls that we could never take down. If we go forward we will fail – God has deceived us. It's time to retreat to Egypt."

The other narrative, given by Joshua and Caleb, went something like this: "There are giants and walls, but it's an amazing land, and God has given it to us. The giants and walls are nothing compared to God and He is going with us. He is so good to give us this spacious land that flows with milk and honey. Let's cross the Jordan and take our land!"

Whichever narrative we agree with will be the reality we live in. God doesn't make anyone go into His promised land for their life. He encourages, He plans, He invites, but He doesn't force us. If we choose to listen to the voice of fear instead of the voice of faith, we will wander in the wilderness and never become all that He wanted us to be.

April 1

Why We aren't the Judge

"All the ways of a man are right in his own eyes, but the Lord weighs the motives." Proverbs 16:2

For years growing up my brother Jimmy and I would come home from school, eat a bowl of cereal, and watch *Gilligan's Island*. From time to time the entire episode would be about something that happened on the island in the past.

Skipper would start telling about the event and all of a sudden we were back there; but it was all from Skipper's perspective. He was in the middle; he was doing the right thing while those around him were doing questionable things. He was the hero; that's how he remembered it.

The episode would return to the present, and then another character would start to give their version of the story (Ginger, the professor, sometimes Mr. Howell) and in their memory they were the hero. And then finally, Gilligan would start talking about it and we'd go back a third time. Where others' versions had Gilligan at blame, Gilligan always had himself being somewhat heroic. Yes, bad things happened but he was actually part of the solution, not the main problem. The funny thing was we were never told what actually happened – only three different perspectives of the same event.

This is why Jesus told us not to judge. (Matthew 7:1) We experience life only from our own perspective and even our own motives are often hidden from us. When we feel others have wronged us, or betrayed us, it's important to realize that that's probably not how they see it. Instead of believing the worst and playing judge, we're called to believe the best and let God be the judge. Where there has been definite sin, we're called to forgive "as God, in Christ, has forgiven us." (Ephesians 4:32)

All things are laid bare before Him to whom we will give an account. (Hebrews 4:13) God calls us to do what's right in His eyes: "To do justly, to love mercy, and to walk humbly with our God." (Micah 6:8) It's humanly natural to have mercy for ourselves, love justice for others, and walk in the pride of being a judge, instead of submitting to God as the only one able to judge rightly. The Holy Spirit wants to help us live differently. He wants us to apply justice to ourselves while giving mercy to others. This is part of what it means to walk humbly with God.

April 2

Loving Righteousness

"Blessed are those who hunger and thirst for righteousness for they will be satisfied." Matthew 5:6

I love stories. In the morning I read the Bible and serious devotionals, but at night before bed, I'm usually reading or sometimes watching a story that inspires me to love righteousness.

A story is a powerful tool (Jesus used them all the time) for good or for evil, so I try to be careful. I have found that some books, shows, and movies actually mock righteousness and empower wickedness, and leave me sad, confused, or even despairing if I embraced their message. I sometimes lament having wasted time on such stories and always promise to use more discernment in the future.

A few years ago I gave an illustration from *The Horse Whisperer* and said it was a good movie and a horrible book. What did I mean by that?

In the book, a woman and the man who healed her horse are drawn to each other, have an affair, and she ends up leaving her husband and her daughter because she has found "true love." The message: Humans are flawed and messy and certainly not to be blamed if their "heart" leads them to break their wedding vows. Horrible.

In the movie, the woman and the man who healed her horse are also drawn to each other and are tempted to be adulterous. Yet they resist the temptation, and in the end she returns to her husband and daughter. We empathize with flawed, emotional human beings, because we relate to them, and then we celebrate when they do what's right in spite of their flaws. It strengthens us and feeds our hunger for righteousness. We too are flawed but we can still do what is right!

I stop reading a book or watching a show when I have no one to cheer for (hopefully sooner rather than later!). I expect people to be flawed because I can't relate to a perfect character. However, I like someone who is trying to do what is right. Someone who is rising above their own comfort, sorrow, or selfish desires to courageously do what is right. Just because something appeals to our love of humor, action, or mystery doesn't make it "good" art. Art that we participate in should inspire our love for righteousness and our hatred for wickedness, not dampen it.

April 3

The Secret Weapon

"Truly I say to you, whatever you bind on earth shall have been bound in heaven; and whatever you loose on earth shall have been loosed in heaven. Again I say to you, that if two of you agree on earth about anything that they may ask, it shall be done for them by My Father who is in heaven. For where two or three have gathered together in My name, I am there in their midst." Matthew 18:18-20

The secret weapon is a game changer. When Popeye is down and out, when all hope seems to be lost and Bluto is certainly going to defeat him, we all wait for the secret weapon – his spinach. The spinach changes everything; once it is eaten, the victory is secured.

Aladdin is trapped in a cave left to die. He tries to escape but it's hopeless until he discovers a lamp. The lamp is a game changer because using it gives access to a genie who can transcend all human limitations.

The church has a secret weapon that changes everything: the Father's response to agreeing prayer. We see it in Acts 2: The church had been in unified prayer for ten days until the Father responded with "a mighty rushing wind" and "tongues of fire" which so empowered the early church that 3,000 were saved in one day.

We see it in Acts 4: The persecuted church gathered and in agreeing prayer asked the Father to "do signs and wonders by Your holy Servant, Jesus." The response: "After they prayed, the place where they were meeting was shaken. And they were all filled with the Holy Spirit and spoke the word of God boldly." (Acts 4:31) Abundant grace was released and signs and wonders were performed (Acts 5:12) while multitudes were saved. (Acts 5:14) Heaven invaded earth in response to agreeing prayer by the church.

But my favorite example of the secret weapon is found in Acts 16. Paul and Silas were put in prison and at the midnight hour began to pray and worship together. Here's the Father's response, "Suddenly there was such a violent earthquake that the foundations of the prison were shaken. At once all the prison doors flew open, and everyone's chains came loose." (Acts 16:26) Natural earthquakes destroy, they don't open doors and release people from chains. Were Paul and Silas asking the Father for everyone's chains to fall off? Unlikely. This is about the extravagance of a God who is able "to do above and beyond all we can think" (Ephesians 3:20) in response to agreeing prayer.

April 4

Getting The Win

"But now Christ has been raised from the dead, the first fruits of those who are asleep... For as in Adam all die, so also in Christ all who are His will be made alive. But each in his own order: Christ the first fruits, after that those who are Christ's at His coming." 1Corinthians 15:19; 22-23

I like to win. If I don't feel I can win, I'd rather not compete, which is why I almost dropped out of the 2011 McFarland Triathlon my brother Mike asked me to be part of.

It was a co-ed competition with three legs to the race: swimming sixteen laps in the pool, running five miles, and riding a bike fifteen miles. Mike's usual swimmer couldn't compete that year, so he asked if I would fill in.

I hastily said "yes" thinking it would motivate me to get in shape, but as I began to practice, I realized it was too much. I almost called Mike, but decided to train in the health club pool a few more weeks before dropping out. I eventually found that I could make the sixteen laps if I did half breaststroke and only half front crawl. I wasn't fast, but I knew I could at least finish. Maybe the other teams weren't that great anyway?

I was wrong. There was a sixteen year old girl sharing my lane who was fast and strong. She didn't just beat me; she lapped me! I was so humiliated by my horrible first leg that I left a message on Mike's phone telling him that I wouldn't be at the awards ceremony. It wasn't just my bad performance that made me feel ashamed; I had ruined it for the team.

Two hours later Mike called to tell me he would be dropping off my gold medal! I was shocked. He told me the story: "You were way behind after the swim and then we were even farther behind after my run, but Darcy (who once tried out for the Olympics) was so fast on the bike that she caught and passed everyone else. We won! We all get a gold medal."

This is the gospel in a nutshell. It isn't about our performance. It's about whose team we're on. Everyone who puts their trust in Christ will win for all eternity. He's that good!

April 5

Feeling Guilty

"When He (Jesus) had made purification of sins, He sat down at the right hand of the Majesty on high..." Hebrews 1:3b

Do you often feel guilty? Do you find that many things you do are really motivated by a sense of guilt and fear instead of love? "Well, I'd better do this, or my husband will be upset." "We better go there or our parents will be disappointed." "If we don't offer to do that for them then they might not do this for us."

It is easy to do the right thing for the wrong reason. God wants to break us of the habit of living out of guilt and fear, so that we can please Him by living in His love. But to get there we need to understand a little theology.

There is one piece of furniture in the heavenly tabernacle, the one Jesus entered into after He died for our sins, that wasn't found in the earthly one: a chair. That's because under the Old Testament sacrificial system the work was never done. The sacrifices the high priest made for sin had to be made again and again, year after year. Sin was covered but never removed. People still felt guilty because the sacrifice was imperfect. Hebrews 10:2 points this out:

"If the law and its sacrifices could make people right with God, would they not have stopped being offered? For the worshipers would have been cleansed once for all, and would no longer have felt guilty for their sins."

The sacrifice Jesus made of Himself on the cross was enough to cleanse you of your sins. He sat down. The work is finished. You don't get right with God by going to church, reading your Bible, doing good deeds, or by being a nice person. You could never be sure you were doing enough. Your own guilt would always demand that you try harder and do more. You couldn't make yourself right with God, only Jesus could. And thank God He did. We must believe that truth to live free from guilt and fear.

"We who have believed enter that rest." (Hebrews 4:2) Jesus has made a rest for you, have you entered it? Have you sat down on His finished work? Once you have you can enjoy going to church, reading your Bible, doing good deeds, and being nice. You're not doing it to get right with God (fear and guilt), but because you are right with God and just want to serve Him out of love. If you blow it, and we all do, you just need to confess your sins and He will cleanse you again. (1John 1:9)

April 6

The Fragrance of Christ

"But thanks be to God, who always leads us in triumph in Christ, and manifests through us the sweet aroma of the knowledge of Him in every place. For we are a fragrance of Christ to God among those who are being saved and among those who are perishing; to the one an aroma from death to death, to the other an aroma from life to life..." 2Corinthians 2:14-16

What do you smell like? Not how do you act or what do you do, but what does the essence of who you are smell like? The Lord's command was not to do witnessing, but to be witnesses. Our very presence should bring people into God's presence if we are releasing the aroma of Christ. If people are invited to "taste and see that the Lord is good," they should at least be able to smell His goodness on us and be drawn to Him the way they would be drawn to a good meal cooking in the oven.

I think it would be a great purpose statement to simply aim to bring the aroma of God's beauty, love, and intimacy to every place we go and in every circumstance we face. We can't control our lives, but we do choose where we turn in the uncontrollable events that happen every day. Will I turn to myself and become anxious and irritable or will I turn to God and allow His presence in me to be released? If you want to get the fragrance out of a tea bag you put it in hot water. Maybe the reason we face all that we do is so God can release more of Himself through our lives.

Paul is using the imagery of a Roman triumph in this passage. The conquering general parades those who he has taken captive through the streets and incense is released throughout the city speaking of the victory that has been won. The captives of Rome were made to follow a general who had conquered them by force. We become part of Christ's triumph when we willingly choose to surrender to His wonderful love and grace. The captives back then lost their old lives and became the prisoners and servants of Rome. We are called to lose our old lives to become prisoners of His love and servants of the kingdom of God.

Are you really His captive? Have you allowed Him to lead you away from your old life into His ways and presence? If not, why not ask Him to fully capture you? Someone might need to smell Him.

April 7

Getting Back Up

"Simon, Simon, behold, Satan has demanded permission to sift you like wheat; but I have prayed for you, that your faith may not fail; and you, when once you have turned again, strengthen your brothers." Luke 22:31-32

Jesus' prayer concern had nothing to do with Peter denying Him three times; in His mind that was a done deal. What He was concerned about was Peter having the faith to get back up after he had fallen. Peter was about to fall hard and he couldn't see it coming. In fact, in the very next verse he tells Jesus that he is "ready to go both to prison and to death" for Him. The reality is that he isn't ready to stand up for Jesus in front of a servant girl. After his failure he would experience the shame and remorse of his actions verses what he had promised. He would loathe himself for a season.

But Jesus prayed that his faith wouldn't fail. That Peter would remember God's love for him and God's wisdom to take even our brokenness and make something good out of it. That he would be able to look beyond himself and see the bigger picture, recognizing God's hand even in allowing his failure.

When God looks at our lives, like He did at Peter's, He sometimes makes a big call for change. It seems like we are put in survival mode when He brings something to bear on us that literally exposes everything inside of us. Sometimes it's a failure that brings this to light, sometimes it's a trial, sometimes it's a difficult relationship, and sometimes it's just God's direct dealing. When God goes there you aren't going to get better until you agree with Him about the depth of the problem and begin to face it with His love and grace.

When we sit in shame, condemnation, and self loathing instead of getting back up again in faith, all it means is that it's going to take that much longer. Proverbs says that a righteous man falls down seven times and gets back up. (Proverbs 24:16) Successful Christians are not those who never fall but those who have learned how to get up quickly!

April 8

Overcoming the Accuser

"The accuser of the brethren has been thrown down, he who accuses them before our God day and night. And they overcame him because of the blood of the Lamb and because of the word of their testimony, and they did not love their life even when faced with death." Revelation 12:10b-11

The enemy of mankind tempts people to justify their sins and independence before they come to Christ, but when they become believers, he switches his strategy to persistent accusation. Notice in the text that he doesn't accuse all people, but only those who call themselves believers. All believers succumb to accusation once in a while, but it is possible to live overcome by so much accusation that there is no joy or sense of victory in our faith. God doesn't want us to live under accusation so He tells us specifically how we overcome it.

First, by the blood of the Lamb. The power of Satan's accusations is the truth in them. We have sinned and failed in the past. He can bring back something we did twenty years ago, or a bad attitude we've had recently, or a failure last week and make it seem like any victory is beyond us. It may be true that we've sinned in the specific way he is accusing us of, but that's not the whole truth. The whole truth is that God loves me anyway which is why Jesus came and died for my sins, and now, His blood washes me completely clean when I confess my sins to Him. (1John 1:9) Remember the song: "Oh happy day, oh happy day, when Jesus washed, He washed my sins away." That's the other side of truth and must be what we agree with to find victory. Trying to defend yourself and your actions will only lead to deeper condemnation. The power to overcome is not in our righteousness, but in His. When we really believe in His cleansing, every day can be a happy day!

Second, by the word of their testimony. We must never lose the power of how our story intersects with God's. His story is the gospel, sending Jesus to die for our sins. Our story is how we were drawn to Christ and became saved. Our testimony is a reminder of the new identity we have in Christ. The enemy will try to tie your identity to your old life in sin, but whenever we recite our testimony (to ourselves or others), we are reminded that our identity isn't in our sin, but in His new life in us. 2Corinthians 5:17 says, "Therefore if anyone is in Christ, he is a new creature; the old things have passed away; behold, new things have come."

April 9

Are You "All In?"

"He died for all, so that they who live might no longer live for themselves, but for Him who died and rose again on their behalf." 2Corinthians 5:15

Our culture is fascinated right now with a game called, "Texas Hold 'em." There are tournaments in bars all over the world and ESPN regularly shows the big events entitled, "The World Series of Poker." Why the craze, and why now? In a regular poker game there is a set limit on the betting, so there's a ceiling on how much a person can lose in a single hand. But in Hold 'em there's no limit. Anyone can go "all in" at any time, so a player either has to match their bet or get out. If you lose after you've gone "all in" you're out of the game. It's all or nothing.

I believe there is something deep inside this generation that wants to go "all in." They don't want to do their "duty," or give some minimal commitment to something that is socially acceptable, or that their mom and dad believe in. If it is real to them, they are ready to give everything. If it's not, they don't want any part of it.

God views the gospel this way. Jesus has died for you and me; He's gone "all in." The response can't be a little religion to ease our guilt. We must go "all in" as well or we won't make much spiritual progress. God is patient so He gives us plenty of time to decide, but He won't lower His wager because we think it's too high. He gave everything for us and He expects everything from us.

If God gave us some dramatic way to show that we were going "all in," I think many of us would be willing to do it. But the way we prove our devotion is by seeking to please Him in the midst of our everyday, ordinary lives instead of just living to please ourselves. It's about our attitudes and decisions each and every day. Will we serve, or seek to control? Will we forgive, or hold a grudge?

We can't say we're going "all in" on Sunday and take the wager back on Monday morning. He wants us to walk with Him 24/7. Because of our sin nature no one will ever do this perfectly, but God's not looking at that. He's looking at the attitude of our hearts: Are we holding back from Him, or are we really seeking to please Him every day?

April 10

Dealing with Guilt

"The law is only a shadow of the good things that are coming - not the realities themselves. For this reason it can never, by the same sacrifices repeated endlessly year after year, make perfect those who draw near to worship. If it could, would they not have stopped being offered? For the worshipers would have been cleansed once for all, and would no longer have felt guilty for their sins." Hebrews 10:1-2

My daughter Christina and I were driving to church early one Sunday morning to help with setup when our windshield started to fog up. I immediately put my glove out to wipe away the clouds when she quickly informed me that I was only going to make it worse, and that we needed to wait for the defrost to do it, which she then turned on high. After just a few minutes, we could see clearly and there weren't any man-made marks that a glove often leaves.

It makes me think of how we often deal with the blinding fog of guilt. The quickest reaction to guilt in most Christians is to try to compensate for it by doing more. I feel I did something bad so maybe doing something good will please God and the bad feeling will go away. Pray more, read more, work more, serve at church more; we just want to feel forgiven again. Actual guilt, which has come because of the Holy Spirit convicting us of sin, will never disappear in this way. You only end up burying it under a bunch of religious works that lead to feelings of fear, rejection, and condemnation. We become spiritually blind when we react to guilt this way even though we still genuinely love the Lord.

Only the blood of Jesus is sufficient to remove the guilt of sin. Trying to work it off is actually us bypassing the blood that was shed on the cross. It may get stuff done, even Christian stuff, but in the end it only does us harm. When genuine guilt comes, instead of reacting quickly with performance, we need to wait for the Spirit to point specifically to the sin we need to repent of. We then need to confess it to the Lord and allow Him to wash the sin, guilt, and shame away, so we can immediately be restored back to a state of righteousness. Is it really that easy? Listen with your heart to 1John 1:9: "If we confess our sins, He is faithful and righteous to forgive us our sins and to cleanse us from all unrighteousness."

April 11

He is Risen!

"Why do you seek the living One among the dead? He is not here, but He has risen." Luke 24:5

Everything has changed because of the resurrection if we only look in the right place. If we live looking at what is spiritually dead and listen to the pessimism of those who can only see what man is doing, we will easily give in to discouragement and despair. But if we remember that He is alive, that God, not man has the final say, and that even that which appears dead can come back to life; we will never cease to have hope.

"Because He lives," the song goes, "I can face tomorrow. Because He lives, all fear is gone. Because I know He holds the future. Life is worth the living, just because He lives."

We often live and work among those who can only see this world. May God help us, as we seek the living One, to bring a little of heaven to earth each day.

April 12

Why a Blood Sacrifice?

"Without the shedding of blood there is no forgiveness of sins." Hebrews 9:22

Recently I received a couple of questions from a young adult about why a loving God would require the blood of His own son in order to accomplish His purpose. Here was my response.

It is critical in thinking about Christ's sacrifice that we leave behind the puny reasoning of man and seek to humbly enter into the thoughts of God. When Jesus was explaining the need for His crucifixion, Peter rebuked Him, and then Jesus said, "Get behind Me Satan for you do not have in mind the things of God but the things of men." (Matthew 16:33)

The things of God. The unfathomable depths of the wisdom of God; who can possibly grasp the fullness of His ways or fully understand His paths? (Romans 11:33) Yet in the cross we see a partial revelation of three important truths:

1. The holiness of God. God is way more holy than you and I could ever grasp. The idea that God should just forgive on the basis of His loving us would deny His holiness. Because He is love, and loves us, He gave His Son to die in our place so that justice for sin would be upheld.

2. The sinfulness of man. We don't realize how sinful we are in the sight of God because we compare ourselves to other people. Jesus called His own disciples "evil" and told the self-righteous rich young ruler that there is no such thing as a good person, only a good God. Satan is the one who tells us we're good people and accuses God of being unjust for calling us guilty.

3. The love of God. "This is love, not that we loved God, but that He loved us and gave His Son to be a propitiation for our sins." (1John 4:10) We will unpack this amazing truth for all eternity!

As far as "why blood." God declares that the life of anything is in its blood and therefore there can be no forgiveness without the shedding of innocent blood on behalf of the guilty. (Hebrews 9:22) In the Old Testament it was the blood of innocent animals that God chose to use to cover over sins from year to year. But all of these sacrifices were only pointing to the Lamb of God whose blood alone could actually take away the sins of the world.

April 13

A Better Message

"You have come...to Jesus, the mediator of a new covenant, and to the sprinkled blood, which speaks better than the blood of Abel." Hebrews 12:22a; 24

Before Cain killed Abel the Bible says that Cain invited him out into a field. (Genesis 4:8) Cain didn't want anyone to know what he was going to do, so he did it in a secret place. But there is no hiding sin from God. The Lord said to Cain, "What have you done? The voice of your brother's blood is crying to Me from the ground." (Genesis 4:10) What was that voice crying to the Judge of the whole universe? It was a cry for justice against Cain. He was guilty of treachery, deceit, jealousy, unbridled anger, and of murdering an innocent victim. When Cain hears that his brother's blood is crying out to God, he becomes afraid and flees the presence of God to go to the land of Nod; translated - the land of "wandering."

Maybe we haven't sinned in the same way Cain did, but our sins also cry out to God for justice. We may be able to justify our sins to ourselves and to other people, but we can't justify them before God. He knows everything, even our motives, and the truth is we're guilty. Can the holy and righteous Judge of the whole universe ignore the cry of justice against us because of our sins?

No, He can't. He has heard the cry of every injustice on this planet, so in His holiness He demanded a just penalty be paid for our sins. He knew that if we paid that price ourselves it would mean we would be separated from Him forever, so in His great love for us, He decided to pay that penalty Himself. Jesus died on the cross and shed His blood to fulfill the cry for justice our sins demanded. Today His blood is speaking a very different message than the blood of Abel.

It speaks to God and to us about our forgiveness because our penalty has already been paid. It speaks to us of a new beginning with God every day. It speaks of my justification – just as if I'd never sinned – before God. Instead of fleeing God's presence in fear, it assures us that we can run to God with confidence. Instead of living a life of wandering without God, the blood of Jesus speaks to us of a life filled with purpose as we partner with God.

Which voice are you listening to today? Is it the one that speaks of fear, guilt, and judgment? That is not God's voice, but only the accuser's. God is speaking to you and me from the cross about His love, His forgiveness, and a new beginning.

April 14

The Shame Chain

"Neither do I condemn you. Go and sin no more." John 8:11

Caught in the act of lust and the betrayal of adultery. Guilt and shame increase as those around pick up the stones of judgment. The holy Son of God up close with a sinner caught in a shameful, sinful act. How does God see the act and how does He see the person?

In my study this week I was reviewing statistics about pornography in the church. 50% of men struggle and 20% of women which is 9% better than those outside the church. The enemy is using our cultural infatuation with sex to erode the moral courage of the people of God.

One statistic I hadn't seen before was that 90% of Christians who struggle in this area feel shame whenever they try to come into God's presence. No wonder the problem is so entrenched! If all I think God is saying to me is "go and sin no more," I am stuck in my shame. If I feel dirty I will eventually return to dirt no matter how hard I try to avoid it.

The power to "go and sin no more" is in hearing "neither do I condemn you." The one Person who has the right to judge you has chosen to die for your sin so that your judgment can be removed. Listen to His heart for you: "Neither do I condemn you." He has given us the "gift of righteousness and of the abundance of His grace so that we can reign in this life through Jesus Christ." (Romans 5:17)

Let Him wash away the shame chain that keeps you going back to the mud. You are a beloved child of God, not a slave to lust. Arise and shine for you Light has come! (Isaiah 60:1)

April 15

Intimacy with God

"This is eternal life, that they may know You the only true God, and Jesus Christ whom You sent." John 17:3

We had an amazing conference a few years ago called "Intimacy with God". We had incredible speakers, but the highlight was a strong awareness of the wonderful presence of God. Here are some of the truths highlighted from our speakers.

1. There is no condemnation for those who are in Christ Jesus. (Romans 8:1) One of the great hindrances to intimacy with God is the feeling that we are only tolerated by God. The truth is that we are not only accepted in Christ, we are a delight to Him. God doesn't just love us, He likes us.

2. God is a Father who wants us to succeed, not just for a little while, but until the end. He wants us to become godly people who overcome the sin nature through vigilance and perseverance. Intimacy with God does not mean everything will be easy for us, it means that God loves us enough to train us for righteousness.

3. Intimacy with God does not mean that we will be famous in front of people. God will give a stone to those who overcome that has a name on it that no one knows accept the one who receives it and God Himself. (Revelation 2:17) There is a privacy in intimacy where you and God share things that no one else gets to share with you. Our culture is often about publicity and appearance before others, but God values those who live to please Him regardless of whether people recognize them.

4. Ultimately intimacy is not about our pursuit of God, but about His pursuit of us. The greatest road to intimacy is in a commitment to following these three words: "Follow the light." As God pursues you, purpose to respond quickly and you will discover an adventure where God reveals Himself to you again and again.

5. There are two wings to the Christian life: Intimacy with God and activity for God. Without both of these wings we will not be able to fly the way we want to or in the way God wants us to. It is easy to focus on one or the other but we need both. James said that faith (intimacy) without works (activity) is dead.

Offering Our Suffering To God

"And the God of all grace, who called you to His eternal glory in Christ, after you have suffered a little while, will Himself restore you and make you strong, firm, and steadfast." 1Peter 5:10

I define suffering as something going on in your life that is not the way you want it right now. You wake up and things aren't the way you want them. You go to bed and things are still not the way you want them, and no matter how hard you try, you can't seem to make these difficult things go away. It might be something physical, financial, relational, emotional, spiritual, or more than one of these at the same time. The gap between how things are compared to how they should be causes us pain until the gap is closed. What we do with the suffering of that time is extremely important to God.

Some get offended with God because they thought if they served God it would mean He would make their lives comfortable. In the text above we see that our calling is to "His eternal glory in Christ." God allows things in our lives because His vision for us is often much higher than ours. We just want to be happy right now; He's making us holy for all eternity.

Some people resent suffering so they feel they have the right to complain to all who will listen. God encourages us to bring our complaint to Him and pour out our hearts before Him (Psalm 62:8), but to be careful how we speak to people. When believers grumble about their lives they are a negative witness for God and betraying the very faith they profess. (Psalm 73:15)

Others minimize their suffering by comparing their trials to what other people are bearing, and scold themselves for being such a cry baby. "What I'm going through is nothing compared to what someone else is going through so I should just suck it up." In this scenario our suffering isn't acknowledged, so it is buried instead of offered to God.

Instead of any of these wrong responses, God is calling each of us to embrace the crosses He brings into our lives and offer them back to Him as an act of worship. I don't have to understand why I am suffering to trust God's purpose in it. Make a bouquet of every problem in your life and give it to God each day, or several times a day, if necessary. "Cast your cares upon Him for He cares for you." (1Peter 5:7)

April 17

Blood Colored Glasses

"The accuser of our brothers, who accuses them before our God day and night, has been hurled down. They overcame him by the blood of the Lamb and by the word of their testimony." Revelation 12:10-11

I'm sure you've heard the phrase, "rose colored glasses." It's a derogatory term signifying that someone refuses to live in the real world. To protect themselves, people can simply choose to not acknowledge evil, pain, and tragedy that is happening all around them. This is a survival device and is convenient because if I don't see problems, I am not responsible to help solve them. If I don't allow for brokenness in human beings, I don't have to be part of their healing.

God's plan for us is not denial, but redemption. The enemy is an accuser and he's very effective because of the truth in his accusations. Things really are bad; you really did commit that sin; that tragedy really did happen… His case seems airtight which allows us to justify a response of despair and even joining with his accusations of those around us in the name of, "I'm just telling the truth."

But the accuser never tells the whole truth. The whole truth includes the fact that God loves us and Jesus died for us. My sins have been paid for on the cross and so have yours and so have the sins of everyone you know. Evil is happening but it won't win. Tragedy happens, but God can also work in and through all things if we allow Him to.

When we put on blood colored glasses, we see the world as God does; through His redemption. There's no person so lost they couldn't be saved; there's no problem so big, it can't be solved; and there is no death that can't be the seed of a greater resurrection. Let's take off the rose colored glasses that cause us to be blind, and let's take off the dark glasses of accusation that cause us to despair. It's time to embrace our redemption and bring the good news to all who are hurting around us in this difficult world.

April 18

Twice His

"Here I am! I stand at the door and knock. If anyone hears My voice and opens the door I will come in..." Revelation 3:20

A boy and his father carved out a toy sailboat from a block of wood. The boy had great delight in his creation so he put his initials on the bottom, and the toy became almost like a friend to him. He carried it with him during the day and kept it by his side when he slept at night.

One day a tragic thing happened. While the son was playing with his boat in the river behind the house, it got away from him. He ran to the house to tell his father, and together they searched downstream to no avail. But months later they attended an auction at a neighboring town farther down the river, and the son saw that a toy sailboat was being auctioned. Could it be? He ran over to it, turned it over, and was overjoyed when he saw his initials. He put it back on the shelf and knew beyond a shadow of a doubt that he would own that boat again. Whatever this toy was worth to someone else, it was worth more to him. He would gladly give all he had to own his boat again.

After winning the auction, we could say that the boat belonged to the boy twice over – once on the basis of creation and a second time on the basis of redemption. God feels the same way about you and me. In great love, the Father and the Son created us by the Spirit and the mark of their design is all over us. Your brain, eyes, skin, muscles, and internal organs are all proof that you are fearfully and wonderfully made. But sin has taken us down the river from a holy God removing us from His presence, but not from His thoughts. He planned our redemption and paid for it when He gave His life for our sins.

He has already paid for our redemption but refuses to make us go with Him. He calls (Matthew 22:14), enlightens (John 1:9), draws (John 12:32), and knocks (Rev.3:20), but He won't push, grab, force, or manipulate. The part of our salvation He delights in is us saying, "yes," in response to His grace, with our own free will. It doesn't matter how far down the river of sin you are. It doesn't matter how deep your doubts, how evil your thoughts, or how blasphemous your words have been. He still loves you and in His mind you belong to Him twice.

April 19

An Intimate Appearance

"Go, tell His disciples and Peter, 'He is going ahead of you into Galilee. There you will see Him just as He told you.'" Mark 16:7

Jesus told His disciples at the last supper that He would meet them in Galilee after His resurrection. The angel is repeating what he overheard Jesus Himself say to them at this last meeting, but he has also witnessed the devastation of Peter. His instructions from heaven evidently include this special reference to the fallen leader who has denied Christ three times after promising to die for Him: "...tell the disciples and Peter."

Jesus appeared first to Mary Magdalene, not in Galilee, but in Jerusalem on the day He was resurrected. This appearance was unpromised and unexpected. He also appeared the same day to two men on the road to Emmaus. And then, that same night, as the two of them were retelling their story, He appeared to all of them (except Thomas), and the details of this visit are given to us in Scripture as well. (See Mark 16, Luke 24 and John 20)

But there is one appearance that happened where we are given no details. Jesus appeared personally, on resurrection day, to Peter. Two different New Testament authors reference this appearance, but give us no specifics. In Luke 24:34, while the men who saw Jesus on the road to Emmaus were telling their story, the disciples respond by saying: "It is true! The Lord has risen and has appeared to Simon (Peter)." In 1Corinthians 15, Paul is referencing all the resurrection appearances to men, and says: "I passed on to you...that He was raised on the third day according to the Scriptures, and that He appeared to Peter, and then to the others..." (1Corinthians 15:4-5)

Why aren't we told of this interaction with Peter? What did Jesus say to him? What did Peter say? Maybe there are some interactions with the Lord that are so intimate they aren't for others to hear about.

Here's what we know for sure: "The Lord is close to the brokenhearted and saves those who are crushed in spirit." (Psalm 34:18) He loved Peter so much that He singled him out on the most important day in history. He took time to come close and restore one who was being crushed by his own sin and failure. Isn't He amazing?

April 20

Stand Firm

"It was for freedom that Christ set us free. Stand firm, therefore, in your freedom and don't become enslaved again to a yoke of bondage." Galatians 5:1

When I was 44 I started having back pain I couldn't get rid of. I complained about it, prayed about it, and had others pray for it, yet it persisted. My wife told me to go to the chiropractor several times, so eventually I humbled myself and went.

The chiropractor made an adjustment to my back that I could never have performed myself. I literally heard something snap in my back and felt something move into place that had been out of alignment. I was thankful and ready to leave, but the doctor wasn't done. He told me to stop carrying a wallet in my back pocket and gave me a list of exercises to start doing so my back would stay in place.

How intrusive! I just wanted to feel better; I wasn't looking for a new lifestyle, so I ignored his instructions and went on with my life. The problem was that my back started hurting again in a few weeks, and I had to return. I didn't want him to know I disobeyed his instructions, so I left my wallet in my coat pocket before going in to see him.

After the appointment, I realized I had a decision to make. I could either spend my life going back for adjustments or change my lifestyle. Today, I use a money clip and have a regimen of exercises I do every morning for my back. I haven't needed an adjustment in years.

God loves us so much He sent Jesus to die on the cross to free us from our sins. Only Jesus can make the adjustment in our lives that aligns us in a right relationship with God, and if we fall back into sin, He is more than willing to forgive us and put us back into alignment. But God has something more for us. He wants us to learn how to live in alignment and not have to be constantly repenting. He wants us to stand firm in the freedom He has won for us and never live in bondage again.

The world is too proud to come to Jesus for an adjustment. The church is often too apathetic to make lifestyle changes that would allow us to walk every day in the freedom Christ died for. Let's shake off unbelief and apathy; let's purpose to get free, and then to live free, for God's glory and our good.

April 21

Encountering Jesus

"Then their eyes were opened and they recognized Him, and He disappeared from their sight. They asked each other: 'Were not our hearts burning within us while He talked with us on the road and opened the Scriptures to us?'" Luke 24:31-32

It was resurrection day but these two disciples were sad and discouraged because they didn't yet believe. It took an encounter, a revelation, for them to truly believe Jesus was alive and the Savior of the world.

A few years ago I was in Belize when I experienced this truth first hand in the life of a young mom. She asked for prayer at the end of the service and told me the problem was her right wrist. A bone had come out of joint and she was very limited in the use of her arm because there was a lot of pain if she twisted it to the left or right. I laid my hands on it and prayed a very short prayer releasing God's healing presence in Jesus Name. I asked her to test it and when she did, she found she could move it back and forth more easily but said there was still some pain. I prayed another short prayer and tears began to flow down her cheeks.

"The pain is gone," she said as she demonstrated full movement of her hand and wrist by twisting them to the right and left. We also prayed that the bone which was sticking up would go back down but nothing additional happened.

This woman (who gave me permission to share her story) works in the kitchen for the missionaries we were visiting so a few days later during breakfast I asked her to tell the story of what happened. She told me that after she became pregnant, a year earlier, the father of her baby was abusive and had twisted her arm in a way that the bone was moved out of joint but she never went to the doctor. She had just lived with the pain and restricted mobility.

The first time I prayed for her she said she felt pain go out of her fingertips. The second time we prayed she felt the rest of the pain leave and knew she was healed.

"The reason for the tears was that I always wanted to believe God was real. When my wrist was healed I knew it for sure." She told me that when she woke up the next morning the bone was back in place as well and then showed me that both wrists now looked the same.

God encountered this precious young woman in a way that she would forever know it was Him. He is risen!

Living from God's Presence

"There remains a Sabbath rest for the people of God; for anyone who enters God's rest also rests from his own works, just as God did from His. Let us, therefore, make every effort to enter that rest..." Hebrews 4:9-11

At the beginning of 2015, I felt the Lord highlight this Scripture with a stream of thoughts about its application in my life. I'm a list person, so God seems to speak to me in lists!

1. I want you to do less and accomplish more.
2. I want you to speak less and say more.
3. I want you to rationalize less and risk more.

I am still unpacking exactly how to live these three phrases out, but I'd love to give a few thoughts on each one that may serve to inspire your journey as well.

1. "Do less and accomplish more." This was a call to stop striving in my own power usually motivated by the fear of not being good enough. Jesus was good enough and He is our Sabbath rest. In the Old Covenant they rested on a day; in the New Covenant we are called to rest in a Person. (Colossians 2:16-17) Remember: God can accomplish more in a moment than man, apart from God, can accomplish in a lifetime.

2. "Speak less and say more." Our life's posture should be listening before speaking. Many words of our own will dilute the power of a few words inspired by God. Isaiah 50:4 is a goal for me: "The Sovereign Lord has given me an instructed tongue, to know the word that sustains the weary. He wakens me morning by morning, wakens my ear to listen..." We live in a culture that is worn out by many words. One "word" that is actually from God has the power to sustain the weary.

3. "Rationalize less and risk more." We are living as the beloved, not as those trying to earn love. This is a safe place. Yet the kingdom can only advance by acts of faith, so someone has to step out of their comfort zone and take a risk when they feel God might be speaking. We were created to live hosting His presence. The more we practice living out of this place, the better we will be at it and the more of the beauty and power of heaven will be released on earth through regular people like you and me.

April 23

Embracing the Cross

"If anyone wishes to come after Me, let him deny himself, and take up his cross, and follow Me. For whoever wishes to save his life shall lose it, and whoever loses his life for My sake and the gospel's shall save it." Mark 8:34-35

Sometimes people refer to their difficulties as, "their cross to bear", and assume that they're bearing it just by going through the trouble. But the cross, to be a cross like our Lord's, is something you must take up and bear of your own free will. Jesus said about His life, "No one has taken it away from Me, but I lay it down on My own initiative." (John 10:18)

You and I don't choose the trouble that comes to us in various forms, but we do choose how we will deal with it. When we grumble, complain, blame, and get frustrated, angry, or depressed it's evidence that we are still very much on the throne of our lives. God's inviting us to embrace suffering like Jesus did, knowing that this identification will lead to knowing Him more intimately, and result in a deeper faith in us. (See Philippians 3:10)

Francois de Fenelon, one of the great spiritual leaders of the 17th century, gave this wisdom to a struggling disciple:

"I am sorry to hear of your troubles, but I am sure you realize that you must carry the cross with Christ in this life. Soon enough there will come a time when you will no longer suffer. You will reign with God and He will wipe away your tears with His own hand. In His presence, pain and sighing will forever flee away. So while you have the opportunity to experience difficult trials, do not lose the slightest opportunity to embrace the cross. Learn to suffer in humility and in peace. Your deep self-love makes the cross too heavy to bear. Learn to suffer with simplicity and a heart full of love. If you do you will not only be happy in spite of the cross, but because of it. Love is pleased to suffer for the Well-Beloved. The cross which conforms you into His image is a consoling bond of love between you and Him." (100 Days in the Secret Place; page 21)

April 24

The Mediator

"He is not a mere mortal like me that I might answer him, that we might confront each other in court. If only there were someone to mediate between us, someone to bring us together, someone to remove God's rod from me, so that his terror would frighten me no more. Then I would speak up without fear of him, but as it now stands with me, I cannot." Job 9:32-35

The longing of Job was for a mediator. Someone who could stand in the gap between him and God. Someone who could remove God's judgment and then place one hand on God and one on him to bring them together. This longing, which is also the need of all human beings, was fulfilled in Jesus Christ.

Jesus was God, the eternal Son. "In the beginning was the Word and the Word was with God and the Word was God... and the Word became flesh and dwelt among us." (John 1:1; 14) Jesus was and is fully God. When the Jews asked Him if He had seen Abraham, He replied, "Before Abraham was born, I am." (John 8:58) This is a clear reference to God's Name in the Old Testament.

But Jesus was also a man. Hebrews 5:9 says that Jesus was "made perfect." How could God be anything less than perfect? He was always perfect as God, but to become the perfect mediator He had to become a human being. "Once made perfect, He became the source of eternal salvation for all who obey Him and was designated by God to be high priest." (Hebrews 5:9) As our priest He offered the perfect sacrifice for sins, Himself. He needed to be God because He had to take the place of the whole human race; and He had to be man because it was man who had sinned. This sacrifice removed God's wrath from all humanity and transformed God's throne into a place of grace instead of judgment. "Let us then approach the throne of grace with confidence, so we may receive mercy and grace to help us in our time of need." (Hebrews 4:16)

Jesus Christ – fully God and fully man. We don't have to understand the mystery of who He is to believe and worship. "There is one God and one mediator between God and human beings, the man Christ Jesus." (1 Timothy 2:5)

The Old Self

"But now you must rid yourself of all such things as these: anger, rage, slander, and filthy language from your lips. Do not lie to each other, since you have taken off your old self with its practices and have put on the new self, which is being renewed in knowledge in the image of its Creator."
Colossians 3:8-10

One day my wife gave me her strong opinion on my favorite apparel, "I don't want you to wear those sweaters any more. They make you look old." She continued with conviction: "In fact, one day they're just not going to be in your closet anymore."

I love sweaters and especially my sweaters. They all fit me perfectly and most were birthday or Christmas presents because my family knows I love to wear them. What's worse is that all of these sweaters were in my winter starting line-up of what to wear to work. They were practically part of me.

Hebrews 12:1 talks about easily besetting sins that need to be put off or they will hinder us in our race. Each of us have different easily besetting or comfortable sins. Think of them as sweaters in your closet – there's one called lust, another anger, there's hatred and slander, lying, filthy talk, and addiction; and then, of course, there's pride. Often there's one that fits so well it seems like it's part of us.

The problem with these sweaters is they make us look like the old self. It's confusing to the world when we claim to be Christians but don't look like Christians. Why didn't Alice just remove those sweaters from my closet? She didn't want to violate relationship. If she removed the sweaters against my will, I might resent it. She gave her opinion but left them there, so that ultimately it would be my choice. God does the same with our old self. Paul is writing to Christians when he says to take off the old self and put on the new. God won't do it for us.

Alice bought me new clothes to wear. She didn't just tell me to put off the old; she purchased new clothes that she likes on me. Jesus has done the same. Here are some of the clothes available for the new self to put on: love, joy, peace, patience, kindness, goodness, faithfulness, gentleness, and self-control. (Galatians 5:22) Jesus bought these clothes with His own blood so we could be and look, new in Him.

Every day we need to look in our closet, reject the old self and put on the new. It will get easier and easier in this life, and in eternity, those sweaters won't even be there anymore!

April 26

Foreshadows

"Take your son, your only son, whom you love, and go to the region of Moriah. Sacrifice him there on one of the mountains I will tell you about."
Genesis 22:2

Genesis promises redemption both by what God says to Abraham, "in your seed all the families of the earth will be blessed," (Genesis 12:3) and by events that foreshadow His bigger plan.

First, God changes Abram's name to Abraham which means, "Father of many nations." Abraham foreshadows what the Father in heaven will do when He takes His Son, His only Son, and sacrifices Him for our salvation.

Isaac foreshadows Jesus, the only beloved Son of God. He goes up a mountain in the region of Moriah (Calvary is one of the mounts in this region) with wood on his back placed there by his father. (Genesis 22:6) When he asks, "Where is the lamb for sacrifice," Abraham responds, "God Himself will provide the lamb." (Genesis 22:7-8) When Abraham lifts the knife to kill his son, an angel stops him, and Abraham then sees a male lamb in a thicket caught by its horns. As that lamb was sacrificed, I can almost see tears in the eyes of the heavenly Father who knows His Son will be the Lamb He provides for the sins of the world.

After this powerful foreshadowing of Calvary, Abraham sends his servant back to his relatives in Haran to get a bride for his son. This unnamed servant represents the Holy Spirit who will be sent back to earth to prepare a bride for the Son of God. The servant brings a small sampling of wealth in his invitation to Rebekah, explaining that his abundantly wealthy master has left everything to his son. (Genesis 25:36) Jesus says, "All that belongs to the Father is mine. That is why I said the Spirit will take from what is Mine and make it known to you." (John 16:15)

Rebekah foreshadows us. The servant asked Abraham, "What if the woman will not come back with me?" Abraham said, "if she refuses, you will be released from my oath." (Genesis 25:41) The Holy Spirit has authority to invite but not to force. When the servant explains that the invitation is urgent and that he will leave the next morning with or without her, her family asks Rebekah, "Will you go with this man?" (Genesis 25:58) Rebekah then leaves all security she has in her circumstances and goes with this servant on a journey that will end in her being the bride of the father's only son. Amazingly, nothing less than this happens when we genuinely answer the Spirit's call today.

April 27

Foreshadows of His Sacrifice

"Therefore, say to the Israelites: 'I am the LORD, and I will bring you out from under the yoke of the Egyptians. I will free you from being slaves to them, and I will redeem you with an outstretched arm and with mighty acts of judgment. I will take you as my own people, and I will be your God. Then you will know that I am the LORD your God, who brought you out from under the yoke of the Egyptians'" Exodus 6:6-7

God's plan from the beginning was to call out a people who would walk with Him in time and for all eternity. He knew before He made us about sin, so His plan all along was redemption – our walk with Him would only be on the terms of His first delivering us. The exodus from Egypt and the journey to the promised land foreshadow our redemption from sin and journey into the promised life we have in Christ. Today I want to reflect on the way Israel was delivered.

There were ten plagues that visited Egypt, but only the tenth set God's people free. The final plague was the death of the first-born male in every house throughout the land unless each home did what God commanded the Israelites to do. Every family was to find a male lamb a year old that had no blemish (Exodus 12:5) and sacrifice it on the 14th day of the month (Exodus 12:6) which was to be their first month from now on. (The Israelites call the month: "Nisan.") Then they were to apply the blood of the lamb to the top and sides of their doors and were to eat the lamb so they would have strength for their journey. That night the final plague would come, but every home that was covered by the blood of the lamb would be passed over. (Exodus 12:13)

On the Friday before Passover in 33 AD, Jesus of Nazareth was inspected early in the morning by Pilate's court. He was found to be innocent and without blemish. Even his accuser declared him innocent when he gave back the money he received from betraying him. (Matthew 27:4)

That afternoon, just as the Passover lambs were being sacrificed in the temple, Jesus died on the cross. John the Baptist had said: "Behold the Lamb of God who takes away the sin of the world." (John 1:29) Paul says that "Christ, our Passover Lamb, has been sacrificed." (1Corinthians 5:7)

April 28

The Key To Fruitfulness – Part One

"The hour has come for the Son of Man to be glorified. Truly, truly, I say to you, unless a grain of wheat falls into the earth and dies, it remains alone; but if it dies, it bears much fruit. He who loves his life loses it, and he who hates his life in this world will keep it to life eternal." John 12:23-25

Jesus speaks first about the necessity of His own death but then He alludes to the necessity of ours. If Jesus chooses to preserve His life, He can't save us. If we choose to live protecting ourselves, we can't bear fruit as Christians. What does death to self look like?

First, we must die to our plans. Proverbs 16:9 says: "Many are the plans of a man's heart, but the Lord's purpose will prevail." We are not discouraged from making plans, but only from clinging to them. Make a plan, give it to God, and then plan on the original plan changing to conform to God's purpose. If our identity is in our plan, we will find ourselves continually disappointed and disillusioned when they don't work out exactly how we thought.

We began a Sunday night service several years ago because we were having to turn people away from overcrowded nurseries in the morning services. Our plan didn't work because we couldn't get families to change to Sunday night, so we ended up solving the Sunday morning problem in another way. But in the process, we recognized God had a different purpose for Sunday nights. It has become the service of choice for many who want more and appreciate the culture of waiting on God at the altar since no one has to pick up their kids.

A second area we need to die to is our property or wealth. Jesus answered the rich young ruler's question about eternal life by telling him to sell everything and give to the poor, and to then, follow Him. He went away sad because he owned much property (one translation: "had great wealth"). The Lord impressed on my wife during a retreat we took, that her great wealth was her children and their unmet needs were what was making her sad. Jesus invited her to really let go of her "great wealth" by giving her children completely to Him, so she could follow Him without sadness anymore.

What's your great wealth? What's holding you back from complete abandonment to God? The reason why God pries things out of our hands is so that we will be open to receive all He has for us. He is not against us owning property, but He insists that our property doesn't own us!

April 29

The Key To Fruitfulness – Part Two

"The hour has come for the Son of Man to be glorified. Truly, truly, I say to you, unless a grain of wheat falls into the earth and dies, it remains alone; but if it dies, it bears much fruit. He who loves his life loses it, and he who hates his life in this world will keep it to life eternal." John 12:23-25

Yesterday we discussed the uncomfortable truth that the only way to real fruit in our lives is through death to self and covered dying to our plans and our property. Today I want to look at dying to our power and our popularity.

When Jesus tells His disciples that they will all forsake Him, Peter insists that he is willing to die even if the others fall away. Jesus then informs Peter that he will actually fall farther than all the others by denying Him three times before the cock crows.

After the resurrection, we can only imagine how ready they were to prove their faithfulness, but Jesus doesn't allow them to minister until they've received power to be witnesses. The word witness in Greek is "martyras," which is where we get our word martyr from, and it means to give witness by life or death. It was only after they received the Holy Spirit that they would have the power to stay loyal to Jesus even to the point of death. We're not all called to be martyrs, but we are all called to die to our own ability to live the Christian life and embrace the power of the Holy Spirit.

The last important thing for us to die to is our desire to be liked. When the crowds following John the Baptist started to diminish, his disciples became concerned and brought this to his attention. His response: "I am the friend of the Bridegroom and my delight is to hear His voice. He must increase and I must decrease." (John 3:29-30)

The best man is not trying to get the bride to like him. He's been chosen by the groom and his desire is to serve him well. He wants the bride to love the bridegroom and recognizes that it doesn't matter if the bride isn't drawn to the best man – she's not marrying him!

To be inordinately caught up with people liking us is to be flirting with the bride of Christ which is a serious betrayal of the Bridegroom. 2Corinthians 4:5 says, "We do not preach ourselves but Christ Jesus as Lord, and ourselves as your bond-servants for Jesus' sake." We're trying to make Jesus famous, not ourselves. Any other attitude will hinder fruitfulness.

April 30

The Beauty of the Church - Part One

"For just as the body is one and has many members, and all the members of the body, though many, are one body, so it is with Christ" 1 Corinthians 12:12

The church is kind of like a jigsaw puzzle. Everyone is a piece, and when each person does their part a beautiful picture is made. When one or two pieces are gone from a puzzle my family is putting together we never say, "oh well, at least most of them are here." No, there is a frantic search for the missing piece, because the picture will not be complete without it. In fact, if we can't find what's missing, we will end up throwing the whole puzzle away because it can never be finished. Each piece, however small, is vital to the whole.

The apostle Paul, in a similar way, says the church is like a body. Each part is very different in looks and function but essential to the whole. He points out two attitudes that can slip into the body of Christ and undermine the unity that God is trying to bring about: rejection and pride (we'll cover pride tomorrow).

First, he deals with rejection which is very prevalent in today's church. "If the foot should say, 'Because I am not a hand, I am not a part of the body,' it is not for this reason any the less a part of the body." (1Corinthians 12:15-16) It is very easy to look around at other people's gifts and feel like yours is inferior. The temptation is to "bury your talent" in a spirit of rejection, because you don't feel like you're "important" anyway.

Rejection can often be the byproduct of jealousy. The jealous ear might be overheard saying something like this: "Oh, how I wish I was an eye. Everyone's always commenting on the beautiful blue eyes, and people look into one another's eyes. Why can't I be an eye? No one comments on ears. No one notices them unless they're too big. Why do I have to be stuck being an ear?" Paul gives the answer of why you were given the part you've been given, "But now God has placed the members, each one of them, in the body, just as He desired." (1Corinthians 12:18) You can either rebel against who you are and be upset and unhappy, or accept your position, serve in it, and experience the joy of the Lord. Joy doesn't come from being important in people's eyes, it comes from being loved and used by God.

May 1

The Beauty of the Church – Part II

"Now you are Christ's body, and individually members of it." 1Corinthians
12:27

One reason that people don't take their place in the body of Christ is rejection (yesterday); another is pride.

Paul addresses this pride in 1Corinthians 12:21: "And the eye cannot say to the hand, 'I have no need of you'; or again the head to the feet, 'I have no need of you.'" It is a temptation for those who are gifted and used by God to feel a little better than those who are not so used. I don't know if there is anything as ugly or as blinding as spiritual pride. Whole churches can feel that they are more important than other churches and look down their noses at those who are not as "spiritual" as they are. This attitude has caused many unnecessary divisions in the body of Christ and has made it hard for the world to believe that the church is any different than they are. God has made us dependent on Him which all Christians believe, but He's also made us interdependent on one another. Many believers today seem to believe that they can be a fulfilled Christian without being part of a local church. This is just another form of spiritual pride.

One of my favorite illustrations of our interdependence is a bird called the Pacific Golden Plover. The PGP has two homes, one in Hawaii, and one in Alaska. They have their children in Alaska during the summer and then take the 90 hour, non-stop flight, to their winter home in Hawaii. Remarkably, the children leave for Hawaii a few weeks later than the adults, making a journey they have never made before. Only God in heaven could direct them to a little dot called Hawaii in the middle of the Pacific Ocean. But they're not just dependent on God, they were also created to be interdependent on one another. Engineers have figured out that the young Pacific Golden Plovers only have body fat (which is their fuel) to make a 70 hour flight. They make up the other 20 hours by flying together in a V, rotating the lead bird to cut down on wind resistance. Without each other they would be 20 hours short of Hawaii and drown in the Pacific. No one of them could ever make it all the way to Hawaii on their own.

Like it or not, you and I have not only been created completely dependent on God (we can't even draw a breath without Him), we have been created to be interdependent on people. You will never completely fulfill your destiny on earth without embracing your part in the body of Christ. Don't drown, humble yourself, and we'll make it to Hawaii together.

May 2

Mother's Day

"Honor your...mother." Ephesians 6:2

My little brother, Jimmy, and I had a disease when we were babies that caused us to vomit up our food. Whenever this difficult period was referenced growing up, all mom would say was: "Never forget Mother's Day!"

To honor my Mom, who is now with Jesus, I'd like to highlight a few of the things she instilled in her children.

Education: For Mom education meant opportunity, so from a very early age, education was celebrated. Each of us read our first book out loud to the family on a blanket Mom laid down on the living room floor while the rest of the children ate popcorn and encouraged the reader.

Instead of getting toys or treats, all of her grandchildren would receive a savings bond every birthday. The bond wouldn't come due until they turned eighteen and was to help them pay for a college education. These seeds produced a harvest as all 18 of her grandchildren went on to graduate from college.

Gratitude: Whenever we received a gift or kindness from anyone, Mom sat us down to write a thank you note. One time all of her six children received $1,000 from our great Aunt Ruth whom we had never met. Mom insisted that we write thank you notes, but we were all in college or beyond at that point, so she couldn't monitor our follow through. Only Sheila ended up writing a beautiful thank you note telling Aunt Ruth how grateful she was and even specifying how she used the money. The rest of us learned a lesson when Sheila alone received a second check from Aunt Ruth!

Faith: Mom didn't spend a lot of time questioning God and she never expected her church to be perfect. Mom and Dad were at church every week, so we were too. When I had a conversion experience and everyone thought I was in a cult, Mom stayed by me even though she didn't understand what I was into. She was proud of me being a pastor and was happy to visit our church, but she remained a faithful Catholic until the end.

I was so blessed to have her as my mom and miss her everyday but I know one day soon we will be together again forever. I hope you take time to honor your mom in some way this Mother's Day.

May 3

Resting and Working in Grace

"By the grace of God I am what I am, and His grace toward me did not prove vain; but I labored even more than all of them, yet not I, but the grace of God with me." 1Corinthians 15:10

Can you feel Paul's liberty in this passage? He's not trying to impress people, or be better than anyone else. He is happy to be himself in the grace of God, "I am what I am." It kind of sounds like God's revelation of Himself to Moses, "I am who I am." While God is self existent, relying on no one else to bring Him into being or to sustain His being; Paul's identity is entirely wrapped up in who God is making him by grace. But grace doesn't just affect who Paul is, it's also the engine for all he does: "I labored..., yet not I, but ...grace..."

Are we as conscious as Paul was of God's grace for our being and doing? Am I performing to gain God's favor, or because I already have His favor by grace? Am I performing to gain self worth, or have I accepted myself as God accepts me in Christ? Can I say with complete self acceptance, "I am what I am by the grace of God?" If I'm resting in grace, no person's opinion can threaten my identity. If I'm working in grace there is no pride of achievement, or fear of underachievement that comes from comparing myself to others.

Whenever we have communion at church and are reminded that it's ultimately not about what we do for God, but what He has done for us through Christ. His body was given, and His blood was poured out, so that we might be forgiven and be able to feast on His grace all of our days.

Free from Condemnation

"Woman, where are they? Did no one condemn you?' She said, 'No one, Lord.' And Jesus said, 'I do not condemn you, either. Go. From now on sin no more.'" John 8:10-11

Today I want to write about the first part of what Jesus said, "I do not condemn you, either." Tomorrow we will look at the second phrase, "From now on sin no more."

The Pharisees witnessed an outward act of sin and were ready to stone this woman who they roughly threw before Jesus. Jesus looked at her and saw not just the act of sin but everything behind the act: the fear, the previous abuse at the hands of men, the financial need, the guilt and shame... whatever it was that brought this precious creation of God to this horrible place of darkness. This is why Jesus warns us about judging people. We simply don't know all of what is going on in a person's heart or the circumstances that are behind their present behavior. When Jesus saw her, He saw the reason that He had come. "For God did not send the Son into the world to judge the world, but that the world might be saved through Him." (John 3:17)

Jesus loves you and me. When He comes to our darkness it is not to punish or condemn us, but to call us into the salvation He has provided. When condemnation rests on our spirit we feel shame and guilt that only serve to keep us doing the things that brought the shame and guilt in the first place. If you think God is only saying in a stern voice, "Sin no more," you won't be able to stay free because the power of freedom is in knowing that He has freed us from condemnation.

Jesus gives the truth that frees us from the slavery of sin later in this same chapter: "The slave does not remain in the house forever; the son does remain forever. So if the Son makes you free, you will be free indeed." (John 8:35-36) The slave's place in the house is only secured by performance and so the slave lives driven by the fear of not being good enough. The way Jesus frees us is by making us children that know they have a permanent place. The key is first believing that we really are children, dearly loved by the Father (1John 3:1-3), and then living out of that identity. This is easy to agree with in our heads, but it's only when it is real in our hearts that we find the power to "sin no more."

May 5

The Seriousness of Sin

"Woman, where are they? Did no one condemn you?' She said, 'No one, Lord.' And Jesus said, 'I do not condemn you, either. Go. From now on sin no more.'" John 8:10-11

Yesterday we looked at how the power to overcome sin is in hearing deeply in our hearts the truth of the cross, "I do not condemn you." Today I want to look at the phrase after forgiveness has been secured, "From now on sin no more."

Sin is not a popular topic in America today. We like to do our own thing, in our own way, and in our own timing without any interference from God. God is fine when we need help, but He had better not encroach on our "freedoms." Hollywood has relentlessly told our culture that there is no sin in immorality and this message has taken a firm hold. Think for a moment of the price America has paid for neglecting God's law in this one area.

If we had obeyed God's boundaries instead of our passions there would have been no abortions (or the guilt and shame that go with them), no venereal diseases, no aids, no pornography industry, no rapes, no molestations, few divorces, few single parent homes, and no need for all the government programs that try to meet all of these needs. There would also be much less heartbreak as well as less depression and despair that often accompany a sexual relationship that has gone bad.

But before we blame America, let's look at the church. The church has seemingly little power to "sin no more" according to all of George Barna's research on church morality. As long as we're acting just like the world, how can the world be expected to repent and turn to Jesus?

What is the gospel's position on sin? Is it, "Go, and keep on sinning because I've died for you?" or "Go, for there is no such thing as sin anymore?" or "Go, sin's not a big deal now that I have died for you?"

Jesus said, "Go. From now on sin no more." He came to wash us of sin and the shame and guilt that accompany it, but He now expects us to be pursuing a lifestyle that is at least seeking to be free from sin. He forgives us again when we are seriously trying but fall because of weakness and immaturity, but that is different from a flippant attitude that presumes on God's grace.

Let's purpose to hear in our hearts His words of grace, "I do not condemn you," and go from that place empowered to live for Jesus free from sin's grip.

May 6

The Righteousness of God

"I am not ashamed of the gospel, because it is the power of God for the salvation of everyone who believes; first for the Jew, then for the Gentile. For in the gospel a righteousness from God is revealed, a righteousness that is by faith from first to last, just as it is written: 'The righteous will live by faith.'" Romans 1:16-17

The good news (gospel) is that a righteousness from God is available to us today because of what Christ did on the cross. This righteousness cannot be earned but only embraced through faith; it is God's gift to those who will receive it. God is so holy that even our seemingly righteous acts appear like filthy rags to Him, (Isaiah 64:6) so He sent His Son to do for us, what we could not do for ourselves. "God made Him who had not sin to be sin for us, so that in Him we might become the righteousness of God." (2Corinthians 5:21)

God's Spirit made this passage in Romans come alive to a young, miserable monk named Martin Luther while studying in Wittenburg, Germany in 1513-1515. Here are his words about the experience:

"I sought day and night to make out the meaning of Paul; and at last I came to apprehend it thus: Through the gospel is revealed the righteousness which availeth with God – a righteousness by which God, in His mercy and compassion, justifieth us; as it is written, 'The just shall live by faith.' Straightway I felt as if I were born anew. It was as if I had found the door of Paradise thrown wide open. Now I saw the Scriptures altogether in a new light – I ran through their whole contents as far as my memory would serve, and compared them, and found that this righteousness was really that by which God makes us righteous, because everything else in Scripture agreed thereunto so well. The expression, 'the righteousness of God,' which I so much hated before, now became dear and precious – my darling and comforting word."

No religious effort or philosophical ideal can produce what God Himself has done for us in Christ. In Him we are righteous! Embrace it, speak it, and walk it out because this simple truth has the power to save everyone who believes.

May 7

The Root of all Fruit

"I am the vine, you are the branches; he who abides in Me and I in him, he bears much fruit, for apart from Me you can do nothing." John 15:5

The problem with this passage is that God allows people to do a lot apart from Him. People are busy everywhere promoting themselves and their ambitions, building their little mini-kingdoms, and constructing towers that reach to heaven just like Babylon of old. And God allows it all, for a time. When Jesus says, "...apart from Me you can do nothing," He means nothing that is born of God, nothing that is beautiful, and nothing that will last. The fruit He would give those who allowed His life to live through them, He promised, would remain, not just through time, but for all eternity. (John 15:16)

The root of this fruit is a humility which agrees with God that we can do nothing truly good apart from Him. Without this agreement our Christianity amounts to sincere people trying to look like Jesus by their own commitment and constantly failing, instead of fully surrendered lives which allow Christ to live His powerful life through them. The gospel doesn't just call us to do good, it shows us the way. We must die to our old selfish nature, not dress it up with the appearance of good, and then we must allow Christ to live through us by the new nature He has given us. Paul, one of the most fruitful Christians who ever lived, said it this way: "I am crucified with Christ and it is no longer I who live but Christ who lives in me; and the life which I now live in the flesh I live by faith in the Son of God, who loved me and gave Himself up for me." (Galatians 2:20)

Jesus gave in the first beatitude the secret to all the other ones, "Blessed are the poor in spirit, for theirs is the kingdom of heaven." (Matthew 5:1) When we agree that we have no righteousness of our own, we are able to embrace His. When we embrace our poverty apart from Him, all of heaven's resources become ours. Four times in the gospels Jesus says the words, "whoever exalts himself will be humbled, but whoever humbles himself will be exalted."

Benjamin Franklin, a deist who never embraced Christianity, sought with all his power to master the virtues. He claimed that after many years of seeking perfection there was only one virtue that escaped him: humility. The difficulty was that whenever he did a good job being humble he found he was proud about it. The pride in a human heart can only be conquered by the Savior.

May 8

The Purpose of Pruning

"Every branch that bears fruit, He prunes it so that it may bear more fruit."
John 15:2

When we lived in Montevideo, MN we had some friends that decided they were going to surprise us while we were away at a conference by working on our yard. Included in their work was the pruning of our front bushes. When I first saw them I was shocked. Our once large, robust bushes looked like they were little, puny twigs stuck in the ground that were about to die. Fortunately one of the women saw my concern and assured me that this was actually a good thing, and that the pruning process was important for the bush. I took her word for it, but still thought that anyone passing by in the near future would be very unimpressed with our bushes.

Jesus said that if we please God by bearing fruit, God will prune us back, so that we will eventually bear more fruit. God always sees things from His eternal perspective. He sees our pain, but He still does what is best for the long term with, what seems to us, little regard for our short term comfort. As human beings we usually consider short term comfort before long term benefit, and can easily be offended that God doesn't see it our way. "If God truly loved people then He would..." Our own ideas of what God's love should look like can easily rob us of faith.

God's end is to transform us into the image of His glorious Son. (Romans 8:29) He is firm in His purpose, so our lives will be a lot easier if we agree with His plan and try to work with it instead of resisting it. Hebrews 12:5 gives the two wrong responses to the pruning process called the Lord's discipline:

1. Don't take it lightly – embrace God's dealings with you and respond quickly. Blowing off conviction will only lead to God bringing the correction at a later time and usually in a bigger way.
2. Don't become discouraged – when life is hard we often conclude that God is angry with us or is somehow not pleased. Don't jump to conclusions! Check your conscience, and if everything is clear then just trust that the God who delights in you is doing a little pruning so that your long term joy will be maximized.

Part of God's plan is that we supply comfort to each other while they are being pruned. Let's be sensitive, gentle, and loving to people who are going through difficulties knowing full well that we may need comfort from them tomorrow.

May 9

Wanting what God Wants

"If you abide in Me, and My words abide in you, ask whatever you wish, and it will be done for you." John 15:7

Jesus gives us here the secret to authority in prayer. When we truly abide in Him by His Spirit, and allow His word to abide in us, our desires are transformed in such a way that what we want will be what God wants. Then we only need to ask with faith, so that heaven's will can be done on earth. The difficulty of course is that no one perfectly abides in Him, nor does His word perfectly abide in anyone, so we are confined to a process of transformation. As we walk with Him there is more and more authority in our prayer life because we become more and more filled with His desires.

This truth also gives light to another remarkable promise: "Until now you have asked for nothing in My name; ask and you will receive, so that your joy may be full." (John 16:24) Some have thought this to be a simple matter of tagging the name of Jesus on to your prayer and you will get whatever you ask for. After praying in this way, you will find that this isn't how it works and may conclude that Jesus exaggerated in His promise because you "... prayed in Jesus name according to this promise and it didn't work!" Praying in His name means more than a postscript to a request we make of God. It means to be in union with Him, it is in fact a matter of the vine (Jesus) giving life to the prayer that comes out of the branches (us). As we live in His name, we will find increasing confidence to pray in His name.

The Old Testament scripture that underlies this truth is found in Psalm 37:4: "Delight yourself in the Lord and He will give you the desires of your heart." When we delight in God by allowing His Spirit to dwell in us and His Word to be our daily food, He gives us His desires and puts them in our hearts, so that what we want is what He wants. True freedom is not just having the power to do what is right; it is having the desire to do what is right. As we become one with God through Jesus our life becomes easier and easier because our own carnal desires are put down and His desires become stronger in us. As Paul said: "It is God at work in you, both to will (desire) and to work for His good pleasure." (Philippians 2:13)

Laying a Solid Foundation

"Let us press on to maturity, not laying again a foundation of repentance from dead works..." Hebrews 6:1

On August 1, 2007 a bridge in Minneapolis that crossed the Mississippi river collapsed killing 13 and injuring 145. The irony was that work was being done on the bridge at the time of the collapse; but it was the wrong work. One article summed up the types of things that were being done: "The construction taking place in the weeks prior to the collapse included replacing lighting, and guard rails. At the time of the collapse, four of the eight lanes were closed for resurfacing." Because the foundational work was left undone, all the other work proved to be in vain. This is how it is in a Christianity that lacks repentance. It doesn't matter how much we do, if we haven't really repented and aren't living a life of repentance, all our works are dead in God's sight.

Hebrews 3:7-8; 3:15 and 4:7 all say the same thing: "Today if you hear His voice, do not harden your hearts." Repentance is not possible until God speaks to us. He can speak through His word as we read it, or through a preacher at church, or by a dream or vision in the night, or through an honest friend, or in difficult circumstances. God has lots of ways to speak to us when He wants to get our attention.

When God speaks we need to agree with Him. David said, "Against You, You only, I have sinned and done what is evil in Your sight, so that You are justified when You speak." (Psalm 51:4) When we agree with what God says we justify Him; when we defend ourselves by making excuses for what we did, we justify ourselves. Hardening your heart toward God can actually mean softening your heart toward you by giving yourself unwarranted and unsanctified mercy for evil you have said, thought, or done. "It wasn't that bad," "he had it coming," "I only spoke the truth," "I was tired," "Yeah, but she did that wrong thing first," are just a few excuses that quickly come into our hearts when we seek to justify ourselves.

Let's not live resurfacing the bridge when what it needs is foundation work. Rather, let's each take time to seek our hearts and fully repent. Isaiah 30:15 gives the blessing that will result, "In repentance and rest you will be saved, in quietness and trust is your strength."

May 11

Is there a Fire in You?

"Be dressed ready for service and keep your lamps burning." Luke 12:35

We are called to carry a fire in us, the very light of life. (John 1:3) It is a fire of grace, meaning that only God can produce it and sustain it, yet we play an important part. Jesus commands all disciples: "keep your lamps burning."

God's revealed presence serves as the spark and lighter fluid to get the fire going. The Word of God in us serves as the kindling (the milk of the Word) and the large logs (the meat of the Word) which brings the fire to a blaze and makes a way for it to keep burning.

Jesus said, "If you abide in Me (His presence), and My word abides in you, you will ask whatever you wish and it will be done." (John 15:7) When the fire of grace is burning in our hearts, our desires become purified to the point that they are unified with what God desires. When this happens there is great authority to bring the kingdom on this earth; our sin nature loses its hold without us having to try hard to fight it; and our lives bring others light and warmth in an effortless way. If you keep your lamp burning, everything else will kind of take care of itself!

So why do so few Christians today seem to have a fire burning in their hearts? Some love the presence of the Spirit but neglect the word. Their hearts are like pouring lighter fluid on a little kindling, lighting it, and watching it burn impressively for a brief period of time. When the fire goes out, they have to look for another meeting where the "Spirit's moving," and so eventually become disillusioned.

Others only want the word and neglect the importance of the presence of God. They presume, like the Pharisees, that because they diligently seek the Scriptures they are close to God. (John 5:39) This is like having a big log in your fireplace that is unlit. It may have great potential, but it can't warm or purify anyone because there's no fire.

Building a good fire is an art; keeping it going is a discipline. Jesus said He would not put out a smoldering wick (Matthew 12:20), so if we acknowledge our need He will bring us His flame again. John the Baptist said He came to "baptize us with the Holy Spirit and fire." (Matthew 3:11)

Grace

"For it is God who is at work in you, both to will and to work for His good pleasure." Philippians 2:13

The Christian life is not difficult, it's impossible. No one can produce what God desires in us other than God Himself. Religion of man may do a great deal of work and have impressive spiritual disciplines, but for all of its efforts, it cannot please God.

True Christianity is about grace through faith in Christ that produces both desire and power within a believer to do the will of God. It leaves no boast in the mouth of the believer except: "I am what I am by the grace of God." (1Corinthians 15:10) In the way of grace, the believer stops "trying" to do good and learns to yield to the goodness of God inside of them.

The verse before the text quoted above reads: "Work out your salvation with fear and trembling..." (Philippians 2:12b) The recognition that God Himself is in us means that our "work" is learning how to yield to, and release, His wonderful grace within us. If we reflect more on what this means, there will be a greater sense of awe (fear and trembling) in our ordinary lives. Think of it: the uncreated God of eternity; the God who created the entire universe – lives in me. Wow!

We don't read our Bibles, pray, worship, go to church, or do good works to gain intimacy with God. Intimacy is His gift to us through the cross. Our part is to accept this gift daily, and to learn how to "do" all spiritual things from the place of freely given grace instead of by a performance mentality of works.

Rejoice in the grace given to you by personalizing the following verse: "In love He predestined us (me) to be adopted as His children (child), in accordance with His pleasure and will – to the praise of His glorious grace which He has freely given us (me) in the One (Christ) He loves." (Ephesians 1:4b-6)

Satisfaction in God

"Blessed are those who hunger and thirst for righteousness, for they shall be satisfied." Matthew 5:6

Jesus knew what it was to hunger and thirst for righteousness, and the deep satisfaction that came when He did the next right thing the Father was calling Him to do. When He was at a well talking to a woman, the disciples offered Him food, but Jesus told them He had food they didn't know about. When they asked about this, He replied, "My food is to do the will of Him who sent Me and to accomplish His work." (John 4:34) When He was tempted in the desert, He told Satan that man lives on "every word that proceeds from the mouth of God." (Matthew 4:4) The will of God and the word of God are how Jesus walked in righteousness and it's how we experience the sustenance and life God gives today.

When natural hunger and thirst is satisfied by a delightful meal and beverage, it doesn't mean that you'll never be hungry and thirsty again. So it is with the will of God, the more you do it, the more satisfaction you have in it, and the more hungry and thirsty you are to have more of that which satisfies in the future.

But to do righteousness, you first have to be righteous. When we believe the gospel, God makes us right with Himself in Christ. He calls it the gift of righteousness. (See 2Corinthians 5:21; Romans 5:17) From this place of right standing with God, we can now hunger and thirst to do righteousness.

The good Shepherd promises to guide us "in the paths of righteousness for His Name's sake." (Psalm 23:3) He will always lead us to do the right thing (righteousness simply means doing what's right) no matter what the circumstance. Even if we walk through the valley of the shadow of death or find ourselves in the very presence of our enemies, we never have to fear; all we have to do is choose to do what is right. If we will be led by righteousness, God promises that "goodness and mercy" will follow us all of our days. Jesus said something similar, "Seek first the kingdom of God and His righteousness, and all these things will be added to you." (Matthew 6:33)

We aren't driven by fear that we won't have the things we need; we are confident that we only need to hunger and thirst for righteousness, and God's abundant provision will follow us. Yet our satisfaction transcends our bills being paid, and our mouths being fed; we get to experience the joy of knowing God and doing His will.

May 14

Glowing in the Dark

"But we all, with unveiled face, beholding as in a mirror the glory of the Lord, are being transformed into the same image from glory to glory, just as from the Lord, the Spirit." 2Corinthians 3:18

My little brother, Jimmy, and I (8 and 10 at the time) were so excited about the Glo-Balls someone gave us that we immediately scampered into our downstairs closet after freeing them from the package. What a horrible disappointment! These balls didn't glow – alright, maybe a little – but certainly not what was promised on the box.

Apparently our disappointment was obvious because we were quickly informed that we had missed a step in the process. First, you have to hold balls near a light source because the balls weren't lights themselves; they only had the capacity to absorb light. We kind of resented an additional step, but I remember holding that ball close to a light bulb willing it to absorb. The second time in the closet was thrilling! Now the balls were brilliant and really did appear like lights in the darkness.

We are not the source of light, but we can absorb light and then carry Him every day into this dark world. Isaiah 60:1-3 describes this beautifully: "Arise, shine; for your light has come, and the glory of the Lord has risen upon you. For behold, darkness will cover the earth and deep darkness the peoples; but the Lord will rise upon you and His glory will appear upon you. Nations will come to your light, and kings to the brightness of your rising."

Every time we look up and behold God's presence we glow a little more. Just like those balls we eventually fade if we don't continue to expose ourselves to His presence. But when we do behold Him, even if dimly as in a mirror (their mirrors were made of brass), we go from glory to glory, and many will be drawn to the Lord and His ways through us. Being His witness is simply glowing in the dark.

May 15

Faith or Fear?

"Then Caleb quieted the people before Moses and said, 'We should by all means go up and take possession of it (the land), for we will surely overcome it.' But the men who had gone up with him said, 'We are not able to go up against the people, for they are too strong for us.' So they gave out to the sons of Israel a bad report of the land which they had spied out..."
Numbers 13:30-33

Every day, in every problem and situation – we have a choice: will we view them through faith or through fear? Caleb and the other spies had gone into the exact same land and were facing the exact same difficulty, yet they saw through two different lenses. God is not just calling us to be saved by faith, but to live by faith. How do we accomplish this in the midst of fears?

1. Faith remembers what God has done in the past. God had already supernaturally delivered the Israelites from Egypt; He parted the Red Sea; He gave them manna out of heaven. Caleb isn't naïve about the size of the giants in the land, it's just that God has proven that there is no difficulty He can't overcome.

2. Faith focuses on the promises and the character of God. It's not that Caleb didn't see the giants that the others saw; he just didn't focus on them. He was focusing on the promise of God who had told Moses that He was planning to bring them into "a spacious land, flowing with milk (needs) and honey (above and beyond)."

3. Faith is not afraid to die. What if disaster happens and we die? The answer is we don't know for sure what the end will look like, so we need to surrender outcomes to God and be willing to do what we think He wants us to by faith. Esther said, "If I perish, I perish." That conviction gave her strength to do what was right even though she couldn't control the outcome.

What are you facing right now? I pray you'll face it with God through the lens of faith, and not through the darkness and isolation of fear.

Redemptive Abandonment

"Now as for me, I said in my prosperity, 'I will never be moved.' O Lord, by Your favor You have made my mountain to stand strong. You hid Your face, I was dismayed. To You O Lord, I called... 'Hear, O Lord, and be gracious to me; O Lord, be my helper.' You have turned for me my mourning into dancing...O Lord my God, I will give thanks to You forever."
Psalm 130:6-8, 10-12

Whenever God favors us we can come to the wrong conclusion that we have life, and God figured out. When things are going well, we can easily assume we are strong, immovable, and in control, but all this is a dangerous deception. Because God loves us so much, He breaks the power of presumption in our lives through something a speaker I heard recently call, "redemptive abandonment." God hides His face during seasons of our lives, not because He doesn't care, but because He cares so much.

Peter declares, "Even though all may fall away, yet I will not... Even if I have to die with You, I will not deny You." (Mark 14:29; 31) Peter has been favored as the top apostle and has come to the wrong conclusion. He believes he is strong, a veritable mountain of faith, immovable from his devotion. We can hear in his words, "all may fall away, yet I will not," disdain for others who aren't as strong as he presumes he is. His future leadership would be very limited if he continues with the false impression that he is somehow better than those he is leading, so Jesus explains to him the reality of prophetic abandonment.

"Simon, Simon, behold, Satan has demanded permission to sift you like wheat; but I have prayed for you, that your faith may not fail; and you, when once you have returned, strengthen your brothers." (Luke 22:31-32) Before he falls, Peter despises the weakness of those around him because he presumes he has it all together. After he falls and is picked up again by God, he will see clearly that the plan is about Divine grace, not human strength. Peter will now be able to lead weak people with gentleness and understanding as a humble servant instead of as a know it all.

Because David (the author of the passage above) and Peter experienced the reality of how weak they were apart from God (abandonment), they were in a position to experience the favor of God (redemption) without becoming proud. Mourning can become dancing when the burden of presumption is broken off our lives.

May 17

Hidden Shame

"The wicked flee when no one is pursuing, but the righteous are as bold as a lion." Proverbs 28:1

A man once described his walk with God as being on a treadmill. He felt he could never make progress because eventually he would stumble again in the area of lust. Every other area, he found, he could set his will and be victorious, but he was utterly defeated in this area and it was robbing him of confidence with God.

How do we overcome immorality and the shame it brings?

1. Wage war against it. Jesus died on the cross so we could be forgiven and have a new beginning. Many today have stopped fighting and changed the gospel to a license to keep sinning in this area. They say something like this to themselves: "God understands how weak I am and why I've stopped even trying to be sexually pure." No, He doesn't. He didn't stop when it was difficult for Him, He shed His blood, He took the shame and pain of the cross and drank the cup of the wrath of God for us. How can we stop fighting to be pure because it's too hard?

2. Wage the right war. After we've set our heart to be pure it is easy to get into wrong thinking, so here is a warning: If we try to wage war against our own sexuality we will become angry with God. God made us sexual beings. The fact that you're attracted to the opposite sex is not sin, it just means all the equipment is working. Jesus said lust in the heart is like adultery, not a thought in the mind. When a lustful thought comes into your mind, you are being tempted, you haven't yet sinned. Don't let the thought have a place; press delete instead of downloading it. It's not a sin to be tempted!

3. Get into the word of God. "Your word have I treasured (hidden) in my heart, so I might not sin against You." (Psalm 119:11) God wants our fantasy life, and all hidden thoughts to be transformed by the word of God.

4. Delight in God's love for you. We are dark but lovely to God. (Song of Songs 1:5) I honestly don't think anyone can win the lust battle without experiencing the higher pleasure of God's love for them. It can be hard for men to connect emotionally with God, but it is really important. In Christ, we are the favored, beloved, children of God. His plan is for our success, not our failure!

The Sacrifice Answered by Fire

"Therefore, I urge you, brothers, in view of God's mercy, to offer your bodies as living sacrifices, holy and pleasing to God - this is your spiritual act of worship." Romans 12:1

At one convention I went to the theme was, "Altared," with a verse from Leviticus 6:12 on never letting the fire go out on the altar. Each speaker brought up the theme and gave reflections on what it looked like to have the fire of God's presence burning in the altar of our hearts.

One speaker asked us to consider what comes into our minds when we hear the word "worship." Then he suggested some possible answers: a too short or too long time of singing before a sermon, hymns or choruses, singing that is too fast or too slow, a key too high or low to sing in, or maybe even the graphics that are now behind the words of songs because of modern technology.

Then he talked about the Bible's version of worship which he said was more PG 13. Worship in the Bible always involved something dying. From Abel's sacrifice to animals required for sacrifice in the tabernacle and the temple; Jews knew that there must be a death to satisfy the holiness of God who said the wages of sin was death. After the sacrifice God required was given, God Himself would answer by fire. The priests didn't need matches.

Elijah said the God who answers by fire, He is God. When the Holy Spirit came after the sacrifice and resurrection of Jesus, there was a tongue of fire that rested on each head. Truly our God is a consuming fire (Hebrews 12:29) and wants to baptize us in His purifying fire so we can easily live for Him.

So here's the problem. The only offering that is answered by fire is death. If we try to give God a partial offering instead of making ourselves living sacrifices, we won't have His fire in our hearts. We will end up with a powerless version of Christianity that looks and acts just like the world. It sounds kind of like the American church today, doesn't it?

In view of His mercy, let's give Him what He died for by offering ourselves as living sacrifices for His glory and our good.

May 19

Standing Firm in Your Faith

"If you don't stand firm in your faith, you won't stand at all." Isaiah 7:9

The words of the text above came to my mind unbidden in June of 2012. Weeks earlier I had received a letter from a lawyer threatening a lawsuit against our church because of some changes we made at our school. I did everything I could to get them to drop it, including begging God to intervene on our behalf, but it was all to no avail. The lawsuit was filed anyway and fear gripped my heart.

As I considered the possible devastation a lawsuit could have on our church, the sentence above came to me. Was this a Scripture? I went to my concordance and found it. The context was a warning to King Ahaz who had two armies mounted against him which had caused his heart to be "shaken as trees of the field are shaken by the wind." (Isaiah 7:2) The same Holy Spirit who was warning him many years ago was now warning me.

It was game time. I talked about trusting God all the time, I'm a preacher after all, but now it was time to actually believe like a Christian should. God didn't tell me how the lawsuit would end, He just warned me that if I gave into the fear speaking to me, it would not go well.

A believer's main job is to believe. Are you facing something right now that is filling you with fear? This is not the time to abandon your faith; it's time to practice it. Tell God you trust Him, speak to the mountain you're facing, and live in the freedom Christ paid for even while the circumstances are unchanged.

That's what I did. Months later I received an email that said the lawsuit was dropped, but the greater miracle was that it wasn't even that big of a relief. I had found rest in God and knew it would be okay, whatever happened.

Why not give God your fears today and claim Psalm 34:4 for your life, "I sought the Lord, and He answered me, and delivered me from all my fears."

The Samuel Generation

"In the last days, God says, I will pour out My Spirit on all people. Your sons and daughters will prophesy, your young men will see visions, your old men will dream dreams." Acts 2:17

A few years ago the pastors of our region decided together to have teens and young adults lead some of our monthly worship gatherings. Why young people? I believe we will never have the fullness of God's presence without the generations coming together. God blesses everything as much as He can and we praise Him for all He's currently doing, but there is a longing in many of our hearts for more.

I am convinced young people need to honor the older generation and value their covering, but am equally convinced that the older generation needs to release their sons and daughters to prophecy. What if they say something that's wrong? What if they become filled with pride? Then we are here to guide them and teach them, but God wants them to speak now, and not just when they're "mature."

In January of 2014 I had the privilege of speaking to our youth group. I told them the church is stuck without them. They are not the "church of tomorrow;" today's church needs them to rise up and grab ahold of God.

In Eli's day there were two types of young people: Hophni and Phineas were one; Samuel the other. So it is today. Hophni and Phineas represent those who are "ungrateful, disobedient to parents,... lovers of pleasure rather than lovers of God," (2Timothy 3:1-4) while Samuel represents a whole generation of young people who love the presence of God (1Samuel 3:3), begin to hear His voice (1 Samuel 3:10), and speak to their culture with great authority. (1Samuel 3:19-20)

We must encourage our young people to become all God desires them to be to have His full blessing in the days to come.

May 21

Trying to Put God on a Leash

"Can you make a pet of him like a bird or put him on a leash for your girls?...Any hope of subduing him is false; the mere sight of him is overpowering. No one is fierce enough to rouse him. Who then is able to stand against Me? Who has a claim against Me that I must pay? Everything under heaven belongs to Me." Job 41:5; 9-11

God is describing to Job an animal called Leviathan in the text above. It's a wild animal that has now gone extinct, but there are many other animals God created to be wild.

Job's friends tried to put God on a leash. "Here's how God works," they argued (my paraphrase). "God blesses the righteous with temporal blessings and punishes the wicked with temporal hardships. Therefore, Job, you clearly have done something wicked because you are suffering."

Job responded to them with equally long arguments that can be summed up by something like this: "You guys have it all wrong. There are many examples where wicked people don't get what's coming to them in this life, and where the righteous suffer – I am example one of this! I have been righteous but am suffering horribly. Your formula for God is wrong."

When God revealed Himself at the end of the book, He said that Job's friends had spoken what was wrong about Him and that Job had said what was right. (Job 42:7) But Job still needed to repent when God confronted him. He felt God somehow owed him something for the righteous life he had led and for the righteous acts he had performed. What was happening to him was "not fair," so he had longed for a face to face encounter with God to tell him so.

God eventually gave Job that encounter and in the text above is rebuking him for trying to put Him on a leash. God will not be told what to do and does not owe mankind anything. Job then apologized: "My ears had heard of You but now my eyes have seen You. Therefore I despise myself and repent in dust and ashes." (Job 42:5-6)

Have you tried to put God on a leash? Have you questioned His ways because you feel entitled to a better life? Why not repent now and lay every sense of entitlement down at the foot of the cross. May the mystery of who He is lead us to worship more than ever.

Set on the Wall

"I have set watchmen on your walls, oh Jerusalem; they will never be silent day or night. You who call on the Lord, give yourselves no rest, and give Him no rest until He establishes Jerusalem and makes her the praise of the earth." Isaiah 62:6-7

Why does God set people on the wall to ask Him to do what He already said He wants to do? He wants His church to agree on earth with His purposes as free moral agents, so that we share with Him in every victory that is won. We cannot bring His kingdom without Him, and He won't bring His kingdom without us wanting it, and asking for it.

In this heaven and hell are alike: both seek agreement on earth from human beings so they can bring their purposes to pass on the earth. "I thought God was sovereign," you may argue. He absolutely is. The only reason it is like this is because He planned it to be this way. "Our God is in heaven, He does whatever pleases Him." (Psalm 115:3) This necessary agreement by earth is what pleases Him.

If hell can get people to live in fear, anger, pride, greed, and lust then this darkness will be increased by demons who will dwell in these strongholds. The Father allows it because He has chosen to not force Himself, or His ways on us.

But listen to the promise heaven gives: "I tell you that if two of you agree about anything you ask for, it will be done for you by My Father in heaven. For where two or three come together in My Name, there I am." (Matthew 18:19-20) When we agree together for the beauty and purposes of heaven to be manifested and ask the Father for this, Jesus Himself will come and establish on earth what we have agreed on.

Our text makes it clear we must persist in our asking and expect a progressive answer as we "give Him no rest" until He has done all He has promised. Some of the greatest heroes of the church are the prayer warriors. Their primary labor is not horizontal but vertical, where God has set them on the wall for this purpose. Without prayer, what we do horizontally as a church will have little lasting effect.

Falling Off the Wall

"The prophet is considered a fool, the inspired man a maniac. The prophet, along with my God, is the watchman over Ephraim, yet snares await him on all his paths, and hostility in the house of his God." Hosea 9:7-8

Even though God sets people on the wall (Isaiah 62:6-7) to align with His purposes and to pray for His will to be done on earth, it's easy to fall off the wall. Here are five reasons why people who are genuinely called to watch over the church in prayer, fall from the ministry God set them in:

1. Self-doubt. Watchmen have prophetic experiences to inspire them to pray, but because everyone doesn't experience the same things they do, they are called "maniacs;" or in our day, made out to be "weird." It's easy to question whether God really did speak and to question why He would tell you and not everyone. "Who do I think I am?" is often an accusing thought.

2. Rejection. "Hostility in the house of God" means everyone doesn't appreciate your intensity. Sometimes church leaders feel threatened by people's "revelations" and seek to shut watchmen down.

3. Suspicion. Revelation 12:10 tells us that Satan is "the accuser of the brethren." He will mimic prophetic experiences (He disguises himself as an angel of light) to watchmen that sow suspicions in their hearts about leaders and churches. He uses things that have actually happened and were actually said to make the case that God is against His own church because of their many sins.

4. Discouragement. In a pragmatic world that supremely values action, it can seem like prayer is a waste of time. When Mary poured precious perfume on Jesus, the church leadership said, "Why this waste?" (Matt. 26:8) Needs will always exist and there will always be time to do practical things after prayer, but please know that the highest calling is to "waste" time worshiping Jesus.

5. Depression. In a place of intercession God shares some of His burden with us. We see clearly how wide the gap is between how things are and how they should be. Our burden must be prayed back to God because the government is on Jesus' shoulders, not ours. (Isaiah 9:6) The enemy would have us be self-proclaimed martyrs who are carrying everyone's burdens for them.

Getting Back on the Wall

"No longer will they call you Deserted, or name you Desolate. But you will be called Hephzibah (My delight is in her)...for the Lord will take delight in you." Isaiah 62:4

Yesterday we gave several ways those God genuinely sets on the wall (in a place of authority to pray) fall off of it. Today we look at how to get back on it. "A righteous man falls seven times, and rises again." (Proverbs 24:16)

1. Accept your calling. Romans 11:29 tells us that God's "gifts and call are irrevocable." Just because you don't like the place God has given you, or feel like you've failed at it, doesn't mean you get a new call. Our lives won't work until we embrace God's plan and flow with it. "It is hard for you to kick against the goads." (Acts 26:14)

2. Forgive as you stand praying. "Whenever you stand praying, forgive, if you have anything against anyone, so that your Father who is in heaven will also forgive your transgressions." (Mark 11:25) If we insist on justice, eventually God will have to give us the justice we want for others. (See Matthew 7:1-4) We don't need someone to be sorry for us to forgive them. If we do, forgiveness will always be difficult. Here's why – let's say someone does say they're sorry for the way they've treated you. How will you know if they're really sorry? And even if they appear to be sorry, are they sorry enough? If they're sorry enough, will that for sure mean they'll never do it again? All we need to forgive is to remember that the greatest injustice didn't happen to me; it happened to Jesus. The truly innocent Lamb of God died in my place – that's injustice. Part of my worship is to lay my injustices at the foot of the cross and freely forgive those who hurt me. This is part of what it means to know Jesus "in the fellowship of His suffering." (Philippians 3:10)

3. Embrace your identity. The strength to stay on the wall is not in seeing your prayers answered; it's in the fact that God's delight is in you. We are favored sons and daughters not because of our works, but because of His great mercy toward us in Christ. (Titus 3:5-6) We don't gain favor by praying; we pray from His favor. Our great reward is not in what He does for us, but in our relationship with Him. Until we grasp this reality it will always be hard to stay on the wall.

May 25

Being Available to God

"But Martha was distracted with all her preparations; and she came up to Him and said, 'Lord, do You not care that my sister has left me to do all the serving alone? Then tell her to help me.' But the Lord answered and said to her, 'Martha, Martha, you are worried and bothered about so many things; but only one thing is necessary, for Mary has chosen the good part, which shall not be taken away from her.'" (Luke 10:40-42)

In the summer of 2010, we were contemplating putting two churches together and I was a bit overwhelmed. I asked a good friend and counselor how I could possibly be in charge of this potentially large church when I was already feeling overwhelmed. He suggested a study day once a week where I would only be available to God, and he told me about his pastor back in Michigan who had done this.

"Because he did this he touched fewer people," he explained. This didn't seem right! Why would it ever be good for a pastor to touch fewer people? But then he went on, "He touched fewer people because he had less availability, but because he did this, God was able to touch many more people through him." He said with great soberness, "I don't remember a Sunday where people didn't get saved, healed, or filled with the Holy Spirit. Somehow God touched him in that time away and then God touched through him Sunday after Sunday."

The next week I asked our elders for a study day every week and it's been part of my regular routine ever since. What does this have to do with Martha and Mary?

Martha is a good person who is doing good work but she is carrying an expectation for her sister. For Mary to continue to do what Jesus wants her to do instead of giving into the pressure Martha is applying will mean at least three things: a Christian sister is going to be disappointed, a real need is seemingly going to go unmet, and Mary's not going to look "good" to anyone observing.

But Mary has chosen the "one thing." She is more available to God and less available to people, so she only serves when God tells her to go. She is no longer called by every need in the world or by every expectation of the people around her. She is listening only for the voice of her Lord.

Because of her devotion something wonderful happens for Martha. She gets her own encounter with Jesus where her motives are revealed and her priorities are challenged.

May 26

A Habitat for Growth

"The kingdom of God is like a man who casts seed upon the soil; and he goes to bed at night and gets up by day, and the seed sprouts and grows - how, he himself does not know." Mark 4:26-27

The seed of the kingdom of God is the Word of God. (Mark 4:14) When the Word of God is in us a change begins to happen from the inside out. Its miracle working power to change us only needs to be in the right habitat for it to complete its wonderful, transforming work. What does that habitat look like?

First, it is a habitat of grace. After the Word is planted, "he goes to bed at night..." We must rest in God instead of continually watching ourselves for growth. Could you imagine that seed surviving if every night the man went out and dug it up to see how it was doing? We need to rest in God and trust that the One who began a good work in us will also finish it. (Philippians 1:6)

Second, it is a habitat focused on God, not man. Jesus said that some seeds dry up when "persecution arises because of the Word." (Mark 4:17) When our focus is on people we try to live up to their expectations and time demands. When we're seeking to follow the Word, God's agenda and man's agenda will come into conflict and then a choice needs to be made. Will we please God or man?

Finally, it's a habitat that is thorn free. Jesus gave three main thorns that will have to be continually weeded out of the garden of our hearts or the Word of God won't grow to maturity in us. (Mark 4:19)

1. "The worries of the world..." Worrying is the opposite of trusting God. If you find yourself anxious, stop, ask God to take control of whatever situation you're anxious about and let go of it.

2. "The deceitfulness of riches..." Money and what money can buy promise happiness and safety but once you get them you find yourself empty and anxious after just a little while. Who's in charge? Is it God or is it money? Choose this day which one you will serve.

3. "The desires for other things..." Anything can choke out the word if it becomes the central focus instead of Jesus. Hold everything you have and want loosely while holding on to Jesus tightly, and you'll find you can enjoy life to the fullest.

May 27

Embracing Our Cross

"And He summoned the crowd with His disciples, and said to them, 'If anyone wishes to come after Me, he must deny himself, and take up his cross and follow Me. For whoever wishes to save his life will lose it, but whoever loses his life for My sake and the gospel's will save it. For what does it profit a man to gain the whole world but forfeit his soul?'" Mark 8:34-36

Jesus went to the cross for our salvation. We must go to the cross for our sanctification. This is a painful and difficult process that requires our participation. We must take up (embrace) the cross for God to do His transforming work in us. When we resist the cross, we change very little over time even though we are Christians. Maybe an illustration will help to understand this.

When my mom reached 80 she began seriously considering moving to an apartment which would require her to sell her house. To prepare the house for a sale she thought that a new dining room floor would be nice because the old one was visibly faded. This change would require minimal cost and could be done fairly painlessly.

Then she brought in a realtor and asked this woman, who was a trusted friend, what she thought needed to be done. Getting a new floor in the dining room would be a good start, this woman advised, but really, all the floors needed to be changed. And not just the floors, but the counters, the cupboards, the appliances and the lighting. All of this would be very expensive, but this woman, who was the professional, felt these things would be the minimum changes needed to get the house ready for a sale.

The realtor didn't demand these changes, but only recommended them. The final decision belonged to my mom because she's the one who would have to pay the price.

God wants to change us for our good and His glory but He won't do it without our participation. He brings difficult circumstances and difficult people into our lives so that they will help us see what is left undone in us. When we embrace the cross by trusting God and asking for His grace in the midst of our trials, His beauty begins to replace our ashes. We can't change ourselves any more than my Mom could rip up flooring and lay tile, but we can invite Him to do whatever it takes.

Let's embrace our cross and let Him do the difficult work of change in us. We'll enjoy the results and so will everyone around us.

May 28

More than Conquerors

"Who shall separate us from the love of Christ? Shall trouble or hardship or persecution or famine or nakedness or danger or sword? As it is written: 'For Your sake we face death all day long: we are considered as sheep to be slaughtered.' No, in all these things we are more than conquerors through Him who loved us." Romans 8:35-37

Bruce and Athena Jarman are pastor friends of ours in Montevideo, MN. They adopted a two year old Chinese boy named Judah who came to them with deformed feet. China had a one child policy at the time, so if parents didn't like the child they birthed they could choose to put them in a state orphanage and try for another child that might be more acceptable to them. Because of Judah's deformity, his parents didn't want him.

Bruce and Athena did. They set their love on this little guy and at great expense brought him back to their home in Montevideo. After much prayer for a physical miracle, they felt God leading them to a different plan. Judah had to have both feet amputated and was fit with prosthetics.

Bruce assured his wife that when he gets older and understands all the facts, he will agree with the decision. But there was no way to explain at the time.

When we "love God and are called according to His purpose" none of our suffering is wasted. It is accomplishing some purpose in us for the glory of God and the good of mankind even when we can't possibly understand how. One day, when we get all the information, we will agree with God's dealings. For now we need to hold on to His great love in the midst of circumstances He's allowing. Nothing can separate us from His love!

Friend of Sinners

"This man is the friend of sinners." Luke 15:2

The speakers at a Power & Love conference a few years ago empowered us with messages of God's love and the worthiness of Jesus, so that we could be sent out and demonstrate His power and love wherever we went. We were taught to be unafraid of people and unapologetic in our approach to them. "The earth is the Lord's and everything in it, the world and all who live it." (Psalm 24:1) Everyone we meet was created by God, redeemed by Christ, and is borrowing air that God gives them to stay alive. We don't need to feel like we're trespassing when we ask them if they'd like prayer.

I approached one woman who was walking with a limp in Panera and asked her politely if I could pray for her. She was upset: "I have my own religion and I'm offended by you and think that you should ask people before praying in the future!" I didn't feel like it was my place to point out that I had asked, so I just smiled at her and told her to have a nice day. It's okay to experience rejection for Jesus' sake!

The day after the conference, my wife and I were walking near our house when I spotted a woman through the pine trees who was sitting on her back porch smoking a cigarette. I raised my voice to say, "Hi, how are you?" She replied, "I just moved here to be close to my mom because my two brothers have died in the last six months and I lost my job in Chicago."

I led the way through the trees up onto her porch. I told her how sorry I was and that God loved her even though these bad things happened and we wanted to pray for her if that would be alright. She was more than willing. As we prayed, tears started to come as the presence of God rested on her. When the prayer time was over and we had invited her to church she was amazed. "Think about it, I just decided to come out here and you were walking past at exactly the right time."

Jesus is the friend of sinners. Let's open our eyes and our hearts and not be afraid to bring His love and power to those around us.

Treadmarks

"Remember your leaders, those who spoke to you the Word of God ... Imitate their faith." Hebrews 13:7

I was late for a pastor's cluster being held at a nearby church, so when the way into the parking lot was blocked by cones, I decided to drive around them even though it meant going over the grass. No one was watching, I thought, but as soon as I had maneuvered my vehicle to the other side of the cones, the worst possible person appeared in the parking lot as if by magic. It was a maintenance person from the church who was a friend of mine from the past. I rolled down the window and told him how sorry I was for ignoring his cones. He was genuinely upset.

"Do you know what happens when people sneak around the cones?" he asked. Not waiting for my reply he continued, "It leaves tread marks in the grass that encourages others to do the same thing. How are we supposed to get people to do the right thing when even the leaders don't do it?"

I told him how sorry I was and asked his forgiveness which he gave (I think). After he left I just sat in the car and let God deal with me. This small event was a picture of my life at the time. I had become very busy running from one meeting to another; meetings at church, meetings with family, meetings at school, meetings with pastors... I didn't seem to be able to stop. What was being cheated was my private time with God where I don't prepare sermons or plan anything, but only worship and enjoy Jesus for His own sake. I still prayed, because I needed God to help me with all of my responsibilities, but I had lost the first love, that delight that finds its reward in who God is and not in what He can do for me.

No one else noticed except my wife and the Holy Spirit. I could continue on in this way and fool most people, but it was clear to me that if I did it would lead to more and more compromise in private that would leave tread marks which others would certainly follow. But I had a choice. It wasn't too late to stop, I felt the Holy Spirit say. I just needed to acknowledge my sin and seek a new passion for God.

What about you? Are you leaving treadmarks of compromise that pave the wrong path for those following you? It's not too late to repent and give a better example.

May 31

Who is the Holy Spirit?

"But when He, the Spirit of truth comes, He will guide you into all the truth; for He will not speak on His own initiative, but whatever He hears, He will speak; and He will disclose to you what is to come. He will glorify Me, for He will take of Mine and will disclose it to you." John 16:13-15

The Lord's vision for the church was not based on His disciples' abilities, but on the ability of the Spirit who would indwell them. Nothing has changed today. God's vision for your life is way beyond your own personality and gifts – you and I were created to have the Holy Spirit indwell us, speak to us, empower us, and guide us. Without the Holy Spirit's presence, we are like cars with no gas in the tank. They may look nice, but they aren't going anywhere.

The Holy Spirit is a Person, not a force. We don't refer to Him as an it, because He is an intimate personality who Jesus says "hears," and "speaks." In other places we find the Spirit rejoicing (Luke 10:21) and grieving. (Ephesians 4:30) He is a Person who feels, communicates, and wills.

He is the Spirit of truth. He will convict us of our deception, and will always bring us back to being real. Sometimes we think God wants us to put our religious best forward when we come before Him. Nothing could be further from the truth. He wants us to be gut wrenchingly honest with Him, so that He can truly forgive us, and truly fill us with His power. If we fake it before God we end up with an empty heart.

Not only will the Holy Spirit tell us the truth about ourselves, He will also bear witness to the truth of the Scriptures and to the Person of Jesus Christ who is the truth. He wants to disclose to us all that Jesus has for us, and guide us in the way we should go. None of us are qualified to be in charge of our own lives. We don't really know ourselves, we don't know the future, and we don't know what other people are going to do to affect us. God, who knows all, invites us to live beyond mere "common sense" as His children. "For all who are being led by the Spirit of God, these are the children of God." (Romans 8:14)

Grieving the Holy Spirit

"Do not grieve the Holy Spirit of God, by whom you were sealed for the day of redemption." Ephesians 4:30

You and I can make the sweet Spirit of God feel sad about how we're living. Although all people can resist Him, no one can bring grief to Him like the children of God He indwells. In a similar way, no can hurt you as much as those who you are closest to. How and when do we grieve the Holy Spirit?

One way is by allowing hatred to fill our hearts, and slander to fill our mouths. The verse immediately after the one quoted above says: "Let all bitterness and wrath and anger and clamor and slander be put away from you, along with all malice." (Ephesians 4:31) God loves, and Jesus died for every person you know and don't know. When we treat others harshly it hurts God and He takes it personally. Jesus said, "whatever you do to the least of these, you are doing to Me." When we accuse and tear down each other we are actually doing the devil's work for him. He is called the "accuser of the brethren," who accuses people to God day and night. When we do the same we are participating in darkness, even if in our opinion the accusations are true. God alone has the right and the purity to pass judgment on others. If you want the Holy Spirit to hang out near you, then learn to be loving and kind in your words. Seek to find the best in others and try to encourage them.

We also grieve the Holy Spirit when we ignore Him or limit what we think He can or should do. Jesus said to His disciples: "You shall receive power when the Holy Spirit comes upon you; and you shall be My witnesses..." (Acts 1:8) In Acts 2 we have the initial pouring out of the Spirit and then the rest of Acts tells how they changed the world through the Spirit's power. Many Christians today seem to be slightly afraid of the Holy Spirit because they've heard of the experiences of others that sound scary. Yet God's plan today is the same as then. He wants to partner with ordinary people to do extraordinary things through the power of His Spirit. God wants to speak through us, heal through us, and bring His gifts through us today. When we say "no" to Him, or try to dictate to Him what He can and can't do through our lives, we grieve the Spirit.

Search your heart and ask God how you may have grieved the Holy Spirit. If you have, ask for the forgiveness He offers us through Jesus, and tell Him you want to walk close to Him again.

Being Filled with the Holy Spirit

"Do not get drunk with wine, for that is dissipation, but be filled with the Spirit." Ephesians 5:18

The greatest need of Christians today is to be filled with the Holy Spirit. Not as a one time event, but each and every day. The literal Greek would read, "be being filled with the Spirit." How can we be filled with the Spirit?

First, by recognizing the need. In Zechariah 4:6 God says, "Not by might, nor by power, but by My Spirit says the Lord of hosts." God's work does not go forward by human strength, will, or cleverness, it requires the operation of His Spirit. We must be convinced this is true, or we will not sincerely seek the Spirit's filling.

Second, we must be thirsty. John 7:37-39 reads, "If anyone is thirsty, let him come to Me (Jesus) and drink. He who believes in Me, as the Scripture said, 'From his innermost being will flow rivers of living water.' But this He spoke of the Spirit, who those who believed in Him were to receive." God wants a river of life flowing out of you and me to bless this hurting and dying world, but it starts when someone is thirsty enough to receive. Are you thirsty for more, or content with what you have? Our hearts are created to thirst for God, but many seek to quench that thirst with stuff, alcohol, entertainment, human relationships, or fill in the blank. If these other things have dampened your thirst for God ask Him to forgive you, and tell Him you want to thirst for Him again.

And finally, we must ask. Jesus said, "If you being evil know how to give good gifts to your children, how much more will your heavenly Father give the Holy Spirit to those who ask Him." (Luke 11:13) The Amplified Bible brings out the Greek tense, "to those who ask and continue to ask Him!" This is not a one time asking, but a continual relationship of dependence. As our cars regularly need to be refilled with gasoline, and our bodies regularly need to be refilled with food, so our spirits need to be regularly refilled with the Holy Spirit.

The main reluctance Christians have about asking is that they don't feel they're good enough to be filled. While God may lead you to repent of areas before He fills you, He wants you and I to know that His Spirit is a gift, not a reward for good behavior. In fact, He starts off this wonderful promise by alluding to his own disciples as "being evil." He's saying that our sinfulness is not preventing Him from pouring out His Spirit, rather the Spirit's filling is actually the solution for our evil. No one washes up before taking a shower – that's the point of the shower!

June 3

The Spirit of Revelation

"The thoughts of God no one knows except the Spirit of God. Now we have received, not the spirit of the world, but the Spirit who is from God, that we might know the things freely given to us by God." 1Corinthians 2:11b-12

In all of our seeking of God we must always remember that any progress we make is not because we're good seekers, but because God is a generous, and merciful revealer. If we don't keep this posture of deep humility, spiritual growth will stop simply because God resists the proud, even if they are His children.

We need to develop a close friendship with the Holy Spirit if we want to seek God in a way that we will find Him. When you fully trust Christ for salvation the Holy Spirit takes up residence in your Spirit. You are, according to the Bible, born again. You have a capacity to know God, hear His voice, and experience His love that an unbeliever doesn't have. But the key is learning to live more and more by, and with, the Person of the Holy Spirit who dwells in you.

He will speak to you through the Scriptures, so devote time each day to reading. He will speak through circumstances if you will only listen. He will speak through whoever's speaking and church friends, so make church a priority. He can also speak in a number of supernatural ways according to the Bible, including: dreams, visions, trances, and through angelic visitations.

Many people wish God would speak louder, but that is not usually His way. When Elijah was waiting to hear God a tornado came, but the Lord wasn't in the wind. Then an earthquake came, but the Lord wasn't in the earthquake. Then a fire, but the Lord wasn't in the fire. It was in a still small voice, a whisper, that God spoke to him. (See 1Kings 19)

If a person yells they can communicate to you from far away. But if they whisper, you have to come very close or you won't hear them. That's what God wants more than anything else, you and I to draw near to Him.

June 4

The Surprise of God

"Now suppose one of you fathers is asked by his son for a fish; he will not give him a snake instead of a fish, will he? Or if he is asked for an egg, he will not give him a scorpion, will he? If you then, being evil, know how to give good gifts to your children, how much more will your heavenly Father give the Holy Spirit to those who ask Him?" Luke 11:11-13

At the beginning of 1996 a group of leaders from the church I was at went to visit the revival in Toronto. Every one of us was dramatically touched by the Holy Spirit, but it all left me a little confused. People were shaking and falling, laughing and crying, and there was prophetic ministry as well as extravagant acts of worship that were more than I was used to.

Although I enjoyed the presence of the Holy Spirit, I questioned the Lord about the need His people have for safety. It was then that the Scripture above came to my mind.

I had gifts for my children in the car to bring home and surprise them with. They would be thrilled about the gifts even though they didn't know what was in the packages. Their safety was not in knowing everything they were getting, but in who was giving it to them. They knew me, and they knew I would never give them anything that could hurt them. I knew they would close their eyes with smiles on their faces, and let me place the gifts in their laps. No fear at all, only anticipation for something good from their father. The Lord spoke clearly in my spirit, "You (church leadership) have sought to keep My people safe through control, and you've taken the surprise out of church."

To me, the number one problem of the church in America is boredom. We are so scheduled and so concerned that everything runs efficiently, we can easily miss the interruption God may want to bring. God wants us to ask for the Holy Spirit again and again so that He can put fresh gifts in His children's laps, reveal His great love, and draw hearts to intimacy. I believe God wants churches and lives that require more than man's best effort. He wants us to always be looking for His surprises!

The Holy Spirit and the Kingdom of God

"The kingdom of God is not eating and drinking, but righteousness and peace and joy in the Holy Spirit." Romans 14:17

Scripture is clear that one day the kingdom of God will come visibly on earth, but for now the way it comes is to human hearts by the power of the Holy Spirit. If you and I want to live and grow in the kingdom of God we must look not to what we can produce in ourselves, but to what God wants to do in us through His Spirit.

The kingdom of God is righteousness in the Holy Spirit. It is appropriate that this is listed first as there will be no joy or peace unless there is first righteousness. The way into the kingdom is through righteousness, not our own, but the righteousness God provides for sinful humanity by the cross of Jesus Christ. The main sin that the Holy Spirit convicts the world of is not believing in Jesus as their Savior. (John 16:9) When we come to Christ our sin becomes His, and His righteousness becomes ours. "He made Him (Jesus) who knew no sin to be sin on our behalf, so that we might become the righteousness of God in Him." (2Corinthians 5:21) Once we are in Christ the Holy Spirit leads us continually away from self righteousness and into the fruits of true righteousness only He can produce.

The kingdom of God is peace in the Holy Spirit. Jesus said "My peace I give to you; not as the world gives do I give to you. Do not let your heart be troubled, nor let it be fearful." (John 14:27) The world only gives you peace when every circumstance in your life is peaceful and under control. Jesus can give us peace through the Spirit in the midst of outward troubles and strife. It is called "the peace that passes understanding" because people that understand your situation can't believe you have peace. True peace doesn't come through being in control, but by trusting the One who is in control!

The kingdom of God is joy in the Holy Spirit. You can do your Christian duty and make your children do theirs on your own, but no one can truly delight in God or in their Christianity apart from the Spirit's touch. "In Your presence is fullness of joy…" (Psalm 16:11) Happiness depends on what's happening in your life. Joy is much deeper, and depends on your relationship with God no matter what's happening outwardly.

The Life of God

"The thief comes only to steal and kill and destroy; I have come that they may have life, and have it to the full." John 10:10

The Greek word for life in this passage is "zoe." Vines' Greek dictionary defines zoe: "Life in the absolute sense, life as God has it, that which the Father has in Himself, and which He gave to the Incarnate Son to have in Himself and which the Son manifested in the world." John 1:4 reads, "In Him was life (zoe) and that life was the light of men." The gospel is not just the forgiveness of our sins or just a promise that we'll go to heaven some day or just a guide that gives us better rules to live by. Praise God it is all of those things, but it's more. The gospel tells the story of Jesus' death and resurrection so that those who believe can receive the very life of God into their spirits. When we are born again we are born of God and His very life resides in us. "I have come that they may have life (zoe)..." Jesus came so that His life could be in you!

The key to the victorious Christian life is to let God's life flow through us instead of getting stuck in our old carnal nature. "Everyone born of God overcomes the world. This is the victory that has overcome the world, even our faith." (1John 5:4) When we try to live by following our emotions, our addictions, our common sense, or our will power we are missing a much bigger plan. Let the life of God rise up in you; drink of Jesus' life so that "rivers of living water" may flow out of your innermost being. (John 7:38) Stop analyzing the old and start meditating on the new.

If we walk in His life we will be lights to those around us without even working at it. "In Him was life and that life was the light of men." (John 1:4) Let's get filled and shine more, so that the people who are around us each day might be drawn to Christ and His wonderful gospel.

Walking in the Spirit

"But a natural man does not accept the things of the Spirit of God, for they are foolishness to him; and he cannot understand them, because they are spiritually appraised. But he who is spiritual appraises all things, yet he himself is appraised by no one. For who has known the mind of the Lord, that he will instruct Him? But we have the mind of Christ." 1Corinthians 2:14-16

Beware of one facet of the carnal nature in you Scripture calls, "the natural man." The natural man wants to believe and obey only what he understands completely. He won't do anything until he knows that he won't look stupid or foolish in front of others, therefore our natural man is incapable of living by faith and cannot please God. (See Hebrews 11:6; Romans 8:8)

It is easy to be born of the Spirit at some point in the past, but not walk in the Spirit today. When that happens we are miserable as Christians, kind of like fish out of water. Our proper habitat is the spirit realm, so when we go back to living like those in the world we become spiritually choked.

Signs of a Christian living in the natural man include anxiety, joylessness, cynicism, discouragement, and feeling spiritually drained all the time. The answer is not complicated; put off the old man and walk in the Spirit. (Ephesians 4:22-23; Galatians 5:25) Start by asking God to forgive you for trying to live the Christian life by the natural man, then remember that your rightful breath is the Holy Spirit, your proper food is the Word of God, and your sure hope for eternity is heaven no matter what happens down here. You have only God to please, so it doesn't matter whether others approve of you or not.

The language of the Spirit does not contradict our minds, but it does transcend it. His many ways of whispering to us must be spiritually appraised, so we must stay alert to the spirit realm. God is in charge of planning, protecting, providing, and guiding. We are in charge of trusting and obeying. It's a nice arrangement when we do our part and don't question His!

June 8

Thirsty for God

"If anyone is thirsty, let him come to Me and drink." John 7:37

Are you thirsty for God? Not thirsty for knowledge about God; not thirsty for God to do something for you; but thirsty for God Himself? The reward for drinking the very presence of God into your spirit is that "rivers of living water" will flow out of your innermost being in blessing to those around you. (John 7:38) Ministry is more than what we do, it is whose strength we do it in. Peter says, "whoever serves is to do so as one who is serving by the strength which God supplies." (1Peter 4:11)

Serving God in our own power will quickly burn us out and leave a chip on our shoulder that says subconsciously, "I did this for God, so now He owes me." We become dry and eventually bitter if we work without drinking. Make no mistake about it – what God gets out of this relationship is not the work we do for Him. Listen to Acts 17:24-25 "The God who made the world and all things in it, since He is Lord of heaven and earth, does not dwell in temples made with hands; nor is He served by human hands, as though He needed anything." God doesn't need us, He's in it for the fellowship we give Him while serving Him.

Several years ago I was overwhelmed by the presence of the Lord in a time of personal worship and kept saying, "I will do anything for you, I will do anything for you...", when I had a clear stream of thoughts interrupt my prayer that went something like this: "I don't want you to do anything for Me; everything I'm calling you to do, I'm calling you to do with Me." Since that time I've tried to remember that God delights in relationship and that I must always drink of Him while working for Him. Make sure you take time to drink today.

June 9

Drinking the Spirit

"If anyone is thirsty, let him come to Me and drink. He who believes in Me, as the Scripture said, 'From his innermost being will flow rivers of living water.'" But this He spoke of the Spirit, whom those who believed in Him were to receive; for the Spirit was not yet given, because Jesus was not yet glorified." John 7:37-39

We will never have rivers flowing out of us into this needy world until we learn how to regularly drink of God's precious Spirit. It is not enough to believe in the Spirit, or even acknowledge our need for the Spirit; we must drink. Why don't we regularly drink of the Spirit?

1. We don't drink because we are often trying to get a drink of something this world offers. "My people have committed two evils; they have forsaken Me, the fountain of living waters, to hew for themselves cisterns, broken cisterns, that can hold no water." (Jeremiah 2:13) Sports, TV, hunting, fishing, video games, work, and education are all neutral things unless we are looking to them for the renewal that only God can give, then they become leaky cisterns. Alcohol, pornography, gambling, smoking, and drugs are often the doorways to addiction for desperate people that started out only knowing that there was a thirst in their souls. God said that He alone is a fountain; an unending supply of renewal and refreshing for those who truly bring their thirst to Him.

2. We don't drink because we presume we already have drunk because we go to church, pray, and read the Bible. One of the saddest pictures in the Bible is Jesus outside the door of His own church knocking in Revelation 3:20. He has everything they need but He's unable to give it to them because they have adjusted their lives and expectations to what they already have so they aren't even asking for more. "I have need of nothing," is what they say.

3. We don't drink because we aren't confident of God's heart toward us. Exodus 34:14 in the New Living Translation says, "The Lord your God is passionate about His relationship with you." God doesn't just love you and me, He likes us. He wants to be with us. Jesus didn't just die so that we could be forgiven and go to heaven some day. He died so that we could come into God's presence now, and regularly drink of His Spirit.

June 10

Judging Prophecy

"Do not quench the Spirit; do not despise prophetic utterances. But examine everything carefully; hold fast to that which is good." 1 Thessalonians 5:19-21

When we despise prophecy we quench the Holy Spirit. Prophecy is God speaking today directly into our lives and situations, so why would people who love God ever despise Him speaking to them?

Some people despise prophecy because they don't think God speaks any more in that way. Today, they reason, God only speaks to us through the Bible so anybody who claims to hear God directly comes under suspicion. The problem with this is that the book of Acts is the New Testament church in action and God speaks directly all the time through visions, dreams, impressions, angels, and prophets. There are no Scriptures which indicate this type of prophetic activity would ever be withdrawn from the church except for a few verses that people quote horribly out of context. People that don't believe God speaks today are arguing from their experience, or rather lack of experience, and not from the Bible.

Others despise prophecy because they have been burned by it. They've seen people use the phrase, "God told me," to enforce their own agenda or to validate their own opinion in such a way that they are deeply suspicious of any prophetic experience. Some have been damaged by following a so-called "prophetic word" when it turned out to only be a person trying to be prophetic, and not God speaking at all. When you've been hurt in that way it is easy to harden your heart.

My opinion is that if you don't feel free to judge the prophetic you will end up despising it. Paul says to "examine everything carefully..." In the Old Testament prophecy came externally to those God appointed and the penalty for being wrong was death. New Testament prophecy, on the other hand, comes from the inside of a believer (where the Holy Spirit lives) and through our yet imperfect souls. Because of this reality we have to be discerning, but should never allow ourselves to become cynical. After Paul tells us to examine everything carefully, he tells us to "hold fast to that which is good."

God loves us and He wants to speak to us. I pray we embrace the potential of hearing God today, and the freedom to exercise discernment so we don't get trapped by anything that is not from the Spirit.

June 11

Doing the Works of Redemption

"As long as it is day, we must do the work of Him who sent Me. Night is coming, when no one can work." John 9:4

The disciples were confronted with a man who had been born blind, so they wanted to seek a reason for this calamity. They asked Jesus, "who sinned, this man or his parents that he should be born blind?" Jesus replied that neither answer was right, "but it was in order that the works of God might be displayed in him." Jesus didn't dwell on those things that sin and Satan have brought into this world. His view was that all situations can be turned around and become a showcase for God's redemption. He wants us to gain the same viewpoint.

Notice that He doesn't say "I" must do the work, but "we." He was modeling for His disciples the kind of works they would be doing after He was gone. A few chapters later He makes the same point in an even clearer way: "Truly, truly I say to you, he who believes in Me, the works that I do shall he do also; and greater works than these shall he do; because I go to the Father." (John 14:12)

Jesus did two kinds of work while He was on planet earth: Isaiah 53 work and Isaiah 61 works. Isaiah 53:5 tells of the work He did on the cross for us: "He was wounded for our transgressions, bruised for our iniquities, the chastening for our well-being fell upon Him, and by His scourging we are healed." This is finished work and it is work that only He could do. All we can do is receive that work and be grateful for the forgiveness of our sins.

Isaiah 61:1 tells of the works of His ministry by the anointing of the Holy Spirit: "The Spirit of the Lord God is upon Me, because the Lord has anointed Me to bring good news to the afflicted; He has sent Me to bind up the brokenhearted, to proclaim liberty to captives, and freedom to prisoners." This work He began while He was on earth but would be carried on by His disciples under the anointing of the same Spirit. Jesus modeled this work for them and then commissioned them to allow Him to continue these same works through them.

The church today preaches Jesus' finished work of Isaiah 53 but largely ignores our responsibility to practice the Isaiah 61 works. I believe God is changing that. He wants us to recognize in a greater way the power of the Holy Spirit in us, and He wants us to gain His viewpoint, so that we can join Him each day in the works of redemption.

June 12

The Authority of the Believer

"Truly, truly, I say to you, he who believes in Me, the works that I do, he will do also; and greater works than these he will do; because I go to the Father. Whatever you ask in My name, that will I do, so that the Father may be glorified in the Son. If you ask Me anything in My name, I will do it." John 14:12-14

One Monday morning I needed to meet someone for an early appointment, but I couldn't leave without my cell phone and it was lost. I looked in all the usual places, but it wasn't there. Everyone else was still sleeping and I certainly didn't want to wake them up, but I could see no other alternative than calling my own number and letting it ring until I found it. I was stunned when after dialing I felt a vibration and heard a ring coming out of my own left pocket.

Almost immediately after finding the "lost" phone in my pocket, I sensed the Lord whispering something in my thoughts: "This is how believers are with authority." Think about it. We as believers are often looking for someone else who can pray for us. or deliver us or who can hear God for us, yet the authority to pray powerfully is already in us. Every believer already has the equipment connecting them to God's voice and power in their hearts, it is God's gift to us in Christ, but it doesn't do much good if we don't recognize that we have it.

God's plan was that those who believe in Jesus would walk in the same authority as He did by using His Name. Jesus gave the first sign of those who believe: "In My Name they will cast out demons..." (Mark 16:17) Not the first sign following apostles, or pastors, or those who have walked with the Lord for at least 30 years; but the first sign following those who "believe." The right to use Jesus' Name is a privilege every one who believes in Him has been given.

Peter was very conscious of this authority when he replied to the lame man who begged him for money: "I do not possess silver and gold, but what I do have I give to you: In the name of Jesus Christ the Nazarene – walk!" (Acts 3:6) Are you conscious that you possess the authority of Jesus Name, or are you still looking around the kingdom to find someone else who has it?

Ministers of Forgiveness

"'Peace be with you; as the Father has sent Me, I also send you.' And when He had said this, He breathed on them and said to them, 'Receive the Holy spirit. If you forgive the sins of any, their sins have been forgiven them; if you retain the sins of any, they have been retained.'" John 20:21-23

I grew up in a tradition that took this verse to mean that there were some men who had the authority to forgive sins on this earth. The truth is that only God can forgive sins, but He has placed the authority to give the conditions of forgiveness to His people. This is John's version of the great commission. Jesus is sending them out to preach the gospel which at its core is about forgiveness that God has made possible. The church has the authority to assure those who meet God's conditions that they are forgiven, and the responsibility of being careful not to promise forgiveness when those conditions are not met.

The first condition is faith in Christ. The idea that I must be forgiven because God is a "forgiving God" is false. God is loving, and God is just, and in His love He sent His only begotten Son to pay the penalty His justice required, so that anyone who believed in Jesus would not perish but have eternal life. (John 3:16) There is no forgiveness outside of Christ, only justice for our sins.

The second condition for forgiveness is repentance. In the exact scene of our text above Luke records a more expansive version of what Jesus said, "Thus it is written, that the Christ would suffer and rise again from the dead the third day, and that repentance for forgiveness of sins would be proclaimed in His name to all the nations, beginning from Jerusalem. You are witnesses of these things." (Luke 24:46-48) The church has no authority to offer forgiveness without repentance which means both a confession and a turning away from sins committed.

In the tradition I grew up in I was regularly told my sins were forgiven when in fact, they weren't. I was living for myself and adding a little religion; that is not repentance. If we don't repent and live for God, it doesn't matter how much religion we add to our lives, we won't be saved in the end.

Does God want us to live in fear? Absolutely not! It's His good pleasure to give us the kingdom. We just need to treat our forgiveness as something precious to be protected by a life that honors God, and not trampled on by a life that presumes that God has to forgive.

June 14

The Michal Spirit

'How the king of Israel distinguished himself today! He uncovered himself today in the eyes of his servants' maids as one of the foolish ones shamelessly uncovers himself!' ... "I will be more lightly esteemed than this and will be humble in my own eyes, but with the maids of whom you have spoken, with them I will be distinguished.' Michal the daughter of Saul had no child to the day of her death." 2Samuel 6:20; 22-23

It was a great moment for the kingdom of God. David had conferred with all the leaders and there was great unity in the decision to bring the ark of God back and to make a place for it in Jerusalem. There was celebrating, rejoicing, dancing, and great wonder in the people of God because something significant was happening in their day and they were privileged to be part of it.

Unfortunately one of the main members of the team, David's own wife, Michal, couldn't participate. Instead of being part of the celebration, she was sitting on the sidelines despising David and everything that was going on. Before we rush to judgment on Michal, I think we need to get in her shoes.

She was a king's daughter. She knew how to do things the right way and she probably wasn't even consulted. What she was seeing was not the way her Dad, the king, had done it, so her own experience and tradition were actually in the way of her accepting what God was doing.

I've been under the Michal spirit before and it is miserable. Here are a few signs that you may be under its influence:

1. You don't enjoy God anymore.
2. You find you can't enjoy people because you're so critical.
3. You can't enjoy church because of what's wrong with the preaching, or the worship, or something else.
4. You are spiritually barren. There's no such thing as being dead and right in Christianity. However right you may think you are, when you're dead, you're not right. (John 5:39-40)

The good news is that if we will agree with God about our sins, He will forgive us, and can remove the barrenness the Michal spirit causes.

June 15

Contending for More

"If you then, though you are evil, know how to give good gifts to your children, how much more will your Father in heaven give the Holy Spirit to those who ask (and continue to ask) Him." Luke 11:13

Our greatest need is more of the power of the Holy Spirit. Jesus lets us know that even though we're sinners ("evil"), we are the children of God and can just ask for more of the One who will overcome our lack and give us what we need for every situation we face. It may seem like God is delaying, but if we are persistent in our asking, He will give us His Holy Spirit. (See Luke 11:5-13) So why don't we ask?

Some fifteen years ago when we lived in Montevideo, MN we got a computer game called, "Raptor." It was straight forward and seemingly easy to play, so I initially loved competing with my ten year old son, Matthew. Then something horrible happened, he started beating me. The game centered around this fighter airplane you operated that shot down enemy aircraft as they tried to destroy you. The enemies increased as you went along, but you could also pick up money packs at different stages to buy more weapons. I always bought the weapons that I understood how to use, bombs and shields. But as I struggled to get through level one and only infrequently made it to level two, Matt started making it to the fourth and fifth levels every time he played.

"Dad, you need to buy different weapons to go higher. Let me show you how to do it." Why was a ten year old having to show me how to do anything? I had a choice to make that day; either I keep my pride intact and continue to struggle, or I humble myself, admit I can't do it on my own, and allow my ten year old son to teach me how to acquire the weapons that will take me to the higher levels. He taught me and I began to gain confidence with my new weapons. That which had seemed impossible before became second nature, and enemies that had intimidated me before were now on the retreat. I was amazed at how much difference having the right weapons made.

The advantage we need to fight the Christian battle more successfully is not going to come from us trying harder, but from us asking more. The Holy Spirit has gifts He is waiting to give us if we would only humble ourselves and start contending for what only He can give.

June 16

A Prophetic Word

"Do not quench the Spirit; do not despise prophetic utterances. But examine everything carefully; hold fast to that which is good..."
1Thessalonians 5:19-21

I think of the whole area of prophecy as being more like art than science. It is messy and difficult because people are involved that still have a sin nature, past wounds, and opinions of their own. "What is truly a word from God and what is just me?" This can be a difficult question to answer when we feel God might be speaking to us directly, or through others. Paul gives us three truths about prophecy in the text quoted above:

1. God does still speak today, so be careful not to quench the Spirit when He is speaking.
2. Just because this is true does not mean that everything said in the name of God is necessarily from God.
3. Examine every supposed prophecy, not as a cynic, but to find what is good (what God is saying).

Years ago I preached a message on Contending for More of God's Presence. Afterwards someone anonymously left me a prophetic word they had received and written down before the preaching. The note left with it only said that they thought the word, "might be for the church from our Lord." I felt a real witness in my heart when reading it, so I submit it to you for consideration and prayer.

"I am looking for a people to pick themselves up, shake themselves, and stir themselves; a people who are passionate, sensitive to My Spirit, and powerful in the realm of My Spirit. I am looking for a generation, a people who will be different, who will be strong, powerful and creative and intense in their knowledge of the Holy and with a genuine persistence for My presence. I want My people to launch out into the deep, into a depth of greater proportion... for I am their portion, and I have much more to impart to My people as they will ready themselves for a greater outpouring of My Spirit. I am calling for the church, My body, to anticipate My agenda and allow My Spirit to do a greater work in and outside any mandated boundaries, and I will show forth the works of My Father as My word promises. So open your hearts and your lives to a freshness of My presence, break down barriers, and expect to be embraced by My presence because as you submit unto Me, I come."

June 17

The Privilege of Partnership

"After me comes One who is mightier than I, and I am not even fit to stoop down and untie the strap of His sandals." Mark 1:7

John the Baptist led a nationwide revival in Israel where his preaching prepared the way for Jesus. Yet he didn't feel like he was doing God a favor, but only that he was immensely privileged to do anything in partnership with the One who was mightier than he was.

Shortly after we moved our family to Montevideo, MN in the mid-nineties, I received a call from a woman in the church I was the pastor of. One of her favorite missionaries was coming to visit and she was hoping I would have him speak on the Sunday morning he was in town. I said I'd pray about it, but the truth was that I was a little miffed about even being asked. I was brand new and trying to establish myself in the pulpit, so I just didn't want to give up a Sunday morning to someone I didn't know, even if he was an established missionary.

One night shortly after my little tantrum I had a dream. A friend of mine was holding a huge missions night at his church and I was to be the "special speaker." It even said that on the posters they had up advertising the event. But after the meal my friend turned to me and said, "Things have changed. We're not going to have you speak tonight." What struck me was that he didn't even say he was sorry, in fact, I could tell he wasn't sorry. That scene stopped and another started.

I was in the foyer of Lake City Church (now City Church) where I was holding a small workshop at a convention. There were only fifteen people there but I could feel the presence of the Holy Spirit all over me. I spoke briefly and then asked if any wanted to receive Christ. Several hands went up and when I asked them to come forward they were so overcome by the power of the Spirit they fell on the floor on their way forward.

I woke up from the dream and a couple of things were very clear to me. The friend in the first scene represented the Holy Spirit and He wanted me to know that whether He uses me or not is His choice, and He doesn't owe anyone an explanation if He decides not to use them. The second truth that filled my heart was that ministry is only special when the Holy Spirit is present. Whether there is one, fifteen, or a thousand – it's His presence and His anointing alone that makes any opportunity meaningful and powerful. We should never care about being "special" in the eyes of people because it's only what God thinks about us that matters.

June 18

The New Wine

"Neither do men pour new wine into old wineskins. If they do, the skins will burst, the wine will run out and the wineskins will be ruined. No, they pour new wine into new wineskins, and both are preserved." Matthew 9:17

God was not able to pour out His Spirit in fullness under the Old Covenant. In fact, He put a veil between His manifest glory and mankind because of their sin. If sinners got too close to His holiness, judgment would break out as it did many times when they were under the cloud of His presence in the wilderness.

God didn't love His people any less under the Old Covenant, but His touch of blessing was limited to people's obedience to the law. The law was the old wineskin and the wine it held was limited to a few people (kings, priests, and prophets) and was only poured out while they performed their functions.

In our text, Jesus is answering a question the Pharisees had. They wondered why Jesus' disciples weren't keeping the fasts they kept. Jesus announced that a change had taken place with His coming. After He was gone His disciples would fast again, He explained, but it would be for a different reason. Under the Old Covenant one fasted in hopes of receiving favor; under the new covenant a person can fast as one who already has favor.

The new wineskin is the new covenant Jesus made with the Father. He died in our place so that we can be forgiven and be adopted as the very children of God. The new wine can be abundantly poured on anyone who believes in Jesus because His shed blood removes the judgment our sin would have automatically triggered under the Old Covenant.

Jesus' death and resurrection frees His Father to pour out the Holy Spirit and allows us to receive more of Him as often as we ask. Jesus said: "If you then, though you are evil, know how to give good gifts to your children, how much more will your Father in heaven give the Holy Spirit to those who ask (and continue to ask) Him." (Luke 11:13)

Own your identity as a child of God and use this favored position to ask for more of heaven's wine. This wine is key to lasting joy and healing unlike the stuff that can only give a short buzz and is often followed by a hangover.

Healing and the Kingdom of God

"And having summoned His twelve disciples, He gave them authority over unclean spirits, to cast them out, and to heal every kind of sickness...And as you go, preach, saying, 'The kingdom of heaven is at hand.' Heal the sick, raise the dead, cleanse the lepers, cast out demons; freely you received, freely give." Matthew 10:1; 7-8

Several years ago, while living in Montevideo, Minnesota, I had a vivid dream about Divine healing. I was in Walmart (in the dream) when I recognized a woman from our church who was walking with another woman who had one leg that was injured. The woman from our church was a brilliant light for Christ and filled with faith as to what God could do, and I knew if she saw me she would ask me to pray for her friend.

I wasn't in the mood. So instead of going toward her I was planning a get away, so she wouldn't see me. Too late. She saw me and immediately came toward me with a big smile on her face. "Would you pray for my friend?" she asked. After agreeing to do so, we went into a room that was right off one of the side aisles (remember, this is a dream), and I began to pray.

This is where things got interesting. I started to pray for her leg and I was filled with the love of God for this person. I could feel the anointing of God go through my hands and knew she was healed but that wasn't what gripped me. It was God's intimate love for people in pain. I woke up with the presence of the Lord still resting on me.

What does this dream mean? I felt like the Lord was saying two things:

1. His end game is not the healing presence of God in our sanctuaries but in the streets. We need to encounter God at church and learn how to minister in church, but He wants us to have a much bigger vision because most of the people He wants to reach don't currently go to church.

2. Healing is not about His power but about His love. Jesus wants to reveal His intimate love for people by touching them in very tangible ways. His healings are not just going to make those who are healed fall in love with Him – they are going to make those who are used to bring the healing fall more in love with Him than ever before.

Let's draw near to the King so we can learn to carry the kingdom everywhere we go!

June 20

The Need to Drink

"If anyone is thirsty, let him come to Me and drink. Whoever believes in Me, as the Scripture has said, streams of living water will flow from within him.' By this He meant the Spirit, whom those who believed in Him were later to receive." John 7:37-39

I want to share two dreams I received in March of 2013. In the first one, I'm in a discussion group where we are talking about the things of God and a man comes up to the group with an empty cup in his hand and is excited. He says to us, "I know what the problem is – we're like this empty cup. We're trying to give people a drink but we're empty so there's nothing to refresh them. The cup itself has to drink (be poured into) before it can give anyone else a drink."

Over a week later I had another dream around the same theme. Two women, one middle aged and one older were receiving prayer and I was watching. Suddenly I knew what God wanted to say to them so I put my hand gently on the head of one and said, "This is the word of the Lord. The enemy's strategy has been to wear you out over a long period of time. The Lord's strategy is now to refresh you over a long period of time; first, by teaching you how to drink, and then by causing you to become addicted to His presence."

I then looked up and she was on the floor basking in the presence of God. I looked over at the older lady and she was beginning to fall, so I caught her and eased her to the floor where she too was enjoying God's tangible presence.

After I woke up I realized that what had happened to those women was just a fresh drink of the Spirit. But the plan was not about one drink; it was about a lifestyle of drinking. Think about this: every other addiction binds and restricts a life, but "where the Spirit of the Lord is (and only there) there is freedom." (2Corinthians 3:17) May the Father teach us how to drink and then cause us to be addicted to His presence.

Should We Expect Miracles?

"Does God give you His Spirit and work miracles among you because you observe the law, or because you believe what you have heard?" Galatians 3:5

The early church was "filled with awe" because of the "many wonders and miraculous signs" done in their midst. (Acts 2:43) From the text above, we can see that miracles continued in the midst of the local church, even in the church at Galatia which was struggling to stay true to the gospel.

A miracle can be defined as an intervention of the immediate presence of God that changes the natural course of things in such a way that transcends human explanation. It is understandable that awe, wonder, and surprise would be the human response to this level of grace. Does God really still want to move in this way today?

If we take the Bible seriously, there's nothing in it that suggests that somehow the Holy Spirit would stop working in these ways in the future, or would in any way change who He is and how He acts. If this is true, why don't we see more? I'm reminded of the old song: "Showers of blessing, showers of blessing we need. Mercy drops round us are falling, but for the showers we plead." God is moving today by His grace in ways which we need to celebrate, but I am convinced we also need to contend for more. The Bible tells us to "pursue love, and desire earnestly spiritual gifts." (1Corinthians 14:1) Maybe we don't see more because we haven't earnestly desired more?

June 22

Hear, and be Healed

"A great number of people from all over Judea came to hear Him and to be healed of their diseases. Those troubled by evil spirits were cured, and the people all tried to touch Him, because power was coming from Him and healing them all." Luke 6:17-19

Health care is a problem today. As we age there are more pains and blockages as well as the risk of external parts and internal organs wearing down and no longer functioning as they should. The medical community can help, and they do what they can, but for many things there is only a pill to treat symptoms and no real promise of healing.

Jesus is a healer. He can and does use doctors, but sometimes He acts apart from them, like in the text above. Two things grip me in this passage – one relates to humanity; the other to Divinity.

The people came to "hear Him and be healed." There is a great tendency in our culture to want to be healed from God without listening to God. The idea that God might want to correct me is offensive in a culture which insists that any correction is being "judgmental." God loves us and wants us to be healed but to Him the heart, the inner person, is more important than the body. When He sees us He looks through the outward appearance to what's really going on inside. (1Samuel 16:7) He wants to speak to us. Jesus' last recorded words are found in the book of Revelation where seven times He repeats the same phrase: "He who has ears let him hear what the Spirit says to the church." (See Revelation 2 and 3)

The second thing about this text that amazes me is the Divine generosity. Divine power flowed from Jesus and it was "healing them all." When Jesus is free to be who He is in our midst, healing power to restore and deliver is available to all. Oftentimes we restrict what He is able to do by our unbelief (Mark 6:5-6), or by our busy schedule which distracts us from ever stopping long enough to hear, or be healed.

June 23

Understanding the Anointing

"He who is thirsty let him come to Me and drink...and out of his innermost being will flow rivers of living water." John 7:37-38

I once heard the late German evangelist, Reinhart Bonnke, tell a story that made a great impression on him when he was a boy. A barge had become stranded on the beach when the tide went out and he and his friends contemplated how impossible it would be for anyone to move it. Yet when the tide came back in, he found he could move this massive rig all by himself. He realized that the laws all change when the tide comes in.

The first crusade he led in Africa was in a city named Gaborone. He only had one pastor join him, yet Reinhart had rented a stadium. The pastor questioned this, "If my whole church came, we would only have 40 people. Why have you rented this stadium?" The answer was, "Because God told me to." The first night, 100 people attended, but while he was preaching the blind began to see, crippled people came off their mats, and the deaf began to hear. Reinhart said the stadium was filled the next night. The success he had in Africa since that time is one of the greatest miracles of our time. There were over 73 million recorded conversions; 58 million since the year 2000.

Jesus wants us to do more than our best for the people around us. He wants us to come and drink of Him, so that He can do His best for them. Paul said to "pursue love and earnestly desire spiritual gifts." (1Corinthians 14:1) This world needs more than our love; it needs to experience heaven's love and in a way that they know God is alive.

The Healing Presence

"'If I just touch His clothes, I will be healed.' Immediately her bleeding stopped and she felt in her body that she was freed from her suffering."
Mark 5:28-29

In the Old Covenant, the immediate presence of a holy God was something to be feared by sinful humanity. God warned people to not get too close and those who were called to draw near had to be very careful or they could die.

Yet in Christ, the presence of God became a healing presence. So much so that this woman disregards the ceremonial law which demanded she stay separate from all around her. (Leviticus 15:25-31) Anyone she touched became unclean according to God's law, yet she instinctively knew that if she touched Jesus she would be healed instead of Him becoming unclean.

In the Savior, the Holy Spirit is a healing presence. In 1997 I did a workshop for our youth camp in Minnesota on the topic of the Holy Spirit. When I was finished speaking, I asked any who wanted a fresh touch of the Spirit to stand. Although I went around and touched the head of each student while praying for them, I wasn't aware of anything special happening.

Three days later, we were in our final evening service and were giving testimonies of what God had done. A ninth grade student from Duluth pulled me into a private room off the sanctuary to tell me what happened to him. He said he was too shy to speak in front of everyone but thought someone should know.

A few years earlier he had fallen down some stairs and hurt his back, but because his mom was so poor he never asked to have a doctor look at it. He had just suffered in silence and learned to live with the pain. "I was the first person you prayed for on Monday," he told me, "and when you touched my head something went through me that took away all my pain. I've tested it for three days and the pain hasn't returned. God healed me."

He was now crying, and so was I. He hadn't asked for healing and I hadn't prayed for healing. Jesus just wanted to heal him, and in a way that he would know for the rest of his life that God is real.

The Open Floodgates

"Now the Lord is the Spirit and where the Spirit of the Lord is, there is freedom. And we, who with unveiled faces all reflect the Lord's glory, are being transformed into His likeness with ever-increasing glory, which comes from the Lord, who is the Spirit." 2Corinthians 3:17-18

A few years ago I was part of a region-wide worship night and we were singing, "Let it Rain." As the congregation sang: "Open the floodgates of heaven," the worship leader kept singing, "The floodgates of heaven are open." She had the words wrong.

Then it hit me. She was the one who had the words right. Sometimes the songs we sing are a reflection of the theology we are currently believing and not how it really is. I am familiar with the: "Open the floodgates", theology; let me explain.

God wants to pour out His Spirit, in this view of things, but He can't. If the church was repentant enough, prayerful enough, worshipful enough, and desperate enough, He then would open the floodgates of heaven and there would be a revival. This is a heavy message and produces Christians who strive harder and harder only to fail again and again. I know, I've been that Christian.

Now let's look at what is true. "Let it rain, let it rain; the floodgates of heaven are open, let it rain." We still must value and ask for the rain of God's presence because He wants to be wanted and will allow us to do church without Him if we think we don't need Him. (See Revelation 3:15-20) But we don't need Him to open the floodgates of heaven, He already has. Jesus' blood opened heaven for us, the veil has been torn down. (See Matthew 27:51)

God pouring out His Spirit in and through us is not a difficult thing; it's the normal Christian life. As His favored sons and daughters, we have easy access to all the riches of His table and can easily drink from His river of delights, if we'll only believe. The floodgates are open, and it's His express purpose to pour out His Spirit on all flesh that we may speak of the glory of God as those who encounter Him regularly. (Acts 2:17-19)

This describes the type of Christians we're increasingly becoming. Favored children, carrying His very presence, and reflecting His glory wherever we go. What a great adventure to be on!

June 26

A Minivan with Wings

"When Gideon came, behold, a man was relating a dream to his friend. And he said, 'Behold, I had a dream, a loaf of barley bread was tumbling into the camp of Midian, and it came to the tent and struck it so that it fell and turned it upside down so the tent lay flat.' His friend replied, 'This is nothing less than the sword of Gideon... God has given Midian and all the camp into his hand." Judges 7:13-14

Three hundred Israelites were facing an army of 135,000 Midianites (Judges 8:10) when God told Gideon to go to the enemy's camp and hear what they were saying. The dream related in the text above encouraged Gideon and led to a mighty victory for Israel. What was it about this dream that instilled such confidence?

Think for a moment of the pressure that weighed upon these three hundred men. The army had started with 32,000, and God Himself had chosen only these three hundred to fight in the battle, a battle whose outcome would determine the future of all Israel. What if they blew it? What if they weren't up to the high calling required of them?

Then this dream comes. A loaf of barley bread tumbling into the camp. God was going to use something very ordinary in a very haphazard way to accomplish His purpose. It wasn't about them or their clever strategy; God was going to do something great through them, but in a way where He would get all the glory. They didn't have to be great; they just had to be willing.

One day my wife, and I were invited to attend a Connect Group from our church and at the end of the night, the group prayed for us. While praying one of the young mom's said God was giving her a vision of a minivan with wings. She said she didn't know why it was a minivan, but prayed that God would give us wings like eagles to soar with Him. (Isaiah 40:31)

It was the word I needed to hear. I don't think I can be a Cadillac or a limousine but I can be a minivan. If the plan is that God can only use super Christians then I'm disqualified, but if He can give a minivan wings, I'm all in! How about you?

God Healing Through Us

"And He sent them (the twelve) out to proclaim the kingdom of God and to perform healing....Whatever city you (the seventy) enter and they receive you, eat what is set before you; and heal those in it who are sick, and say to them, 'the kingdom of God has come near to you." Luke 9:2; 10:8-9

Are you willing to have God heal through you even if you haven't experienced God's healing to you? This message from Jesus to His disciples wasn't about their healing, but about the importance of healing in advancing the kingdom of God. Healing was to be a key to let people know the kingdom of God had drawn near, it's God's calling card. Mark 16:20 says that the disciples "preached everywhere, while the Lord worked with them, and confirmed the word by the signs that followed." God wants to do things only He can do to help people know the gospel is true.

One day I went to breakfast with a friend and noticed that the man who took us to our table was limping. When he faced us I could see his hand and wrist were bound with some type of bandage, so I asked him what happened. He told me he had an accident on his bike the Monday before.

Now what. Maybe God wants to heal him right there so I should pray for him, but how awkward will it be in front of everyone? "Before leaving today, I'd really like to pray for you," is what I said, and then tried to measure his reaction. All during breakfast I tried to envision how I would go about praying for him, or if I should. Maybe he was hiding in the kitchen waiting for me to leave for all I knew.

It turned out he was the one who checked us out and there was no line behind us, so I asked if he would come over to a private corner to be prayed for. He came, and I prayed a brief prayer of healing over him and then told him God loved him. He said thanks and went his way while we left the restaurant.

Did God heal him? I don't know. What I do know is that I tried to love him with God's love and tried to give God an opportunity to do something only He can do. Was I pushing too hard to get God to do something He didn't want to do? According to the text above, I don't think so. The bottom line is I don't want to live a safe, comfortable, sheltered faith; I want to be on the front lines bringing the kingdom of God everywhere I go, even if I'm not that good at it yet. How about you?

June 28

"Now Herod the tetrarch heard of all that was happening; and he was greatly perplexed, because it was said by some that John had risen from the dead, and by some that Elijah had appeared, and by others that one of the prophets of old had risen again. Herod said, 'I myself had John beheaded; but who is this man about whom I hear such things?' And he kept trying to see Him." Luke 9:7-9

Herod Antipas was a "somebody." After his father died, he was made a tetrarch in Israel (tetrarch means one fourth) and given the region of Galilee to rule. Why couldn't he see Jesus who was from his own region?

In the chapter before the text above, a woman with an issue of blood saw Him. While Herod was curious, she was desperate. She had no options left because she had spent her life savings on doctors and had only become worse. She told herself that if she could get to Jesus, she would be healed. She pressed through the crowds until she found Him and when she did, was immediately healed. It's not the curious who see Jesus apparently, it's the desperate.

Herod Anitpas wanted to see Jesus but he was a busy man, maybe there wasn't ever a convenient time for the two of them to meet? Yet Jairus, a ruler in the synagogue, saw Him. His only daughter was at the point of death and he knew the only One on earth who could help was Jesus. All of a sudden, this official had only one thing on his schedule: seeing Jesus. Maybe that's why he found Him and Herod didn't? Maybe Jesus can't be seen unless He's our top priority?

When Herod finally does see Jesus, he puts him on trial and asks for a miracle to be done in front of him. (Luke 23:8) Jesus came to serve mankind, not perform for us. Human pride puts God on trial and demands Him to prove Himself so we will believe, but Jesus didn't submit to Herod's request. In fact, He wouldn't speak to him at all. (Luke 23:9) "The proud He knows from afar, but He is close to the humble of heart." (Psalm 138:6) If we want to see Jesus, we must humble ourselves like children and ask Him to reveal Himself in whatever way He desires. "I praise You, Father, Lord of heaven and earth, that You have hidden these things from the wise and intelligent and have revealed them to children. Yes, Father, for this way was well-pleasing in Your sight." (Luke 10:21)

The Orphan Spirit

"I will not leave you as orphans; I will come to you." John 14:18 "For you did not receive a spirit that makes you a slave again to fear, but you received the Spirit of sonship. And by Him we cry, 'Abba, Father.' The Spirit Himself testifies with our spirit that we are God's children." Romans 8:15-16

As I was preparing a sermon on the prodigal son returning home, I remembered a family in Minnesota who had adopted three siblings from Guatemala. The three came from an orphanage where there was never enough into a family where provision was abundant.

All three children had trouble grasping their new identity. They used to hide food and lie about it when confronted by their new parents. I couldn't help wondering how long it took for them to be totally free of the orphan spirit, so I found a phone number and had an opportunity to chat with the mom. (She gave me permission to share their story.)

"How long," I asked her, "did it take for the kids to stop hiding food?"

"Two years," was her sober response. Think about it. Adopted into a home, loved and favored by their new parents, abundance surrounding them, yet it took two years to actually believe that they didn't have to be afraid of not having enough to eat.

"When do you think they were completely free of the orphan spirit?" was my second question.

There was a long pause. Finally she replied, "That spirit's a bugger. Two of them have been able to find their identity in Christ, but I don't know if any of them are completely free in all areas of their lives."

Our heavenly Father has chosen to adopt us and to give us the full inheritance and privileges of the children of God. (Galatians 4:5-7) He has given us the best robe (the righteousness of Christ), put sandals on our feet (removing shame), put a ring on our finger (access to heaven's resources), and has thrown a party for us (the Father's joy in having us home).

Only eternity will reveal all this entails, but for now He wants each of us to know we don't have to live in fear. We're home, we're accepted, there's always going to be enough, and He will never abandon us!

June 30

Embracing God's Priorities

"Oh that My people would listen to Me, that Israel would walk in My ways! I would quickly subdue their enemies, and turn My hand against their adversaries...I would feed you with the finest of the wheat; and with honey from the rock I would satisfy you." Psalm 81:13-14,16

I believe God's ways are His priorities. To walk in His ways is to change our priorities so that they line up with His. In the book of Haggai the Lord asks His people to examine the way they're living their lives: "Give careful thought to your ways. You have planted much, but have harvested little. You eat, but never have enough. You drink, but never have your fill. You put on clothes, but are not warm. You earn wages, only to put them in a purse with holes. This is what the Lord Almighty says: Give careful thought to your ways." (Haggai 1:5-7)

He tells them that He was the One controlling this to try to get their attention. They had put their houses, before His house; their plans, before His plan and were experiencing the discipline of the Lord. He was trying to get their attention, so that they would make the necessary changes to have His full blessing again.

I received a call at church from a lady who needed financial help. She described at length how the situation had occurred and why there was nowhere else to turn to for this emergency need. The church was in a position to help, so I told her what we would do and she was relieved. Before hanging up I asked her where she went to church, to which she replied, "no where." I told her that I thought the financial gift was only a band-aid while the long term solution would require a rearranging of life so that she could respond to God, and not just to her needs. She said she agreed.

Maybe as you read this you wonder if God is trying to speak to you about your own life? Maybe you've been putting band-aids on your finances and relationships for so long that you're getting weary of it? Maybe you're tired, as Saul of Tarsus was, of "kicking against the goads?" (Acts 26:16) Maybe you're ready for the radical solution of changing your priorities to line up with God's?

The Jewish people were ready. They listened to Haggai and started putting God's things first by working on the house of the Lord. After three months of this change in their lives the Lord declared: "From this day on I will bless you." (Haggai 2:19) I think He's waiting to bless you and me as well!

July 1

Shake to Wake

"'Yet once more I will shake not only the earth, but also the heaven.' This expression, 'Yet once more,' denotes the removing of those things which can be shaken, as of created things, so that those things which cannot be shaken may remain. Therefore, since we receive a kingdom which cannot be shaken, let us show gratitude, by which we may offer to God an acceptable service with reverence and awe..." Hebrews 12:26-28

Have you ever been driving along and before you know it you realize that drowsiness is beginning to overtake you? Immediately you become awake and fear grips you because of the possible consequences of falling asleep at the wheel. Not only would you and anyone in your car be at risk, but also innocent people in other cars who hadn't fallen asleep. When I know I'm a bit sleep deprived on a long trip I make sure that I've got caffeine and somebody to talk to who keeps me properly alert.

God is shaking America right now. We have gone our own way and done our own thing, yet He is calling out to us. I don't believe He is shaking us to punish us as much as He is shaking us to wake us up. Some people feel like God would have to apologize to Sodom and Gomorrah if He didn't send His wrath on America. I disagree. Scripture is clear that Sodom wasn't destroyed because of how evil the worldly people were, but because God couldn't find a remnant of His people to preserve it. As Abraham sought God's face for mercy, the Lord promised him that if He could find a remnant of just ten, He would spare the whole city. (Genesis 18:32)

Well God has a huge remnant in America; people that love God, serve God, and seek God day in and day out. His heart is for this remnant to wake up from the spiritual sleeping pills this culture has given us through compromise and idolatry. As Hebrews says, "Let us consider how to stimulate one another to love and good deeds, not forsaking our own assembling together, as is the habit of some, but encouraging one another; and all the more as you see the day drawing near." (Hebrews 10:24-25)

July 2

America: Judgment or Mercy?

The people of the land have practiced oppression and committed robbery, and they have wronged the poor and needy and have oppressed the sojourner without justice. I searched for a man among them who would build up the wall and stand in the gap before Me for the land, so that I would not destroy it; but I found no one. Thus I have poured out My indignation on them; I have consumed them with the fire of My wrath; their way I have brought upon their heads declares the Lord God." Ezekiel 22:29-31

Because of failed leadership and a population that only sought its own interest, Israel was on the brink of judgment. Yet the wrath that eventually came on them was not only because of their sin; it came because God couldn't find anyone to stand in the gap before Him. Even with Israel fully deserving wrath, God's heart was still mercy, but He needed someone on earth to confess these sins; to agree with His right to judge; and then to ask for mercy instead. He actually searched for someone to do this for Him but couldn't find anyone. What a tragedy!

America is in trouble today. We have many signs of present discipline and indications that things are going to get worse if something doesn't change. Instead of trembling at His word we have often ignored it, and in some cases publicly contradicted it at the highest levels. Instead of caring for the poor, we have often made the rich, richer, and created a system where the gap between the "haves" and the "have-nots" is ever increasing.

When a nation gets in danger of judgment God doesn't look for the heathen to change things, He looks to His own people. We are the key! "If My people, who are called by My Name, will humble themselves, and pray, and seek My face, and turn from their wicked ways; then I will hear from heaven, forgive their sin, and heal their land." (2Chronicles 7:14) Lord, let there be a revival and let it start with me.

Pray for America

"If My people who are called by My Name will humble themselves and pray and seek My face and turn from their wicked ways, then I will hear from heaven, will forgive their sin and will heal their land." 2Chronicles 7:14

God tells us here that the future of our nation lies in the hands of His people. Sometimes as Christians we think that worldly people are the reason our nation is going down hill. We think God's eyes are on the sins of the world and that He is planning judgment on America because of it.

The truth is that God's eyes are on His church. Yes, if the church does nothing then America will receive the judgment of God because of all its sins. But what if the people who are called by God's own name (Christians) humble themselves before God and repent on behalf of the church and the country? What if we sincerely ask Him for a revival in our country and welcome Him to start with us? Could God give, in this critical hour, undeserved mercy instead of deserved judgment and save this nation? Absolutely.

So let's purpose to repent:

1. For the pride in our hearts and the pride of the church that has said in its heart, "I need nothing." (Revelation 3:17) Let's humble ourselves and acknowledge our desperate need for God personally and corporately.

2. For the prayerlessness that has come out of our pride. Let's start praying more often and for longer times. Let's ask Jesus like His disciples did, "Lord, teach us to pray."

3. For seeking God's hand (what He can do for us) instead of His face (who He is and what ways bring Him pleasure). We've often wanted to use God for our ends instead of submitting to God for His ends. Dear Lord, forgive us.

4. For our wicked ways. Everything that we do that God has already said is wrong in His word: immorality, lying, stealing, contentiousness, selfish ambition, slandering fellow human beings, etc. Ask for forgiveness for these things and then purpose to stop doing them.

Now as you pray for America, believe that He wants to hear from heaven, forgive our sins, and heal our land.

July 4

Willing and Obedient

"So then, my beloved, just as you have always obeyed, not as in my presence only, but now much more in my absence, work out your salvation with fear and trembling; for it is God who is at work in you, both to will and to work for His good pleasure." Philippians 2:12-13

What God has worked in us, we now need to work out in our everyday lives. By grace He is in us to create both the desire and the ability to do His will. When we cooperate with His grace by being willing and obedient, grace flows freely in and through us. Isaiah 1:19 says, "If you are willing and obedient, you will eat the best from the land." I don't know about you but I want God's best. The key is to be willing and obedient.

Sometimes we are willing, but not obedient. We love God, we worship God, we say "yes" to God when someone's preaching, but we don't do what He says to do. We won't forgive, we won't throw the porn away, we won't cut off the destructive relationship, we won't give money He's asked us to give, we won't check our speech, we won't lay down our judgments on others, etc. Being willing but not obedient leads to self deception which is why James said, "Prove yourselves doers of the word, and not merely hearers who delude themselves." (James 1:22) Worship must be more than a song or a prayer to touch God's heart; it has to include costly obedience.

Others are obedient, but not willing. This person says, "I do the right things but have no joy or love in doing them any more." If this applies, you need to return to your first love and ask God for a new grace to make you willing. Just going through the motions leaves you and I very vulnerable to sin and the schemes of the enemy. After David sinned horribly he prayed to God, "Restore to me the joy of Your salvation and grant me a willing spirit, to sustain me." (Psalm 51:12) Notice he didn't just ask for forgiveness, but prayed for a change of attitude so that it wouldn't happen again.

Check your life right now. Are you willing, or do you spend most of your time complaining to God? Are you obedient, or has your life become one compromise after another? God wants His very best for you. If something is off ask Him now to pour out more grace, so you can make it right.

Beholding the Glory of God

"Now the Lord is the Spirit, and where the Spirit of the Lord is, there is liberty. But we all, with unveiled face, beholding as in a mirror the glory of the Lord, are being transformed into the same image from glory to glory, just as from the Lord, the Spirit." 2Corinthians 3:17-18

Whatever we behold we eventually become. If you behold, or "keep before your eyes," your worries, you will become anxious. If you keep anger before your eyes, you will become bitter. If you keep pornography before your eyes, you will become lustful. But if you and I keep the glory of the Lord before us, we will be transformed from one level of glory to the next. It sounds easy but there are a few problems.

"As in a mirror" is a problem. The mirrors back then were made of brass and the image they gave was very dim. Paul says earlier in Corinthians, "we see in a mirror dimly." (1Corinthians 13:12) Even though we have nothing between us and God (unveiled faces), in this current time we live more by faith than sight. Yet even now a glimpse of His glory will transform us. Are we willing to behold Him even if it isn't always powerful or instantly rewarding? Are we willing to spend time in His Word and prayer seeking to behold Him even when it seems like He's hiding Himself? Will we prioritize church over a thousand other things we could do on the weekend even though it's kind of boring to us? The more we behold Him, the more others will be able to behold Him through us.

The other problem is the abundance of other things to look at. Hollywood and the internet are filled with images that you can easily behold without doing any work at all; excitement and entertainment at the click of a button. We were made to behold and our hearts will always behold something. Even as a Christian, the only way you and I will behold the Lord is if we make it our priority. The man after God's own heart said, "One thing have I desired and that I will seek after, that I may dwell in the house of the Lord all the days of my life, to behold the beauty of the Lord and to meditate in His temple." (Psalm 27:4) It isn't enough to desire, we must act on that desire by actively seeking or something else will easily creep in.

Am I saying that it's wrong to enjoy a movie, a game, or other legitimate pleasures? Absolutely not. What I am saying is that when we make beholding the Lord our first priority, everything else takes its proper place and won't become an idol.

July 6

Honoring the Son

"For not even the Father judges anyone, but He has given all judgment to the Son, so that all will honor the Son even as they honor the Father. He who does not honor the Son does not honor the Father who sent Him. Truly, truly I say to you, he who hears My word, and believes Him who sent Me, has eternal life, and does not come into judgment, but has passed out of death into life." John 5:22-24

Honor means to give esteem, respect, and to place a high value on someone. Do you honor the Son? Does your life bring honor to His Name? To truly honor Jesus we must honor His position as our Judge, honor His word as the final authority in our lives, and honor His work as the only way to eternal life.

All judgment has been given to the Son. This means that at the end of our lives only One opinion of our thoughts, words, and deeds will matter, and that is the Son's. Paul defines living in view of Christ's judgment of our lives as the fear of the Lord: "For we must all appear before the judgment seat of Christ, so that each one may be recompensed for his deeds in the body, according to what he has done, whether good or bad. Therefore, knowing the fear of the Lord..." (2Corinthians 5:10-11) We honor Him by acknowledging His right to judge us.

In our text Jesus talks about the importance of hearing and believing His word. In fact, in John 12:48 He says that He won't personally judge us but will only judge us by the word He has spoken. He has made His sayings known to the human race through the Bible. We cannot honor the Son without honoring His word.

The One who sent Jesus, the Father, sent Him to die on the cross so that those who believed in Him would not perish but have everlasting life. (John 3:16) In fact, the reason the Father gave the Son the right to judge the human race was that He became a Son of man. (John 5:27) He is the only One worthy to open the scroll which brings the final day of the Lord because He was the Lamb who was slain. (Revelation 5:9) We honor His work on the cross when we put our trust in Christ for our salvation and trust Him for every need we have in this life. Because of His work, Hebrews 4:16 says we can come with confidence to a throne of grace whenever we have something we need help with. We aren't bothering God when we ask, we're actually honoring Christ's work.

July 7

Free Indeed

"Jesus therefore was saying to those Jews who had believed in Him, 'If you abide in My word, then you are truly disciples of Mine; and you shall know the truth and the truth shall make you free.'" John 8:31-32

All that believe in Jesus are promised forgiveness, but only disciples are promised freedom. "I thought all believers were disciples?" Apparently not, because Jesus said to believers that they would only be disciples if they abided or continued in His word. Just because someone believes in Jesus doesn't mean they have disciplined their lives to learn and live out of His truth.

What is the truth that will make us free? Jesus first talks about the slavery of sin and then gives the plan for freedom: "The slave does not remain in the house forever; the son does remain forever. If therefore the Son shall make you free, you shall be free indeed." (John 8:35-36) A slave is only secure while he performs – his master uses him to get work done but makes no long term commitment. A son, on the other hand, is loved just because he was born. He is born into favor and has nothing to prove.

Jesus frees us by making us the very children of God. Knowing this in our heads may be the beginning of freedom, but it's when we continue in this truth until the Father fills our hearts with it that we experience the "free indeed." Are you living your Christianity from the privileged position of favored child, or are you still struggling to perform well enough to be accepted? Let's persevere in the truth of our favored position until our hearts fully catch it and we become free indeed.

Mary's Worship

"In Your Presence is fullness of joy..." Psalm 16:11

Have you ever had a one-way friendship? Someone you genuinely like, but whenever they contact you it's only because they need something? They are so busy and focused on their own lives that they may not realize they treat you like a means to an end instead of like a true friend. Once in a while, true friends just want to be with you with no other agenda except to be together. In our weekly prayer meeting we begin by emptying our thoughts, worries, and desires at the cross and just worship for a half an hour. The goal is not to get something but to just be with Him.

What does God do during this time of concentrated worship? It doesn't matter because it's not about us, it's about Him. No doubt He will transform us and bless us with a new joy in His presence, but that's His agenda, not ours. We just want to be with Him and pour out our worship and thanksgiving for who He is. Even the disciples said, "Why this waste?" (Matthew 26:8), when Mary poured out her costly perfume on Jesus. The great temptation of the church today is to make God and our worship a means to an end instead of the main event. Please listen to Jesus' response to Mary's worship: "Wherever the gospel is preached I want this story told." (Matthew 26:13)

Finally, in this act of worship, Jesus saw the response God is looking for to the gospel. Abandoned worship that isn't looking at its watch or at the crowd for approval; someone who just wanted to spend herself on Jesus for His sake. I want to join Mary's worship, don't you?

July 9

The Untamable God

"No one is so fierce that he dares to arouse him; who then is he that can stand against Me? Who has given to Me that I should repay him? Whatever is under the whole heaven is Mine." "I am angry at you and your two friends, because you have not spoken of Me what is right as My servant Job has." Job 41:10-11; Job 42:7

The first passage quoted above is a comparison God makes between Himself and Leviathan, a sea monster He created. (This animal that Job was familiar with has clearly gone extinct as no living animal compares to all God says about this creature.) In His lengthy description of this animal God makes it clear that no one can tame the Leviathan, no one can put him on a leash for his girls, no one can frighten him with spears or arrows, and no one dares to rouse him. The point of the argument is that if this is true about a created animal, how much more is it true about the God who made it and everything else that exists.

The Lord is angry with Job's three friends because they have sought to tame God by their theology. They were sure that they understood what was going on in this world and how God would act in any given situation. They were confident that what was happening to Job was brought on by something Job had done because surely God would never allow so much suffering to one who was innocent. Their theology put God in a box that ultimately was about their own protection. God was angry by their short-sighted, man-made beliefs which sought to limit His sovereignty, so we must be careful not to make God out to be something that He is not today.

"You have not spoken of Me what is right as My servant Job has." What did Job say? That it's not always fair in this life; that sometimes sin isn't punished in this life; that sometimes righteousness doesn't seem to pay off in this life; and that it often feels like God is indifferent to the injustices that are happening on His planet.

Part of learning to be meek of heart, like Jesus, is to trust God's heart even when you don't understand His ways. He is accomplishing a good purpose in every judgment He brings, every circumstance He allows, and in every test that He orchestrates. He gets no pleasure from our pain, but He will use our pain to speak to us eternal truths that will in the long run save us from greater pain. God is good, but He won't be tamed, and that's one reason that it is an adventure being one of His children.

July 10

A World at Spiritual War

"I have given them Your word and the world has hated them, for they are not of the world any more than I am of the world." John 17:14

When Morpheus offers Neo the choice of two pills in *The Matrix* he explains that the blue pill will put him back in his bed and back under the deception the world lives under. The red pill will give him the truth and a life of discomfort because he will see "how deep the rabbit hole is in Wonderland." Neo said earlier that he sensed deep within himself that something was wrong with the world, but the reality of how bad it is will be shocking to him.

When John says that "...the whole world lies in the power of the evil one," (1John 5:19) he is only expounding on the worldview of Jesus. There is something deeply wrong in the world around us beyond what the eyes can see. The spirit of the world, "the lust of the flesh, the lust of the eyes, and the boastful pride of life," (1John 2:15) is being breathed on by spiritual darkness that is in opposition to God and His rule. Human beings have been born into this conflict and every one of us has to choose each day whether we will pretend all is well, or to embrace the truth. If Neo chooses the blue pill, Morpheus tells him he will find himself back in the comfort of his bed and then he can "believe whatever he wants to believe." A lot of that is going on today, even in Christian circles.

It becomes us to embrace the worldview of Jesus so that we will live wisely in this present age, and be a light to those in darkness. The only way those under the world's spirit will be able to see Jesus is if we look different than them yet continue to love them. This is the challenge in a world at spiritual war.

The Key to Great Peace

"The meek inherit the land and enjoy great peace." Psalm 37:11

The proud seek to be in control and are continually trying to get what they want. If they can't get it now, they live in grasping anxiety that blames and complains about everyone in their way.

The meek of heart yield to the One who really is in control. They trust they will inherit everything God has promised in God's timing, and find great peace in the assurance that God will have His way eventually, even if it seems darkness is winning right now.

A few verses before our text, David writes: "Be still before the Lord and wait patiently for Him; do not fret when men succeed in their ways, when they carry out their wicked schemes." (Psalm 37:7) This may sound like the meek are called to do "nothing" while evil is growing around them, but this is not the case. Here is our part when we those around us are making destructive choices:

1. Patiently wait on God. We don't pretend evil isn't happening; we take that evil to God in prayer.
2. Don't fret because of the evil. We don't just pray, we actually believe God hears us and that He will reverse the evil that seems to be succeeding in the short run.
3. Walk in peace now. We don't have to wait for everything to work out because our peace isn't in our circumstances, it's in our God.

The New Testament scripture that puts all this together for us is Philippians 4:6-7: "Be anxious for nothing, but in everything by prayer and supplication with thanksgiving let your requests be made known to God. And the peace of God, which surpasses all comprehension, will guard your hearts and your minds in Christ Jesus."

July 12

Our Mutual Debt

"I am a debtor both to the Greeks and to the Barbarians; both to the wise, and to the unwise. So, as much as I am able, I am ready to preach the gospel to you that are in Rome also." Romans 1:14-15

How can Paul owe people he has never met? There are two ways to owe a debt (Timothy Keller's commentary on Romans): one is when someone lends you money and you owe them until it is repaid; the other is where someone gives you something to give to someone else. Until you have given them what was entrusted to you for them, you are in their debt. This is how Paul, and we, are in debt to all those who have not heard the gospel. Think of when UPS is given a package for someone else. They could be said to be in debt until the package is delivered and signed for.

To all those God has graciously saved, He has given a charge: "Go into all the world and make disciples of everyone." (Matthew 28:19-20) "Go" is to be understood as plural because He is speaking to the redeemed community. Go together, and take the gospel that has saved you, and give it to everyone in the world for My sake.

I don't like being in debt; but if I have a debt, I certainly want to know about it. In Charles Dickens' *Christmas Carol,* Scrooge's dead business partner, Jacob Marley, appears to Scrooge as a ghost with a chain he must carry around as a punishment for how he lived on earth. Scrooge feels the chain is unfair.

"You were a good man, Jacob. A man of business."

At this Marly screams his response, "Business! Mankind was my business!"

Marley had a debt while on earth even if he didn't own it. We don't get to bury our heads in the sand and say to ourselves, "that's not my problem." If you are a real Christian, it is your problem. We have a mutual debt to reach the nations with the gospel of Jesus Christ. Let's own it together and then pray to the Lord of the harvest, "Send us to fulfill whatever assignment you have for us to fulfill." (Matthew 9:38)

The Lost Sheep

"Suppose one of you has a hundred sheep and loses one of them. Doesn't he leave the ninety-nine in the open country and go after the lost sheep until he finds it?" Luke 15:4

Jesus came to seek and to save the lost (Luke 19:10) and won't take "no" for an answer. When He invites people to follow Him and they choose to go further into darkness instead, He just keeps looking for them like the shepherd looks for his lost sheep, "until he finds it."

If Jesus doesn't give up on people then we can't either. If people don't want to be found right now, pray for them, knowing that the time is soon coming when they will need Him. We are to give this world a taste of His goodness and unconditional love. God reveals Himself as "an ever present help in the time of trouble," (Psalm 46:1) so let's join Him in being present to people when their lives are hard.

If it's difficult for you to envision God saving someone you know, remember that He saved you. He kept looking, kept knocking, kept seeking until you finally gave your life to Him. Remember those who were used by God to help you come to Him, and purpose to be that to someone else.

When I think back on how I came to the Lord, I am amazed. There was so much darkness around me, yet the Divine pull was stronger. He used so many different people and books to secure me. It's funny because my gratefulness to God doesn't reduce my gratefulness to those He used to help me. It really was God, and it really was the people He worked and loved through.

July 14

Eden Restored

"He brought me out into a spacious place; He rescued me because He delighted in me." Psalm 18:19

Eden means delight. We were created to be the delight of God and to find our delight in Him. Delight means, "to be greatly pleased in."

Why did David believe that God delighted in him? I think it was because he refused to hide anything from God. We see his prayer life in Psalms and nothing is hidden. His joys, his sins, his pains, his loneliness, his anger and frustration; whatever David was going through, he was going through with God.

Delight was lost in Eden when Adam and Eve hid from God because of shame. And then even the word delight is almost entirely lost in Scripture until David, who believed he was a delight to God, and who invited all of us to "delight" ourselves in the Lord. (Psalm 37:4)

I see a picture of how God can delight in us when I observe my wife with our grandsons. They make huge messes and make constant demands, yet how does she treat them after they treated her in this way? Pure delight, and there's seemingly nothing they can do to change this. She can't stop smiling when she holds them, changes them, feeds them, and reads to them. Everything new they do requires a picture, so she now has a thousand pictures and videos on her phone.

This is how God feels about us when we don't live hiding from Him. He can handle the mess we make and do all the work required to take care of us. Our ways may please or displease Him from time to time, but make no mistake about this: we are His delight!

July 15

God's Timing

"Humble yourselves therefore under the mighty hand of God and in due time He will exalt you." 1Peter 5:6

Timing is very important to God. We want everything right now. I remember when our daughter Christina was only about three years old holding up her cup toward me saying, "Daddy, get me some milk." Wanting to teach her good manners I replied, "What do you say, Sweetheart?" I'll never forget that cherubic face that seemed to be a contradiction to her demanding tone as she uttered only one word: "NOW!"

It is the pride in us that demands God and people to do what we want them to do, now. God is gracious and loves us more than we can imagine, yet He wants more for us than we often want for ourselves. We think about our short term circumstances while He thinks about our long term character. Our Father wants to break off our pride, so that we can take on the beauty of His Son who is "meek and lowly of heart." (Matthew 11:29)

One way He does this is timing. In our text the words, "due time," are a translation of the Greek word, "kairos." "Chronos" is the Greek word that measures epochs and periods of time, but "kairos" is a specific point of time; "an opportune time," "at the proper time," or as the NIV translates, "in due time." They all mean the same thing: "In God's timing." Ours is to humble ourselves knowing that God's hand is mighty and able to do whatever we have asked, if we will only wait for Him instead of trying to manipulate things ourselves.

The next verse gives us instruction on how to humble ourselves: "Cast all your anxiety on Him because He cares for you." We are to rest in His love and know that He is going to be active in taking care of what we have trusted to Him while we wait expectantly.

July 16

The Main Character

"So Joseph's master took him and put him into jail. But the Lord was with Joseph." Genesis 39:20-21

"The Horse Whisperer" is a movie about a guy who can train horses that have been wild, spooked, or abused in their past. His method does not require violence or yelling, but only the power of a gentle whisper. Over time, the horses begin to trust his gentle ways so they will do what he asks until they are eventually fully trained for any one to ride.

Robert Redford is not only the director of the movie, he's the main character. In the story of Joseph, God isn't just the One who sovereignly directs events in Joseph's life from above, He is with Joseph in the prison. God, the Divine director, has cast Himself as the main character, not just in Joseph's life, but in ours as well.

The problem with human beings is that we often want to be the star of our own story. God is fine as long as He is helping us look good, but we still want to be the center. Through the gospel the Father has cast His own Son, Jesus, as the star of the human race. You and I can't reinvent the story, but we are invited to join it.

Jesus is the "sinner" whisperer. Darkness has broken us, abused us, and spooked us, yet He has continued to love us. He draws us to the Father with great gentleness and whispers to our spirits in His still small voice. Our healing doesn't come all at once, but He is patient. The more grace changes us the less people see of our brokenness and the more they see that the Healer has touched us. The Father wants to make Jesus the main character of their story as well.

July 17

Shutting the Door

"When you pray, go into your inner room, shut your door and pray to your Father who is in secret, and your Father who sees what is done in secret will reward you." Matthew 6:6

Think about the words "shut your door." Are we too available to this world and to the people of this world? Are we so connected that we struggle to shut the door on human contact to make ourselves fully available for fellowship with God? Bob Sorge says: "God's not disappointed in you when you fail to spend time with Him alone; He's disappointed for you." He has so much to give us in the secret place. We lose our fear of man, we hear His whispers, He changes our desires, He adjusts our perspectives, He removes our weights, and of course, He hears our prayers.

Sometimes people do get alone with God and find their time disappointing because they don't feel they really make a connection. Jesus said, "If anyone loves Me, he will keep My word; and My Father will love him, and We will come to him and make Our abode with him." (John 14:23) If you are a believer the Holy Spirit lives in your spirit and that is where God wants to meet you. Sometimes we close the physical door but we have trouble closing the door of our souls (mind, will, and emotions) so that we can really commune with God in our spirits.

Our emotions, anxieties, and continual thinking can keep us from true communion. Shut the door! Ask the Holy Spirit to help you and become comfortable with the fact that God lives in you. The challenge is to live from our spirits, so that the presence of God and the word of God dominate our souls instead of our carnal nature. When we take time to shut the door to have alone time with God it gets much easier to shut the door of our souls during the day when we need to drink from the Spirit.

The cool thing about disconnecting from this world and its relationships is how much more we will have to bring to them when we reconnect.

July 18

Keeping the Bats Out

"Now when the unclean spirit goes out of a man, it passes through waterless places seeking rest, and does not find it. Then it says, 'I will return to my house from which I came': and when it comes, it finds it unoccupied, swept, and put in order. Then it goes and takes along with it seven other spirits more wicked than itself, and they go in and live there; and the last state of that man becomes worse than the first." Matthew 12:43-45

We had a bat problem in our house in Montevideo, MN. There's nothing creepier than a bat slithering into your house and flying around in your bedroom. I remember being awakened one night, and then commanded by my wife to "do something" while she left the room and made sure the door was shut. She snuck a broom back into the room a few minutes later, so I wouldn't be completely defenseless.

The bat was dealt with that night, but the next morning came with a more difficult problem to solve: how did the bat get in? We ended up hiring a company who came out to bat proof our house. A few days later I was sleeping peacefully when I thought I heard something swooshing around the room. My first thought was a bat but I comforted myself that we had already solved that problem. Surely it's only a dream.

I wasn't dreaming. The morning after fighting with the second bat, I called the bat proof company and they assured me that they would come back out and that I didn't need to be alarmed because this sort of thing happens all the time. He told me something like this: "When bats get evicted from a house they circle that home for up to three days trying to find a way back in. We will find the new way they snuck in and plug it and continue to do so until they find a different home."

If you're a believer, the enemy can't possess you, but if you believe a lie he can bring oppression. When you and I grab hold of the word of God in any area he loses his hold temporarily, but he doesn't give up easily. He will circle and persecute and test the truth we started believing because he wants his place of influence back.

When we actively believe the truth we plug up any holes that would allow the enemy's influence back into our lives. Paul told us to "stand firm in our freedom and not be enslaved again to any yoke of bondage." (Galatians 5:1) So stand firm in the truth and don't let the bats back in!

July 19

Watch!

"Watch therefore, for you do not know what hour your Lord is coming. But know this, that if the master of the house had known what hour the thief would come, he would have watched and not allowed his house to be broken into." Matthew 24:42-43

The word watch means to "keep awake" and be "spiritually alert." (Vine's Expository Dictionary) It is the main instruction Jesus gives to His people about the end times. So how does one watch?

First, I think it is important to realize how easy it is to fall asleep spiritually. The flesh or carnal nature is weak and when it's in control of our lives we go to sleep. It can be hard to recognize you're asleep because you can still be busy doing stuff, maybe even religious duties. But when we put our identity in doing instead of in the Lord Himself, we start falling asleep spiritually.

Jesus said we have to "keep watching," so we have to ask ourselves regularly: Have I fallen asleep? Do I find myself compromising in situations that I wouldn't have in the past? Have I stopped reading the Bible and praying on my own? Do I think most about this world or the one to come? Am I more concerned about what people think or about what God thinks? These are important questions because they warn us when we're getting sleepy.

If you're fairly certain you've fallen asleep then tell yourself it's time to wake up. Sound the alarm and don't hit the snooze button or turn it off until you are all the way out of bed. Take time to repent and ask the Holy Spirit to fill you again. Consider fasting a meal or a day to grab a hold of eternal life in a determined fashion. I'm struck by this verse in Hebrews, "There is a Sabbath rest for the people of God... so make every effort to enter that rest." (Hebrews 4:9-11) It really is a paradox – we are fully awake only when we're resting in Christ's finished work. Once we're awake we need to "keep watching."

July 20

God's Heart for Israel - Part I

"For I do not want you, brethren, to be uninformed of this mystery–so that you will not be wise in your own estimation–that a partial hardening has happened to Israel until the fullness of the Gentiles has come in; and so all Israel will be saved...from the standpoint of the gospel they are enemies for your sake, but from the standpoint of God's choice they are beloved for the sake of the fathers; for the gifts and the calling of God are irrevocable."
Romans 11:25; 28-29

The Larson's had a prosperous farm in the early 1920's and were thrilled with their first born son, Bobby. Seven years after Bobby's birth they welcomed four more children, one after another, and then the depression hit. Bobby was not able to go to high school because he had to help his Dad on the farm to make ends meet. Because of his sacrifice, the other kids were all able to stay in school and prospered greatly. When World War II came, Bobby had to go off to war and when he came back, something had changed in him.

He had a bad attitude and became violent at times. His Dad warned him again and again that to be in this house there were rules that had to be followed, but Bobby persisted in his rebellion. It finally came to a head one day when Bobby, in the midst of one of his tantrums, hit his mom in the face and made her bleed. His Dad then told him to leave. Bobby left angry and promised to never return.

Years went past and the four younger siblings developed different attitudes toward Bobby. One felt that Dad and Mom were still angry and holding a grudge against Bobby; one felt that Dad and Mom had completely forgotten Bobby in the joy of the children that remained; and one, although aware that Dad and Mom were still sending money anonymously to Bobby, felt that it didn't involve him.

The last child knew that losing Bobby had broken Dad and Mom's heart and that they would never feel the family was whole until Bobby returned. He would find Dad and Mom praying for Bobby with tears, and would often join them in prayer as well as do whatever he could to reach out to him even though Bobby still claimed he wanted nothing to do with the family.

Israel was God's first chosen family. He hasn't forgotten them anymore than Bobby's parents had forgotten Bobby. Pray for Israel.

July 21

God's Heart for Israel - Part II

"Remember that you were at that time separate from Christ, excluded from the commonwealth of Israel, and strangers to the covenants of promise, having no hope and without God in the world. But now in Christ Jesus you who formerly were far off have been brought near by the blood of Christ. Ephesians 2:12-14

When Christ came there was a tremendous spiritual war in Israel and the leadership ended up rejecting their own Messiah. The Father gave them the consequences of their choice and they became isolated from the New Covenant which was promised to them. The Gentiles, God's second family of choice, then came in and benefited greatly from all the hard work Israel had done and actually came into the covenant promised to Israel instead of Israel. Today there is confusion in the body of Christ as to how God feels about Israel.

1. Some feel God is still angry at them because of their rejection of Christ and continues to punish them for their bad attitude.
2. Some feel that the church has replaced Israel; God has forgotten His firstborn – they were just a means to the end of His present family.
3. Some know that God still loves Israel and is taking care of them anonymously even though they still refuse to recognize their Messiah, but see the continued independence of the Jews as a problem that doesn't involve them.
4. Some have seen the sorrow in God's heart and have joined Him by intercession and kindness toward the Jewish people.

Whatever the responses of the children, the Larson family will not be complete to Dad and Mom until Bobby comes home. Whatever joy they have in their remaining children, none of them can replace Bobby. In the same way, God's family won't ever feel complete to Him until Israel comes home. He wants our hearts to be engaged with His for Israel. We have great spiritual wealth today in Christ because of their sacrifice. We need to remember that sacrifice and honor it by praying for Israel, weeping for Israel, and blessing Israel. God's kindness to them through the church is going to help bring them home.

July 22

Confidence through Victory

"When David was told, 'Look, the Philistines are fighting against Keilah and are looting the threshing floors,' he inquired of the Lord, saying, 'Shall I go and attack these Philistines?' The Lord answered him, 'Go, attack the Philistines and save Keilah.' But David's men said to him, "here in Judah we are afraid. How much more, then, if we go to Keilah against the Philistine forces! Once again David inquired of the Lord, and the Lord answered him, 'Go down to Keilah, for I am going to give the Philistines into your hand.' So David and his men went to Keilah, fought the Philistines and carried off their livestock. He inflicted heavy losses on the Philistines and saved the people of Keilah." 1Samuel 23:1-5

David's men are afraid and having a hard time believing that God really wants them to reach beyond their fears. When David brings the Word of the Lord, they say in essence: "We're already afraid here in Judah which we know; now you think God wants us to go into enemy territory and fight there? You'd better ask God again because we don't think He would ask us to go that far out of our comfort zone."

David asks again and sure enough, it is God's plan. Why? Is God mean? Does He like seeing His children miserable? No, it's just that the only way to remove fear is to face it and discover that the prison it was making around your life was artificial. They obeyed God in spite of their fears and God gave them victory. Eventually these very men became David's mighty men and became known for their fearlessness.

Did you know God is on a mission to make us fearless? He wants us to face every trial and challenge with a confidence that says: "I can do all things through Christ who strengthens me." (Philippians 4:13) Do not let fear set the limits of your life but only the will of God.

If fear has been your automatic default mode I want to encourage you to regularly take up the confession of Hebrews 13:5-6: "God has said, 'Never will I leave you; never will I forsake you.' So we say with confidence, 'The Lord is my helper; I will not be afraid. What can man do to me?'"

The Alternate Reality

"For our struggle is not against flesh and blood, but against the rulers, against the authorities, against the powers of this dark world and against the spiritual forces of evil in the heavenly realms." Ephesians 6:12

The Narnia books are all about an alternate reality; another realm where there is a continual conflict between good and evil. C.S. Lewis was describing for us the spirit world that is actually around us all the time. Jesus lived physically and engaged physical realities, but He was equally conscious of the spirit realm and in a moment would expose and address darkness with complete authority.

Whether releasing a woman that Satan had bound for eighteen long years (See Luke 13), delivering a man so tormented that he lived in total isolation (See Luke 9), or rebuking His own disciples when they were listening to the wrong voice (See Mark 8); Jesus was never surprised by the need to address the alternate reality.

After He rose from the dead He entrusted those who believe His authority and gave as the first sign of believers: "In My Name, they will cast out demons." (Mark 16:17) Have you embraced the alternate reality? It is easy in the American church to theologically believe in the spirit world but functionally live as if it's "make believe" and irrational.

The problem is we will never win a war we haven't fully engaged in. In fact, we will end up thinking flesh and blood is our enemy and feel the solution to our problems lies in manipulating people to get our way, or even, to get "God's" way. (It is easy to equate our agenda with God's will when we really want something.) This often leads to bitterness, frustration, or idolatry, and a life of striving which is actually under the influence of darkness instead of light.

"Get behind Me Satan; for you are not setting your mind on God's interests, but man's." (Mark 8:33)

July 24

Facing Your Fears

"You will not have to fight this battle. Take up your positions; stand firm and see the deliverance the Lord will give you, O Judah and Jerusalem. Do not be afraid; do not be discouraged. Go out to face them tomorrow, and the Lord will be with you." 2Chronicles 20:17

It appeared to be a disastrous day for Israel. Three armies were attacking it at once. One, they could possibly have handled; two, unlikely; but three? No way. Have you ever had a day like this? So much is happening at once, you feel like you're going to collapse unless God does something.

Instead of calling the nation to war, the king called them to prayer. The prayer had two basic thoughts:

1. We're in big trouble. "We have no power to face this vast army that is attacking us. We do not know what to do, but our eyes are upon You." (2Chronicles 20:12)

2. God is our only hope. "Power and might are in Your hand, and no one can withstand You...We will stand in Your Presence before this temple that bears Your Name and will cry out to You in our distress, and You will hear and save us." (2Chronicles 20:6, 9)

God spoke the words quoted above through a prophet in response to this prayer. Please notice God didn't tell them to hide while He took care of their problems for them. He told them to face what they were afraid of with confidence that He would be with them. He told them to stop fearing and to start trusting, He had a victory planned for His children.

It's the same today. God wants to give us victory and in the process teach us how to trust Him. What are you afraid of today? Why not bring it before God in real prayer and ask for His help? Then go out and face your problems and impossibilities with courage because God is with you, and there is no difficulty too large for Him.

The Israelites faced this vast army the next day with their eyes on God. The worshipers went out front saying, "give thanks to the Lord, for His love endures forever," and as they began to sing and praise, "the Lord set ambushes" against their enemies. (2Chronicles 20:22)

Let's lift our eyes above what is making us afraid and see the God who loves us, helps us, and gives us strength.

July 25

The Bigger Message

"'Behold now, I (Naaman) know that there is no God in all the earth, but in Israel; so please take a present from your servant now.' But he (Elisha) said, 'As the Lord lives, before whom I stand, I will take nothing.' And he urged him to take it, but he refused." 2Kings 5:15-16

Naaman was a famous general in the army of Aram and everyone knew he had leprosy. A young Israeli girl who had been taken captive by him said that she wished he would go to the prophet in Israel, so he could be healed. This was the beginning of God's message to Naaman. Here is a girl who should want his death but instead wants his healing.

He goes to Elisha and is sure that his position before men will be recognized and honored by the prophet, but it's not. In fact, Elisha doesn't even come out but only gives the message to go dunk seven times in the Jordan river, and then he will be healed. Naaman is furious. He thought Elisha would "surely come out to me and stand and call on the name of the Lord his God, and wave his hand over the place and cure the leper." (2Kings 5:11) Do you see how dangerous it is when we dictate to God how He should do what only He can do? One of his officers said to him, "My father, had the prophet told you to do some great thing, would you not have done it? How much more then, when he says to you, 'Wash, and be clean'?" (2Kings 5:13) So finally Naaman goes and does what God tells him to do and is completely healed.

In the text above he wants to pay for his healing, but Elisha has been instructed to take nothing. Everyone in Aram will want to know how Naaman got healed and he is to tell the story and to let everyone know that it came absolutely free when he submitted to God's conditions. But Gehazi, Elisha's servant, thinks that Naaman got off too easy so he follows him and receives a gift from what Naaman wanted to pay. This stirred God's judgment because Gehazi's greed blurred the message God wanted to speak to the people of Aram about His grace.

Gehazi completely missed the bigger message because of human reasoning and selfishness. Did you know that God's speaking a message through your life that's bigger than you? It's important for us to obey even when we don't understand.

July 26

Drawing Near

"Draw near to God and He will draw near to you." James 4:8

The remarkable thing about the New Covenant is that it gives us as much of God as we want. The Old Covenant featured a veil which stood between sinful humanity and a holy God. It served as a reminder that God needed to keep a safe distance from us, or we might easily be struck down by the consuming fire He is. (Hebrews 12:29)

Everything today has changed because of Jesus' death and resurrection. The veil, it turns out, was a picture of Christ's body. (Hebrews 10:20) When Jesus was crucified as the sacrifice for our sins, the veil in the temple was torn from top to bottom. (Matthew 27:51) We now have access to God 24/7 and are encouraged to "draw near with confidence having our hearts cleansed from a guilty conscience." (Hebrews 10:22)

We don't have to live far from God! Don't let fear, confusion, regrets, discouragement, distractions, or even struggles with sin keep you away from nearness to God. No one cleans up before they take a shower – the purpose of the shower is to clean you up. Don't clean up for God, draw near and God will clean up your life without you even focusing on it. Here's how He cleans us up in His Presence:

1. His perfect love casts out fear. (1John 4:18)
2. The clouds of confusion are cleared by the lens of eternity. (2Corinthians 4:18)
3. He gives us His beauty in place of the ashes of our regrets. (Isaiah 61:3)
4. He releases joy which replaces discouragement. (Isaiah 61:3)
5. His blood silences every accusation against us and gives us a new beginning without sin. (Revelation 12:10-11)

God likes us, and He has done everything to welcome us into His presence which is the ultimate answer to every one of our problems. To live far away from God is to miss the main purpose for living.

Reexamining Our Faith

"Did God really say?" Genesis 3:1

The first attack of the enemy was not to question the existence of God, but the word of God. So it is today. The Word of God is being questioned and challenged at every level. This is a sobering time for the church in this country which should cause all Christians to pause and reexamine their own faith. Here are three questions we should ask ourselves:

1. Am I really a Christian? Do I believe the Word of God as it is or have I twisted it to say something it doesn't say? The enemy followed up the question above with a promise: "You will surely not die." (Genesis 3:4) If we don't really believe the wages of sin is death, I don't think we will see our need to receive the gift of eternal life. If we don't really believe in sin, why would we need forgiveness?

2. Do I fear God? We can live in the fear of God and change our thinking to embrace His ways, or we can rebel against His commands and make a new god in our own image. Paul says we are to "behold the kindness and severity of God." (Romans 11:22) Have we done this, or have we tamed God and made Him something He isn't?

3. Am I willing to be persecuted for my faith? Am I willing to go against the grain? Am I willing to be mocked and laughed at or put in prison for my faith? The late missionary, Elizabeth Elliott, said this in her journal: "If something isn't worth dying for, it isn't worth living for." Am I willing to die for my faith?

This is not a time for Christians to become afraid; it's time for us to shine. It's not a time for us to be angry because America isn't Christian; it's time to wake up ourselves and make sure we're Christians. Isaiah 60:1-3 says: "Arise, shine, for your light has come and the glory of the Lord rises upon you. See, darkness covers the earth and thick darkness is over the peoples, but the Lord rises upon you and His glory appears over you. Nations will come to your light, and kings to the brightness of your dawn." This is to be the church's greatest hour.

July 28

Confidence in Prayer

"Will not God bring about justice for His chosen ones, who cry out to Him day and night? Will He keep putting them off? I tell you, He will see that they get justice, and quickly. However, when the Son of man comes, will He find faith on the earth?" Luke 18:7-8

One of the devices Jesus used to teach us truth is giving a human scenario we can easily understand, and then comparing it to our relationship with God.

In Luke 18, Jesus tells the story of a widow who keeps coming to an unjust judge who doesn't fear God or care about the widow, but eventually gives her justice because she won't give up. In the text above, He's trying to instill confidence in us because we are His chosen, not widows, and we are coming before a God who deeply loves us and wants justice on the earth more than we do. Where the unjust judge delays unnecessarily, Jesus says the chosen can expect justice quickly as they cry out to God.

Yet the whole story is about how we deal with delay. Luke gives us the point before he tells the parable: "Then Jesus told his disciples a parable to show them that they should always pray and not give up." (Luke 18:1) We will feel at times like God doesn't care and that we have no position of importance before Him which will tempt us to give up on our prayers. Jesus is encouraging us to fight through these feelings and to keep believing.

He ends the parable with a question for us to consider: "When the Son of man comes, will He find faith on the earth?" In essence, here's what I think He's saying: "The Father is always good and will never give up on you. He can be counted on to do His part, but will you do yours? Will you give up on God because it seems He doesn't hear?"

Jesus wants us to believe that God can change any circumstance where darkness has tried to "kill, steal, and destroy" us or our loved ones. He wants us to believe while we pray, and to keep believing during delays. Asking for justice is similar to praying: "Your kingdom come, Your will be done on earth as it is in heaven." May all of our hearts be filled with confidence that this is possible no matter how long evil seems to have its way. A believer's job is to believe. Let's believe and keep believing for His glory, and our good.

July 29

Whose House?

"Submit to God, resist the devil and he will flee." James 4:7

One day the owner of a beautiful house heard a knock at the door and when he opened it he found the Lord of glory, Jesus Himself, waiting to be welcomed in. "Do you want to come into my house?" the man asked in wonder. "Please come in; I am so honored to have you in my home." Jesus came in and then the man led Jesus to the best, cleanest room in the house for Him to live in.

The next day, there was another knock at the door and this time it was the devil. The man slammed the door shut, but the devil got a foot in the door, pushed it open, and began to wrestle with this homeowner. The wrestling match went on all day long until finally the man got Satan back out the door. He was totally exhausted and couldn't help wondering why Jesus hadn't done anything.

The next morning, he heard the knock again and planned to ignore it. But there was something alluring about the knock, so he decided to take a small peek. He opened the door a crack, and before he knew it, the devil was back in. While wrestling all day, he couldn't help but be offended by Jesus. "Why isn't He doing anything?" So when he finally got Satan out the door, he walked up the stairs and knocked on Jesus' door.

The Lord of glory opened the door, and the man was careful to be respectful: "Sir, I didn't want to disturb You, but I thought You should know the devil's been here the last two days. I have exhausted myself fighting him and was hoping to get some help in the future."

"My Son," Jesus said with love in His eyes, "you have invited me to live in your house, but the truth is that I have already paid for this house with My own blood. Why don't you get the deed and give it to Me, so instead of Me living in your house; you live in Mine."

The next morning the knock came again and fear grabbed the man's heart. He was so tired he didn't know if he could resist the knock or get the devil out again if he opened the door. Then he heard steps on the stairs. It was Jesus and He didn't look happy. "Son," he said, "I want you to open the door and not just a crack. I will stand right behind you. Ask him what he wants." There was fire in the eyes of Jesus.

The man opened the door wide and there was the devil in all his hideousness. "What do you want?" the man asked. The devil started trembling. "Nothing," he said, as he turned to flee.

July 30

Civil Authority

"Let everyone be subject to the governing authorities, for there is no authority except that which God has established. The authorities that exist have been established by God. Consequently, whoever rebels against the authority is rebelling against what God has instituted, and those who do so will bring judgment on themselves... Therefore, it is necessary to submit to the authorities, not only because of possible punishment but also as a matter of conscience." Romans 13:1–2; 5

Civil authority was God's idea, not man's. To be a good citizen of heaven and a pleasing child of God, we must also aim to be a good citizen of whatever country we live in.

Our goal is not just to stay out of the trouble that comes when we break the law, but to keep a clear conscience before God. We honor positions of civil authority because God established them to restrain evil in this present time. To honor civil authorities, therefore, is part of honoring God.

But our duty to civil government goes beyond blind obedience. Conscience limits us when government asks us to do something that is against God's commands. When this happens, we appeal with honor toward them, and if they still will not relent, we must disobey and be willing to suffer the penalty.

This is what happened in Acts 4. Civil authority commanded the apostles to stop speaking in Jesus Name (Acts 4:17), but this was in contradiction to Christ's command to go into the whole world and preach the gospel. Here was Peter and John's response: "Judge for yourselves whether it is right in God's sight to obey you rather than God. For we cannot help speaking about what we have seen or heard." (Acts 4:19-20)

For Jesus' sake we should be model citizens of America. We should pay taxes, we should stay within the limits of the law, and we should pray for all who are in positions of authority. Yet if the government in the future makes laws that force us to disobey God, it will be our duty to follow God, not men.

All over the world we have brothers and sisters who are being persecuted and martyred for just this reason. Let's pray for them, thank God for the freedom we enjoy in America, and continue to pray for all those in authority.

The First Great Awakening – Part One

"Unless one is born again he cannot see the kingdom of God." John 3:3

Between the years of 1730-1770, there was a spiritual awakening that swept over the American colonies and England. Many were used greatly by God, but none stand out so clearly as Jonathan Edwards, George Whitefield, and John Wesley. We will look at each of these over the next three days.

Jonathan Edwards was the pastor of a congregational church in Northampton, Massachusetts in 1734. He inherited the pulpit from his maternal grandfather, Solomon Stoddard, who had introduced a way for the unconverted to become members.

This reduced their Christianity to an outward form that lacked the power of an experience with God and led to an atmosphere of frivolity and immorality. So when one popular young man was stricken down with an illness that led to his sudden death, Edwards seized the opportunity. Depicting an image of strikingly beautiful flowers of the field that are mowed over and ruined by the end of the day, Edwards reminded the weeping congregation of the fleeting beauty of youth. How foolish it was to center one's life on short-lived pleasures. How much wiser it would be to trust in Christ, whose beauty far outshone the highest earthly glory, and in whom one's joy would be for all eternity. (A Short Life of Jonathan Edwards; pg. 46)

As this spark grew to a fire, people started meeting during the week to pray, sing, and read. Lines of awakened young people gathered at Edward's study door seeking spiritual counsel. People in Northampton talked of almost nothing but spiritual things. They dwelt on other topics only so long as it was necessary to conduct their daily work, and sometimes even neglected their work so that they could spend more time in spiritual activities. For a time, sickness almost disappeared. Astonished by the phenomena that surrounded him, Edwards wrote a booklet called: "A Faithful Narrative of this Surprising Work of God." Wherever this account went, similar spiritual hunger broke out.

A fire had been lit that would eventually travel far and wide in the colonies and in England. These early moves of the Spirit would pale in comparison to what would happen in the next decade through an evangelist from England named George Whitefield who God would raise up to put gasoline on these early embers.

The Great Awakening – Part Two

"You must be born again." John 3:3

George Whitefield (1714-1770) was eleven years younger than Jonathan Edwards and was born in England, but God would use him in the American colonies to bring the spark Edwards had lit to a raging spiritual fire that would wake up souls everywhere he preached.

While reading a book lent to him in college called, "The Life of God in the Soul of Man," Whitefield became convinced that it wasn't religious works that made one right with God; you needed to be born again. He wrote, "A ray of Divine light was instantaneously darted in my soul, and from that moment did I know that I must be a new creature." (George Whitefield's Journals, pg. 47)

From that time on crowds were drawn to Whitefield's preaching and the message that we must be born again. In 1738 he made the first of seven trips to America and started an orphanage near Savannah, Georgia. When he returned to England to raise money for his orphans, crowds were waiting to hear him preach. Although he was ordained as an Anglican minister no one offered him a pulpit, so he began preaching in the fields. Thousands came to hear him in the open air in Bristol and coal miners wept as they were converted to Christ.

When he returned to America in 1740, the reports of his popularity in England preceded his arrival in Philadelphia, so crowds quickly gathered to hear him. He preached every day for months to thousands gathered from New York City to Charleston, riding from city to city on horseback. When he was invited by Jonathan Edwards to visit Northampton, all heaven broke loose as people wailed, wept, fainted, and rejoiced as they experienced the manifestation of God's presence during Whitefield's preaching.

In 1740 Benjamin Franklin wrote these words about Philadelphia: "The alteration in the fact of religion here is altogether surprising. Religion has become the subject of most conversations. No books are in request but those of piety and devotion; and instead of idle songs and ballads, the people everywhere are entertaining themselves with psalms, and hymns, and spiritual songs." (Pennsylvania Gazette, June, 1740)

In 1770, the 55 year old Whitefield continued preaching in spite of poor health. He said, "I would rather wear out than rust out." His last sermon was preached in Newburyport, Massachusetts, which is where he died. It is estimated that he preached over 18,000 sermons in his lifetime primarily in England, America, and Scotland.

August 2

The Great Awakening – Part III

"You must be born again." John 3:3

John Wesley (1703-1791) was the fifteenth of nineteen children of Samuel and Susannah Wesley. His dad was an Anglican preacher and poet, but John took mostly after his mom. Susannah believed in discipline, though rigidly maintained, it was never the cruel discipline of a tyrant. The methodical way of living Susannah taught was the same intentional way John would train his disciples in the years to come.

On May 24, 1738, Wesley went to a meeting on Aldersgate Street in London, England where his life would be forever changed. Although he grew up in a godly home and had earnestly pursued God for thirteen years (he began a group known as the "Holy Club" at Oxford), he had no assurance of being right with God. That night, as Luther's Preface to Romans was read, he felt his heart "strangely warmed," and for the first time knew that Jesus was his Savior (not just the Savior of the world), and that his sins were forgiven.

He was so excited about being born again that this became his central message. After reading Jonathan Edwards' account of revival in Northampton, the same types of conversions started happening in his meetings. Then his friend from the Holy Club, George Whitefield, invited him to come to Bristol where thousands were gathering in the fields to hear him preach. Whitefield needed to move on but didn't want to abandon all the new converts. "Would Wesley take over for him?"

In a time when "enthusiasm" was frowned upon in church circles, Wesley found that wherever he went people were dramatically and often emotionally converted. He recorded that, while preaching on the text that it's God's will for all to be saved (2Peter 3:9), one after another would sink to the earth, "They dropped on every side as if thunderstruck." At other times there would be a "curious prevalence of uncontrollable laughter accompanied by a shocking violence of movement." The experiences were followed, as a rule, "by a state of religious well-being, of happiness and composure, nor was there any difficulty in resuming the business of ordinary life."

It is estimated that John Wesley road on horseback a total of 400,000 miles between 1738-1790. He preached at least twice a day; often three or four times, and gave over 40,000 sermons in his lifetime. In England he established 240 circuits with an attendance of over 240,000, and in America he had 114 circuits with an attendance of over 57,000. He was the apostolic organizer of the first great awakening in America and his efforts are still bearing fruit today.

August 3

Overreaching

"The creation waits in eager expectation for the sons of God to be revealed...We who have the first-fruits of the Spirit, groan inwardly as we wait eagerly for our adoption as sons, the redemption of our bodies." Romans 8:19; 23

My favorite board game is called Ticket to Ride. It involves "tickets" you choose to keep or throw away based on whether you think you can build the trains necessary to connect the two cities listed on the card; it's all about risk and reward. The problem, of course, is that if you overreach and take a ticket you can't fulfill, it counts against you in the end. You can be having a great game but then, in a moment of presumption, overreach in a way that causes you to lose in the end.

Overreaching in preaching leads people to disillusionment. Some very zealous teachers today believe that this is the time that the sons of God are going to be fully revealed and begin to remove the curse on creation. As we walk in our full authority, they maintain, everything will change for the better on this earth.

While it is critically important for us to know our identity in Christ, the event creation is longing for only occurs at the return of Christ where our adoption is completed and our bodies are redeemed. The full manifestation of the sons of God happens at the second coming; not in this present age. John said it like this: "Beloved, now we are children of God, and it has not yet appeared as yet what we will be. We know that when He appears, we will be like Him, because we will see Him just as He is." (1John 3:2)

Right now we groan with all of creation and the Holy Spirit within us also groans (Romans 8:26-27) because things aren't right yet and they won't be until Jesus comes back. Life in this present age is hard, but God is still good. When Jesus described the time we're now living in He said the wind and the waves were going to hit every life. He promised that those who obeyed His words would survive the storms, not be saved from them ever happening. (Matthew 7:24-27)

I love it when people are excited about Jesus, but we never have permission to overstate what we have been promised. No matter how much we may like a preacher, we have a responsibility to judge all that we hear by what the Word of God actually says. (Acts 17:11)

August 4

Keeping the Fire Burning

"When the day of Pentecost came, they were all together in one place. Suddenly a sound like the blowing of a violent wind came from heaven and filled the whole house where they were sitting. They saw what seemed to be tongues of fire that separated and came to rest on each one of them and they began to speak in tongues as the Spirit enabled them." Acts 2:1-4

Every year I do a study leave in late January with three pastor friends at a cabin without any heat except for a little wood stove. Our friend who owns the cabin goes a day before the rest of us to get the fire going, so the place is warmed up for our arrival.

Another one of the pastors brings a minivan full of wood because the fire needs to keep going 24/7 while we're there. All events that week take place near the fire – study, worship, cards, our ministry to one another – everything happens in front of the light and heat that come from the fire. Each of us take a part in keeping it going which involves opening the door and throwing another log on, and once in a while, removing excess ash.

What does all this have to do with us? This cold, dark world needs the fire of God's Presence to draw them to Christ, and to melt the hardness of heart that easily occurs in our culture. The church is to be carriers of the Spirit's fire. How do we do this?

1. Recognize that human energy and zeal don't start the fire, the Holy Spirit does. A tongue of fire "came to rest on each one of them." The Holy Spirit is the Friend who gets the fire going for us, all we have to do is tend it and remove excess ash once in a while.

2. Fellowship together is like wood on the fire. We are warned to not forsake regular meetings together (Hebrews 10:24-25) and are told to "encourage one another, day after day, so that none of you may be hardened by the deceitfulness of sin." (Hebrews 3:13) The fire fell when "they were all together in one place." God has designed us to need Him, and to need each other. We all know that an ember separated from the fire will quickly burn out.

August 5

Living from Victory

"Very soon the God of peace will crush Satan under your feet." Romans 16:20

From God's perspective, darkness has already been defeated through Christ's triumph on the cross. (Colossians 2:15) Jesus is not at war with Satan; He's already won the war and now, through the gospel, is inviting us to live from His victory.

The key is walking in peace. We must first acquire the peace of God, and then we must learn to walk in the peace of God. When we do this, we become like a thermostat in our environment. "Very soon . . ." the darkness around us is crushed as the kingdom of God and Christ's victory permeate the atmosphere we bring Christ's peace to. Notice from the text, Satan will be crushed – his work, his plans, his voice – under our feet. Jesus wants us to share His victory.

So how does one get the peace of God? It starts with salvation where God offers us peace with Him through the sacrifice of Jesus for our sins on the cross. (Romans 5:1) Once we are saved, we have continual access to God through Christ and have peace available to us if we give our anxieties to God in prayer. "Be anxious for nothing but in everything make your requests known to God with thanksgiving, and the peace of God which transcends understanding will guard over your hearts and minds in Christ Jesus." (Philippians 4:6-7)

Getting peace is easier than walking in peace. How does one stay in peace in a world that creates so much uncertainty, fear, and anxiety? I believe the key is in the verse before our text in Romans 16 and in the verse following the reference in Philippians. Notice how similar they are: "I want you to be wise about what is good, and innocent about what is evil." (Romans 16:19) "Brothers and sisters, whatever is true, whatever is noble, whatever is right, whatever is pure, whatever is lovely, whatever is admirable – if anything is excellent or praiseworthy – think about such things... And the God of peace will be with you." (Philippians 4:8-9)

To stay in peace, we have to keep ourselves from focusing on evil and on what evil is doing. When we focus on darkness we end up empowering it. Jesus focused on what the Father was doing and saying (John 5:19); to walk in peace we need to do the same.

If we lose our peace, all we have to do is bring our anxieties back to God and He will restore it again. Let's practice living from victory until it becomes our lifestyle!

August 6

God's Delight in You

"The Lord disciplines those He loves, as a father the child he delights in." Proverbs 3:12

God doesn't correct us because we irritate Him. We are His delight and He wants us to be better for our own sake, not so He can like us more. You are unconditionally loved by God and totally liked; not some day when you're mature, but as you are right now!

I was with a father recently who gave me permission to share what happened with his five year old daughter recently. She was caught hitting her three year old brother, so Dad gave her a time out. When the time out was done he invited her, as always after discipline, to sit on his lap to talk about it. But she wouldn't come immediately. She had taken his correction as rejection, so she didn't have confidence that his lap was safe for her.

When he saw this, his heart felt nothing but compassion for his daughter. He urged her to come and finally she gave in, so they cuddled first, and then talked about why hitting her brother was wrong. In this place of security, she was able to say she was sorry to her brother, he forgave her, and the family was restored to Dad's delight.

Don't ever mistake correction for rejection because Your Father in heaven is crazy about you!

Concerning Spiritual Gifts

"Pursue love and earnestly desire spiritual gifts." 1Corinthians 14:1

The world needs more than what you're good at; it needs what only God is good at. God has placed each of us in His body (1Corinthians 12:18) just as He pleased. We don't choose our part; we can only, at best, discover and embrace it. This is called our ministry. Paul said there were a variety of ministries (1Corinthians 12:5) and a variety of expressions of similar ministries. (1Corinthians 12:6) God loves to reveal Himself through our differing, unique contributions to His body, so we must accept our part and learn to honor everyone else's part.

But the supernatural gifts are different from our ministries. These work "as the Spirit wills" (1Corinthians 12:11) and are dependent on His moving, not ours. Whereas your ministry has already been set, the gifts of the Holy Spirit are dynamic. Every believer has the potential of being used in any one of the nine supernatural gifts Paul lists. We are to pursue loving people so much that we want more for them than what we can do. While loving them, we are to "earnestly desire spiritual gifts," those things that require the supernatural.

Paul gives nine gifts and each is powerful when meeting the needs of the person we're ministering to. The gifts can be divided into three general categories:

The revelation gifts: Word of knowledge, word of wisdom, and discerning of spirits. (1Corinthians 12:8, 10)

The power gifts: the gift of faith, gifts of healings, and the working of miracles. (1Corinthians 12:9-10)

The oral gifts: prophecy, diversity of tongues, and the interpretation of tongues. (1Corinthians 12:10)

When we cease to love people, we grieve the Holy Spirit (Ephesians 4:30), and when we don't make a place for the manifestation of God's power, we quench the Holy Spirit. (1Thessalonians 5:19) God wants both His beauty and His power revealed through the church.

Jesus is so great that He can use flawed, normal people to do His amazing works through. This was His plan! We can't do His works without Him, and He won't do them without us. He's calling us into an adventure of walking with Him. Let's say "yes" to the beauty of His character and to His desire to use us in power.

August 8

Spiritual Gifts

"Pursue love and earnestly desire spiritual gifts." 1Corinthians 14:1

Part of God's increased Presence among us is the manifestation of spiritual gifts. God wants us to love people so much that we want more for them than what is humanly possible. He wants us to desire what only He can do for them.

In 2013, I was on a team that went to Belize and was in charge of a "Healing Service" we had announced. Before the service, a group of us were praying and earnestly desiring spiritual gifts. The only way it would actually be a healing service was if God did something beyond our preaching and praying. Only Jesus heals!

As we were worshiping, I had a dim picture in my mind's eye of a woman holding an infant on her hip accompanied by a feeling of compassion. I asked for more, and somehow instantly knew two facts about this woman: she was a mom, but old enough to be a grandma, and she had a horrible back problem that made every day miserable.

At the end of the service I asked whoever this was to come forward, and it turned out to be our missionary, Linda. Her and her husband, Ron, had grandchildren but also had an infant they had adopted. Linda's back was so bad she was afraid to sit down because she didn't know when she'd be able to get up again. When we laid hands on her, Jesus instantly healed her so she gave testimony to the group. (She was still healed the rest of the week and three months later when she came to our mission's conference!)

Then I asked our team if God was showing them anything. One of our leaders said he saw someone's right arm in an x-ray and there was a crack in the bone. A young man named John came up and was instantly healed by the power of God. I found out his story from his mom a few days later when we were taking a bus to a region-wide prayer event.

John was 24 and had fallen away from God and the church. His mom kept begging him to come back to church, so he made a deal with her – "You stop nagging me and I will go back one time." John had an ongoing problem with his right arm, so this was the service she chose.

I was stunned by her story of his healing and told her I'd love to talk to John himself about it. She said that would be easy because he was on the bus heading to the prayer meeting! God hadn't just healed his arm; He had restored John's faith.

August 9

Believing in Hell

"Do not fear those who kill the body but are unable to kill the soul; but rather fear Him who is able to destroy both soul and body in hell." Matthew 10:28

It is tempting for human beings to pick and choose the parts of the Bible they like and kind of ignore the rest. Everyone wants to believe in heaven; that God is watching lovingly over us; and that there is meaning to our lives. Jesus gives us all those things, but He also told us there is a hell.

On November 23, 1998 a man named Bill Wiese had a prophetic experience where he was sent to hell for twenty-three minutes. (Google "23 Minutes in Hell" to hear him tell the story.) Near the end of this dramatic experience the Lord spoke to Him about why this had happened: "Because many people do not believe that hell truly exists. Even some of My own people do not believe that hell is real." (23 Minutes in Hell; pg 33)

To not believe in hell puts one at greater risk of ending up there. This would be the most tragic thing that could happen to any of us. We need to believe in hell, fear God, and make sure that we cling to Christ and His salvation so that we stay off the wide road that leads to destruction.

August 10

Answered Prayer

"Until now you have asked for nothing in My name; ask and you will receive, so that your joy may be made full." John 16:24

Oswald Chambers is convinced that prayer is more about coming into union with God than it is about getting things. The condition Jesus places on answered prayer is to ask "in My name." What does that mean? Is it just a postscript at the end of a prayer, "...and we ask this in Jesus Name. Amen.", or is it something more? Jesus makes another reference to answered prayer in the chapter before: "If you abide in Me, and My words abide in you, ask whatever you wish, and it will be done for you." (John 15:7) Two conditions: union with His presence, "if you abide in Me;" and with His word, "... and My words abide in you." What if "in My name" means "in union with My nature and purpose to the degree that it is no longer your prayer but our prayer?" Jesus always gets His prayers answered and we always get ours answered when we are so in union with Him that two have become one, and our prayer is indistinguishable from His.

1John 5:14-15 would be in agreement with this thought: "This is the confidence which we have before Him, that if we ask anything according to His will, He hears us. And if we know that He hears us in whatever we ask, we know that we have the requests which we have asked from Him." The key is being one with His will which means intimacy before asking. We shouldn't be trying to get what we want from God, but rather, trying to get what He wants inside of us. Before His will is done on earth someone needs to voluntarily pray it from here but I don't think we can do that unless we are intimate enough to really pray in His name. Prayer is vital, but for it to be effective our first goal must be union with God. Only then will our joy be full.

August 11

The God of Midnight

"But about midnight Paul and Silas were praying and singing hymns of praise to God, and the prisoners were listening to them; and suddenly there came a great earthquake, so that the foundations of the prison house were shaken; and immediately all the doors were opened and everyone's chains were unfastened."
Acts 16:25-26

In Luke 11 a friend comes to a friend at midnight because he has no bread. Even though he has nothing to give his midnight visitor he knows someone who does. He goes to this rich friend and after shamelessly, persistently knocking on his door, he secures provision for his other friend. Jesus said that this was how prayer worked and said that if we keep on knocking, seeking, and asking, the Father will give the Holy Spirit to us in a way that will reach our friends who have no bread in their hour of need. The point is to stay connected in friendship with unbelievers and don't be discouraged if they don't seem to be responding right now because midnight, the darkest hour, will come to their lives at some point, and then they will seek someone who they think might be able to help.

In our text Paul and Silas could easily have been despairing. While they were evangelizing, doing the very work God had told them to do, they were thrown into prison and chained up. They could have easily fallen into doubt and asked the question: "Why did God let this happen?" The Scripture mentions that it was "about midnight." Maybe you're in the middle of some dark circumstance right now and at the end of yourself. You have a choice just like Paul and Silas did.

They decided to trust God in the midst of their circumstances and began to pray and worship instead of grumble and complain. God's response is astounding. There was a supernatural earthquake whereby the prison doors all opened and everyone's chains fell off, yet no one got hurt. He is the God of midnight. When man is at the end of himself and there seems to be no hope, God is there, waiting to set people free and bring them to Himself.

August 12

Part of the Bride

"For this reason a man shall leave his father and mother and shall be joined to his wife, and the two shall become one flesh. This mystery is great; but I am speaking with reference to Christ and the church." Ephesians 5:31-32

If you have accepted Christ you are a son or daughter of God, but you are not a bride of Christ. Jesus doesn't have many brides, only one. The two will become one – Jesus is one and the church together is the other one. When we accept Christ we become part of the bride so to fulfill our destiny we must learn how to connect with each other. When we become one unified church, the beauty of the bride will go forth drawing people to Christ, the Spirit and the bride will announce the gospel, and finally, Jesus will come back and take us to the marriage supper of the Lamb. We don't need anyone but Jesus to become a child of God, but we need one another to really be the bride. That's why He is so insistent on unity.

Ephesians 4:3 says, "Make every effort to keep the unity of the Spirit through the bond of peace." "Make every effort" means work at it! Jesus said if someone has sinned against us we are to forgive them without even going to them. "And when you stand praying, if you hold anything against anyone, forgive him, so that your Father in heaven may forgive you your sins." (Mark 11:25) He said if someone has something against us and we know about it, we are to go to them and try to make it right. "If you are offering your gift at the altar and there remember that your brother has something against you, leave your gift there in front of the altar. First go and be reconciled to your brother; then come and offer your gift." (Matthew 5:23-24)

This is real Christianity that really shows God we are serious. When we make things right, even if we don't feel like it, the Father is able to bring healing to the bride and prepare us for the coming Bridegroom.

August 13

Getting Over Grief

"Now the Lord said to Samuel, 'How long will you grieve over Saul...? Fill your horn with oil and go; I will send you to Jesse the Bethlehemite, for I have selected a king for Myself among his sons.'" 1Samuel 16:1

Samuel was stuck in his grief. He had prophesied to Saul, anointed Saul, and saw him get off to a great start as Israel's king, but now Saul had turned his back on God. God had allowed a time of grief to pass so that Samuel could rightfully mourn Saul's backslidden condition and the negative results all Israel was experiencing, but now He wanted Samuel to move on. "How long will you grieve over Saul?" It's as if God was asking, "Is this your new life? Are you going to be depressed and live in regret every day because someone you love isn't walking with God?" God had stuff He wanted Samuel to do for Him, new people for him to anoint, but Samuel couldn't do anything if he wasn't willing to leave the place of grief.

Have you been there? I sure have. It's a dark and heavy place that taints all of life in a negative way. How do you get over the failure of someone close to you? The answer is not forgetting them, but giving them to God in prayer recognizing that only He can reach them. While you ask God to touch the one you love, you also need to be willing to leave the place of grief and go touch someone else He loves. "Fill your horn with oil and go..." Part of our healing comes from getting filled again with His Spirit to touch someone He leads us to in Jesus Name. The way He touches through us is often as simple as a word of encouragement, a prayer, a good deed, or just a listening ear.

It's a strange thing in the kingdom, but often true. The ones we love the most are often the hardest for us to reach, so we need to trust them with God, and let Him raise up someone else to speak into their lives. As life and people disappoint us we can allow our grief to paralyze us, or we can give it to God, fill our horns with oil, and ask God to use us again for His glory.

August 14

Destiny or Comparison?

"So Peter seeing him said to Jesus, 'Lord, and what about this man?' Jesus said to him, 'If I want him to remain until I come, what is that to you? You follow Me!"
John 21:21-22

My wife and I were at a pastor's convention and one of the speakers preached from Psalm 29 on the voice of God. His point was that we are formed by whatever voice we regularly listen to. He asked if we were listening to the voice of destiny or comparison.

He said that when we stop listening to the voice of destiny, the voice of comparison will take over. The fruit of operating out of comparison will either be a competitiveness that wins by making sure others lose, or a complacency that comes from self pity because we don't think we're as good as someone else.

The problem is how deeply ingrained comparison is in our hearts. Jesus told the disciples at the last supper that one of them would betray Him. Luke 22:23 says that "they began to discuss among themselves which one of them it might be who was going to do this thing." But the argument about who was the worst quickly gave way to another one about who was the best because the very next verse says, "And there arose also a dispute among them as to which one of them was regarded to be greatest." (Luke 22:24) We know Peter thought he was on top from his statement to Jesus, "Even though all may fall away, yet I will not." (Mark 14:29)

But the text above from John 21 finds Peter in a very different place. He has denied the Lord and has gone back to fishing. He used to think he was the best, but by now, we can imagine, he is convinced he is the worst. To bring him back to his destiny Jesus asks Peter if he loves Him. When he says he does, Jesus recalls him into the ministry; "...feed My sheep; ...tend My flock; ...shepherd my lambs." It's not about whether Peter thinks he's as good at it as someone else, it's only about loving Jesus and doing what Jesus told him to do. Denying Jesus didn't change his destiny any more than our failures change God's destiny for us. God has factored our weaknesses, mistakes, and even our sins into His plan.

After receiving his instructions Peter did what we usually do, he looked at the guy next to him and asked, "What about him?" Jesus said, "What's that to you? You follow me." Our job isn't to keep track of anyone else's destiny, that's between them and God. Our job is to get our eyes off of people and on to Jesus. Let's fight off the persistent voice of comparison, so we can fulfill God's purpose for our lives.

August 15

What are You Wearing?

"Put on the Lord Jesus Christ, and make no provision for the flesh in regard to its lusts." Romans 13:14

Just because you have a new outfit in your closet doesn't mean that you chose to put it on today. When we accept Christ into our hearts God gives us a new nature, but He doesn't remove the old one. Christians have the ability to "put on the Lord Jesus Christ," or to not put Him on. When we don't put Him on we live governed by the same appetites, desires, fears, manipulations, and agendas that those in the world function under every day. Our lives become, "the survival of the fittest," with a little God added on here and there.

But when we get up in the morning and put on the Lord Jesus, our new nature responds and transformation occurs, little by little, from glory to glory, until those around us can sense something different about us. It's not just reflected in what we do but in who we are. They begin to smell the fragrance of His life in us even as we go about our daily responsibilities.

So what does it mean to put Him on? First, it means to die to self. When Paul said he, "died daily," he was referring to dying to the carnal nature. Before you put on a new outfit you take off the old one. We have to do it every day because we won't lose the old nature until heaven. Second, it means to choose an attitude that puts God first instead of self. Humility instead of pride, loving instead of competing, praying instead of presuming, serving instead of consuming, and thanking God for what's good instead of whining about what's bad.

We can't produce any of these on our own, but we can choose an attitude that activates the new nature inside of us. In Christ, you have become a partaker in the divine nature (2Peter 1:4), so that what is easy for God can eventually become easy for you and me. We must practice putting on the Lord Jesus. The world around us rarely gets a glimpse of Christ even from those who call themselves Christians, so our lives stick out like a brand new outfit when we truly put Him on. Peter wrote: "Be ready to give an answer to anyone who asks you a reason for the hope that is in you." (1Peter 3:15) When they see Him, they will ask.

August 16

Difficult Questions

"And His disciples asked Him, 'Rabbi, who sinned, this man or his parents, that he would be born blind?'" John 9:2

The disciples asked Jesus a difficult question and He answered them. I'm so glad they asked it, so that we could all hear the answer. The church can either welcome questions or see them as a threat to the established system. God is very secure in Himself, and I think He likes questions when they are accompanied by a heart that wants to know the truth. Asking often leads to study which can lead to deeper convictions than those who never bothered to ask.

There are some people, I am convinced, that want to not believe. They have another issue with God and may use difficult questions to hide the real problem. Sometimes people are mad at God because of unresolved pain, so their questions are really only accusations against God. Others seem to resent that they are not the ones who ultimately decide what is right and wrong. They question God to justify their own lifestyle.

But there are others who are genuinely open to believe, and some who actually want to believe, but they have honest questions that hinder them. God does not ask us to set aside our minds to believe in Him. In fact, He calls us to love Him with all of our minds. Faith does not contradict our minds, but it does transcend them. For these people, it can be very helpful to give the mind rational answers for troubling questions. Explanations for difficult questions will not give a person faith, but they can give a person's mind permission to exercise the childlike faith it takes to connect with God. He is so much higher than us, and His ways so beyond us, that we must humble ourselves like children to experience the fullness of His love and salvation.

August 17

Science Proving God

"For since the creation of the world His invisible attributes, His eternal power and Divine nature, have been clearly seen, being understood through what has been made." Romans 1:20

On December 26, 2014, the Wall Street Journal ran an article called: "Science Increasingly Makes the Case for God," by Eric Metaxas. The article tells of Carl Sagan's original announcement in the 1960s that there were two important factors for a planet to support life: The right kind of star, and a planet the right distance from that star. With this easily attainable goal in a universe as vast as ours, there was a project put together with both public and private funds called: "Search for Extraterrestrial Intelligence" (SETI).

The enthusiasm to find life on other planets has diminished since then as scientists have discovered that there aren't just two factors necessary for life on a planet; there's actually more than two hundred. The probability of life existing on any planet, including ours, turns out to be zero. I will now go to direct excerpts from the article:

Metaxas writes: "As factors continued to be discovered, the number of possible planets (that could sustain life) hit zero, and kept going. In other words, the odds turned against any planet in the universe supporting life, including this one. Probability said that even we shouldn't be here. Today there are more than 200 known parameters necessary for a planet to support life – every single one of which must be perfectly met, or the whole thing falls apart."

"Theoretical physicist Paul Davies has said that 'the appearance of design is overwhelming' and Oxford professor Dr. John Lennox has said 'the more we get to know about our universe, the more the hypothesis that there is a Creator gains credibility as the best explanation of why we are here.'"

God is speaking through creation about His own existence. It turns out that it takes more faith to believe He doesn't exist than to believe He does.

August 18

The Great Designer

"For since the creation of the world God's invisible qualities - His eternal power and Divine nature - have been clearly seen, being understood from what has been made." Romans 1:20

C.S. Lewis tells about a man who stumbles over a watch in the middle of a desert. Where did it come from? He didn't see anyone leave it there and no footprints are visible around it in any direction. There are no video tapes of what happened beforehand, and there is no scientific experiment that can be run to test why this watch appeared. Any explanation concerning this watch will have to be based on faith.

The man examines the watch more carefully. The metal band is elastic and can be stretched so that it fits snugly on the wrist. There is a plastic, clear covering that appears to be designed to protect the face of the watch. There are ordered numbers going around in a perfect circle and three hands pointing to different numbers. Hold it! One of them is moving – this object is ticking!

Here are the two faith explanations available to our man. One is that the watch is the result of a designer and has been left here by someone. The other is that over an immense period of time the sand blew together in such a way to form the band, face, and plastic covering of the watch. In a freak accident, numbers were etched on the face, remarkably in order, and by some natural stimulus (who knows what it could be), it started ticking all by itself. The appearance of design is deceiving because it is the result of nothing more than time and chance.

Both of these are faith explanations, but I submit, one of them is much easier to believe than the other. Our universe is so clearly designed at so many levels, it is incredible to me that anyone can believe it is only the result of random coincidences over a long period of time.

August 19

The Age of the Earth – Part I

"In the beginning God created the heavens and the earth. Now the earth was (or possibly became) formless and empty, darkness was over the surface of the deep, and the Spirit of God was hovering over the waters." Genesis 1:1-2

Many have felt that a straightforward reading of the Bible leads to an earth/universe which is less than 10,000 years old. Any other explanation is often seen as a compromise with the scientific community who believe the earth is billions of years old. Do we have to choose between the Bible and what most scientists believe about the age of the earth?

Genesis One gives six days of creation and describes each day by the words, "There was evening and there was morning," giving the impression of a 24-hour period. Some make the point that the sun and moon are not created until day four so there is no reason to believe that "evening and morning" are describing a solar day. This group would say that each day, the Hebrew word "yom," is describing an indefinite period where God creates through a long process that is only generally summarized in the text. There need be no conflict with scientists, in this view, because Genesis One is only concerned about "who" created, not about "how" He created.

Although I have some sympathy with this argument, I think it is unnecessary when one looks closely at the text. If we subtract all six days of creation given in Genesis One, notice that we still have an earth even though it's covered with water and darkness. Before day one, the earth is already here. The only verse that references the creation of the earth is Genesis 1:1: "In the beginning God created the heavens and the earth."

Is this an introduction to what the author is going to describe as happening during the six days, or is the actual creation of the heavens and the earth being referenced before the six days? Since the earth isn't created during any one of the six days, I think we have to conclude that Genesis 1:1 is describing the act of God in creating the original heavens and earth. If this is the case, and the heavens, including the stars, sun and moon, are already here before day one, day four cannot be describing their creation. Tomorrow I will give four reasons I believe this is true.

August 20

The Age of the Earth – Part II

"In the beginning God created the heavens and the earth. Now the earth was (or possibly became) formless and empty, darkness was over the surface of the deep, and the Spirit of God was hovering over the waters." Genesis 1:1-2

Here are the four reasons I believe the heavens were already in existence before the six days of Genesis one:

1. Darkness is only on the face of the earth in verse two; it isn't filling the universe. Job 38 describes the earth at some time after it was created as having clouds as its garments and being "wrapped in thick darkness." (Job 38:9)

2. When God says, "Let there be light," on day one, He was not creating light, He was allowing the light that was already filling the universe to appear on the earth.* Evening and morning on earth are describing a solar day as the clouds dissipate enough at God's command for light to appear again on the face of the earth.

3. The difference between "bara" and "asah." In Genesis 1:1, God creates the heavens; on the fourth day He only works on them. The word "create" in Hebrew is "bara," the word used on the fourth day in connection to the stars, sun, and moon is "asah" (often translated "made"). Bara indicates something brand new while asah never involves something new, but rather something preexisting that is being worked on.

4. On day four God doesn't create the heavens, He only works on them by completely removing the cloud cover so they can be seen from the earth. This is similar to the work He does on the earth in day three. He doesn't create the earth on the third day, He gathers the water so that dry land appears, and then calls the dry land, "earth." In a similar way, on day four He doesn't create the heavens, He removes the clouds so the heavens can be seen from the earth.

*Scofield Study Bible: "And God said, Let there be light: and there was light." Comments: "Neither here nor in verses 14-18 is an original creative act implied. A different word is used. The sense is made to appear; made visible. The sun and moon were created 'in the beginning.' The 'light' of course came from the sun, but the vapor diffused the light. Later the sun appeared in an unclouded sky."

The Age of the Earth - Part III

"You are of your father the devil, and you want to do the desires of your father. He was a murderer from the beginning..." John 8:44

Satan was already Satan at the beginning; not his beginning, but our beginning. Even though God called everything He made good, there was something evil left over from another time. The story of Satan's fall is an untold story in Scripture even though we are repeatedly assured of the presence of an evil kingdom and given many instructions on how to stand against evil and how to exercise authority over demons.

So when did he fall? Genesis 1:2 says that after creation; "The earth was formless and void." The greatest Hebrew scholars in the world say that the word "hayah" translated "was" in this text, can just as easily be translated, "became." (See the footnote in the 1984 translation of the NIV Bible) In fact, the King James Bible translates "hayah" as "became" in 67 other places. Is it possible that God didn't create the earth formless and void but that it became formless and void sometime after the creation?

The Hebrew words translated "formless and void" are "tohu va bohu." The phrase "tohu va bohu" is only used in two other places in Scripture. One is in Jeremiah 4:23 where God is describing the result of His desolating judgment on Israel's rebellion. Because they rebelled, God left Israel "tohu va bohu." The other place this phrase is used is in Isaiah 34:11 where God is describing the result of His desolating judgment on Edom. Because Edom rebelled, God left the land "tohu va bohu."

What if Genesis 1:2 is describing the result of God's desolating judgment on the earth following Lucifer's (Satan's) rebellion? God created the early earth perfectly and it was inhabited by angels and animals but when Lucifer fell, God's judgment followed. We don't know when or how long until other angels followed him, we only know that a third did fall (Revelation 12:4, 7) and that judgment did come. The earth is covered with water and darkness in Genesis 1:2, not because God created it that way, but because it became that way after Satan's rebellion.

August 22

Generational Telephone

"God waited patiently in the days of Noah while the ark was being built. In it only a few people, eight in all were saved." 1Peter 3:20

Do you remember playing "telephone" as a kid? Someone comes up with an original statement that they whisper into the next person's ear. That person, in turn, tells the next until it goes all the way around the circle. At the end you have the last person tell what they heard and then compare it to the original to see how much it's changed.

Less than 5,000 years ago there was a world-wide flood on this earth and only eight people survived it. Five generations later people had strayed so far from God they built a tower to make a name for themselves, so God confused the languages. Five generations after that God spoke to Abraham and from there the Jewish race was established who carried the promise of Messiah and were entrusted with the story of what actually happened in the early years of mankind. Moses was the one who finally wrote it down.

Most cultures that arose out of the original eight people eventually wrote down their version of what happened as it had come down from their ancestors. Today we have over 300 different versions of a flood story from people who live all over the earth.* After so many retellings it is amazing how similar they are. Of the over 300 accounts:

95% are worldwide floods
88% favor one family
66% the family was forewarned
66% it was the result of man's sin
70% survival was by a boat
67% animals were saved
57% survivors landed on a mountain
35% birds were sent out

Georges Cuvier, the father of modern geology (he was the first who recognized mass extinctions in the earth's past), maintained that catastrophes had happened in the earth's history, the most recent being a world-wide flood. He wrote an essay called: "The Concurrence of historical and traditionary testimonies, respecting a comparatively recent renewal of the human race, and their agreement with the proofs that are furnished by the operations of nature." To Cuvier the evidence of these testimonies meant there had to be an original. Noah's flood is not a children's story; it's part of the history of our planet.

August 23

Patterns of Evidence

"Know this for certain that your descendants will be strangers in a country not their own, and they will be enslaved and mistreated four hundred years. But I will punish the nation they will serve as slaves, and afterward they will come out with great possessions . . . In the fourth generation your descendants will come back here, for the sin of the Amorites has not reached its full measure." Genesis 15:13–16

Filmmaker Timothy Mahoney went on a journey to discover whether the exodus the Bible describes is actual history or only a myth. What he found after more than a decade of traveling all over the world interviewing top scholars and Egyptologists is patterns of evidence affirming the Biblical account.

But the evidence was not in the time period archeologists were looking in and this led to much skepticism toward the Biblical account. Because of Exodus 1:11, "They built Pithom and Ramses as store cities for Pharaoh," scholars assumed that Ramses was the Pharaoh of the exodus, so that was the city they were excavating. Many problems became evident: No sign of a Semite (Israelites are called Semites) population, no signs of distress in Egypt, and nothing that indicated any people group who were there, up and left.

Yet other Egyptologists call the text of Exodus 1:11 an "anachronism," something added to the text by a later editor to help their readers understand where they were referring to. What the later editor was actually saying was something like this: "This is the place where the Israelites built the store city and we know it today as Ramses." Evidence of a similar anachronism is found in Genesis 47:11 where Joseph settles his family in Goshen and the text refers to it as "the best part of the land, the district of Ramses." This was hundreds of years earlier than the Exodus 2:11 text, long before any Ramses could possibly have been Pharaoh, or named a city after himself.

For the last thirty years, archeologists have been digging in another city, also in the area of Goshen, but at a lower level than Ramses, called "Avaris." This city existed hundreds of years earlier than Ramses, in what Egyptologists call "The Middle Kingdom," and in it is found every evidence Ramses was lacking. (Mahoney's movie is called: Patterns of Evidence)

Let's Talk about Politics

"My kingdom is not of this world. If it were, My servants would fight to prevent my arrest by the Jews. But now my kingdom is from another place." John 18:36

"You would have no power over Me if it were not given to you from above. Therefore the one who handed me over to you is guilty of a greater sin." John 19:11

In our texts above we see that there are two kingdoms – the kingdom of God and the kingdom of man. Jesus says that the kingdom of God is from another place and that it does not advance with physical force at the present time. The kingdom of God isn't here to overthrow governments; it's here to change hearts. "The kingdom of God is righteousness, peace, and joy in the Holy Spirit." (Romans 14:17) Only the kingdom of God can bring real hope and change to a human being.

But God is also over the kingdom of man, so Pilate is assured that he would have no authority to judge if it wasn't given to him from above. Paul says: "The authorities that exist have been established by God. Consequently he who rebels against authority is rebelling against what God has instituted, and those who do so will bring judgment on themselves. For rulers hold no terror for those who do right, but for those who do wrong...For he is God's servant to do you good. But if you do wrong, be afraid, for he does not bear the sword for nothing. He is God's servant, an agent of wrath to bring punishment on the wrongdoer." (Romans 13:2-5) Because of the power and possibility of sin, God has appointed civil government to limit the evil man is able to do while on this earth.

The kingdom of God alone can redeem; the kingdom of man can only restrain. If we don't believe in redemption, we tend to see government as the solution for all mankind's problems. For Democrats the answer usually means more government involvement, and for the Republicans, less. When problems continue there is a lot of time spent blaming each other because "if there was only more", or "if there was only less", things would get better.

I don't think God is looking at Democrats or Republicans to turn America around; He's looking at His people, the church. "If My people, who are called by My name, will humble themselves and pray and seek my face and turn from their wicked ways, then will I hear from heaven and will forgive their sin and will heal their land." (2Chronicles 7:14)

August 25

Raising Hell - Part I

"Do not fear those who kill the body but are unable to kill the soul; but rather fear Him who is able to destroy both soul and body in hell." Matthew 10:28

Two years ago I approached our elder board with a desire to present a position on the nature of hell that is different from what most of the traditional church believes. The elders asked me to wait on doing the talk publicly until they had a chance to study and discuss the topic with me. So I waited, and we went through Scripture together. Here are some of the points we were in full agreement about:

1. Hell is a place of punishment where those who reject Christ will go.
2. Hell is a place of conscious torment.
3. Hell is a place of eternal, irreversible judgment or punishment. There isn't a second chance nor is its punishment remedial.

What some respectfully disagreed with is the duration of conscious torment. I believe Scripture teaches ultimate annihilation after souls have paid a just penalty for their sins while others believe the traditional opinion that the torment of hell goes on forever. Of course, they would argue that in God's economy, this too is a just penalty.

I was given the freedom to do the talk as long as I was clear that we were in agreement on the essentials and that the exact nature of hell's punishment is a non-essential that Bible believing evangelicals can agree to disagree on. (I ended up writing an ebook on the topic called: Raising Hell: A closer look at the church's darkest doctrine)

God wants us to behold His severity so that we will never experience it. He loves us and has made a way for all of us to be saved through Christ, so that all we ever need to know is His kindness. Yet we are to behold His severity, so that we never forget that He is a holy Judge. If we choose to turn our backs on Christ, Paul warns, we will experience His severity along with all those who have hardened their hearts to His love.

It is important that we believe in hell. There is a heaven, Jesus said so, and He even said that if it wasn't so He would have told us. (See John 14:2) But the One who is the truth also said there is a hell. In fact, He warned us many times about hell urging us to make sure we didn't end up there.

August 26

Raising Hell - Part II

"He must not be allowed to reach out his hand and take also from the tree of life and eat and live forever." Genesis 3:22b

Part of becoming a Christian for me was accepting the Bible as the final authority on every area of life and doctrine. I was brought up in the Lord by people who believed that the Bible was clear on the nature of hell's punishment, so I never even questioned it.

The argument went something like this: Because men and women are made in the image of God they are automatically eternal beings. The great tragedy of someone rejecting Christ, therefore, was that they would live in conscious torment for all eternity. No one chooses, whether they are eternal, I was taught, it is just a by-product of being in the image of God. Everyone is born with eternal life – they either spend it in heaven with Jesus or in the conscious torment of hell with Satan and his angels.

In the last few years I've questioned whether this is true Biblically or if it is only a tradition of man that was passed down. The context of the passage quoted above was God putting Cherubim with swords at the entrance to Eden because He wanted to ensure that Adam and Eve would not eat from the tree of life and live forever apart from Him.

Apparently being in the image of God didn't mean Adam and Eve would automatically live forever, but only that they had the potential of being eternal. According to the text, to live forever they would have to eat of the tree of life.

Jesus said, "For God so loved the world that He gave His only begotten Son that whoever believes in Him would not perish, but have eternal life." (John 3:16) Eternal life is God's gift to humanity in Christ; without it, I believe, you and I will eventually perish. It was never in God's heart that we would be able to live forever apart from Him.

August 27

Raising Hell - Part III

"Do not be afraid of those who kill the body but cannot kill the soul. Rather be afraid of the One who can destroy both soul and body in hell." Matthew 10:28

As I have explored the church's traditional view of hell, I've learned a lot about the power of confirmation bias. Once we believe something, it's hard for us to consider something that contradicts it, no matter how much evidence there is. It leads us away from "believing what we read," into a place where we only, "read what we already believe." It's hard to learn or grow in this place because we already think we know how things are.

At the foundation of the doctrine of eternal torment is a belief that our souls are eternal. The early church didn't explicitly comment on this topic, but two later church fathers did. Tertullian and Augustine both referenced our eternal souls, but as proof they quoted Plato, not Scripture! (Tertullian; Resurrection of the Flesh; 3; The Fire that Consumes; 300). The Old Testament described man as a transient being: "For all men are like grass, and all their glory is like the flowers of the field; the grass withers and the flowers fall, but the word of the Lord stands forever." (Isaiah 40:6-7) Only Greek philosophy describes us as automatically having an eternal soul.

The New Testament gives many descriptions of what eventually happens to souls who reject Christ, if we will only listen:

1. The body and soul will be destroyed. (Quoted above)
2. The chaff will be burned up in eternal fire. (Matthew 3:12)
3. The enemies of God will be consumed by fire. (Hebrews 10:27)
4. The wicked will perish like beasts. (2Peter 2:6)
5. The wicked will be burned to ashes like Sodom and Gomorrah by eternal fire. (2Peter 2:12; Jude 7)
6. Those whose names are not in the book of life will experience the second death in the lake of fire. (Revelation 20:15)

This is what Scripture says, but if we believe the soul is eternal then destroy can't mean destroy, consumed must not mean consumed, burned up doesn't mean burned up, perish must mean something different then perish, and death can no longer mean death.

August 28

Born Broken

"As He passed by, He saw a man blind from birth. And His disciples asked Him, 'Rabbi, who sinned, this man or his parents, that he would be born blind?' Jesus answered, ' It was neither that this man sinned, nor his parents; but it was so that the works of God might be displayed in him.'" John 9:1-3

Many people become blind because of an accident or disease, but some are born blind. The disciples are troubled by this because they think bad things only happen to bad people and this doesn't fit their formula. When they ask if it was this man's sin you see how predisposed they were to this thinking. You can almost hear their thoughts: *It absolutely has to be this man's fault that he's blind... but he was born blind... maybe he sinned in the womb!*

Jesus says that it wasn't his sin or his parents' sin. He also says that the work of God is not his blindness, but him being healed and made whole. So why was he born blind? I think it's just the brokenness that sin has caused to the human race passed down from generation to generation. It has affected everything, including our DNA, so much so that some people are born blind even though Adam and Eve weren't created blind and no one will be blind in heaven.

We have spiritual DNA as well as physical and it too has been broken by sin. In fact, the Bible says that the effects of sin multiply over generations. The sin nature passed down will become worse and worse if given into by the previous generation, so much so that people can be born with strong tendencies toward addictions even though they themselves haven't done anything wrong yet. It doesn't seem fair, but the truth is all of us are born broken in some way.

Although God has allowed this, He has promised to be close to the broken (Psalm 34:18) and He sent Jesus to redeem us from our sins and to bind up our brokenness. He doesn't judge us for being broken, but invites us to make our identity in Him instead of in how broken we are. The work of God is that we become whole. Although blind eyes can be instantly made whole, spiritual wholeness is a process that won't be completed until heaven.

August 29

Knowing in Part

"Now I know in part, but then I will know fully just as I also have been fully known." 1Corinthians 13:12b

I've seen a great evil in the body of Christ that has plagued the church throughout the ages. Those who know in part often presume they know fully and so divide themselves from other Christians who don't see things exactly their way.

Jesus prayed in John 17:17 that we would be sanctified (set apart) by the truth and then defined truth for us: "Your word is truth." The word of God was given to set us apart from the corrupt value system, perspective, and ungodliness of this present age, so that we would reflect God and His ways in the darkness of this world.

Christians have taken the word that was given to separate or divide us from the world's system, and instead used it to divide the body of Christ. In the very chapter that Jesus prayed we would be sanctified, He also prays that the Father would make us one. The result of this oneness, He said, would be that the world would believe in Jesus.

Instead of accepting each other, the body of Christ is often found rejecting each other on things that aren't essential to the gospel. Pride makes us "strain at gnats and swallow camels." (Matthew 23:24) There are essential truths that unite us and divide us from the world and these need to be embraced with a passion we are willing to die for: the authority of Scripture; Jesus is the Son of God and Savior of the world; the gospel calls all people to repent and put their trust in Christ for salvation; Christians are called to love God and love people; everyone will stand before the judgment seat of Christ and go irreversibly to heaven or hell. Even these clear truths in the word of God are only known in part, yet Christians through all the ages have established these as essentials that define one as a Christian.

Matters like communion, baptism, how the second coming will unfold, how predestination is defined, spiritual gifts, the age of the earth, etc. are all examples of issues that sincere believers disagree as to how the Bible should be interpreted. You probably have an opinion on every one of these topics and you more than likely think you're right. (If you didn't it wouldn't be your opinion) Yet, we need to hold these opinions with humility or our attitude can end up bringing division to the church instead of the unity that Jesus prayed for.

August 30

Natural Disasters

"For the creation was subjected to futility, not willingly, but because of Him who subjected it, in hope that the creation itself also will be set free from its slavery to corruption into the freedom of the glory of the children of God. For we know that the whole creation groans and suffers the pains of childbirth together until now."
Romans 8:20-22

As we witness earthquakes, volcanoes, and hurricanes around the world, the age old question arises: Is this an act of God? Was this somehow God judging people for not responding to the gospel? Or maybe His way of preparing them for the gospel? We know God could have stopped the disaster, but did He intentionally plan it? Or was this an act of Satan? Do demonic forces somehow have the power to bring about disasters according to their mission statement of "kill, steal, and destroy?" (John 10:10)

I believe it's neither God or the devil, but a result of the curse which came on this earth when Adam and Eve sinned. In nature we see evidence of the beauty of our God, but also evidence of the ravages of the fall. Very similar to what we see in mankind.

Although neither God nor Satan directly causes disasters, in my opinion, both kingdoms are very active in the aftermath. Darkness will use tragedy in human minds as proof that God doesn't love them, or that God doesn't exist at all. It will try to bring despair, survivor's guilt, bitterness, etc., anything to lead precious people who Jesus died for away from the help only He can bring.

What is God doing? "The Lord is close to the brokenhearted and saves those who are crushed in spirit." (Psalm 34:18) Notice it doesn't say, "Close to the brokenhearted if they're Christians," or "if they're praying." He is unconditionally close to the brokenhearted whether or not they even believe in Him. He is speaking gently to hearts about His love; He is bringing comfort beyond comprehension; He is raising up individuals and governments to help; and yes, He will use tragedy to show people that they can't put their trust in anything man builds or guarantees.

One day soon Jesus will not only liberate the children of God from their sin nature, He will remove the curse from creation itself, and then the lion will lay with the lamb.

August 31

Working to Rest

"There remains a Sabbath rest for the people of God. For the one who has entered His rest has himself also ceased from his works, as God did from His. Therefore let us be diligent to enter that rest, so that no one will fall, through following the same example of disobedience." Hebrews 4:9-11

Confronted with the demands of ministry, I've thought a lot about the importance of rest. The center of Christianity is not our work, but Christ's finished work on the cross. Our victory comes not from our human efforts but from learning to rest in Him, and allowing His life to overcome through us.

Our text tells us that if we tend to this one relationship, ("Be diligent to enter that rest...") we will no longer be under the striving of our own works but be in a position where God can work through us. Working without entering that rest will always lead to unbelief and disobedience because only Christ in us can live the Christian life. On our own we can clean up the outside of the cup and even impress a few people, but real cleansing requires our ceasing from what we can do and yielding to the Holy Spirit's presence in us.

Are you tired? Are you slowly burning out? Has your Christianity become one more burden instead of the lifter of all your other burdens? Jesus has some advice for all of us: "Come to Me, all who are weary and heavy-laden, and I will give you rest. Take My yoke upon you and learn from Me, for I am gentle and humble in heart, and you will find rest for your souls. For My yoke is easy and My burden is light." (Matthew 11:28-30)

September 1

Being Honest

"Faithful are the wounds of a friend, but deceitful are the kisses of an enemy." Proverbs 27:6

"Charm is deceitful..." Proverbs 31:30

We live in a culture where people are often offended so it is easy to become comfortable with being less than honest. Little white lies may smooth things over in the short run, but they eat away at our integrity. Charm is deceitful because it appears to be kindness; but it's not. Charm has an agenda! It's nice to you because it wants something from you. If you don't give charm what it desires, watch out. All those kisses had an agenda behind them that had nothing to do with loving you for your sake.

An enemy appears nice to you in person and then gossips behind your back. A friend wounds you in person, if they have to, and will defend you to the death behind your back. You and I can't make people be loyal or genuine to us – that's in their hands. What is ours to decide is what kind of person we are going to be. Are we always about our own agenda or are we willing to lay ourselves out for the sake of others? Will we say what needs to be said or only stick with what others want to hear so they'll like us?

The truth can hurt which is why Paul encourages us to "speak the truth in love." (Ephesians 4:15) Just because something is true does not mean I need to say it right now or in front of other people. We need to be careful how we speak the truth, but we do need to speak it!

When I was in high school, Billy Joel was one of my favorite artists. Some lines from a song he wrote called *Honesty* come back to me: "Honesty is such a lonely word, everyone is so untrue; Honesty is hardly ever heard, it's mostly what I need from you."

Let's purpose to be honest to God and honest to people. If we have an agenda let's be forthright about it and not play games. I think we'll stand out in a world that seems comfortable with deceit.

September 2

Responding to the Light

"This is the judgment, that the Light has come into the world, and men loved the darkness rather than the Light, for their deeds were evil." John 3:19

People are not judged because they are in darkness or because their deeds are evil. They are judged on their response to the Light who has come into their darkness to save and transform them. It is not being in darkness that brings ultimate judgment, but staying in it when God has made a way out. The Holy Spirit convicts the world of the central sin of not believing in Jesus. (John 16:9) Without Christ, who is the Light (John 1:4), there can be no real relationship with God.

When a relationship with God is established, the Holy Spirit brings light into the remaining darkness of a believer. It is not ours to make ourselves better, but rather to cooperate with the Spirit who alone can bring us into closer union with Jesus and internally conform us to His beautiful image.

I have marveled for years at how wonderful Christ is yet how long it seems to take us to change. Here are four wrong responses to the conviction of the Holy Spirit in a believer's life:

1. "Not now..." This is the response of procrastination. "You are right, I need to work on that area, but not now because I'm busy." We are often able to put off conviction by simply involving ourselves in something else.

2. "Relax, it's not that bad..." This is the response of justification. "Everybody does this, in fact, I even know pastors who do this so it's not a big deal." God doesn't compare us to other people so it is very dangerous to base your righteousness on what you think other people get away with.

3. "It's not my fault..." This is the response of blame. "What I am doing is okay because I'm in a lot of pain right now; pain, by the way, that You allowed." God has compassion on our hurts and pains – He is the friend of sinners. However, our pain does not excuse our sin.

4. "I agree, so I will now punish myself..." This is the response of works. "I will do more so this bad feeling will go away." Don't bypass the cross by punishing yourself. Jesus took the punishment so we could be free from the guilt, shame, and power of sin.

September 3

The Narrow Road

"Watch out for the leaven of the Pharisees and Sadducees." Matthew 16:6

The Christian life truly lived out in the power of the Holy Spirit will discover the truth of Jesus' words: "My yoke is easy and My burden is light." (Matthew 11:28) It is the wide road which leads to destruction that is the heavy, hard way. The problem with the road to life is not that it's hard, but that it's narrow; in other words, easy to get off of.

In our text the Lord gives the two sides of the road to life that Christians can easily fall into. The first is the leaven of the Pharisees which is legalism. It's easy to fall into this ditch and not realize you're in it because outwardly you're still doing all the stuff. I'm going to church, reading my Bible, staying away from known sin, and keeping all the rules; but that's the problem. God's not calling us to rules but to a relationship with Himself. Another reason it's hard to discern legalism is that there is often a lot of passion involved. Jesus said the Pharisees were willing to travel over land and sea to make one disciple. That's passion! But legalism's passion isn't really for the Lord Himself, but only for it's version of Christianity. My church, my group, and my doctrine all become more central than Jesus.

The other side of the road Jesus says is the leaven of the Sadducees. These were religious people who made a compromise with the world's system. They no longer really went by the Bible and saw nothing wrong with fully embracing the ways of a godless culture. When we listen to the world our passion for the Lord goes out, and it becomes all about us and what we want. Christianity and even the Lord Himself become a means to our personal happiness. Going this way you end up with a form of godliness but lose the power that changes your life.

The good news is that it's easy to get back on the narrow road when we realize we have drifted off it. Because of what Jesus did on the cross we just need to repent and ask Him to forgive us and fill us again. The church in Ephesus had fallen into legalism and Jesus told them to repent and remember their first love. (Revelation 2:1-6) The church at Laodicea had fallen into license and the Lord told them to be zealous (wage war on compromise) and repent because He was standing at the door knocking wanting to be the center again. (Revelation 3:15-20)

Here's how I check myself for leaven: legalism produces anxiety before God while license produces apathy before God. The fruit of truly being on the road to life is to be "awake" (spiritually alert with our lamps filled with oil), and "at rest" (confident in Christ's love and finished work on our behalf).

September 4

Two Very Different Judgments

"Do not marvel at this; for an hour is coming, in which all who are in the tombs will hear His voice, and will come forth; those who did good to a resurrection of life, those who committed evil to a resurrection of judgment." John 5:28-29

Our souls go to heaven or hades when we die but our bodies are held by death until the second coming of Christ. Every human being that ever lived will receive a new body, of which their body on earth was a seed (it doesn't matter if people were cremated or buried); and then will be judged by Jesus Christ, the Son of God. The judgment of those who trusted Him as their Savior will be very different from those who rejected Him in three ways.

1. The timing of the judgment. Those who trusted Christ will be raised first and that will begin at what is commonly known as the rapture of the church. Paul tells us that "..the dead in Christ will rise first. Then we who are alive and remain will be caught up together with them in the clouds to meet the Lord in the air, and so we shall always be with the Lord." (1Thessalonians 4:16-17) The second resurrection doesn't happen until after the millennium: "And the sea gave up the dead which were in it, and death and Hades gave up the dead which were in them; and they were judged, every one of them according to their deeds. (Revelation 20:13)

2. In what is being judged. Those who trusted Christ will not be judged for their sins – that judgment happened already on the cross. Jesus, in the text above, says their resurrection is to life, not judgment. However, believers will be judged for their works and 1Corinthians 3 says that some will have all their works burned up in the fire of God's judgment, even though their souls will still be saved. The righteous are only judged to determine their rewards, not their salvation. Those who reject Christ will be judged for all their sins. They chose to pay their own penalty, so they will.

3. The kind of body received. The righteous are raised immortal and their new bodies are imperishable. (1Corinthians 15:42) Those who reject Christ are given a new body but it is perishable like the one they had on earth. Jesus says they will perish – John 3:16; Paul says they will perish – 1Corinthians 1:18; and Peter says they will "perish like the beasts." (2Peter 2:12)

September 5

What's Your Assignment?

"I have brought You glory on earth by completing the work You gave Me to do." John 17:4

The Message brings out the truth that our "work" is simply the assignment God has given us. The way we bring glory to God on this earth is by working on the assignment He's given us to do. When my daughter was in high school it was amazing how many different things she could occupy herself with instead of the homework that was assigned by her teacher. I think we are often the same way in life.

God has assigned us to be His witnesses wherever we are. Not to "do" witnessing, but to "be" witnesses. He tells us that before this can happen we must be filled with the Holy Spirit (Acts 1:8), so part of our assignment is cultivating a relationship where we stay filled with Him. Being His witness is going to look different in different spheres, but it always involves bringing a sense of God's presence, love, and beauty to whatever setting we are in.

There is a fresh anointing of the Spirit for every new assignment God might ask of you. Sometimes it's a new person He wants you to love, sometimes it's a new stage of life He wants you to embrace, and sometimes it's a new job or responsibility He's given you to do. Let's not waste our time feeling sorry for ourselves or worrying about future scenarios that may never happen. Let's be about the work He's given us to do, in the strength He has supplied, so He is glorified. We don't ever have to out-produce or impress anyone else. It's enough that we work on our assignment.

September 6

Sinners or Saints?

"Paul,...to the saints that are at Ephesus." Ephesians 1:1

"Cleanse your hands, you sinners; and purify your hearts, you double-minded." James 4:8

So which are we sinners or saints? I think we're both and need to keep in touch with both identities.

Some go by the saying, "only a sinner saved by grace." If all we are is forgiven sinners then the only message we have to the world is forgiveness. However important this message is, it is often hard for unbelievers to see their need when they don't see any difference between their lives and ours. The "sinner" identity certainly makes you relatable to people, but it won't change your life. We are more than sinners saved by grace. In Christ we are new creations who have His very life in us transforming us from glory to glory. If we have a message of forgiveness but no real changes in our life to back it up, why would anyone think that our message is any more true than what they're already believing?

Others are so excited about being "saints," they no longer want to be identified as sinners. One group in Christianity changed the words of Amazing Grace because they felt the words "saved a wretch like me" no longer described them. The problem with the saint's only identity is that it eventually leads to hypocrisy because Christianity never promises to take away our sinful nature. God's plan was not to replace the old with the new but to add the new to the old leaving believers the daily choice of which nature they live out of. We need to die daily to the old nature because it's still there. Pretending that real Christians shouldn't struggle any more, does nothing to help new believers who are trying to figure out what is going on inside of them. The other problem with the "saints only" identity is that it tends to divide the world into "good" people and "bad" people. When we believe we're good and others are bad we become hard and self-righteous and lose any possible chance of reaching the people Jesus died for.

So who are we? We are saints that have been set aside for God's glory and have been given a new nature which is slowly transforming our minds and souls into the image of Jesus. But we're also sinners that need Jesus' blood and forgiveness as much now as we did on the first day we said "yes" to Him!

September 7

Falling Away

"Those on the rocky soil are those who, when they hear, receive the word with joy; and these have no firm root; they believe for a while, and in time of temptation fall away." Luke 8:13

Few things are as distressing to me as those who fall away from faith after once walking with Jesus. How can we help people get a firm root down, so that they don't fall away when things get difficult? Instead of giving my opinion, I want to quote a man who led over a half million people to Christ in the 19th century. The notable thing about Charles Finney was that a survey taken at the time showed that 85% of those who responded to Christ in his meetings were still walking with the Lord ten years later. Compare these results to surveys of Moody's converts that showed only 30% remained, and one survey of Billy Graham's converts that showed only 3% were still faithful to the Lord a year after coming to the altar. Here's how Finney preached the gospel:

"We should present to their minds the character of God, his government, Christ, the Holy Spirit, the plan of salvation, any such thing that is calculated to charm the sinner away from his sins, and from pursuing his own interests, and that is calculated to excite him to exercise unselfish and universal love. On the other hand, his own deformity, selfishness, self-will, pride, ambition, enmity, lusts, guilt, loathsomeness, hatefulness, spiritual death; all these things should be brought to bear in a burning focus on his mind. Man's depravity should then be held up against the great love, the infinite compassion, the meekness, condescension, purity, holiness, truthfulness, and justice, of the blessed God. These should be held before him like a mirror until they press on him with such mountain weight as to break his heart." (Reflections on Revival Pg 40-41)

I will close with precious words from Jude 24: "Now to Him who is able to keep you from falling, and to present you before His glorious presence without fault and with great joy – to the only God our Savior be glory, majesty, power and authority, through Jesus Christ our Lord, before all ages, now and forevermore! Amen."

September 8

Discernment and Accusation

"...the accuser of our brethren has been thrown down, he who accuses them before our God day and night." (Revelation 12:10)

If there has ever been a time that we need discernment, it is today. There are many with tickling ears and many who will tell those ears whatever they want to hear for a price. There are many abuses that need to be called out and stood against, but there is another abuse that has slipped into the body of Christ under the guise of discernment, and that is accusation.

This spirit has caused fear and division in the church and has kept many people from experiencing the genuine power of God. People under this "wisdom" content themselves with the fact that they go by Scripture, but Scripture is not an end in itself; it's supposed to lead us to a living relationship with Jesus. Jesus said to the Pharisees: "You diligently study the Scriptures because you think that by them you possess eternal life. These are the Scriptures that testify about me, yet you refuse to come to me to have life." (John 5:39)

I had fried chicken this week. Because it had been in the refrigerator for a while I looked it over closely before I ate it. If I had seen any trace of mold on it I would have immediately thrown it away – that is discernment. However, I fully expected that there would be bones in with the chicken that I would have to throw away. Even though there were bones, it was worth it for the meat. Any ministry you receive from will have bones with it. Either you won't agree with everything, or you won't agree with the way it was presented, or some quirk in the person delivering it. It takes humility to receive from any ministry, but if we will humble ourselves God can teach us through anyone.

In my mind we all "know in part" now and have to give each other some room to disagree on non-essentials. One of my favorite sayings from church history goes like this: "In essentials, unity; in non-essentials, liberty; and in all things, charity."

September 9

The Power of Your Calling

"Faithful is He who calls you, and He also will bring it to pass."
1Thessalonians 5:24

The power to fulfill your calling lies in the One who called you. We can either live before God out of our calling, or live before men out of guilt, man-pleasing, or fear of rejection. Because we all naturally tend toward the latter, we need to remind ourselves to come back continually to the One who calls us.

Even though I have been given responsibility to provide accountability for our pastoral staff, I don't want them working for me. If they do their work for a man then they will probably only do the minimum he requires, and the quality of their work will probably fluctuate proportionate to whether "the boss" is watching or not. It is too low a calling to work for any person.

Colossians 3:23 reads: "Whatever you do, do your work wholeheartedly for the Lord rather than for men, knowing that from the Lord you will receive the reward." Everything you and I do can be holy if we do it for the right Person. It doesn't matter whether we're at church, school, work, or even at play – if we're living for God we will find His energy, pleasure and reward. Paul tells us that it even applies to eating meals! "He who eats does so for the Lord for he gives thanks to God..." (Romans 14:6)

What has God called you to do? Not, "what do you want to do," or "what do your parents want you to do," but what has God called you to do? If you're not sure, I think you should review your history and see if He hasn't given some hints. Come back to that calling and to the One who gave it, and watch Him bring it to pass. There is power in our calling!

The Humility of our Humanity

"Come now, you who say, 'Today or tomorrow we will go to such and such a city, and spend a year there and engage in business and make a profit.' Yet you do not know what your life will be like tomorrow. You are just a vapor that appears for a little while and then vanishes away. Instead, you ought to say, 'If the Lord wills, we will live and also do this or that.' But as it is, you boast in your arrogance; all such boasting is evil." James 4:13–16

God gave King Nebuchadnezzar a dream and then gave Daniel the interpretation to warn him about the brevity of his life. In the dream he was pictured as a head of gold, but Daniel explained that the reason why the metal changed at the shoulders was: "after you will arise another kingdom..." (Daniel 2:39) The king didn't like this reminder of his humanity so he ordered that a ninety foot statue be made of himself out of pure gold, and then ordered those in his kingdom to bow down and worship it. He had those who would address him use this phrase before stating their business; "O king, live forever!" (Daniel 2:9)

God was very patient with this proud king revealing Himself in many ways until he finally came to a place of worship. Daniel records his words: "I, Nebuchadnezzar, praise, exalt and honor the King of heaven, for all His works are true and His ways just, and He is able to humble those who walk in pride." (Daniel 4:37) I wonder if he had his servants remind him by changing the greeting to something like: "O king, you won't live forever."

When we remember how short our time on earth is, it is easier to live for the important things of eternity instead of the temporal things of this world. No wonder David prayed, "Lord, make me to know my end and what is the extent of my days; let me know how transient I am;" (Psalm 39:4) and Moses prayed, "Teach us to number our days, that we may present to You a heart of wisdom." (Psalm 90:12)

When we're right with God we have no anxiety about the brevity of our lives because the best is yet to come!

September 11

God or Money?

"No one can serve two masters; for either he will hate the one and love the other, or he will hold to one and despise the other. You cannot serve God and money." Matthew 6:24

Perhaps the greatest distraction to pure devotion to Jesus Christ in this day and age is money. Who is ruling all things in our lives? Is it Jesus, before whom "every knee shall bow and every tongue shall confess," or is it money? The one who actually rules our lives is not necessarily what our religion states; it's the one we make our decisions by and find our comfort in.

Jesus said, "Seek first the kingdom of God and His righteousness; and all these things shall be added to you." (Matthew 6:33) Unfortunately, we in America are often guilty of seeking first "all these things" and adding a little religion on the side. Our money says, "In God we trust," but do we really?

Jesus came across a very moral and religious young man who was bound by the power of money. The Scripture tells us that, "Jesus felt a love for him, and said to him, 'One thing you lack; go and sell all you possess, and give to the poor, and you shall have treasure in heaven; and come follow Me.' But at these words his face fell, and he went away grieved, for he was one who owned much property." (Mark 10:21-22)

God wanted to free this man from money's subtle power over him. His property wasn't the real problem, it was his heart. In the very same chapter Jesus promises that those who have left, "houses...and farms," for Him will receive back a hundred times, "houses...and farms," in this life. (Mark 10:29-30) Ultimately Jesus didn't want his money; He wanted his heart.

Matthew 6:21 says, "Where your treasure is, there will your heart be also." Does God have your money, or are you holding on tightly to it trying to add a little religion on the side? In these difficult days of shaking it is vital for us to be trusting God in every area of our lives.

September 12

What's Your Dream?

"One thing I ask of the Lord, this is what I seek; that I may dwell in the house of the Lord all the days of my life, to gaze upon the beauty of the Lord and to seek Him in His temple." Psalm 27:4

David's dream was that he would know the intimacy of God's presence which is why he was called the man after God's own heart. His dream was to know God Himself. What's yours?

David also had an assignment, in fact, it was a big one. He was appointed by God to be king in Israel which meant that he was responsible to lead and shepherd them, which he did with integrity and diligence (Psalm 78:72), but his assignment was never his dream.

This became evident when he sinned against God and was in danger of losing everything. In his prayer recorded in Psalm 51, he pleaded with God about his dream but never even mentioned his assignment: "Do not cast me from Your presence or take your Holy Spirit from me..." (Psalm 51:11) When Absalom was seeking to overthrow the kingdom, David fled, but made Zadok keep the ark in Jerusalem: "If I find favor in the Lord's eyes, He will bring me back...", but if not, "I am ready; let Him do whatever seems good to Him." (2Samuel 15:26) David's identity wasn't in being king but in being God's child. He didn't have to fight to be or do something, He just wanted to be where God wanted him.

Acts tells us that David completed his assignment while on earth (Acts 13:36) and you should aim to fulfill yours as well, but I hope you don't make it your dream. Making your assignment your dream will burn you out and all those who are around you because burn out is always the end result of putting the second commandment (Love your neighbor) before the first (Love God). But if we seek God Himself as our dream, like David did, we will find an abundance of grace to complete His assignment and all the glory will belong to Him.

September 13

Breaking Intimidation

"Then the Philistine (Goliath) said, 'This day I defy the ranks of Israel! Give me a man and let us fight each other.' On hearing this, Saul and all the Israelites were dismayed and terrified." 1Samuel 17:10-11

I believe there was a spirit of intimidation behind Goliath's threats that still seeks to paralyze the people of God today. If we listen to our fears we will do little to advance the kingdom of God in our lives. The Bible tells us that David, "served the purpose of God in his own generation." (Acts 13:36) He didn't live a sinless life, but God was able to accomplish what He wanted through him. If we fulfill our purpose, it will be because we broke intimidation the same way David did. Consider with me three common sources of intimidation:

1. The opinions of family. "When Eliab, David's brother, heard him speaking with the men, he burned with anger at him and asked, 'Why have you come down here? And with whom did you leave those few sheep in the desert? I know how conceited you are and how wicked your heart is; you came down only to watch the battle.'" (1Samuel 17:28) We love our families but we dare not allow their expectations to determine our destinies. It's hard for them to see us beyond the role we played in the family growing up.

2. The way others have done it. "'I cannot go in these,' David said to Saul, 'because I am not used to them.' So he took them off." (1Samuel 17:39) Saul put his own armor on David because that's what Saul would have worn if he was fighting. Others have an opinion about us but it's often based more on who they are then on who we are. We will never fulfill God's purpose trying to be someone we're not.

3. The taunts of the enemy. How did David boldly confront the same enemy who had paralyzed the entire Israelite army for forty days? I believe the key is found in the previous chapter: "So Samuel took the horn of oil and anointed him in the presence of his brothers, and from that day on the Spirit of the Lord came upon David in power." (1Samuel 16:13) The key to breaking intimidation is being filled with the Holy Spirit. We have nothing to fear, God has given us the Spirit of power, love, and a sound mind. (2Timothy 1:7) Be yourself, filled with the Holy Spirit, and know with confidence that you and God can accomplish anything together.

September 14

The Sovereignty of God and Salvation

"For those God foreknew he also predestined to be conformed to the image of his Son, that he might be the firstborn among many brothers and sisters. And those he predestined, he also called; those he called, he also justified; those he justified, he also glorified." Romans 8:29-30

A mighty ship named Salvation is crossing the ocean; its Captain is Jesus and its destination is heaven. Two men tell Jesus they are going overboard because they resent the confinement of the ship. Each swims away from the ship in a different direction, and at some point, both will surely drown if not rescued. What will the Captain do?

There are two main Christian views of how and of who God saves as well as two different definitions of what predestination means. Both believe in God's sovereignty but differ in how He chooses to exercise it.

In one view, the Captain sends out a professional swimmer (the Holy Spirit) with a life preserver (the gospel) to one of the two men. The professional swimmer wakes up (the call of God) the man who has passed out and informs him of the Captain's great love and rescue. He then places him on the top of the life preserver while holding him on it. Jesus pulls the rope connected to the life preserver until this man is safely on the ship. This man had no part in his own salvation – Jesus did it all.

In the other view, the Captain sends out a professional swimmer (the Holy Spirit) to both men and brings a life preserver (the gospel) to both. The professional swimmer has been instructed by the Captain to wake up (the call of God) both men and to inform them of the great danger they're in as well as of the rescue the Captain has arranged for them both because of His great love. Each man is told by the swimmer that he must participate in his own salvation by grabbing the life preserver. The swimmer will assist them in holding onto the life preserver while the Captain pulls them to the ship, but if they don't want to return to the ship, He will eventually have to leave them alone, and let them drown. In this scenario, the Captain once again knew before the ship sailed that both men would go overboard, but instead of predestining one to be saved, He predestined that salvation would be offered to both.

I believe the latter is the true definition of predestination and the way God exercises His sovereignty in salvation. Only you can decide what you believe.

September 15

The Gospel Guarantee

"For while we are in this tent, we groan and are burdened, because we do not wish to be unclothed but to be clothed instead with our heavenly dwelling, so that what is mortal may be swallowed up by life. Now the one who has fashioned us for this very purpose is God, who has given us the Spirit as a deposit, guaranteeing what is to come." 2Corinthians 5:4-5

The gospel guarantee for our bodies is resurrection when Jesus comes back, not physical healing in this present age. While healing is available now and should be prayed and believed for, the bigger plan for our bodies is that they be raised at Christ's coming.

Our current bodies are referred to as tents – they are temporary. God has a redeemed, perfect body for us who believe that is permanent. "Now we know that if this earthly tent we live in is destroyed, we have a building from God, an eternal house in heaven." (2Corinthians 5:1) All physical healing now is evidence of the resurrection power that will one day raise our earthly bodies (whether we've died or are still alive) and give us the redeemed body that can't be worn down or worn out. (See 1Corinthians 15:52)

In Jesus first coming, He secured forgiveness for our sins and peace for our souls. At His second coming, He will reverse the curse that causes our bodies to "waste away" in this present age. (2Corinthians 4:16) We need to live in our tents until we die, so I thank God for His power for us to be healed now, but it's really important that we don't guarantee the wrong thing to people.

A dear friend at a former church was dying and on his deathbed started to doubt his salvation. He was such a brilliant, giving Christian, so I couldn't understand why he was struggling at the time he most needed his faith. He explained: "If Jesus died for my sicknesses the same way He died for my sins, then how can I believe I'm forgiven if I'm not healed?"

Those of us who believe in healing need to be careful to not overreach in what we promise or we create confusion in those God loves. I told him that God loved him and Jesus died so that he could be forgiven and go to heaven whether he got physically healed or not. Physical healing now is available to be asked for but when it doesn't happen, we thank God that a more complete healing is coming - our resurrection.

September 16

Continual Devotion

"They were continually devoting themselves to the apostles' teaching and to fellowship, to the breaking of bread and to prayer." Acts 2:42

God is wholehearted toward you. He gave everything on the cross before we gave anything to Him, just because He loves us. The goal of the Christian is to have the same wholehearted love for God that He has for us. When we do we will have energy and joy to do whatever God wants us to do without even noticing the sacrifices we make. As Jesus endured the cross for the joy set before Him (Hebrews 12:2), even so, our burning love for Him will make any difficulty just one more chance to embrace the cross for His sake.

Continual devotion is a great definition of being wholehearted. Continual means a 24/7 relationship instead of a religion that puts God in a box that you only bring out once or twice a week.

When you are devoted to something it is of the highest value to you and you will pay any price to protect it. God wants this fire for Him in our hearts. Our text then gives four things they were continually devoted to that produce an atmosphere of being wholehearted lovers.

1. The apostle's teaching – they weren't devoted to the apostles but to their teaching which we have today in the New Testament. We must not be devoted to our favorite preacher but to the Word of God. Men are like the grass of the field but the Word of God abides forever. Do you read His word daily? I encourage you to start if you don't.

2. Fellowship – we must make some Christian friends that are seeking to be wholehearted as well. Go to church, get in a small group, and look for opportunities to grow.

3. The breaking of bread – this is a reference to communion and the centrality of the cross. Christianity is not about how good we are but about how good Jesus was on our behalf. It is not about our great love, but that He loved us first.

4. Prayer – spending time listening and talking to God. Allow His presence to be your breath and make prayer a moment by moment conversation as well as a special time set aside each day.

Through these four disciplines God will ignite a fire in us and grow it until our hearts are completely healed and completely His.

September 17

The Benefits of the Good Shepherd

"The Lord is my shepherd, I shall not want..." Psalm 23:1

In John 10 Jesus revealed that He was the good shepherd Psalm 23 was written about. There are three tremendous benefits in making the Lord our Shepherd:

1. Security – Sheep are timid creatures and don't eat or rest well when they're afraid. When Jesus is truly our Shepherd we have somewhere to take our fears and can learn how to live our daily lives free from anxiety. "Though I walk through the valley of the shadow of death I will fear no evil; Your rod and your staff they comfort me." Through the forgiveness offered in the cross, Jesus takes away the fear of death by giving us eternal life now. Death becomes a promotion instead of an end and getting older no longer means we're past our prime; we're only getting closer to coming into it. In Christ, our best days are before us because we were created for eternity and not just time.

2. Success – When the shepherd is not close by, sheep immediately form a butting order by which each sheep learns its place. Sheep won't even lie down without the shepherd nearby because they're afraid they'll lose their place. The world's definition of success is often about power, money, and fame, and it requires a lot of energy to protect one's place. But Jesus redefines success for His people – "He leads me in paths of righteousness for His Name's sake." We only have to do the right thing in each situation we are in and live to honor His Name. When we live to please God and make that our priority, "goodness and mercy will follow." We always get in trouble when we seek God's blessings instead of letting them follow us. Jesus said it this way: "Seek first the kingdom of God and His righteousness and all these things will be added to you." (Matthew 6:33)

3. Satisfaction – "My cup overflows." Jesus said, "I came that you might have life, and have it abundantly." (John 10:10) God's idea was that witnessing would be a very natural outflow of our satisfaction in Him. Is it a burden to tell someone about a movie or book you loved? The witness is spontaneous because you want those who you love to experience the blessing that you enjoyed in watching or reading. George Mueller said, "I consider the first duty of every day is to get my soul happy in God." Let's do the same!

September 18

Liking People

"Accept one another, then, just as Christ accepted you, in order to bring praise to God." Romans 15:7

One of the most liberating truths of Scripture is that God accepts me just as I am in Christ. He doesn't just love me, He likes me and wants to be around me. One phrase I've heard Christians say is: "I love them, but I don't have to like them." I don't think that's right. What if someone came up to you and said, "I love you, but I don't like you." Wouldn't that make you feel totally rejected? God wants us to learn how to like and enjoy people the way He does.

My family is very into the Myers-Briggs personality test. Here's how it works: you answer a number of questions and based on your responses they let you know which one of sixteen different personalities you fit most closely into. The interesting thing about the result is that it is unrelated to how you were raised, rather it reflects only who you have made to be as a personality. Many books have been written recently around these sixteen different types that include strengths and weaknesses of each personality, how each personality views life, how to raise children of different personalities, and one interesting study which identified famous people of each personality type.

This study gave a name for each of the sixteen personalities. The six in my family include: "the mystic" (deep but trouble doing regular life), "the enforcer" (a love for rules and discipline), "the counselor" (empathetic for others pain), "the messiah" (sees self as the solution to other's problems), "the architect" (dreams of ways things could be and desires to change them), and "the field marshal" (goal oriented and wants to take others along). The test identified me as "the field marshal" (surprise, surprise) and gave the two famous examples of Napoleon and Hillary Clinton.

My point is that God made everyone of the sixteen personality types and He likes every model even though some are harder to get along with than others. We need to accept each other and enjoy the diversity God has made instead of trying to make everyone the same. My advice has always been: "Don't try to be like someone else, only seek to be yourself filled with the Holy Spirit."

September 19

Free From Shame

"I advise you to buy from Me... white garments so that you may clothe yourself, and that the shame of your nakedness will not be revealed."
Revelation 3:18

Jesus is speaking to the church at Laodicea who has lost any place of deep connection with Him. He actually pictures Himself outside the door of their hearts, knocking to gain entrance. Part of what is keeping them from opening the door is shame.

"The shame of your nakedness" is a reference to Adam and Eve in the garden of Eden. When God first placed them there, they were "naked and unashamed." (Genesis 2:24) It was when they disobeyed God that shame came into their spirits and they looked around for things to hide themselves with.

When shame is on our spirit, even as Christians who love God, we live in a fear of being exposed as not good enough. Living in fear reduces our lives, so many don't ever know or develop who they really are. Jesus is ready and waiting to take away the fear shame brings, so His children can put on the righteous robes He paid for. Paul writes: "He (the Father) made Him who knew no sin (Jesus) to be sin on our behalf, so that we might become the righteousness of God in Him." (2Corinthians 5:21)

If you feel dirty, you will live dirty. Jesus wants us to feel clean on the inside so we don't have to hide or pretend any more. He delights in us even though we are weak and immature – He's knocking on the door because He wants to free us from the power of shame. Let's open our hearts wide to His love and break all agreement with the enemy's accusations over our lives.

September 20

Setting Your Heart

"...if you do not set your heart to honor My name, ' says the Lord Almighty, "I will send a curse upon you, and I will curse your blessings. Yes, I have already cursed them, because you have not set your heart to honor Me." Malachi 2:2

It needs to be about Him. In Malachi's day the priests who made sacrifices and represented God to the people were living in a place where God couldn't bless them. They were sacrificing their lame and blind animals to God, and saving the good ones for themselves. Their lives were very religious, but it was all self centered instead of God honoring.

God loves us and wants to bless us, but our lives won't work right if they are about us. Jesus taught us to pray first, "Our Father who art in heaven, hallowed (honored) be Thy Name," and then to pray "give us this day our daily bread." When we set our hearts to honor God and re-orient our lives around this theme, a huge weight comes off of us.

It no longer matters how we appear to others but only how He appears through us. We no longer have a mortgage or a car payment, everything belongs to Him, so we trust Him to help us fulfill obligations we have made. If we do our best and fail, it's fine, because it's about His success which often looks very different than ours.

We were created to be second, not first. Our sin nature is such that we easily put ourselves first without even thinking about it, which is why we often need to reset our hearts to honor Him. We do it by sincere prayer: "Father, honor Your Name through Me. May Your kingdom advance (not mine), may Your will be done (not mine), for Yours (not mine) is the kingdom, power, and glory forever."

You may think that you lose all sense of yourself by setting your heart to honor God, but the opposite is true. Jesus said that whoever loses their life for His sake, will end up finding it. We were made to honor God so when we aim to do it, everything feels right.

September 21

Keeping the Treasure Safe

"I know whom I have believed and I am convinced that He is able to guard what I have entrusted to Him until that day...Guard, through the Holy Spirit who dwells in us, the treasure which has been entrusted to you."
2Timothy 1:12, 14

Paul writes about two things: something we entrust to God that He guards; and something that He entrusts to us which we guard. Let's look a little closer at both of these.

First, Paul recounts to Timothy the suffering he has had to go through and is going through for the sake of the gospel. He is not having an easy or comfortable life, and in fact, is currently in prison for his faith. He assures Timothy that it will be worth it. God has seen every sacrifice; He has witnessed every accusation and every injustice. God knows that Paul has persevered and continued to turn away from self-pity or bitterness and has tried to be faithful to his calling. Paul believes he will be generously rewarded for his attitudes and actions on the judgment day, and that God Himself is guarding over his reward.

After telling us about something valuable God guards for us, Paul writes about a treasure God expects us to guard. The treasure includes our "sincere faith" (1Timothy 1:5); our ministry "gift" that needs to be continually stirred up (1Timothy 1:6); and the salvation that God has given us "not according to our works, but according to His own purpose and grace which was granted us in Christ Jesus." (1Timothy 1:9) How do we keep this treasure safe?

1. Value that which you have in Christ above everything else. If you don't recognize the treasure you have it becomes vulnerable to the enemy who Jesus called a thief. (John 10:10)
2. Stir up your faith by reading, praying, and obeying every day.
3. Don't become offended with God when you go through trials, confusion, or persecution. Remember Jesus didn't promise a lack of trouble, but peace within it. (See John 16:33) My favorite bumper sticker: "Life is hard, but God is good."
4. Plan to persevere. "So do not throw away your confidence; it will be richly rewarded. You need to persevere so that when you have done the will of God, you will receive what he has promised." (Hebrews 10:35-36)
5. Ask for help. One of the things the Holy Spirit does for us, according to the text above, is to help us guard the treasure.

September 22

Have You Gone Back to Performance?

"You foolish Galatians! Who has bewitched you? Before your very eyes Jesus Christ was clearly portrayed as crucified. I would like to learn just one thing from you: Did you receive the Spirit by the works of the law, or by believing what you heard? Are you so foolish? After beginning by means of the Spirit, are you now trying to finish by means of the flesh? Have you experienced so much in vain–if it really was in vain? So again I ask, does God give you his Spirit and work miracles among you by the works of the law, or by your believing what you heard? Galatians 3:1-5

The Galatian Christians started well, but at some point retreated from "grace through faith" living back to, "trying to be good enough for God," living. Are you there as well? Here are some symptoms:

1. You find you are no longer focused on what Jesus did for you on the cross. You punish yourself instead of accepting His forgiveness easily, and find it hard to forgive others who have hurt you.

2. Your focus is more on your discipline than on the Spirit's power. You are more conscious of what you're doing for Him than what He is doing in and through you.

3. The miracles and the sense of the supernatural are gone. There is no awe, no wonder, and no surprise any more. Jesus said there should be rivers flowing from our inmost being, but you feel like you are plugged up, and anything spiritual is hard.

4. You struggle to believe God loves you; Jesus died for you; and that God wants you to be with Him more than anything else.

If you see yourself in this list let me give you a few practical things to do. First, repent, and ask God to forgive you for going back into performance based religion. Take time to thank Him again for His love, for the cross and for the grace He wants to lavish upon you. Then ask for a fresh filling of the Holy Spirit in simple faith and tell Him you want to be near Jesus. Wait quietly in His presence, stilling every other distraction, and let Him fill you to overflowing. Repeat as necessary.

September 23

War Horses

"I am meek and lowly of heart, take My yoke upon you and learn from Me and you will find rest in your souls. For My yoke is easy and My burden is light." Matthew 11:29-30

The Greek word "praus" is translated "meek" in our text, but it is difficult to find an exact English word to match what it means. Ancient Greeks used this word to describe a stallion that was broken and could be ridden. One commentator writes: "The horse was perfectly trained and ready, it would obey the master, the rider, no matter what was going on around it, so that it could be trusted in the heat of battle not to do something stupid or foolish; once the rider knew that he could trust the animal, and that it would obey him no matter what, he called it a meek horse even though it could have been a powerful, thoroughbred stallion, capable of killing enemies in battle."

Jesus is saying that He's like the war horse. He didn't fear anything, whatever the Father showed Him, He did (John 5:19). If the Father told Him to go right into hell itself to cast out a demon, He would go there. He walked in perfect rest because He only had to pay attention to His Father and had no fear of anyone or anything else.

Why did God describe a meek horse to Job? (Job 39:19-25) I think it's because all that God had allowed in Job's life was for the purpose of making him meek and fearless, like this horse. Job walked uprightly before God but he still had things that he was afraid of. "What I fear comes upon me, and what I dread befalls me." (Job 3:25) After all of this trial was over, I am convinced, Job was unafraid of anything. The worst had happened and God had brought him through.

What if we face what we face because God is trying to destroy the power of fear in our lives? I believe God wants to make us war horses the Holy Spirit can lead into any battle, at any time, knowing that we won't go by our emotions, our past experiences, or our opinions, but only by His prompting. The Father doesn't want us hiding in fear until Jesus rescues us out of this wicked, scary world – He wants to lead us right into the midst of darkness to bring His kingdom on earth, as it is in heaven!

September 24

The Value of Jesus

"Truly I say to you, wherever this gospel is preached in the whole world, what this woman has done will also be spoken of in memory of her."
Matthew 26:13

When Mary of Bethany poured costly oil on Jesus' head in a spontaneous act of worship, the disciples were "indignant" and said, "Why this waste? For this perfume might have been sold for a high price and then given to the poor." (Matthew 26:8-9) Yet there was something in this act that captured the whole-hearted response the value of Jesus calls for, so our text says the gospel itself is to now include the retelling of this event.

Earlier Jesus had compared the kingdom of heaven to a "treasure hidden in the field, which a man found and hid again; and from joy over it he goes and sells all that he has and buys that field." (Matthew 13:44) In this act of devotion, Mary modeled this truth before everyone's eyes. Mary had found treasure in her relationship with Jesus and could not contain her worship. To the others, even those closest to Him, it was as if the treasure was hidden. "Why this waste?" is what they said in the face of such an extravagant offering.

Today our costly oil is our time. Do you ever just "waste" time worshipping Jesus? Beware of a voice in your head that will speak to you whenever you want to spend time alone with the Lord: "Why this waste? You've got things to do, needs to meet, responsibilities to fulfill, calls to make, and items to check off of your list. You don't have time for this." Yet when we set a higher value on God than on all the things we have to do, we bring pleasure to Jesus, like Mary did.

"What about all the urgent other things?" you ask. Jesus replied, "you always have the poor with you." (Matthew 26:11) In other words, the needs will still be there after you take time for devotion. The reality is you and I are much more equipped to handle all of the pressures around us after we have "wasted" time with Jesus because His presence, blessing, and wisdom will then flow more freely. Jesus said that the result of us drinking of Him would be "rivers of living water flowing out of our innermost being." (John 7:37-39)

September 25

Seeking Prayer

"Seek, and you will find." Matthew 7:7

Jesus describes three types of prayer that we will look at over the next three days. The first is seeking prayer which is a description of prayer that seeks after God for who He is. Jeremiah 29:13 gives the essence of this kind of prayer: "You will seek Me and find Me when you search for Me with all your heart."

Singing worship songs is considered part of seeking prayer because it is God focused instead of need centered. Jesus gave us an outline for prayer which starts with who God is: "Our Father who lives in heaven; hallowed by Your Name." Seeking prayer is when we remember it's not about us or our name (reputation), but about God and His Name.

The best selling book The Purpose Driven Life, starts with the words, "It's not about you." In seeking prayer we remember this truth and long to find our satisfaction and identity in God, instead of in ourselves.

"When you said, 'Seek My face,' my heart said to You, 'Your face, O Lord, I shall seek.'" (Psalm 27:8) God invites us to come after Him and find a deeper faith based more and more on His character and less and less on our momentary feelings about Him.

People often start prayer by asking for God's hand which is fine, but the real action comes when we prioritize seeking His face. Consider one of the greatest promises in the Bible: "If My people, who are called by My Name, will humble themselves, and pray, and seek My face and turn from their wicked ways, then I will hear from heaven, forgive their sin and heal their land." (2Chronicles 7:14) Isn't it interesting that this verse never mentions anyone asking God to heal the land? If you seek His face, you will see His hand move on your behalf without even having to ask!

I remember when my kids were young. A lot of their interaction with me was because they needed something, but once in a while they would bring a picture that they made "just for me." It didn't matter what was on that paper, it was a masterpiece that was going on the refrigerator because of their loving intent. I think that's how God feels when we seek His face!

September 26

Knocking Prayer

"Suppose one of you has a friend, and he goes to him at midnight and says, 'Friend, lend me three loaves of bread, because a friend of mine on a journey has come to me, and I have nothing to set before him.' Then the one inside answers, 'Don't bother me. The door is already locked, and my children are with me in bed. I can't get up and give you anything." I tell you, though he will not get up and give him the bread because he is his friend, yet because of the man's boldness (shameless persistence) he will get up and give him as much as he needs." Luke 11:5-8

Years ago my daughter told me that she wanted to have an operation on her jaw. Her teeth didn't line up right so she lived with constant pain and had difficulty chewing things. There were two possible solutions: One was affordable and would cut down the pain as well as slow the deterioration; the other was expensive but would actually make her better.

We didn't have the money. I told the Lord in prayer that we didn't have the money to do what really needed to be done. We were already making sacrifices to put her and her siblings through college and I just felt like all my resources were tapped. "Not all your resources," was the whisper I heard in my spirit. Was there a bank account somewhere I had forgotten about? As I began to think about other resources, I thought of my relationship with my mom.

To do everything for my daughter didn't just mean using money we had, it had to include me humbling myself before my mom and asking her if she would help. To say "no" to my daughter without at least asking my mom for help, would not be doing everything possible. Because of my mom's generosity, I rejoice to say that my daughter had that operation, and now, years later, has no trouble with her jaw.

Have you included your relationship with God when you think about your resources? You may not have what others need, but you know Someone who does.

September 27

Asking Prayer

"Ask and it will be given to you." Matthew 7:7

In seeking prayer we seek God for who He is; in knocking prayer we persistently knock for the influence of the Holy Spirit on others; and in asking prayer we ask for our own needs. Jesus said we didn't need to use many words in asking prayer because "your Father knows what you need before you ask Him." If He already knows, why ask? God wants us to get to know His generosity and love through answered prayer, and He strategically uses delays in answers to refine our character.

Believing is especially central to asking prayer. Jesus said, "And all things you ask in prayer, believing, you will receive." (Matthew 21:22) Believing what? Believing that God will give it exactly when and how you want it? Or do we simply believe God is good; He hears our prayer and He will answer it in His own way and in His own time? Martin Luther believed it was the latter:

"We are to lay our need before God in prayer but not prescribe to God a measure, manner, time, or place. We must leave that to God, for He may wish to give it to us in another, perhaps better, way than we think is best. Frequently we do not know what to pray as St. Paul says in Romans 8, and we know that God's ways are above all that we can ever understand as He says in Ephesians 3. Therefore, we should have no doubt that our prayer is acceptable and heard, and we must leave to God the measure, manner, time, and place, for God will surely do what is right." (Devotional Classics; pg 117)

A couple of months ago I was praying about a frustrating situation and instructing God exactly when He needed to have this problem fixed by, and if not, I was going to have to do something drastic. After I was done with my little tirade, I heard a one word whisper in my mind that I believe was the Holy Spirit speaking: "Really?" I was instantly repentant of my attitude. *I'm not going to take over; I'm going to wait for God's timing and allow the process to refine my soul.*

Ephesians 3:20 is a verse that gives God a lot of latitude in how He answers prayer: "God is able to do far above all you ask or think..." We don't have to ask perfectly or even think of how God might do it; our part is to pray with childlike faith and trust that our God will take it from there. Ask and it will be given to you.

September 28

To Speak or not to Speak?

"The women are to keep silent in the churches; for they are not permitted to speak, but are to subject themselves, just as the Law also says. If they desire to learn anything, let them ask their own husbands at home; for it is improper for a woman to speak in church." 1Corinthians 14:34

Why would Paul, who insisted that we are free from the law in the New Covenant, reference the law as the reason why women should be silent in the church? The motivation of all his ministry is explained to us just a few chapters earlier: "To the Jews I became as a Jew, so that I might win Jews; to those under the Law, ... so that I might win those who are under the Law; ... I do all things for the sake of the gospel, so that I may become a fellow partaker of it." (1Corinthians 9:19-23)

The church in Corinth is reaching out to Jewish unbelievers. It is already difficult for unbelieving Jews to have women sitting alongside men in the same meeting; but to have them speaking would be so offensive to them they would have no chance to respond to Christ. Because Paul is concerned about reaching these people who are under the law, he puts the churches reaching them under the law, even though they aren't under the law, so that they might win those under the law.

Acts 2 is about the freedom God has brought to both men and women through the gospel. (Acts 2:17-18) 1Corinthians 14 is a reminder that we live in culture and we need to honor culture so that we can win people to Christ. A few years ago one of my daughters went to Oman on a missions trip. While there, she always wore a dress in public with a head covering. Why? It wouldn't have been illegal in that country to wear whatever she wanted, but her team was trying to reach unbelievers for Christ. Dishonoring the Muslim culture in Oman would have made it very difficult for the team to share Jesus. Once you offend someone, it's hard for them to hear anything else you are saying.

Paul goes on to say in 1Corinthians 9 by saying, "to those without the law I become like those who do not have the law... so that I may win some." Do you think Paul would allow women to speak in church if he lived in 21st century America?

September 29

God's Timing

"It is not for you to know the times (chronos) or dates (kairos) which the Father has set by His own authority." Acts 1:7

Two of the Greek words for time in the New Testament are "chronos" and "kairos." Chronos is the word for sequential time which is how mankind usually thinks about time. There are twenty-four hours in a day, seven days in a week, and fifty two weeks in a year. We make plans and appointments in sequential time and live our lives trying to fulfill them.

Kairos is a word we don't have one English word to describe. It is not sequential time, but rather, God's time for something to happen.

Vine's Expository dictionary gives this distinction: "Chronos marks quantity (of time), kairos, marks quality." (554) So how does recognizing God's kairos time practically make a difference in our lives? Let me give a number of ways.

1. Although we live in sequential time our priority should be kairos time. Jesus waited for God's time to go to the feast while his unbelieving brothers had no such concern. "The right time (kairos) for Me has not yet come; for you any time is right." (John 7:1-2)

2. We should not be frustrated by our present difficulties but can have confidence that if we keep doing what's right, the time (kairos) will come when we will see God's deliverance. "Humble yourselves therefore under the mighty hand of God and in due time (kairos) He will exalt you." (1Peter 5:6) "Let us not become weary in doing good, for at the proper time (kairos) we will reap a harvest if we don't give up." (Galatians 6:9)

3. History has a purpose and a direction way bigger than us, so we should be able to put all of our minor irritations in perspective. Jesus died at the "right time" (kairos) for us (Romans 5:6); and we can be assured that Jesus will come back in God's "appointed time" (kairos – Mark 13:33).

4. As we respond to God's dealings with us with a spirit of repentance, He desires "times" (kairos) of refreshing to come to us from the presence of the Lord. (Acts 3:19)

September 30

Living on God's Time

"When He (Jesus) approached Jerusalem, he saw the city and wept over it, saying, 'If you had known in this day, even you, the things which make for Peace! But now they have been hidden from your eyes...you did not recognize the time (kairos) of your visitation." (Luke 19:41–42; 44b)

Yesterday we discussed the difference between sequential time (chronos) and God's special time (kairos). How do we live on God's time?

1. We have to recognize the trap of becoming enslaved to chronos time. I am a very scheduled person and it's easy for me to define success as keeping all my appointments and fulfilling all my priorities for any given day. God wants to free me from that mindset, so I can begin to look more and more for His kairos appointments. Jesus was the master at this. He would often be interrupted on His way somewhere, but instead of driving on, He would recognize the timing of God and minister to the interruption. This is how many were healed and delivered in the gospels. He said that His secret was only giving Himself to what He saw the Father doing. (John 5:19)

2. We need to recognize our utter dependence on God to "see." Most of the Jewish people missed what God was doing in their day and then it became "hidden" from their eyes. The Laodiceans were also "blind," yet Jesus promised, "eye salve to anoint your eyes so that you may see" (Revelation 3:18) if they would only repent. Why couldn't they see? They had stopped acknowledging their continual dependence on God and had said in their hearts, "I need nothing." To see we must continually humble ourselves and recognize we need God's grace to see what He is doing.

3. We need to fear God enough to respond quickly and wholeheartedly when a kairos opportunity is available. Jesus wept when He entered Jerusalem because His people had missed the time (kairos) of their visitation and had missed the mercy God wanted for them. The Israelites missed the kairos of God when they were on the edge of the promised land. When they finally decided they wanted to go in, the opportunity had been removed and it was too late. Let's not hold back when opportunities are open to speak, or love, or give, or pray. Let's seize the kairos of God and make sure Jesus never has to weep over us for the mercies we missed.

October 1

Pregnant with God's Purposes

"We know that creation has been groaning as in the pains of childbirth right up to the present time...In the same way the Spirit helps us in our weakness. We do not know what we ought to pray for, but the Spirit Himself intercedes for us with groans that words cannot express. And He who searches our hearts knows the mind of the Spirit, because the Spirit intercedes for the saints in accordance with God's will." Romans 8:22; 26-27

Effective prayer is like pregnancy. Humility recognizes that we don't really know what to pray so it starts by asking, "God, what do You want to do in this situation?" As we open our hearts in sincerity and surrender, the Holy Spirit plants in us the very word of God concerning the situation we're praying about and we become pregnant with the answer.

God's Word to us, Peter says, is an imperishable seed that will stand forever. (1Peter 1:23-25) The only question once God has impregnated us with His purpose is will we persevere with Him in the place of prayer and agreement until heaven's purpose becomes a reality on earth? There is a weight when we carry His purposes; there is an inward groaning when the very opposite of what we have prayed seems to be happening. Will we continue to travail until God's full purpose is accomplished or will we give up and allow that vulnerable seed to be aborted before birth?

"If God wants to do something why doesn't He just do it?" you may ask. He chooses to co-labor with us and has purposed that His plan will not be done on this earth unless someone on earth wants it, prays for it, and does whatever is necessary to birth it. Why else would He tell us to pray, "Your kingdom come, Your will be done on earth as it is in heaven?"

Are you just surviving day to day or are you pregnant with God's purposes for your life? Women that are pregnant don't do things others do and don't eat things other people eat because they don't want to injure the baby. They limit their freedom because they don't want to put what they are carrying at risk. Are you conscious that your life is not just about you, but about the One you are carrying and the purposes He has for you on this earth?

Now that's something to pray about!

October 2

Perseverance

"Do not bother me; the door has already been shut and my children and I are in bed; I cannot get up and give you anything." Luke 11:7

Jesus is teaching about prayer and He tells this story of a friend who seems unwilling to help. In Luke 18 He again is talking about prayer when He describes an unjust judge. In both instances the point is perseverance in prayer. "Then Jesus told His disciples a parable to show them that they should always pray and not give up." (Luke 18:1)

You and I need to be confident in who God is and how He views us because prayer is a battle. I think Jesus is giving us insight on emotions we will face when God delays answers to our prayers. We may feel like God is sleeping and telling us to go away because we're bothering Him. We may feel like God is a callous, unjust judge who doesn't care about our needs, but only His own kingdom. What do we do when God's character is attacked in our minds and emotions?

Jesus told us to press through them and keep praying because God isn't like that, and those feelings are not reliable. The truth is that He is the friend that sticks closer than a brother, who never slumbers or sleeps. (Psalm 121:4) I read a plaque on a wall recently that said: "When you go to bed, leave your problems with God. He's going to be up all night any way."

Fight through the accusations that God isn't just and keep praying and believing because Jesus assures us that God does hear our prayers. "Will not God bring about justice for His elect who cry to Him day and night and will He delay long over them? I tell you that He will bring about justice for them quickly. However, when the Son of Man comes, will He find faith on the earth?" (Luke 18:7-8)

In essence Jesus is saying this: "God will be faithful to do His part, the real question is will we be faithful to do ours'?" Our part is to have faith in the character and promises of God even when our circumstances seem to contradict them. Will the Son of Man find us persevering, or will we give up?

Let's stir ourselves to pray and not waver in the midst of our trials and emotions.

October 3

The Will of God

"My food is to do the will of Him who sent Me and accomplish His work."
John 4:34

Consider with me three things about the will of God: the delight, the cost, and the result.

The delight. David said that when Messiah came He would proclaim, "I delight to do Your will O My God, Your law is within My heart." (Psalm 40:8) In the text above we have Jesus saying that the will of God is His hidden food, sustenance, and supply. Jesus' yoke was easy and His burden was light because He never measured Himself by anything or anyone else – it was enough to do the will of God. Life can be very complicated, but when your passion is the will of God the questions change. It is no longer "what will I choose to do," but only, "what is the will of God so I can obey." Deciding to do God's will, whatever it is, answers a thousand other questions for you. For instance, you don't have to decide whether to forgive someone or not. You always forgive because He's forgiven you.

The cost. Jesus prayed, "not My will, but Yours be done." He didn't finish the work God gave Him to do until He said, "It is finished," on the cross. He did work for us that we couldn't do for ourselves which is why the beginning of us doing the will of God must be putting our faith in Christ. But there's a cross for us as well if we really want to accomplish God's plan. Romans 12:1-2 says, "In view of God's mercy, present your bodies as a living and holy sacrifice, acceptable to God, which is your spiritual service of worship. And do not be conformed to this world, but be transformed by the renewing of your mind, so that you may prove what the will of God is, that which is good and acceptable and perfect." We must offer ourselves before God as a sacrifice willing to do anything, before we will be able to walk out the specific plan He has for us.

The result. Because Jesus obeyed He was given the highest Name and the greatest place in all the universe. (Philippians 2:11) When we do the will of God we end up sharing in His glory forever and ever. "The world is passing away, and also its lusts; but the one who does the will of God lives forever." (1John 2:17)

October 4

Passing God's Tests

"Do not be afraid of what you are about to suffer. I tell you, the devil will put some of you in prison to test you, and you will suffer persecution for ten days. Be faithful, even to the point of death, and I will give you the crown of life." Revelation 2:10

This is kind of a disturbing passage. These are people God is pleased with, yet He is allowing a time of testing at the hands of the devil in which they will be put in prison. Do you feel like you are in some type of prison right now? A situation that you can't change, an affliction that you can't remove, or some type of thorn in your flesh that God doesn't seem to be delivering you from? I want to encourage you, it's just a test. God wanted the church at Smyrna to know that He, the One who loved them, was allowing it, and that He had rewards for those who passed it. How do you pass God's tests?

1. Know that God has limited them. Jesus said there would be a beginning and an end – it would last 10 days and then be over. When you are in a test it is tempting to despair because it feels like this will be the rest of your life. Don't worry, this too will pass. We can't shorten God's tests but we can lengthen them by having a horrible attitude. (See Israelites in the desert for 40 years) 1Corinthians 10:13 promises that in all temptations (same Greek word as tests) "God is faithful; He will not allow you to be tempted beyond what you can bear. But when you are tempted, He will also provide a way out so that you can stand up under it."

2. Don't be afraid. Satan works through fear and God works to free us from fear. Trust God in your prison and don't give into fear. Oftentimes the purpose of the test is to get us in a situation where we would normally be afraid, so that we can learn to walk in faith.

3. Be faithful. Keep doing what you know is right even if it doesn't seem to be working. Keep praying, reading, loving, and obeying – God wants to see if we will be faithful when things are rough, or if we're only fair weather Christians. What's the worst that can happen – you dying? Jesus said to be faithful even to the point of death. What's so bad about being home with Jesus forever in the eternal city where the streets are made of gold, and where we rule and reign with Him for all eternity?

October 5

Long Term Joy

"Though the fig tree should not blossom and there be no fruit on the vines, though the yield of the olive should fail and the fields produce no food, though the flock should be cut off from the fold and there be no cattle in the stalls, yet I will rejoice in the God of my salvation. The Lord God is my strength, and He has made my feet like hinds' feet, and makes me walk on my high places." Habakkuk 3:17-19

God wants you and I to have a joy in His love and union with us that transcends our circumstances. Habakkuk is declaring an absolute freedom from God having to do anything a certain way or give a certain outcome. God is Sovereign and it doesn't matter what's going on in my life or on this planet, it really doesn't change anything. He loves me, He delights in me, and His joy and salvation are my strength. Whatever faces me, God will show me how to walk on my "high places," or as the Amplified version says, "make me to walk (not stand in terror, but to walk) and make (spiritual) progress upon my high places (of trouble, suffering, or responsibility)!"

We live in a culture that is addicted to short-term pleasure and has often lost the ability to sacrifice for long term joy. Paul said that in the end times people would be "lovers of pleasure rather than lovers of God..." (2Timothy 3:4) God is all about pleasure, "at His right hand are pleasures forevermore" (Psalm 16:11), yet He is more concerned about the long term than the right now. This is a problem for us because we want pleasure now, and if we aren't having it we can be tempted to think that God has left us or is somehow mad at us because obviously, in our minds, "He's not blessing me now!"

Yet to become godly we will go through much suffering, internal and external, and often be called to sacrifice short term success in man's eyes for Christ's sake. We can resent this, or like Moses, we can by faith "see Him who is invisible" and choose to embrace ill treatment with the people of God rather than live for the passing pleasures of sin. (see Hebrews 11:25-27)

God does care about what we're going through. He cares so much that He will not short-change a process that He knows will lead to our long term joy.

October 6

Standing Firm in Your Faith

"If you do not stand firm in your faith, you will not stand at all." Isaiah 7:9b

News that Ephraim and Aram had joined forces to attack Judah resulted in king Ahaz being gripped with fear. The Bible says his heart was "...shaken, as the trees of the forest are shaken by the wind." (Isaiah 7:2) He would either stand firm in his faith, or he would fall – those were the only two options. In easier more peaceful times you can get by without really believing, but when everything is shaking around you, you either believe God, for real, or you become a victim of fear.

"Trust in the Lord with all your heart and lean not on your own understanding." (Proverbs 3:5) When our situation is confusing and intimidating we must lean on God directly, not on our understanding of the circumstances, or even on our understanding of God. He is able to make us stand in the storm, and after we have passed His test, is equally able to speak "peace, be still," to our situation. When He does the wind and waves of our circumstances will calm down, and we will see the deliverance of God. But it all starts with us standing in faith while everything still looks bad.

"Therefore put on the full armor of God, so that when the day of evil comes, you may be able to stand your ground, and after you have done everything, to stand. Stand firm then..." (Ephesians 6:13-14a) If God tells you to do something, do it, but after doing it, only "stand firm." Don't worry, don't strive, don't doubt, don't wrestle... just stand. Evil will take its swing at you and me, and God will allow it, but if we stand in our faith, it will come to nothing. Believe in God's promises; trust in His character; and then "stand still and see the salvation of the Lord on your behalf." (2Chronicles 20:17)

The Cave of Desolation

"Then he (Elijah) came to a cave and lodged there (Mt. Horeb); and behold, the word of the Lord came to him, and God said to him, 'What are you doing here, Elijah?' Elijah answered, 'I have been very zealous for the Lord, the God of hosts; for the sons of Israel have forsaken Your covenant, torn down Your altars and killed Your prophets with the sword. And I alone am left; and they seek my life, to take it away.'" 1Kings 19:9-10

For over three years Elijah had only gone where God specifically told him to go, but now he has run to Mt. Horeb on his own initiative. Horeb means "desolation," and Elijah was in a desolate place, not just geographically, but spiritually. God never sends us to a cave of desolation, but He will follow us when we end up there.

Have you ever been in this cave? Feeling isolated in your faith and feeling like all you have done is in vain? No one is getting saved; no one cares about God; in fact, they're getting worse right in front of your eyes. Have you ever felt like you've been diligent to do your part, but God has seemingly dropped the ball? How do we get out of the cave of desolation?

1. Get a fresh word from God. If we aren't hearing God it is easy to live under the voice of frustration, condemnation, despair, or anxiety. God took Elijah out on a ledge and spoke to him again in a gentle whisper. We all need to hear that gentle whisper of God's love and grace toward us again.

2. Get a fresh perspective. God tells Elijah that there are 7,000 in Israel who have not bowed down to Baal. (1Kings 19:18) Elijah's ministry has been way more fruitful than he knew. He isn't alone, there are a lot of people serving God with him, praying for him, and wanting the same revival he wants. The kingdom of God isn't losing, it's going forward, no matter how you and I may feel today.

3. Get a fresh assignment. The Lord says, "Go, return on your way to the wilderness...and you shall anoint Hazael...and Jehu...and Elisha...." (1Kings 19:15-16) God will take care of the big plan, but Elijah needs to keep doing his part. It's as if God is saying: "You don't have to change the whole world, just be filled with My Spirit and go to the people I send you to one at a time."

October 8

Hidden Treasure – Part I

"The kingdom of heaven is like a treasure hidden in the field, which a man found and hid again; and from joy over it he goes and sells all that he has and buys that field." Matthew 13:44

You can be in the field of church and seldom see the treasure that's hidden in it. Without seeing the treasure there will be little joy in your faith and your Christianity will seem more of a burden added to your life, than that which removes every burden and gives you joy. So what is the treasure and what hides it from our hearts?

The first treasure the gospel reveals is God's unconditional love for us, but it is hidden from those who have their identity in performance. It's very difficult for humans to grasp God's love because we are used to conditions. Paul says it would be rare for someone to die for a good man, but at least we can conceive of the possibility because a good person deserves to be loved. He goes on to explain God's love: "But God demonstrates His own love for us in this: while we were still sinners, Christ died for us." (Romans 5:6-8)

God doesn't just love everyone; He loves you. Whether you've been good or bad in man's eyes, He loves you. Whether you feel like a success or a continual failure, He loves you. And nothing you can do or fail to do can change that.

The prodigal son (Luke 15) represented the prostitutes, tax gatherers, and "sinners" who felt God would never want them near because of their bad performance. Even when the prodigal repented he planned on asking to be made a "hired man." The hired man made the wages of a slave but didn't live in the house. Yet when he returned he received an unexpected welcome and restoration to his father. The Father sees us, even when we're far away, and when we take a step toward Him, He runs toward us. Is it hard for you to believe that this is how emotional God is over you every time you try to draw near to Him? Ask Him to heal whatever is keeping you from believing in His love.

The older brother missed the party because he thought his good performance earned him something. He represented the Pharisees and Scribes who were listening and thought they were better than other people. Self-righteousness will keep you busy as a Christian, but it will prevent you from experiencing the Father's love and out of the party of His joy.

October 9

Hidden Treasure – Part II

"The kingdom of heaven is like a treasure hidden in the field, which a man found and hid again; and from joy over it he goes and sells all that he has and buys that field." Matthew 13:44

Yesterday we saw that the treasure of God's unconditional love is hidden from our experience when our identity is in our performance. The second treasure the gospel reveals is salvation in Christ, yet this remains hidden from our experience when we cling to unbelief.

Jesus said that the Holy Spirit would convict the world of their sin "because men do not believe in Me." (John 16:9) No one minds believing in the historical existence of Jesus or in the inspirational teaching and example He gave. What people struggle with is that He claims to be the Savior. (The name Jesus means savior)

To believe in Jesus as Savior means I'm not a good person who just needs a little instruction and encouragement. I am a sinner who needs saving. Really believing in Jesus means that I am no longer the hero in my own story which is why the self-righteous often persist in unbelief even when God has given them ample evidence that they are sinners.

Some people struggle with the simplicity of receiving salvation as a gift, yet this is the only way one can experience this treasure. "The wages of sin is death, but the gift of God is eternal life through Jesus Christ our Lord." (Romans 6:23) Think of someone who loves you and has bought you an expensive gift for your birthday. When they give it to you, you don't try to pay for it, do you? That would be an insult to the giver. You say, "thank you," and unwrap it and when they see you enjoying the gift they freely gave, it makes the price they paid worth it to them.

God saw our need and paid a very high price (the blood of Jesus) to get us an "indescribable gift" (2Corinthians 9:15) called eternal life. To own it we just have to admit we're sinners and receive it with the faith of a child. When we begin walking in the relationship that is included in this gift, we bring joy to the One who purchased it for us.

October 10

Hidden Treasure – Part III

"The kingdom of heaven is like a treasure hidden in the field, which a man found and hid again; and from joy over it he goes and sells all that he has and buys that field." Matthew 13:44

David said, "in Your presence is fullness of joy," (Psalm 16:11) and when he had sinned, prayed: "Cast me not away from Your presence and take not Your Holy Spirit from me. Restore to me the joy of Your salvation and sustain me with a willing spirit." (Psalm 51:11-12) God's presence restores the joy of truths we may not have believed for years. It takes the "have to" out of our faith, and turns it into a "want to". It makes our spirit "willing." Yet God will not force His people to value His presence.

In October of 2009 I had a dream where I was fighting a man with no face because he had stolen the tabernacle and I was trying to get it back. I was at the point of exhaustion when I finally knocked him out and then secured the suitcase that held the tabernacle. (Don't ask me how it fits in a suitcase!)

In the second scene of the dream the tabernacle was all set up and on a pallet waiting for a ship to come and pick it up. But there was a problem; the ark wasn't in it (the ark was where God's manifest presence dwelled). I was scurrying around trying to find where the ark was hidden, fearful that this enemy would soon wake up to fight again.

Then I had an idea. I called the ship that was coming and asked if they would pick up the tabernacle without the ark. They said they would. The last part of the dream was me hanging up the phone and thinking about the enemy, "He never would have guessed we'd sail without the ark."

In January of 2010 I was given the interpretation – the dream was about me. For years my vision was for genuine revival where God's Spirit would be poured out in such a way that people would see God and not man. Wherever I went, this was what I contended for.

But in Madison I had become tired. People had disappointed me, God hadn't done things I asked Him to do, and the responsibilities of ministry had taken a toll on me. I still talked the talk, but was in grave danger of settling for life and church without God's manifest presence.

This dream and its interpretation were just what I needed to get a new beginning. Isn't God good!

October 11

Is Your Calling Hard?

"Then I heard the voice of the Lord saying, 'whom shall I send? And who will go for us?' And I said, 'Here am I. Send me!' He said, 'Go and tell this to the people: be ever hearing, but never understanding; be ever seeing, but never perceiving. Make the heart of this people calloused; make their ears dull and close their eyes. Otherwise they might see with their eyes, hear with their ears, understand with their hearts and turn and be healed.'"
Isaiah 6:8-11

Is it hard to do what you do day in and day out? Do you ever find yourself growing weary and falling into self pity? I sure have. In times like these it's helpful to remember some of those who have gone before us.

Consider Isaiah's calling in the text above. Basically God is telling Isaiah that if he does exactly what God wants, and says exactly what God says, people will get worse. God is in essence saying: "They don't want the light so your ministry will actually make them harder but I want you to go to them anyway." Really? And I thought my calling was hard.

Consider Paul's calling. "Five times I received from the Jews the forty lashes minus one. Three times I was beaten with rods, once I was stoned, three times I was shipwrecked, I spent a night and a day in the open sea, I have been constantly on the move. I have been in danger from rivers, in danger from bandits, in danger from my own countrymen, in danger from Gentiles; I've been in danger in the city, in danger in the country, in danger at sea; and in danger from false brothers. I have labored and toiled and have often gone without sleep; I have known hunger and thirst and have often gone without food; I have been cold and naked. Besides everything else, I face daily the pressure of my concern for all the churches." (2Corinthians 11:24-28) Maybe my calling isn't that hard?

Consider David's calling. Psalm 54 was written by David when he was in the wilderness being chased by Saul and about to be betrayed by some of his own people, the Ziphites. This is the David who God had anointed king and had been called because his heart was after God's heart. At this point he had not disobeyed in any way, yet he is not only not king but is living day by day with an army chasing him down.

How is your life compared to these? It's amazing what a little perspective will do!

October 12

The Heartbeat of Missions

"I pray that the eyes of your heart may be enlightened, so that you will know what is the hope of His calling, what are the riches of the glory of His inheritance in the saints." Ephesians 1:18

The modern missions movement is often cited as beginning in 1732 when two Moravians by the names of Johann Dober and David Nitschmann were willing to sell themselves into slavery to reach the natives of the West Indies with the gospel. It wasn't their act of going that became the heartbeat of missions, it was why they were going. Why would they leave the comfort of their homes and families to go reach people they had never met?

It is said that they called out to their loved ones on shore as the ship pulled away, "May the Lamb that was slain receive the reward of His suffering!" It wasn't their love for humanity that called to them; or the fear that people would perish in hell if they weren't reached with the gospel; it was their burning love for Jesus.

The gospel promises forgiveness and eternal life for us, but the Father isn't just thinking of what we get; He's thinking about what His Son gets. He had promised Him in eternity that if He would be born as a son of man, He would be given the nations as His inheritance. (Psalm 2:7-8) Think of it: Jesus died and shed His blood for every human being that you know. If He got His full inheritance, everyone would worship Him, love Him, serve Him, and follow Him.

We all have loved ones we want to reach for the gospel because we want them to be with us in heaven. Maybe instead of praying God would save them for their sake, or for our sake, we should pray that the Father would draw them, so that the Lamb of God might receive the reward of His suffering!

October 13

Prolonging God's Discipline

"My son, do not make light of the Lord's discipline, and do not lose heart when He rebukes you, because the Lord disciplines those He loves and He punishes those He accepts. Endure hardship as discipline." Hebrews 12:6-7

God doesn't want to constantly discipline his children any more than earthly parents want to. He tells us in Psalm 32 He wants to guide us with only His eye, but He also assures us that He will use bit and bridle if He has to. Earthly parents tend to either under or over discipline, but our Father in heaven disciplines us perfectly for our good. (Hebrews 12:10)

What is often imperfect is our response which can lead to a prolonged discipline that was never intended. Here are two natural, but wrong responses to discipline:

1. "Do not make light of the Lord's discipline." We sometimes miss what God is trying to do in our lives, so we end up blaming people, the devil, or "bad luck" for something that God is trying to use to get our attention. Don't just plow through life; listen for what God is saying. He wants to use our unhappiness to drive us close to Him so He can make us holy. (Hebrews 12:10) He uses hardship to soften us and beautify us if we will let Him. If we keep running away from difficulties He wants us to face, He will just bring larger ones until we finally slow down and listen to Him.

2. "Do not lose heart when He rebukes you." God loves us so much that He won't let us go the wrong way without eventually intervening. If you think hardship is evidence that God has rejected you, you will become disabled by the very thing God intended for your healing. (Hebrews 12:13) When we believe the lie that God has rejected us, we end up on the disabled list and God waits for us to come back to Him like the father waited for the prodigal. When we doubt God's love, darkness keeps us from the intimacy and adventure that should be ours in Jesus.

Let's respond quickly to our Father and come out of the wilderness leaning on our Beloved. (Song of Songs 8:5)

October 14

Equipped with Peace

"Peace I leave with you; My peace I give you. I do not give to you as the world gives. Do not let your hearts be troubled and do not be afraid." John 14:27

The peace, or shalom (Hebrew) of Jesus, is vital equipment for the Christian life. It is to act as a guard for us, and as a thermostat for others.

1. A guard for us. "Do not be anxious about anything, but in everything, by prayer and petition, with thanksgiving, present your requests to God. And the peace of God, which transcends all understanding, will guard your hearts and minds in Christ Jesus." (Philippians 4:6-7) The world only gives you peace when all your troubles are solved. The peace Jesus gives is in the midst of troubles. His peace guards us from leading anxious lives that end up burning us out. This is not merely a positive attitude that things will get better, but a tangible presence that acts as a guard against fear and anxiety. We must grow in His peace; we must break the habit of living anxious, fearful lives and learn to practice His presence in the midst of the storm. We put clothes on every morning; let's not forget to put on the peace He has given us for a guard.

2. A thermostat for others. When Jesus said, "My peace...", I think the disciples remembered the power of His peace. When the storm was threatening their lives, Jesus stood and said, "Peace be still." Then the peace that allowed Jesus to sleep in the storm acted like a thermostat until the entire environment was as at peace as He was. The disciples were living as thermometers (a thermometer only reflects what is in the environment), like the world does, a storm outside had led to a storm of anxiety and fear inside their hearts to the point that they thought they would perish. When they reached the other side they met a demoniac who was so restless, not even chains could hold him. Once again, the peace of Jesus acted like a thermostat until the man came into his right mind and came to share the very peace of God. Think of it: "My peace I give to you."

To give peace, we must have peace. I don't know your circumstances today, but I do know that God wants to give you peace in the midst of them. He then wants us to be a portal of His peace to those around us so that the very atmosphere is filled with the presence of redemption.

October 15

Hungry in the Kingdom

"Of those born of women no one is greater than John the Baptist, but he who is least in the kingdom of heaven is greater than he. From John until now the kingdom of God suffers violence, and violent men take it by force."
Matthew 11:11–12

John the Baptist was marked by a spiritual hunger that was willing to do anything to live close to God. He lived in the desert separate from all the contaminating forces of this world. He embraced a life of simplicity and was committed to pleasing God and speaking what God wanted, even if it resulted in prison and death.

How could the least of us in the kingdom of God possibly be greater than John? John prepared the way for the kingdom but couldn't enter it himself. He lived under a covenant that could only restrain evil behavior but lacked power to redeem the human heart. Even though John had an anointed birth and led an exemplary life that made him the best there ever was under the old system, that system could only get him to the doorway of the kingdom of God.

The least person born into this kingdom immediately has greater privilege before God, and greater access to God than anyone in the Old Covenant could ever reach.

John approached God on the basis of the annual temple sacrifices of sheep, goats, and bulls while we approach the throne of grace with a confidence based on the once and for all sacrifice Jesus made of Himself. (Hebrews 10:19-22)

Isn't it tragic when we as Christians live as though we're still on the outside trying to get in? What if we combined confidence in what Jesus did for us, with the spiritual hunger of John? What if we lived hungry in the kingdom and used that hunger to easily access all those things that were out of John's reach? I think we'd change our world!

October 16

The Mystery of Giving

"You (Philippians) sent me aid again and again when I was in need. Not that I am looking for a gift, but I am looking for what may be credited to your account. I have received full payment and even more, I am amply supplied...Your gifts are a fragrant offering, an acceptable sacrifice, pleasing to God. And my God will supply all your needs according to His glorious riches in Christ Jesus." Philippians 4:16-19

We use giving boxes at our church instead of receiving offerings and rarely even talk about the importance of giving as part of our worship. It's our response to a culture where many believe the church just wants their money. God loves people and He doesn't want a system where anyone thinks you have to "pay" to stay in His grace.

Yet the self-sufficient God is mysteriously interested in our giving. He has placed, in giving, a number of incentives so His people will want to give freely to that which He values. Paul gives us three in the passage above:

1. We increase our heavenly account. "I am looking for what may be credited to your account." In Matthew 6:20 Jesus invites us to "store up for yourselves treasures in heaven" in the context of giving, not to be seen by men, but by the Father in heaven. You can't take money with you, but mysteriously, it seems we can send it ahead by investing in God's interests.

2. We please God by our sacrifice. "Your gifts are a fragrant offering, an acceptable sacrifice, pleasing to God." Money is real to us, and God knows it. For most of us, giving more to God's work means choosing for the present to have less stuff, or go on fewer vacations, or at least, having less in our retirement account. It is meaningful to God, a fragrant offering, when we choose to worship Him in this very tangible way.

3. We secure future provision. "God will supply all your needs according to His glorious riches in Christ." Although we make a present sacrifice, God is committed to being the only true Benefactor in His kingdom. Those who give do not need to fear, He Himself has resources to draw on and will see to it that all our needs are provided for. He encourages all of us to test Him in the area of tithing, for instance, and promises to "throw open the floodgates of heaven and pour out so much blessing that you will not have room enough for it." (Malachi 3:10)

October 17

Monopoly Money

"Naked a man comes from his mother's womb; and as he comes, so he departs. He takes nothing from his labor that he can carry in his hand."
Ecclesiastes 5:15

If you play Monopoly by the real rules a game should take about an hour. During that brief period Monopoly money has value – you can buy property, improve property, and pay your debts with its currency. But when the game is over you put everything away, put the box on the shelf, and there is no longer any worth in those dollars. It will be seen that the same is true of our money on planet earth.

Compared to eternity our time here is called a breath or a vapor. Money has value during this time and how we use it is one way God tests our hearts. Jesus said, "If you have not been trustworthy in handling worldly wealth who will trust you with true riches." (Luke 16:11) A few verses later He went on to say: "No servant can serve two masters. Either he will hate the one and love the other, or he will be devoted to the one and despise the other. You cannot serve both God and money." (Luke 16:13)

How do we pass God's money test?

1. Recognize we are stewards, not owners. We are to love God and use money; not love money while trying to use God.
2. We are to give back to God the first fruits of our income (Proverbs 3:9-10) which Scripture defines as a tithe or ten percent. (Genesis 14:20; Malachi 3:10-11)
3. We are to be willing to share in any good deed as God leads us. (2Corinthians 9:7-8)
4. As riches increase, we are to guard our hearts. (Psalm 62:10) Money is a useful servant but a terrible master.
5. We are to trust God as our Source and be thankful because He "richly provides us with everything for our enjoyment." (1Timothy 6:17)

October 18

Thinking Right

"But the Jews who refused to believe stirred up the Gentiles and poisoned their minds against the brothers." Acts 14:2

Belize and Mexico are two places I regularly go for missions trips and in both places you can't drink the tap water. It looks fine but is contaminated, so you can't drink it or you become sick. A few years ago our whole team got sick and it was traced back to a restaurant where they had cooked the chicken we ate in contaminated water. You only have to get sick once to become very careful about what you drink!

Are we as careful about our thoughts? In our text we have a group of Jews who "refused to believe" the good news of God's love and redemption through Christ and then poisoned others with their judgments. When we stop seeing ourselves and others as loved and worth redeeming, we tend to take up the enemy's accusations instead. (Revelation 12:10) This is poison. Satan sows suspicion and bitterness toward others in our minds if we let him, and he can even use us to divide homes, friends and churches. He knows that a kingdom divided will not stand and is the master at using poisonous thoughts to bring offense, isolation, envy, and jealousy.

The judgments we make appear to be "the truth," so we justify ourselves in thinking them and even speaking them, but judgment isn't the whole truth. God loves people and sent His Son into the world to save us, not to condemn us. (John 3:17) We overcome the accuser by testifying about the blood of the Lamb (Revelation 12:11) which was shed for us and for everyone we know. The whole truth, therefore, is not just what is wrong with people, but must include what God has done through His Son to make them right. (2Corinthians 5:19)

When the children of Israel came out of Egypt, they drank from a water source that was poisonous. Moses cried out to God, and God showed him a tree. (Exodus 15:25) He cut it down, threw it in the water, and it became sweet. God didn't show him a different place to drink that had pure water; He redeemed that which was bitter and made it sweet. He wants to do the same thing with our thinking. Why don't we identify our poison, bring it to the cross, and allow God to sweeten our thoughts toward even the most difficult sinners in our lives.

October 19

Is God Awakening the Muslim World?

"I revealed Myself to those who did not ask for Me; I was found by those who did not seek Me." Isaiah 65:1

A few years ago we had Tom Doyle speak at our missions conference. Tom has spent eleven years as a full-time missionary to the Middle East and has authored the book *Dreams and Visions: Is Jesus Awakening the Muslim World?* Below is one of the stories he relates in his book. My heart soars as I contemplate God's love for people and the measures He is willing to take.

Hassan had a heart for Muslims and had studied for years to reach them for Christ but the results were disappointing. He had lived in the old part of Cairo, Egypt for two years and although he talked about Christ daily, he had not seen a single convert. Early one morning he was abducted and taken against his will across rooftops to a hatch door that he was commanded to open. Hassan was praying the prayer of a martyr, "Jesus, into your hands I commit my spirit," but something extraordinary awaited him inside the foreboding room he entered.

The man who had kidnapped Hassan explained: "We are imams, and we all studied at Al-Azhar University. During our time there, each of us had a dream about Jesus, and each of us has privately become a follower of Christ. For a time, we didn't dare tell anyone about this. It would, of course, have been our own death sentences. But finally, we could hide it no longer.

"We each prayed to Jesus for His help to learn what it means to be His follower. Over time, He brought us together, and you can imagine our amazement when the Holy Spirit revealed that there are other imams who have found Jesus as well. Now we meet here three times a week at night to pray for our families and for the people in our mosques to find Jesus too. We know you follow Christ. He has led us to you.

"I'm very sorry I had to frighten you with the mask and the gun, but I knew it was the only way to get you here. It was just too dangerous any other way. I apologize. But now our question is, will you teach us the Bible?"

October 20

The Father's Joy

"He brought me out into a spacious place; He rescued me because He delighted in me." Psalm 18:19

David experienced the positive side of God's passion. Knowing this delight is the secret to great faith.

God's love and delight in me means that, of course, "The Lord who delivered me from the paw of the lion and the paw of the bear will deliver me from the hand of this Philistine." (1Samuel 17:37) Perfect love casts out all fear. (1John 4:18) Perfect love is not my love for God, it's His love for me. When this truth goes from being our theology to our identity, great faith is easy.

Yet this truth can be hard to grasp in our hearts, so Jesus gave us three stories in Luke 15 to explain the Father's joy in us. The Father is like a shepherd looking for a lost sheep. When he finds it there is great joy and this is how all of heaven feels when one sinner repents. God feels like the woman who searches for a lost coin of precious value (Notice that it doesn't lose its value because it's lost!). When she finds it, she rejoices, because that which was lost to her has been found.

And then He tells of an earthly father that runs to welcome back his prodigal son. Instead of reminding him of the hurt the son has caused, the father, in his joy, throws an extravagant party for him.

The prodigal thought it was all about his bad behavior so he planned on coming back as a hired man instead of as a son. (Luke 15:19) The older brother thought it was about his good behavior so he was confused as to why he hadn't received more, and was angry about his father's welcome of the prodigal. (Luke 15:29-30) But it's not about behavior; it's about relationship. God knows that apart from grace we can't be good, and that when we're in Christ we can't help but bear good fruit. (John 15:5)

The Father's joy is in you! Have you come into the party called grace or are you standing outside because of the shame of sin, or the self-righteousness of pride?

Say it to yourself: "I am God's delight. Not because I'm good, but because I'm His." This is not just our experience when we first receive forgiveness; this is our name, our very identity. Believe it!

October 21

The World's Mold

"Don't let the world around you squeeze you into its own mold, but let God re-mold your minds from within." Romans 12:2 Phillips Translation

I was in Belize sitting at a picnic table with six fifth grade boys. We had just done a drama of Samuel coming to Jesse's house to anoint the next king. Jesse didn't know which of his eight sons it would be but he had decided which son it wouldn't be. David, his youngest, wasn't even invited to the party because someone needed to stay with the sheep.

So the question I asked these fifth graders was: "Give a time when you felt left out, lonely, or rejected."

The boys spent a lot of time looking at each other, but no one would answer me, so I finally called on the one next to me. His answer was "never."

"Let me get this straight," I asked. "You've never felt lonely, left out, or rejected, in your whole life?"

Nope; and the funny thing was, as I made each answer, it turned out that none of them had ever felt lonely, left out, or rejected – amazing.

Then we moved on to the part of the story where God tells Samuel: "Do not consider his appearance or his height, for I have rejected him. The Lord does not look at the things people look at. People look at the outward appearance, but the Lord looks at the heart." (1Samuel 16:7)

"For instance," I told them, "God knows that every one of you lied to me a few minutes ago. You might be able to fool me and each other, but God sees your heart, and you can't fool him."

These weren't bad kids, they were just being squeezed by peer pressure to maintain a certain image so they didn't want to be vulnerable in front of each other. When our time was ending I asked them to close their eyes and put their heads down.

"God saw David when man didn't," I told them. "He saw that David wanted to please Him so God chose him and poured out the Holy Spirit on him. If you want to please God and have God pour His Spirit on you, I want you to lift up your head and look me in the eyes."

Do you know that every one of those six boys looked up without hesitation! They knew they had lied, but that's not who they wanted to be. They wanted to please God and knew they needed the Holy Spirit to help them do that. What a privilege it was to pray over each of them.

October 22

Idolizing Leaders

"For when one says, 'I am of Paul,' and 'I am of Apollos,' are you not mere men? What then is Apollos? And what is Paul? Servants through whom you believed, even as the Lord gave opportunity to each one. I planted, Apollos watered, but God was causing the growth. So then neither the one who plants nor the one who waters is anything, but God who causes the growth." 1Corinthians 3:4-7

We are in danger of erring in two ways in our attitude toward those leading us. We can dishonor them and lose the benefit God wanted to bring through them, or we can idolize them and lose the benefit God wanted to bring through other leaders who are different from them. Let's look at the second one today.

Paul says that when we identify with only one leader and set Christian leaders in some type of a contest against each other, we are acting like mere men. God has called us to the high calling of favored sons or daughters who are carriers of God's own presence. We are the very temple of God! (2Corinthians 6:16) Yet when we reduce Christianity to our favorite speaker we have missed the whole point.

To say you follow Paul instead of Apollos means that you are missing out on what God wanted to give you through Apollos. From God's perspective, Paul, Apollos, and Cephas (Peter) belong to you; they were raised up and anointed for your benefit so you could come into fullness. To choose one over another or exalt one over another is to miss what the other one was supposed to bring to your life.

To idolize a leader is to set them up for a fall. A few years ago a man was set up as the greatest prophet in America so much so that it was thought he didn't even need to be part of a local church. He would come from his place of being alone with God and tell us the word of the Lord and we honored his unique place; many times in an idolatrous way. He succumbed to an addiction to alcohol and also was found to be involved in sexual sin. Would this have happened if we had prayed for him more instead of idolizing him? I don't know.

What I do know is that at the end of the day those who plant and water, however gifted they may be, are nothing, but only instruments that help you grow in the grace of God. Honor leaders, receive from leaders, but please don't idolize them. It puts them at greater risk and it keeps you from seeing the reason for their existence.

October 23

Right Leadership

"Peter asked, 'Lord, are you telling this parable to us, or to everyone?' The Lord answered, 'Who then is the faithful and wise manager, whom the master puts in charge of his servants to give them their food allowance at the proper time? It will be good for that servant whom the master finds doing so when he returns.'" Luke 12:41-43

Many in the church today have been hurt by leaders. Leaders have at times abused their God given authority by manipulating, profiting, abusing, and/or politicizing instead of serving. This has created a response of cynicism in many Christians and has caused some to question whether we even need leaders other than Jesus Himself.

In the text above Jesus has just warned people that He's coming back unexpectedly like a thief in the night, so they need to live ready. Peter is asking who the parable is directed towards – is this for the leaders, or for the general public? Jesus then applies what He has said specifically to the leadership; those He's putting "in charge."

The first thing I want to point out in our text is that Jesus says God is going to put some people "in charge." The church Jesus is building has elders in it who are responsible for the care of His people.

Just because someone has been hurt by leadership in the past doesn't mean they get a lifetime pass from being part of a local church. People need to learn how to forgive, and if necessary, find a different fellowship where they can trust, serve, and be fruitful in. Why do you think God tells people who are sick to call for the elders of the church? (James 5:14) I think it's because when people are desperate and nothing else is working, they become willing to do anything, even making their attitude right toward leadership who has offended them. God doesn't just want your body healed, He wants His body healed.

The second thing we observe in our text is that the manager who is put in charge of the servants is also called a servant himself. He/she is called to serve the master by serving the other servants and giving them their food at the proper time.

Leadership is for the purpose of servanthood, not entitlement. May God raise up leaders in this hour who are willing to wash the feet of those who are under their care.

October 24

Profitable Lives

"What will it profit a man to gain the whole world and forfeit his soul?"
Matthew 16:26

God wants us to see the big picture and give ourselves to those things that will ultimately lead to our own profit. So what will lead us to a profitable life before God and man? Here are four observations from the passage in Matthew 16 where the verse above is taken from.

1. It involves a revelation of who Jesus is. "Blessed are you, Simon son of Jonah, for this was not revealed to you by man, but by My Father in heaven." (Matthew 16:17) The foundation of a profitable life is Jesus Christ. Building your life on anything else will eventually be revealed as sinking sand.

2. It involves a personal cross. "If anyone would come after me he must deny himself and take up his cross and follow Me." (Matthew 16:24) Thank God that Jesus went to the cross for us, and made the payment for our sins required by a holy God. But that doesn't change the fact that each of us will have a personal cross and a Gethsemane where we will either choose to trust God in the midst of our pain, or turn from God and reject His purpose for us. Joni Erickson Tada said: "Sometimes God allows what He hates to accomplish what He loves." This sounds like a good definition of the cross.

3. It involves freedom from self preservation. "Whoever wants to save his life will lose it but whoever loses his life for Me will find it." (Matthew 16:25) Don't try to make your own life; grab a hold of Jesus and He will make you exactly who you were originally designed to be.

4. It involves a process. "Get behind me, Satan! You are a stumbling block to Me; you do not have in mind the things of God, but the things of men." (Matthew 16:23) Shortly after Jesus speaks into Peter's destiny, Peter must be rebuked for going the wrong way, a way that came naturally to him. We must accept the fact that our natural way of thinking is often wrong. This is not a one time event, but a way of life for a disciple. Jesus wasn't discouraged with Peter. He was only keeping His promise to him: "Follow Me and I will make you..." He makes the same promise to you and me.

October 25

The Role of Mordecai

"If you remain silent at this time, relief and deliverance will arise for the Jews from another place, but you and your father's family will perish. And who knows but that you have come to a royal position for such a time as this?" Esther 4:14 (Esther's uncle Mordecai is the one who gave her this message.)

Without Mordecai the story of Esther becomes a tragedy because Esther is so much like us. News comes about Haman's plot to destroy the Jews and Esther feels bad about it and even wishes she could do something about it, but "any man or woman who approaches the king in the inner court without being summoned by the king has but one law: that he be put to death." (Esther 4:11) Esther is saying in essence what many of us believe about ourselves: "I'm sorry that the world is going to hell, but circumstances are such that I can't do anything about it right now. Wish I could, but I can't." Without Mordecai, Esther probably would have done nothing, wouldn't have become a heroine, and most likely, there wouldn't even be a book of Esther.

Think for a moment about the role of Mordecai. He's the one who calls Esther to fulfill her God ordained destiny. He's the one who encourages her to risk her life and promises to fast with her as she steps way out of her comfort zone. Because of his encouragement, she moves from an attitude of self-preservation to a willingness to lay her life down. The one who initially says, "I can't," now says I'll try and "if I perish, I perish." (Esther 4:16)

We are called to be Mordecai to the people in our lives. We are to see their destinies and to speak into them. We're to encourage them to take risks and to know that God loves them and will help them. We're to pray and fast for others, so they will seize the day and not let their lives pass by with the regret of never doing anything heroic to help those around them.

October 26

The Glove

"I am crucified with Christ and it is no longer I who live but Christ who lives in me. The life I live in this body I live by faith in the Son of God who loved me and gave Himself for me." Galatians 2:20

A few years ago at a men's conference, a speaker told of a Sunday school teacher he had when he was in middle school. This teacher used magician's tricks to keep the students' attention, so everyone was intrigued the day he brought in a magic glove and declared that the glove was able to pick up the Bible.

He laid the glove on the Bible and started saying magic words but it didn't work; the glove did nothing. What's wrong? He picked up the glove and looked it over, put it back on the Bible, said the magic words, but once again, nothing. What's wrong with this glove?

Finally, he took the glove, turned it around and put it on, said the magic words and lo and behold, the glove picked up the Bible. One of the kids in the class was not impressed: "Do you think we're stupid?" he asked. Everyone in the class recognized that even though the glove did pick up the Bible, it wasn't really the work of the glove. It was all about the hand inside the glove.

Then the teacher read Galatians 2:20 and explained that we are the glove and Jesus is the hand inside the glove. We are powerless to live the Christian life on our own, but if we will identify our lives with Jesus' crucifixion and resurrection, and then trust Him day by day, He will live in us and make all things possible.

The speaker went on to say we would hear many things during the day about how we could be better Christians, better fathers, and better husbands which would make us feel worse than we already did unless we remember the hand in the glove. The Christian life isn't about us trying to live like Jesus, it's about Jesus living His life in and through us.

October 27

Dealing with Differences

"'Master,' said John, 'we saw a man driving out demons in Your Name and we tried to stop him, because he is not one of us.' 'Do not stop him,' Jesus said, 'for whoever is not against you is for you.'" Luke 9:49-50

When I first came to Christ, I was part of a church that believed we were the only pure expression of Christianity in our city. Every sermon featured some way we were better than everyone else. We only used the King James Bible, for instance, and believed every other translation was defiled and leading people into heresy. We were "it," and everyone else was deceived at some level.

Looking back, I feel sadness for how proud and blind we were; not just about ourselves, but about who God is. We had made the God of all grace so small and picky that if you didn't believe exactly like we did you were on the outside. The truth is that we were small and picky, not God.

John is clearly proud of his rebuke of this man who wasn't, "one of us." Jesus had a wider circle of those who are with Him.

People come to me with accusations against Christian leaders across the body of Christ. Sometimes it's about what a leader said and sometimes it's about something questionable they did. I'm almost always in agreement with those who are bringing the charge, leaders are flawed and often say things and do things that are a little off. But once in a while the person bringing the accusation wants more than agreement, they want me to publicly renounce that leader and their group.

At this point I become a disappointment to them. Jesus is not ashamed to call me His brother (Hebrews 2:11) with all of my flaws and errors, so I want to be unashamed to stand next to brothers and sisters who love Jesus, but aren't just like our group.

I understand and value the desire for truth and the need to be on guard against deception, but we must be very careful before pointing the finger at others lest we condemn someone who Jesus accepts and delights in. May God help us be humble and generous toward all those who are different from us. "Accept one another," Paul says to Christians who were judging each other over minor differences, "just as Christ has accepted you." (Romans 15:7)

October 28

Believing God

"Against all hope, Abraham in hope believed and so became the father of many nations, just as it had been said to him, 'So shall your offspring be.' Without weakening in his faith, he faced the fact that his body was as good as dead-since he was about a hundred years old-and that Sarah's womb was also dead. Yet he did not waver through unbelief regarding the promise of God, but was strengthened in his faith and gave glory to God, being fully persuaded that God had power to do what he had promised." Romans 4:18-21

There's a difference between believing in God and believing God. Let's look at Abraham's process of believing God, so we can learn how to believe God as well.

He heard from God. "So shall your offspring be," was a reference to Abraham gazing at the stars and hearing the voice of God. This is the beginning of faith – God speaking. (Romans 10:17)

He faced his circumstances. He was a hundred years old, and Sarah was barren – it would take a miracle. All human hope of the promise coming true was extinguished; it would take direct intervention from God. Faith never asks us to live in denial of our circumstances, but it often does ask us to believe God in spite of them.

He kept believing. The beginning of faith is exciting, but what if what was promised doesn't happen right away? "He did not waver through unbelief." He didn't but he could have. He could have questioned whether God had really spoken at all, or whether He really meant what He said. He could have thought of all the others who had prayed and didn't seem to be answered. It's easy to waver through unbelief. He chose to believe God and to keep believing God.

What has God promised you? If nothing, then get into His word and ask Him what He has for you. Position your life to hear the whispers of the Holy Spirit and you'll be surprised at how alive Jesus is today. When He speaks, I encourage you to go from believing in God to believing God. Whether it's for salvation, healing, restoration, provision, or a direction He's leading you in. Time in His word and in His presence will purify our thoughts, so we can know the difference between what God is actually speaking and what we are only imagining. Take what is truly of God and believe Him for the great things He wants to do in us, for us, and through us.

October 29

Generations Coming Together

The company of the prophets said to Elisha, "Look, the place where we meet with you is too small for us. Let us go to the Jordan, where each of us can get a pole; and let us build a place there for us to meet." And he said, "Go." Then one of them said, "Won't you please come with your servants?" "I will," Elisha replied. And he went with them. 2Kings 6:1-3

Every year, Alice and I go to our National Conference where we hear a number of speakers. The final message of last year's conference was from the above text. The first message of this year's conference was also from this exact text. Can you imagine how we felt when the second night's message this year was also from 2Kings 6:1-7? Three straight speakers all speaking from the same obscure text! Only God could arrange this, so the question becomes, why? I think it has to do with the generations coming together.

Here are three encouragements for the older generation:

1. Have something to give from God that the younger generation needs. Elisha had burned his plow and pressed in for a double anointing which he had received from Elijah. The younger generation doesn't need information from us – they can just Google to get that. But Google can't supply the wisdom that comes from an ongoing relationship with God. We must keep pressing in for all God has for us to be "relevant" to the generations behind us. They asked Elisha to come because they needed what he had.

2. Release the younger generation to go beyond where we've been. The idea to build bigger came from the young prophets. The place they were currently living in was probably built by Elisha and now it wasn't good enough. Instead of being offended, Elisha releases them to do something more than he'd done. King Saul had become jealous of the next generation and feared they would be greater than he was, so he tried to kill David. Elijah believed that God could take His anointing and double it in the next generation – let's believe as well and release the coming generation into even more grace than we've experienced.

3. We need to go with the next generation to ensure their success. In their zeal, mistakes are made, but Elisha was there to show them that every problem is actually an opportunity to encounter the faithfulness and power of God.

October 30

The Narrow Way

"I am the way, the truth, and the life; no one comes to the Father except through Me." John 14:6

Alice and I were flying back from a conference in New York a few years ago, and the lady across the aisle was flipping through index cards, so I asked her what she was doing.

"I'm learning to speak German," she said. "My son married a German woman and we're going over to Germany soon for her ordination as a Lutheran pastor."

She was more than willing to talk, so I asked about her own background and found out she was raised Southern Baptist but had since become a Unitarian.

"As I grew intellectually I realized that all religions were equally sincere and therefore, equally true," she explained.

So I asked her about the resurrection, and she said she wasn't sure about it and didn't know if anyone could be. I gave her a couple of historical arguments for Jesus' resurrection and then asked her to rethink her premise of "sincerity" being the proof of truth. We know that in mathematics one plus one equals two and that it doesn't matter how sincerely someone may think it's three – there's only one right answer. Truth, by definition, is narrow. If Jesus rose from the dead then He was who He said He was, and if so, He is the only way to God.

At this point the man in front of me turned around and asked me to keep my voice down because it was "projecting." I finished talking with the woman, trying to keep my voice down, by sharing C.S. Lewis' *Liar, lunatic, or Lord* argument. We don't have the intellectual option of believing Jesus was a good man, or even a great prophet. Jesus claimed to be God in the flesh so He was either a liar, He knew He was just a man so lied about being God; a lunatic, He really thought He was God but wasn't; or He was and is Lord of all.

At this we finished our conversation and after a minute of silence, I felt a tug on my sleeve from the man directly behind me. When I turned around, he told me he wished that our conversation had lasted for two more hours.

Some believe, some don't believe, and some aren't sure what they believe. But the truth stands on its own regardless of how people react to it. The sun still exists on a cloudy day whether we believe in it or not!

October 31

Give Thanks

"In everything give thanks, for this is God's will for you in Christ Jesus."
1 Thessalonians 5:18

Many times we aren't sure what God's perfect will is for a situation, so we waver between one direction and another. "God, couldn't you speak more clearly so that I would know for sure?" Well, this passage is crystal clear and it's right in the word of God; "In everything give thanks, for this is God's will..." The interesting thing about God's will is that it is not as much about what we do, as it is about how we do what we do. Listen to this verse: "And whatever you do in word or deed, do all in the name of the Lord Jesus, giving thanks through Him to God the Father." (Colossians 3:23) Whatever you do! Praying, eating, playing, watching football, shopping.... whatever.

Our text doesn't say "for everything," evil does happen, but rather, "in everything." How can we thank God in every single circumstance we are in?

We can always thank Him for His love which endures forever. God loves you and me right now no matter what we're going through! How wonderful is that?

We can thank Him that He is in control. However bad things may seem, everything that is happening has at least been allowed by God and has not surprised Him. We can thank Him for always having a plan for good no matter how badly we have messed things up. (Jeremiah 29:11) We can thank Him for His wisdom which is able to work "all" things for our good. (Romans 8:28) He will use our trials (self inflicted or God ordained) to make us complete and content in Christ alone. (James 1:2-4)

No matter what is going on we can thank Him that our real life is, "hidden with Christ in God," (Colossians 3:1) and that our real home is in heaven. We can thank Him for the forgiveness of our sins and for His guiding presence in our future. We can thank Him for the cross, and that whatever hardship we are going through is nothing compared to what He went through for us. We can thank Him for being good, for being our Father, for being our Savior – for being our everything. As the Psalmist has said, "Oh give thanks to the Lord, for He is good; for His loving-kindness is everlasting." (Psalm 107:1)

November 1

Emotionally Content

"There is a time for everything, and a season for every activity under heaven...He has made everything beautiful in its time. He has also set eternity in the hearts of men; yet they cannot fathom what God has done from beginning to end." Ecclesiastes 3:1, 11 NIV

I want to learn how to enjoy the season that I am currently experiencing instead of fighting it. Why is it so easy to pine over what once was, or to long for a future that is different than my life right now? God has made right now beautiful if I'm willing to see it. He has you and me where we are right now. Can we agree with Him in our emotions and even learn to enjoy this season? Or do we fight with God, advise God, disagree with God, and basically go against the grain of the season we're in with the slivers to prove it? Jesus said to Saul, "It is hard for you to kick against the goads." (Acts 26:14)

We can't fathom the whole of what God is doing in our lives and because of that we aren't capable of judging how the present season fits. Why not trust God and get into the flow of what He is doing? Maybe you're like me, frustrated by your seeming lack of control over what happens in your circumstances. If we surrender our need for control we are free to trust the One who really is in control. Easier said than done, but it's only when we truly let go that we experience His peace. Here's His promise to us in Philippians 4:6-7: "Be anxious for nothing, but in everything by prayer and supplication with thanksgiving let your requests be made known to God. And the peace of God, which surpasses all comprehension, will guard your hearts and your minds in Christ Jesus."

Whether you are old or young, married or single, employed or unemployed, in school or out of school, happy or sad, on the top or on the bottom... whatever your life is like right now, I challenge you to find God's beauty in it and to be at peace.

November 2

Taking Time to Give Thanks

"Now one of them, when he saw that he had been healed, turned back, glorifying God with a loud voice, and he fell on his face at His feet, giving thanks to Him. And he was a Samaritan. Then Jesus answered and said, 'Were there not ten cleansed? But the nine - where are they?'" Luke 17:15-17

We glorify God when we recognize what He has done for us by giving thanks. God's not looking for a repayment which would be impossible, but He is looking for our sincere thanks for the good things He does for us. How sad that Jesus would have to ask, "The nine – where are they?" Why didn't they come back and thank Jesus? Probably for some of the same reasons you and I don't spend more time giving thanks.

1. Maybe they were too busy. Now that they received their healing there were a hundred things they needed to do. They needed to return to their families; they needed to look for work; they needed to make up for lost time. Thanksgiving is a simple thing but it does take time which is a precious commodity. Make it a priority to devote time every day to just stop and give thanks to God.

2. Maybe they had a chip on their shoulder. "God owes me..." When we feel like God owes us anything we start taking His blessings as payments for our devotion and service instead of that which He has freely given us out of His love and grace. Maybe the nine were angry at God because of their leprosy so when they were healed it didn't produce gratefulness, but more like, "it's about time." It is good to remember that God owes you and me nothing. "Who has first given to Him that it might be paid back to him again?" (Romans 11:35)

3. Maybe they were overly focused on themselves. When our lives are all about us we miss the big picture and fall into the delusion that we are independent. Remember, every breath we draw comes from the God who made us, and we continue to exist only due to His mercy. He's the sun we orbit around, so we need to be careful not to make ourselves the middle. There is no greater use of the breath He has lent us than to give thanks back to God.

November 3

The Sacrifice of Thanksgiving

"He who sacrifices thank offerings honors Me, and he prepares the way so that I may show him the salvation of God." Psalm 50:23

Sometimes it's a sacrifice to give thanks. Maybe it's because things aren't going well right now, or because God hasn't done the big thing you're asking Him to do. Yet the word of God encourages us to give thanks even when we're not in the mood, and it still honors Him. My number one defense against discouragement is thanksgiving. When I find myself down I will recount God's blessings starting with salvation, then family, health, job, and every blessing I can think of. It's difficult to be both depressed and thankful at the same time.

Thanksgiving brings us quickly into God's Presence. "I will enter His gates with thanksgiving in my heart..." (Psalm 100:4) No wonder our sacrifice of thanksgiving prepares the way for God's salvation. Think about human relationships. Isn't it easy to give to a thankful person and hard to give to someone who takes you and your gifts for granted? I think it's the same way for God. He encourages us to pray when we are anxious about anything and "with thanksgiving, present your requests to God." (Philippians 4:6) Before we have even received what we are praying for, we are to give thanks. For what? How about for the last time God answered your prayer, or for who God is and that He even cares about our needs, or for the promises He has given that we can believe and pray back to Him as we ask.

The word says that after we turn our anxiety into prayer with thanksgiving, "the peace of God which transcends all understanding, will guard your hearts and your minds in Christ Jesus." (Philippians 4:7) I wonder if thanksgiving is the key to breaking through to peace. Prayer without thanksgiving can actually just be worrying in front of God. Thanksgiving brings in an element of faith and victory even if we haven't seen the answer yet.

November 4

Preparing the Way

"He who sacrifices thank offerings honors Me, and he prepares the way so that I may show him the salvation of God." Psalm 50:23

It is easy to give to a grateful person and difficult to give to one that takes what you do for granted. Many years ago now our great Aunt Ruth decided to disperse some of her enormous estate. From the money she gave her sister, our grandmother, $100 was sent to me and to each one of my five siblings. I had never met Aunt Ruth but I was very excited about the $100 because at the time I was a broke college student. With the money there was a note from my mom that said to be sure to send Aunt Ruth a thank you note.

I was thankful and certainly planned on sending a note, but it just never happened. Sometimes stopping to say thank you is just unintentionally forgotten because of our busy lives that are always rushing to the next thing. Well it turns out that none of my siblings ended up sending Aunt Ruth a thank you note either, except for my sister Sheila. Sheila didn't just send a note, she wrote a letter, detailing what she was doing with the generous gift sent to her. A month later, Sheila received a second check for $100 directly from Aunt Ruth. None of the rest of us got one. We certainly didn't deserve a second check, in fact, we hadn't deserved the first one.

And that's how it is with God's blessings as well. Sometimes I think it helps to remember that we are owed nothing, and that every blessing that comes to us is because of God's generous love. He doesn't want us to live in guilt because of His gifts, but He does want us to be thankful. The only sacrifice a thank offering requires is the time it takes to stop and reflect on our blessings. It won't only honor God, it also prepares the way for His continued blessings.

November 5

Living in the Party

"The older brother became angry and refused to go in. So his father went out and pleaded with him. But he answered his father, 'Look! All these years I've been slaving for you and never disobeyed your orders. Yet you never gave me a young goat so I could celebrate with my friends." Luke 15:28-30

There is a party going on, but the older brother refused to enter it because it wasn't the party he wanted. There are people at the party, but not the friends he would have chosen to be there. He has become a victim of his own sense of entitlement and is now alone in the isolation of self-pity.

In His great love the Father has thrown an extravagant party for the human race called "grace." Through Christ's death and resurrection, we can experience forgiveness of sins, new life, the assurance of heaven when we die, and a present fellowship with the Holy Spirit no matter what circumstances we're living in.

But often this isn't good enough for us! We want God to prove His love by doing certain things and healing or saving certain people ("my friends") within the time frame we've given Him. We can feel like we deserve this because we've been faithful and obedient, prayed and believed "right," or because we go to church regularly and even give money.

We don't try to be ungrateful, entitlement just creeps up on us and makes us feel like we're somehow being cheated. Then we find ourselves, even as Christians who love God, living outside of the party.

The father is not put off by the older brother's self-pity. He goes out to him and reminds him of all the blessings that are his: "My son, you are always with me, and everything I have is yours." He explains that the party he's throwing is not an endorsement of the prodigal's sin, but a celebration of redemption. "We had to celebrate and be glad, because this brother of yours was dead and is alive again; he was lost and is found."

"We" are supposed to be celebrating; God and us, because of the grace He has lavished on us and on all who repent and believe in Christ. Are you missing the party God's throwing because it isn't exactly the party you wanted? Why not surrender your expectations to God, lay down that sense of entitlement that comes from self-righteousness, and enter fully into the celebration of God's grace today?

November 6

A Sign to Examine

"He has fixed a day in which He will judge the world in righteousness through a Man whom He has appointed, having furnished proof to all men by raising Him from the dead." Acts 17:31

Usually in church we are called to believe in our hearts something that we can't see with our eyes. But there is one case where God encourages us to examine something we can see with the logic of our minds – the resurrection. God has "furnished proof" that Jesus is the judge of all mankind by raising Him from the dead.

In John 2 Jesus clears the temple and the religious leaders ask, "What sign do you show us as your authority for doing these things?" (John 2:18) The only person on earth that might have authority to move temple furniture around was the high priest. Outside of him, only God himself would have that kind of authority. "Who do you think you are?" is what they're asking. Jesus answered, "Destroy this temple, and in three days I will raise it up." (John 2:19) The sign He gave of His authority was the resurrection. In Matthew 12 again He is asked for a sign but replies that no sign will be given except the sign of His death and resurrection as prefigured in the story of Jonah. (Matthew 12:39-40)

Paul says that all of Christianity hinges on the actual, historical resurrection of Jesus. "If Christ has not been raised, your faith is futile; you are still in your sins... if only for this life we have hope in Christ, we are to be pitied more than all men." (1Corinthians 15:17-19) I've heard people say that they'd be a Christian "even if it wasn't true." Paul wouldn't be. He's only in if it's true and to him it's true because of a historical proof that God gave. Paul didn't believe in Jesus because he was afraid he'd go to hell if he didn't, and he didn't ultimately believe because of the subjective encounter he had on the road to Damascus. He believed because it was the truth; not just his truth, but everyone's. The evidence is the resurrection.

November 7

What Happened?

What has happened to all your joy?" Galatians 3:15

Joy is a good measure of our Christianity because true joy is only found in the presence of God. (Psalm 16:11) Apparently the early joy the Galatian church experienced had faded. In the text above, Paul is bringing this fact to their attention so he can get to the source of the problem.

They were still living; they were still religious; and maybe even still zealous for the faith, but the joy was gone. What happened? Have you ever been there? Still doing what you're supposed to be doing, but over time, losing the heartfelt energy that comes from the joy of the Lord?

Paul identifies the freedom the gospel brings as the source of releasing God's joy, and the loss of that freedom as the block to it. Jesus came to free them from the slavery of a performance identity, so they could know what it is to be the beloved children of God. (Galatians 4:6-7)

They knew this joy once but are now being seduced by teachers who are preaching a different gospel. The gospel these teachers are promoting makes more sense because it involves them keeping more rules and "earning their keep" instead of the free gift of grace through faith alone. Paul exposes the deception and calls them to return to the true gospel and to stand firm in it. The central verse of Galatians is chapter five, verse one: "It was for freedom that Christ set you free. Stand firm therefore in your freedom and do not be enslaved again by a yoke of bondage."

Do you know you're a beloved child of God with the full rights of an heir of God? (Galatians 4:6) If you understand the gospel correctly it should make you laugh. Paul says that we, like Isaac (whose name means laughter), were born of a promise. (Galatians 4:28) Sinners deserving death were saved, not by any work of their own, but just by believing God's love and promise to us in Christ!

May God restore to each of us the joy of our salvation and may that joy overflow to all those who are around us every day.

November 8

Who Inherits?

"Get rid of the slave woman and her son, for the slave woman's son will never share in the inheritance with the free woman's son." Galatians 4:30

You cannot earn as a reward what is yours by inheritance, so when we go back to performing for God, the benefits of grace dry up. The Old Covenant, the slave woman, only blesses those who keep the law. Because no one can keep the law, all of her children become slaves of the fear and guilt which come from never being good enough.

Paul is stunned that the Galatians are allowing anyone to seduce them back into a performance identity because the fruit is so bad. "You foolish Galatians, who has bewitched you... are you so foolish? Having begun by the Spirit, are you now being perfected by the flesh?... Does He who provides you with the Spirit and works miracles among you, do it by the works of the Law, or by the hearing of faith?" (Galatians 3:1-4)

In Luke 15 Jesus tells us about the older brother who becomes angry at the Father's generosity toward the prodigal: "Look! All these years I've been slaving for you and never disobeyed your orders. Yet you never gave me even a young goat so I could celebrate with my friends." Listen to the Father's response, not just to the older brother, but to all His children who are living like slaves in His house: "My son, you are always with me and everything I have is yours."

Did you know that in Christ you have an abundant inheritance as a favored child of God? "Because you are sons, God sent the Spirit of His Son into our hearts who calls out, 'Abba, Father.' (you are always with me) So you are no longer a slave but a son; since you are a son, God has made you also an heir." (and everything I have is yours) (Galatians 4:7)

"So why don't I feel like an heir?" you may ask. Maybe it's because you haven't once and for all put away the performance identity. Maybe you've been seduced in your heart and are still trying to perform for God's approval instead of accepting it by faith. It's time to take decisive action and "get rid of the slave woman and her son!"

I am so ready to walk in favored son status instead of being a slave to performance. How about you?

November 9

No Compromise

"Do not seal up the words of the prophecy of this book, because the time is near. Let him who does wrong continue to do wrong; let him who is vile continue to be vile; let him who does right continue to do right; and let him who is holy continue to be holy." Revelation 22:10–11

Why is God telling those who do wrong to continue to do wrong? Shouldn't He tell them to repent? He's not writing to those who are in the world in this book, but to "His servants" (Revelation 1:1) who are living in a culture of compromise and will be tempted to backslide.

The message of this passage could be paraphrased like this: "Don't plan on the people around you changing – they might not. Instead, make sure you don't change and give in to the culture of compromise around you. Be separate in your desire and make sure the pursuit of your life is different from the worldly people around you."

This text is from the last chapter of the New Testament and is amazingly close to another passage in the last book of the Old Testament. "'They will be mine', says the Lord Almighty, 'on the day when I make up My treasure possession. I will spare them, just as in compassion a man spares his son who serves him. And you will again see the distinction between the righteous and the wicked, between those who serve God and those who don't.'" (Malachi 3:17-18)

Whatever else you do, choose to live holy before the God who saved you and before the generation around you. Make sure you don't just believe differently, but actually live differently. Anything less is deception.

November 10

A Tale of Two Cities - Part I

"For those who say such things make it clear that they are seeking a country of their own. And indeed if they had been thinking of that country from which they went out, they would have had the opportunity to return. But as it is, they desire a better country, that is, a heavenly one. Therefore God is not ashamed to be called their God; for He has prepared a city for them." Hebrews 11:14-16

Once upon a time there was a city called "Worldly Values" where people were born and lived until the time came when they died and were thrown off the precipice. It was a beautiful and exciting city with many pleasures, especially for those who were young. You see, everyone born in this city started on one side and were forced to move their tents across the city year by year, until they were near the precipice that overlooked the chasm of fire.

The rules of the city prevented anyone from moving their tent away from the precipice. You could look back, but you could never move back, which was why so many took pictures. Pictures helped them remember the early days when the city gave great promises of abundant life. The pictures also helped to keep their minds off of the precipice they were constantly moving toward.

There's another city called, "Eternal Joy," rumored to be on the other side of the chasm. I say rumored because there is a great fog which lies over the chasm of fire so it's usually impossible to see over to the other side. A few have had glimpses through the centuries, however, and have reported seeing a city of pure gold where everyone lives forever.

The clearest testimony of this city came years ago when the king of Eternal Joy had a son born in the city of Worldly Values. This son made a path during his brief life which he said would lead anyone who chose it to the city of Eternal Joy. When he was pushed off the precipice after his tragic death, it is rumored that he rose again, and then built a bridge from Worldly Values, over the chasm of fire, into Eternal Joy.

Some are sure that people who take this path never have to die. They don't have to live looking back like the rest do, because the best for them is yet to come.

Whenever someone chooses to stay on this path, they never really fit into the society of Worldly Values again. It's as if they're citizens of Eternal Joy before even arriving in the city.

November 11

A Tale of Two Cities – Part II

"Enter through the narrow gate; for the gate is wide and the way is broad that leads to destruction, and there are many who enter through it. For the gate is small and the way is narrow that leads to life, and there are few who find it." Matthew 7:13-14

Many began on the narrow path the king's son had made but then became discontent. Some began to doubt if this was really the right path because they were sure that the right path would be easy, yet the son's path had many turns in it as well as high mountains and dangerous valleys.

Others didn't like the humility required to stay on the son's path. They wanted to make their own way and have their own following. Many set out on their own and took others with them often with promises of pleasure and wealth people could have "right here" in Worldly Values.

Some resented the king, and his son for making only one path and one bridge over the chasm of fire. Why couldn't he make more bridges? Why shouldn't all paths lead to Eternal Joy? These people accused those on the path of arrogance and self-righteousness. "Who do you think you are," they would angrily yell, "to maintain your path is the only right one?"

Some began to shoot at those on the path, while others made laws which made it illegal to encourage anyone new to get on the path. A new religion formed which said there was only one sin and that was the sin of intolerance, therefore every path was to be tolerated except the son's path because of its claim to be the only way to the city of Eternal Joy.

Yet even in this climate of hostility, more and more were drawn to the path and willingly gave up their pride to embrace the son's way. The more they were shot at, mocked, or ignored, the more joyous and confident they seemed to become. No one stayed on the path perfectly, yet those who had walked on it for a long time seemed to instinctively know when they were off the path and quickly returned to it.

The king's son gave them writings and inspired songs from Eternal Joy that became well known to those on the path. The more these writings were proclaimed, and the more these songs were sung, the brighter the path became. In fact, one of the songs had a verse that went something like this: "Oh how bright the path grows from day to day, leaning on the everlasting arms."

November 12

Are You Willing?

"If you are willing and obedient you will eat the best from the land." Isaiah 1:19

A minister in the 1950's was complaining to God saying, "God, you said if I was willing and obedient, I would eat the best of the land and I've been obedient."

He had been a pastor when God told him to start traveling because he wasn't really a pastor, he was a prophet and a teacher. Even though it was difficult to leave the security of a pastorate, he obeyed God. The problem was that he wasn't making it. His shoes were worn out, his wife and kids were barely surviving, and there was constant financial pressure on his home. All this when he had only obeyed God and stepped out in faith.

The Lord answered this man with a whisper: "You've been obedient, but you haven't been willing." When he told this story, he said that he instantly became willing in response to God's prompting, and it started to change everything in his life.

Did you know you can be obedient and not be willing? You can do the will of God and carry out your responsibilities as "have tos," but that's not good enough for God. He only releases His full blessing over us when we "want to." It's not enough for Him that we serve Him; He wants us to be happy about it.

The sweet Spirit of God was given so we would have both power to God's will as well as the "want to." Philippians 2:13 says, "It is God who works in you to will (the want to) and to act (the power to do) according to His good purpose."

The way we change all of the "have tos," in our lives into "want tos," is by embracing the cross and doing them for God instead of for man. Jesus said that no one took His life from Him; "I lay it down of my own accord." (John 10:18). You and I have the choice of resenting our "have tos," or of making them "want tos," by doing them for God.

How we do what we do changes everything and puts us in the place of God's full blessing. "Whatever you do, work at it with all your heart, as working for the Lord, not for men, since you know that you know that you will receive an inheritance from the Lord as a reward. It is the Lord Christ you are serving." (Colossians 3:23-24).

November 13

The Joy Serving

"Now that you know these things, you will be blessed (happy, joy-filled) if you do them." John 13:17

When people arrived at a feast in that time, it was customary for a slave to wash everyone's feet as they entered, but in all the preparations for the last supper the disciples had missed this detail. Each of them apparently felt that this job was below them, so it appeared it would go undone. Then the unthinkable happened. One far above them went lower than they were willing to go. Not only did Jesus wash their feet, He called them to wash each other's feet (willingly serve each other), and in the text above said this was the key to their happiness.

He explained that this attitude was also the key to their greatness: "The kings of the Gentiles lord it over them; and those who exercise authority over them call themselves Benefactors. But you are not to be like that. Instead the greatest among you should be like the youngest, and the one who rules like one who serves." (Luke 22:25-26)

Our level of joy is not to be a victim of our own sense of entitlement. In other words, we don't have to wait until we are treated in a certain way to have joy. Our joy can be found in God's delight in us regardless of how other people are treating us. I found out this truth the hard way while pastoring in northern Minnesota.

A group of thirty wanted me out of the church and had started a secret campaign of visiting members in their homes to try to get the necessary votes to remove me. God was moving in the congregation and so was the enemy. There was a deacon who represented the thirty, but whenever I tried to meet with them it got postponed. It finally occurred to me that they didn't want to be reconciled, they wanted me gone. This was their church and they weren't going to leave, so I would have to.

How do you pastor a church Sunday after Sunday when this is happening? The Lord made it clear that they didn't have to like or respect me, for me to serve them. I wasn't to defend myself or be offended by their attitudes. I was to serve them for His sake. (2Corinthians 4:5) His affirmation was better than theirs anyway!

Emptying ourselves, rolling up our sleeves, and serving whoever God puts in front of us is the key to lasting joy.

November 14

The Generosity of God

"Who has ever given to God, that God should repay him?" Romans 8:32

Any sense of entitlement in us will undermine our faith. God never gives to us because He has to; He gives because He wants to. The gospel starts by revealing to us that God owes us nothing but hell because of our sins, and then proceeds to show us His kind intention of adopting us as His sons and daughters. (Ephesians 1:4-6)

I was speaking in Uganda about entitlement and told a story where God revealed to me that I had been waiting for an apology from Him. I felt I had been mistreated just like Job and the older brother did (Luke 15:26-31), and that attitude was keeping me from experiencing the generosity of God.

After I was done speaking a woman found me and said I had to talk with her friend, Annette. Annette was laying on a mat on the floor of the church and was unable to get up because of crippling pain in her back. Through an interpreter, Annette told me that God spoke to her through the message. She had experienced a number of setbacks and had been angry with God. Now she was free because God showed her she needed to let go of her bad attitude.

I felt in my heart that God now wanted to heal her body, so I asked if I could pray for her back. After a brief prayer, I told her to move her back around and eventually told her to stand up. As she did, tears started to pour down her face.

"Ask her why she's crying," I said to the interpreter.

The answer was what I was hoping: "She says God is healing her back."

Before my next teaching, she came to the front with the joy of the Lord on her face and gave testimony to what God had done in her heart and then in her body. Everyone then rejoiced in the generosity of God.

Sometimes we become focused on the outward miracle we need while having the wrong attitude in our heart. Do you feel God owes you something because of your obedience, sacrifice, or prayers? Why not lay down your disappointment, acknowledge that God is not in your debt, and focus on His generosity?

"He who did not spare His own Son, but gave Him up for us all – how will He not, also along with Him, graciously give us all things" (Romans 8:32)

November 15

The Puzzle of the End Times

"Blessed is the one who reads the words of this prophecy and all who listen to its message and obey what it says, for the time is near." Revelation 1:3

The God who helps us with our smallest problems is the Ruler over history. History will one day be seen to be His story, and knowing that brings a blessing to our lives especially at times when they seem pointless or chaotic. John wrote Revelation from Patmos, an island prison where the emperor, Domitian, had sent him because of "the word of God and the testimony of Jesus." (Revelation 1:9) As God revealed His bigger plan, we can imagine John's comfort in the soon coming of the Lord and the assurance of His ultimate victory.

The evil and darkness of this world will be short lived. As surely as Jesus came the first time to save us from our sins, He will come a second time to secure His bride, judge the world, and set up His kingdom. (2Timothy 4:1) Just how these events will unfold is unclear. There are many pieces to the end times' puzzle and no one but God knows exactly how they fit together, yet John tells us in the text above that there's a blessing in just contemplating the mystery. What exactly is the blessing? I believe it's more of the fear of the Lord. Let me explain.

Paul tells us to "behold both the kindness and severity of God" in Romans 11:22. Our tendency is to only behold His kindness because it's pleasant, but it's in beholding His severity that we grow in the fear of the Lord and stay in a place where we will only experience His kindness. The end of Romans 11:22 goes like this: "...to those who fell, severity, but to you, God's kindness; otherwise you also will be cut off." Jesus wants nothing for us but kindness, but to ensure that blessing, we must have the courage to behold His severity. When someone warns me of danger I feel love, not offense.

Jesus came the first time as a Lamb to save the world; He's coming a second time as a Lion to judge it. At that time it won't matter how close our theology about the end times matches what actually happens, but only that we are in a right relationship with God. May God engage both your mind and heart as you join me in contemplating the end times' puzzle over the next few days.

November 16

Two Events of Judgment

"Truly I say to you, this generation will not pass away until all these things take place. Heaven and earth will pass away, but My words will not pass away. But of that day and hour no one knows, not even the angels of heaven, nor the Son, but the Father alone. For the coming of the Son of Man will be just like the days of Noah." Matthew 24:34–37

I have come to believe that Jesus is describing two events of judgment in His discourse on the future (Matthew 24; Mark 13; Luke 17 and 21) and that they are very different to prepare for.

One event, the destruction of Jerusalem, will happen in their lifetime, or their "generation." It is a time of God's wrath on the Jewish people for rejecting Christ (Luke 21:22-24); it will feature an abomination of desolation being set up in the holy place (Matthew 24:15); and it will be horrible but "cut short," otherwise all of the Jewish elect would be wiped out.

The rescue for the church at this time is to flee Jerusalem when you see these things happening. "All these things" were to be expected within their generation and they would be as visible as a fig tree budding indicating that summer is near. There will be a fulfillment of "all that is written" (Luke 21:22), a reference to Daniel's seventieth 'seven' (Daniel 9:27), and Jeremiah's allusion to a time of Jacob's trouble. (Jeremiah 30:7)

The second event Jesus describes is not just in Judea, it's world-wide (Luke 21:35); Jesus doesn't know when it's going to happen; the elect don't have to flee, they are taken; and there are no signs to prepare for it, so people have to live ready. This coming event is not a judgment on the Jews for rejecting Christ (that already happened in the destruction of Jerusalem), but on the Gentiles who have rejected Christ. (Luke 21:24)

By the end of their generation this second judgment will be imminent, or "at the door," (Matthew 24:33-34) because it will occur immediately after Jesus appears in the clouds. We are now living between the first and second judgment events in a time of God's favor. (2Corinthians 6:2) This is the time to respond to God's salvation!

November 17

The First Sixty-nine 'Sevens'

"Seventy 'sevens' are decreed for your people and your holy city..."Know and understand this: From the time the word goes out to restore and rebuild Jerusalem until the Anointed One, the ruler, comes, there will be seven 'sevens,' and sixty-two 'sevens'...After the sixty-two 'sevens,' the Anointed One will be put to death and will have nothing." Daniel 9:24-26

One of the most remarkable prophecies of the Old Testament is found in Daniel 9:24-27. The seventy years of captivity in Babylon are finished, so Daniel is praying for the deliverance from their exile when the angel Gabriel appears to him and gives the message above. After telling about the first 69 'sevens' he describes the 70th 'seven' but makes it clear that there will be a gap – Messiah will be "put to death and have nothing" after the 69 'sevens,' but before the 70th seven. The seven 'sevens' and the sixty-two 'sevens' are consecutive and are only split up so Daniel will know how long it will take to restore and rebuild the Jerusalem – 49 years (seven 'sevens'). The 62 'sevens' or 434 years immediately follow the 49 after which Messiah will be put to death and have nothing. Forty-nine and 434 equals 483 years – not solar years which we use today, but the 360 day lunar years they used then.

We find the decree Gabriel references in the book of Nehemiah. Nehemiah is the Persian king Artaxerxes' cupbearer and he is sad because "the city, the place of my father's tombs, lies desolate and its gates have been consumed by fire." (2:3) So in Artaxerxes 20th year, in the month of Nisan (April), a decree is made to rebuild the city. (2:1-9)

Artaxerxes began his reign in 465 BC (Encyclopedia Britannica), so his 20th year would be 445 BC according to our calendar (444 BC because Daniel used accessional dating to count his reign). To convert from lunar to solar we begin by figuring out how many days there are in 483 lunar years: 483 times 360 equals 173,880 days. Then we divide 173,880 by 365.242 (the days in a solar year) to determine the number of solar years so we can get a date that corresponds to our dates in history – it comes to 476 solar years. So when we start the prophetic clock in 444 BC and begin with the first 444 years we come to 1 AD because there is no year "0". (The year after 1 BC is 1 AD) That leaves 32 (476 minus 444 equals 32) years which when added to 1 AD brings us to 33 AD. The Messiah would die after the 69 sevens - the time most scholars give for Jesus' death is Passover of 33 AD.

November 18

Daniel's Seventieth 'Seven' - Part I

"Tell us, when will these things be, and what will be the sign when all these things are going to be fulfilled?...when you see the abomination of desolation standing where it should not be...then those in Judea must flee to the mountains....truly I say to you this generation will not pass away until all these things take place." Mark 13:4; 14; 30

When Jesus talks about the abomination of desolation as being the sign that the temple will be destroyed, he is referencing an event that happens in Daniel's seventieth 'seven.' He says that this would all be fulfilled in the generation He was speaking to. So what happened?

A Jewish rebellion to Rome occurred in 66 AD causing the emperor, Nero, to send his general, Vespasian, to subdue it using whatever means were necessary. Vespasian first went to Galilee where he took some of its cities "by treaties, and on terms." (Josephus, The Jewish War, Preface 8). Josephus tells us that "Sepphoris, the largest city of Galilee, received Vespasian, the Roman general very kindly, and readily promised that they would assist him." (III:ix:8)

But most of the Jews dug in their heels, so Vespasian pursued them through war. In 69 AD there were three Roman emperors after Nero's suicide – Galba, Ortho, and Vitellius who eventually gave way to Vespasian – the fourth emperor in one year. The Jewish war continued with Vespasian's son, Titus, leading the charge on his behalf. In 70 AD, at the three and a half year point of the war, Titus destroyed and burned the temple so completely that not one stone was left upon another. A Roman ensign with Vespasian's image on it was set up in the wing of the temple area declaring Caesar to be Divine (the outer wing, not part of the temple itself, was all that was left at the time).

Even though the temple was destroyed and all sacrifices ceased, the war continued for three and a half more years as Titus ran down the Jews to wherever they went. The final siege was in the stronghold of Masada. When Titus broke through in 73 AD almost 1,000 Jews had already committed suicide ending the pursuit, and the war against the Jews. Josephus wrote that over a million Jews died during that seven year span by sword, famine, crucifixtion, or suicide. All this was completed 40 years from when Jesus said, "this generation will not pass away until all these things happen."

November 19

Daniel's Seventieth 'Seven' - Part II

"He (a coming prince) will confirm a covenant with many for one 'seven.'
In the middle of the 'seven' he will put an end to sacrifice and offering. And
at the temple he will set up an abomination that causes desolation, until the
end that is decreed is poured out on him." Daniel 9:27

After the Messiah is put to death, Gabriel says "the people of the prince who is to come will destroy the city and the sanctuary and its end will come like a flood." (Daniel 9:26) The next verse, quoted above, is a description of this event that will happen during the seventieth 'seven.'

Jesus said that this "abomination of desolation," spoken by Daniel the prophet (Matthew 24:15) would be fulfilled in the generation that He lived in. "Truly I say to you, this generation will not pass away until all these things take place." (Mark 13:30)

Many commentators don't believe the seventieth 'seven' occurred in Jesus' generation so they put it off until the generation before the Lord's return. They treat the fall of Jerusalem as a foreshadowing of the events that will happen again before the coming of the Lord which is why so many are certain the Jewish temple has to be rebuilt. But all this is conjecture and not in the text. In Mark's gospel only one question is asked and it's about the destruction of the temple (not about His coming or about the end times) and the sign they should look for: "the abomination of desolation." (Mark 13:14)

Yesterday we looked at what actually happened in their generation and the abomination that was set up in the destroyed temple. Now let's reread Daniel's seventieth 'seven' in light of this history:

"And he (Vespasian) will make a firm covenant with many (Galilean Jews) for one 'seven.' (The war went from 66-73 AD) In the middle of the 'seven' he will put an end to sacrifice and offering. (The temple was destroyed at the three and a half year mark, so sacrifices could no longer be made.) And at the temple he will set up an abomination that causes desolation (the Roman ensign was sacrificed to where the temple had been), until the end that is decreed is poured out on him." Daniel's seventieth 'seven' was fulfilled in the first century, just like Jesus said it would be.

November 20

The Little Horn

"While I was thinking about the horns, there before me was another horn, a little one, which came up among them; and three of the first horns were uprooted before it." Daniel 7:8   "The ten horns are ten kings who will rule that empire. Then another king will arise, different from the other ten who will subdue three of them." Daniel 7:24-25

Almost all scholars identify the fourth beast of Daniel 7 as the Roman Empire who would have "iron teeth" (7:19) and would "devour the whole world, trampling and crushing everything in its path." (7:23) What they disagree on is who the ten kings were and who the eleventh king was who began as a little horn. Instead of trying to figure out when the ten successive kings begin, I propose we focus on how he comes to power. He begins as "the little horn" and doesn't become king until three of the other horns or kings are subdued before him.

Remarkably there is an event in our history that fits this description. When Nero committed suicide in 68 AD, the leadership of the Roman Empire was up for grabs. Sixty-nine AD has become known as the year of four emperors. Galba, Otho, and Vitellius all seized control for a time but eventually they were subdued before Vespasian. Vespasian began as Nero's general (a little horn – a leader, but not a king) and was then the emperor for ten years after coming to power. If he is the eleventh king all we need to do is count backwards to find the first. Five of the kings have already been accounted for (Nero, Galba, Otho, Vitellius, and Vespasian), so who were the other six?

Before Nero was Claudius, then Caligula, before him was Tiberius (the emperor during Jesus' ministry), then Augustus (emperor when Jesus was born), before him was Julius Caesar who wasn't called an emperor but "Dictator", and finally, before Caesar was Pompey, who wasn't called emperor or dictator, but "Sole Counsel."

Is there any logical reason why God would identify Pompey as the first of the eleven kings when there were many other Roman leaders before him? There is. Israel did not belong to the Roman Empire until 63 BC when Pompey invaded Jerusalem and desecrated the temple. He was the first leader (king) in Rome when God's people, Israel, came under the rule of the Roman Empire.

November 21

The Beast

"The beast which you saw, once was, now is not, and will come out of the abyss and go to his destruction." Revelation 17:8

In Daniel 7 the beast has its body destroyed and is thrown into the blazing fire when the Messiah returns to the earth. (Daniel 7:11; 13) How can Vespasian be the beast when Jesus didn't return to end his reign? In fact, after the Jewish war ended Vespasian reigned six more years until his peaceful death in 79 AD. How can he be the beast when everything that was supposed to happen to the beast didn't happen to him?

Is it possible that the beast is both the one who appeared in history using Vespasian and the one who inspires and possesses a future anti-Christ? The beast, according to the text above, is more than a human being; it is a creature of darkness that has been released in the past, now is restricted, and will be released again before the coming of Christ.

The Apostle John writes Revelation after one of the judgment events has already occurred in history (the fall of Jerusalem), and before the final one (after the second coming). John assures us that the beast who comes up out of the abyss, and once was (had already appeared), now is not (is not presently active in the world), yet will appear again before he is destroyed.

What Daniel sees is a composite of both comings of the beast. Just like Old Testament prophecies about Jesus are sometimes confusing because they don't distinguish or even see two comings of the Messiah; Daniel can't see two comings of the beast. He can only see what God shows him, so what he describes is everything that the beast will do until God destroys him.

In Daniel we're told that after the beast changes Jewish law (Vespasian did this at the destruction of the temple), the saints will be placed under his control for a time, times, and half a time. (Daniel 7:25) This is a reference to his second appearance where John sees a future anti-Christ speaking "great blasphemies against God," waging "war against God's holy people and conquering them," and being "given authority to do whatever he wants for forty-two months." (Revelation 13:5-7)   Revelation 12:14 calls this same period, "time, times, and half a time," the same words used in Daniel seven.

November 22

The Seven Seals Of Revelation

"When he opened the seventh seal, there was silence in heaven for about half an hour." Revelation 8:1

If Revelation stood alone, I would conclude that the seven seals are all future as many commentators believe, but the rule of Scripture is that clear truth interprets obscure passages, and not the other way around.

I believe the first five seals of Revelation have already been opened by Jesus. The five seals correspond exactly to what Christ said would happen in their generation before the fall of Jerusalem. (Deception; wars and rumors of wars; earthquakes and famines; death; martyrdom) They were opened by Jesus in the first century; they were already opened when John wrote Revelation from Patmos in 95 AD; and they're still open today.

The fifth seal is the martyrdom of those who were killed "because of the word of God and because of the testimony they maintained." John is writing to people that are in danger of being martyred under Domitian's rule. He writes to them as one who is a fellow partaker "in the tribulation and kingdom and perseverance which are in Jesus." He is on the island because of "the word of God and the testimony of Jesus," the same reason the martyrs were killed. (Revelation 1:9)

He is writing because the Lord's coming is very near – He ends the book with the words of Jesus, "I am coming quickly." After the fifth seal has been opened, John sees those who have been martyred and hears their question, "How much longer?" There has been a delay and they are waiting for the coming day of the Lord to avenge their deaths. The answer: "a little while longer until all those who will be killed like you is complete." (Revelation 6:11)

The second coming is imminent but delayed. Then John sees the sixth seal opened and the very signs Jesus gave for the rapture happen before his eyes. The earth prepares for the wrath of God while the saints are suddenly found before the throne of God. Jews come to Christ as a Spirit of mourning comes upon every tribe when they see the One they had pierced. One Hundred forty-four thousand Jews become evangelists who "follow the Lamb wherever He goes." (Revelation 14:4)

Those who were ready for the Bridegroom's coming are kept "from the hour of testing, that hour which is about to come upon the whole world," (Revelation 3:10) while everyone else must endure it. Let's live ready!

November 23

Choosing Jesus In The Darkness

"As I watched the Lamb broke the first of the seven seals on the scroll."
Revelation 6:1

In Matthew 24, Jesus gives to us the conditions on earth while the gospel is preached: false religion, wars, natural disasters, and persecution of the truth that in some instances ends in martyrdom.

In Revelation 6, we see these same four conditions but they are seen from heaven's perspective. They are not incidental; they are necessary before the day of the Lord can come.

Seals were not part of a Jewish legal document – they were on the outside and represented conditions that had to be met before the document could be opened or enforced. Jesus is the only One who is worthy to break the seals which lead to the coming day of the Lord, but we must ask, "Why?" Why has God insisted that the gospel be preached in such darkness before He comes to actively rule the world?

Here's my opinion: He wanted us to choose Him in the darkness, so we never reject Him again for all eternity. The first group, the angels, chose Him in the light and eventually a third fell away. Angels have free will even as we do, and a third of them chose self-rule over God's rule even while living in a perfect heaven, and beholding God's beauty face to face.

By having us choose Him in the midst of darkness, in the midst of the worst conditions and the ugliness of sin and horrors of the curse, it will be almost impossible for us to reject Him when we see Him face to face in the light and glory of heaven.

Ephesians 3:10-11 says this: "God's purpose was to use the church to display His wisdom in its rich variety to all the unseen rulers and authorities in heavenly places. This was His eternal plan, which He carried out through Christ Jesus our Lord." "All" means both the angels that fell away and those who remained true.

Those who fell away are judged as they see the church choose Him even while they can barely see Him, when they had rejected Him while seeing the beauty, glory, and power with absolute clarity. Those who remained loyal see through Christ's coming and the church's devotion more of the beauty of God's love and humility. This strengthens them, I can imagine, and further secures them from the danger of ever falling away in the future.

When the day of the Lord begins, every eye will be able to see God's active judgment and redemption, but right now we must choose Him in the darkness. God Himself has ordained this!

November 24

The Next Event

"When you see all these things, you know that it (His coming) is near, right at the door. I tell you the truth this generation will certainly not pass away until all these things have happened." Matthew 24:33-34

Jesus does not say His coming will be in their generation; He says it will be "at the door" in their generation. He says the sign of His coming will appear "immediately after the distress of those days..." (Matthew 24:29) Immediately, on God's calendar, means imminently; His coming is the next prophetic event and has been since the fall of Jerusalem.

While the first rescue and judgment event was preceded by an abundance of signs so that God's people would be prepared for the distress of their generation, the second rescue and judgment event will come unexpectedly.

While first century Christians were warned not to be trapped in Jerusalem, Jesus warns us not to be trapped in the things of this world before His coming in the clouds: "Be careful, or your hearts will be weighed down with carousing, drunkenness and the anxieties of life, and that day will close on you suddenly like a trap. For it will come on all those who live on the face of the whole earth." (Luke 21:34-35) We need to live ready for His coming!

The rescue in the first century required Christians to leave Jerusalem. The rescue at the Lord's coming won't require anyone to leave, we'll be taken. "Two men will be in the field; one will be taken and the other left. Two women will be grinding with a hand mill; one will be taken and the other left." (Matthew 24:40-41) The word translated "taken" is "paralambano" in the Greek and means: "to receive near to one's self in any intimate act." (Strong's, 55) It is used in Matthew 1:24 when Joseph "took Mary home as his wife."

It is used of the rapture again in John 14:3 where Jesus makes this promise to His disciples: "And if I go and prepare a place for you, I will come back and take (paralambano) you to be with me that you also may be where I am." Jesus is coming for His beloved bride. If He came today would you be ready?

November 25

Living Ready for His Return

"Now while the bridegroom was delaying, they all got drowsy and began to sleep. But at midnight there was a shout, 'Behold, the bridegroom! Come out to meet him.' Then all those virgins rose and trimmed their lamps. The foolish said to the prudent, 'Give us some of your oil, for our lamps are going out.' But the prudent answered, 'No, there will not be enough for us and you too; go instead to the dealer and buy some for yourselves.'"
Matthew 25:5-9

The great work of this life is to live ready for Christ's return. He has delayed His return because He doesn't want anyone to perish (2Peter 3:9) and is even now calling sinners to repent and turn to God. But what about the danger to those who have begun their journey but are now distracted by other things? How do we ensure we don't end up like the foolish virgins Jesus describes in Matthew 25? There are three things we can do daily, so that we're living ready for His return.

1. We must stay awake. Jesus said that before Noah's flood and the judgment of Sodom and Gomorrah, people were "eating, they were drinking, they were marrying...they were buying, they were selling, they were planting, they were building." (Luke 17:27-28) The problem was that these legitimate things were all they were doing – they had lost track of a living faith in God. The busyness of this world easily lulls us to sleep and pretty soon we are relying on past experience instead of present relationship.

2. We must trim our wicks. Yesterday's sins, regrets, and successes have to be trimmed away to walk with God today. Listen to Paul's encouragement: "One thing I do: forgetting what lies behind and reaching forward to what lies ahead, I press on toward the goal for the prize of the upward call of Christ Jesus." (Philippians 3:13-14)

3. We must have fresh oil. The foolish virgins think they can get oil from other people – it's not possible. You can't get your relationship with God from your grandma, parents, or pastor, however godly they may be. Go to the dealer Himself. He has fresh oil for every single day. The cost is only the time and effort it takes to seek Him for it. Jesus has already paid the price, so we can always be filled with the Holy Spirit. Your Father loves you, Jesus died for you, so all you need to do is ask each day.

November 26

The Glasses of Faith

"I would have despaired unless I had believed that I would see the goodness of the Lord in the land of the living. Wait for the Lord; be strong, and let your heart take courage; yes, wait for the Lord." Psalm 27:13-14

My daughter, Anne, and I went out for a date together during one Christmas break and saw the movie, "Partly Cloudy with a Chance of Meatballs." The main reason we wanted to go was that it was in 3-D and required special glasses to view. I loved it. A couple of times I took my glasses off to see what the screen looked like without them. Although you could tell something was there it was all hazy and confusing. If people had slipped into the wrong theater they never would have guessed the beauty that was there right in front of them. You can't see right if you don't have the right glasses.

Life is like that. If you put on the glasses of faith you are able to see God everywhere and behind everything. Even bad things that He allows are able to be worked for something good if we will give them to Him. (Romans 8:28) Jesus said in John 5:17: "My Father is working until now, and I Myself am working." God is working – He may not be doing what we want Him to do, He may not be moving at the pace we'd like Him to move at, but He is working if we choose to see Him.

Now the devil is also working all the time. Much of what he does in this world is quickly reported on the news, so if we get the wrong glasses on we can easily fall into despair. It takes discipline in this world to keep seeing God because our God glasses easily fall off in the midst of life's difficulties. Without the glasses of faith you easily focus on your problems and that only leads to anxiety and discouragement. Church, prayer, and Bible reading are important because they help us keep our glasses on, or to get them back on if they've fallen off.

David said, "I would have despaired unless I had believed..." He had to choose to believe that God was in control and that His goodness would be revealed at some time in the future even though his present circumstances were horrible.

The need of the hour was to wait for God to come through. There was nothing he could do to make his circumstances better, only God could. He needed to courageously trust God and refuse to give into despair. Is that where you are today? Let me encourage you to wait for God. You will see the goodness of the Lord in your circumstances if you'll just remember to keep putting on the glasses of faith.

November 27

Kingdom Mode

"Of the increase of His government and peace (shalom) there will be no end... The zeal of the Lord Almighty will accomplish this." Isaiah 9:7

The Father has promised the Son that His kingdom (government) and His presence (peace) will continually increase. The Father's own zeal will accomplish this – not man's efforts or programs. Where will this increase happen? In and through you and me, His adopted children. We are carriers of the kingdom and the Presence of the King Himself!

When the world goes into crisis mode, we can go into kingdom mode. On September 11th, 2001, I received a phone call from the manager of the area wide Christian radio station. The church secretary had to find me because I was in the sanctuary praying and meditating on the morning's One Year Bible reading from Isaiah 8:12-14: "Do not call conspiracy everything that these people call conspiracy; do not fear what they fear, and do not dread it. The Lord Almighty is the one you are to regard as holy, He is the One you are to fear...and He will be a sanctuary (for you)."

The manager told me that one of the twin towers was hit by terrorists and that another plane was hijacked and he was asking pastors to pray over the air. There was such a presence of God on me because I knew that He had prepared me for this. Darkness was having its day, but God didn't want us to focus on what the world was focusing on, or respond in the way the world would respond. We were to fix our eyes on Him and find sanctuary in Him, and that's what I prayed for everyone who was in the midst of this horrible crisis.

The world goes into crisis mode when there is a crisis and many wrong decisions are made because they are based on the hurt, fear, anger, or frustration the situation has caused. This is when Jesus wants to increase His government and peace in us – we are to fix our eyes on Him and go into kingdom mode. Don't focus on darkness or respond to it. What is God saying? What does God want you to do? All you need to do to break darkness is bring a light into it. Light is always stronger than darkness.

"In Me you may have peace, in the world you will have trouble. Let your heart take courage for I have overcome the world." (John 16:33) In every situation around us we are either a thermometer that simply reflects the environment, or a thermostat that sets it. God's plan is that we would so host His presence, and have such confidence in Him that we would automatically go into kingdom mode when a crisis arises and be thermostats of His kingdom and peace.

November 28

Trees and Flowers

"A man of many companions may come to ruin, but there is a friend who sticks closer than a brother." Proverbs 18:24

How do we navigate all the relationships in our lives? How can we love people and be loyal to people when we have so little time to share between so many? How can we reach out and love new people yet still give the necessary time and investment to the valued friendships we already have? Only by giving all our relationships to God, and by discerning His purpose in each one. Each of us will be called to have a few trees in our lives, and many flowers. Likewise, each of us will be called to be a tree to a few people and a flower to many others. Let me explain.

A tree is someone who is with you the rest of your life. A tree may not be as beautiful, or as fragrant as a flower, but they are steady through good times and through bad. They are the friend who sticks closer than a brother, the friend who loves at all times (Proverbs 17:17), the friend who is willing to speak the truth even if it hurts (Proverbs 27:6), and the friend who believes in your destiny in God even though they know all your sins and faults. A tree is a blessing from God and should be valued and not taken for granted. As someone said, "you can make new friends, but you can't make old ones."

Flowers are temporary. They are beautiful and fragrant and they enrich our lives by the grace they impart even though they aren't called to be trees. These are people God brings into our lives at just the right time to give us a message, to pray for us, or to pick us up when we're down. We must thank God for them and not resent their seemingly temporary nature in our lives. All of them will be trees in eternity, but down here they are called to be someone else's tree. If you think everyone should be a tree to you then you will go through life feeling hurt and betrayed by those God called to be only flowers to you. "Why did they move away?" "Why did they send such a short response to my email?" "Why did they pretend to be my friend when they obviously weren't?" We can easily judge flowers we wanted to be trees and end up shutting our hearts down in self-protection so we don't get hurt again.

You and I will be disappointed with some people and be a disappointment to others, but there is One we can always please who is the ultimate Tree – Jesus!

November 29

The Value of Godliness

"Train yourself to be godly. Physical training is of some value, but godliness has value for all things, holding promise for both the present life and the life to come." 1Timothy 4:7-8

To train ourselves to be godly is to reorder our lives in a way that makes living close to God our highest priority. Asaph said, "the nearness of God is my good." (Psalm 73:28) In what way is godliness good for us?

First, Paul says it's valuable in this present life. Later in his letter he gives a qualifier: "Godliness with contentment is great gain, for we brought nothing into this world, and we cannot take anything out." (6:6-7) The more we pursue godliness with contentment the more we live defined by God and the more all other definitions fade away. We are not our financial net worth, or what other people think we are, or even how we define ourselves – we are God's masterpiece! (Ephesians 2:10) Only the godly grow away from the traps of this world into their true identity. Letting the One who loved us and gave Himself up for us (Galatians 2:20) be the One who defines us is tremendously liberating. His perfect love drives out fear and insecurity (1John 4:18), so that we can simply be ourselves filled with His Holy Spirit.

Then Paul says godliness has value for the life to come. Asaph says that those who live "far from You will perish; You put an end to everyone who is unfaithful to You." (Psalm 73:27) The ungodly will "perish like beasts" (2Peter 2:12) and "be consumed" eventually in the eternal fire (Hebrews 10:27), but the godly will share eternal life with God. This is the simple gospel: "For God so loved the world, that He gave His only begotten Son, that whoever believes in Him shall not perish, but have eternal life." (John 3:16)

Godliness begins by forsaking our own works and by putting our trust in Jesus Christ because salvation is God's gift to us. "Now to the one who works, wages are not credited as a gift but as an obligation. However, to the one who does not work but trusts God who justifies the ungodly, their faith is credited as righteousness (right standing with God!)." (Romans 4:4-5)

November 30

The Way Forward

"In repentance and rest you will be saved; in quietness and confidence is your strength." Isaiah 30:15

Sometimes the way forward is to go back. Repentance is when we return to God and find our rest in His forgiveness and acceptance again. The new beginning He gives requires an exchange of strength. Instead of seeing our activity and energy as the way forward, we learn to quiet ourselves and to find our strength in God.

"Cease striving and know that I am God..." (Psalm 46:10) Quieting ourselves and encountering God will produce a new confidence to face life's challenges that isn't based on our ability to control, but on God's ability to work all things for His glory and our good. Here's the end of Psalm 46:10, "Then I will be exalted in the nations; I will be exalted in all the earth."

In our text above, Israel was unwilling to repent. They decided to go forward even faster than they had begun, and they became a sign to others of what not to do. (Isaiah 30:17)

What was God doing while they rejected His counsel? "Therefore the Lord longs to be gracious to you, and He waits on high to have compassion on you..." God is waiting for you and me to come to the end of ourselves and our own devices, so He can have compassion on us! Sometimes the way forward is to recognize we're eating pig's food, come to our senses, and then return to our Father no matter what it looks like. (see Luke 15)

It turns out that the One who owes us nothing, longs to give us everything, if we'll just come home!

December 1

The One Behind the Scriptures

"All Scripture is God breathed..." 2 Timothy 3:16

The Bible is one of God's most startling revelations of Himself. It was written over a period of 1600 years by over 40 different human authors with a variety of backgrounds, from three different continents, and in three different languages, yet it is one story, one history, with one message. It is by far the best selling book in history. You probably have one, or maybe even a few, lying around your house. The question is how does one read the Bible in a way that he will find God and not just be frustrated by the seeking?

There were two major religious groups at the time of Christ that had access to the Scriptures but didn't find God: The Sadducees and the Pharisees. To the Sadducees Jesus said, "You are mistaken, not understanding the Scriptures, or the power of God." (Matthew 22:29) They were a group that had exalted intellect and human wisdom above the word of God. They didn't believe in angels, miracles, or the resurrection of the dead, even though the Old Testament Scriptures taught these things. Because of this grave error they lost all understanding of spiritual things. Many in America have made a similar mistake. When you put your opinion above the word of God and only believe the parts of the Bible that agree with your thinking, you make yourself out to be the final authority and end up denying the God of the Scriptures. Submit your heart to the Scriptures, humble your mind before God, and you will find yourself being changed by God's word as you seek to apply it to your life.

The other group who had access to the Scriptures was the Pharisees. Jesus said to them, "You search the Scriptures, because you think that in them you have eternal life; and it is these that bear witness of Me; and you are unwilling to come to Me, that you may have life." (John 5:39) The Pharisees believed every jot and tittle of the Scriptures from Genesis to Malachi, but they had exalted them to the place of God. They lived for rules and interpretations and spent much of their time arguing doctrines and splitting hairs over who was the most right, while attacking anyone who didn't share their insights. Unfortunately many Bible believing people get caught in this trap today. The Bible is not an end in itself. Its purpose is to reveal a living Person who is in love with us. Truth itself, Jesus said, was not a belief system, but found in His Person. He said, "I am the truth..." (John 14:6) He is the Word that became flesh. He is the One that the Scriptures were written to reveal. Read your Bible to find the One behind it and you will find life in Jesus Christ.

December 2

An Inconvenient Truth

"For we must all appear before the judgment seat of Christ, so that each of us may receive what is due us for the things done while in the body, whether good or bad. Since then, we know what it is to fear the Lord, we try to persuade others." 2Corinthians 5:10-11

In 2006 Al Gore released a documentary on global warming called, "An Inconvenient Truth," urging us to do something to make changes in the environment before it's too late. It's not just about us, he urged, it's about the world we're giving to our children.

While I'm all for stewardship of the earth and reducing carbon emissions, there's another inconvenient truth that troubles me way more than global warming – it's the final judgment. It turns out that our lives on this planet will one day appear like a vapor in light of eternity, and that the choices we're making now determine how our judgment will go then. To live in light of that day is to know the fear of the Lord. To live ignoring our accountability to God is reckless and dangerous. As Hebrews 10:30-31 says, "For we know Him who said, 'It is Mine to avenge; I will repay,' and again, 'The Lord will judge His people.' It is a terrifying thing to fall into the hands of the living God." That is, it's terrifying to be completely unprepared for our judgment day.

Here's the inconvenient truth that must be told: Jesus came the first time as a Lamb to save the world, but He's coming the second time as a Lion to judge it. I want to be ready for that day and I want to persuade others to be ready as well. Let's change our lives now, let's serve God now, and let's seek His presence now before it's too late. Jesus took God's judgment on sin when He died on the cross, so that we could be forgiven. Let's make our identity in Him and receive His love now instead of being exposed by His holiness then.

December 3

Abiding in Christ

"Abide in Me and I in you. As the branch cannot bear fruit of itself, unless it abides in the vine, neither can you, unless you abide in Me." John 15:4

The Greek word for abide, meno, is from the noun, mone, which means home. The noun form is used a few verses earlier, "If anyone loves Me, he will keep My word, and My Father will love him, and we will come and make Our home with him." (John 14:23) When I say to a guest, "make yourself at home," I'm telling them to relax because they belong here. Have we given God that kind of welcome? Do we believe He gives us that kind of welcome?

Jesus invites us to make a new home with Him. He doesn't want to be a hotel we visit on Sundays, and He doesn't want to be an apartment we rent from month to month to keep our options open. He wants us to make the investment of our lives by building a home together with Him, and He gives us the blueprint of what the new home will look like.

First, it will be large. It must be because there seems to be room for everyone. "This is My command, love another." (15:12) There's room for all Christians, for strangers, and even for enemies. It turns out Jesus is planning on inviting a lot of people over to the new home!

Secondly, it's a happy home. "These things I command you so that My joy may be in you, and your joy may be full." (15:11) If we aren't there yet it's not because it's not part of the blueprint, it's only because the new home isn't fully built yet.

Thirdly, it's a unique home. "If you abide in Me and My word abides in you, ask whatever you desire and it will be done." (15:7) His presence and His word so purify our desires that who God has uniquely made us, becomes part of the new home. The life of Jesus is going to be expressed differently in each of us, so it's important not to compare ourselves with each other. The home you build with Jesus will look different than the home I build with Jesus.

December 4

The Power of Words

"Have faith in God. Truly, I say to you, whoever says to this mountain, 'Be taken up and thrown into the sea,' and does not doubt in his heart, but believes that what he says will come to pass, it will be done for him." Mark 11:22-23

When God speaks everything changes! There may be darkness and chaos, but when God speaks, light and order come in response to His word transforming the world. (See Genesis 1) But what happens when we speak? I don't believe there is intrinsic power in our words, but I do believe that our words can be filled with power if we speak out loud what God has spoken to our hearts.

Speaking expresses faith. Romans 10:10 says we believe with our hearts and then speak with our mouths resulting in salvation. What we believe about God and the world will affect what we speak and what we speak will then affect the world around us. Proverbs 18:21 says, "life and death are in the power of the tongue."

So what is God speaking to this world? May our hearts be filled with the truth of John 3:17: "For God did not send His Son into the world to condemn the world, but in order that the world might be saved through Him." We are not called to be positive in a negative world; we are called to be redemptive in a fallen world. We don't ever have to live in a bubble that denies the brokenness and darkness all around us; we only have to believe that God has a redemptive plan for everything and everyone who is broken and dark.

Moses allowed himself to become frustrated and hit the rock when God told him to speak to it. The rock, which represented Christ (1Corinthians 10:4), had already been struck (a picture of Jesus dying on the cross), so God wanted Moses to have enough faith to just speak. If he had spoken to the rock it would have flowed with water for all the people, for God was the One telling him to speak.

Today He's telling us to speak His redemption over our own lives, the lives of our loved ones, and over this nation. What are you speaking?

December 5

The Gift God is Offering

"What must I do to inherit eternal life?... One thing you lack: go and sell what you possess and give it to the poor... and come follow Me." Mark 10:17; 21

What if the gift we are asking God for is different than the one He's offering? The rich young ruler already had a good life but saw it could be better if he had the promise of eternal life. He asked Jesus what He had to do to ensure that gift but didn't like the answer. "But at these words he was saddened, and he went away grieving, for he was one who owned much property." (Mark 10:22)

He was willing to do something, but Jesus asked him to let go of something. He wanted to improve his life, but Jesus wanted to become his life. He wanted to add a room to his house, but Jesus wanted to tear down the house he had built and start over with Himself as the foundation of a new building.

He ended up walking away sad. The gift he asked for was different than the one God was offering. I wonder if we have answered Jesus' call to let go of our control, or if we have redefined what He's offering to accommodate our own desires?

Better to be sad than deceived. I wonder if the rich young ruler ever reconsidered and followed Jesus on His terms? If he did, he would have found that God is not opposed to us having stuff; He just doesn't want our stuff to have control over us.

A few verses after this young man walked away sad, Peter said: "We have left everything and followed You." Here was Jesus' response to him: "Truly I say to you, there is no one who has left house or brothers or sisters or mother or father or children or farms, for My sake and for the gospel's sake, but that he will receive a hundred times as much now in the present age, houses and brothers and sisters and mothers and children and farms, along with persecutions; and in the age to come, eternal life." (Mark 10:29-30)

When we withhold nothing from Him, He will withhold no good thing from us! (See Psalm 84:11)

December 6

Saying "Thanks"

"Jesus asked, Didn't I heal ten men? Where are the other nine?" Luke 17:17

Jesus marvels at the ungratefulness of the human race. Ten cried out in great distress; ten were miraculously healed by the mercy of God; yet only one returned to say, "thank you."

In 1987 I was a youth pastor in Grand de tour, Illinois, and we were doing a fundraiser in a town 30 miles away from our church. After we packed up the teens and took off, a seventh grade girl called my wife at our apartment and explained that she had missed the bus, but still wanted to go. Could Alice pick her up and drive her to the event?

Alice felt compassion for her and agreed to do it even though it would be difficult. It meant loading up our two little ones, driving 15 minutes in the wrong direction, and then 45 miles to get to the event. It took most of the morning to do this good deed.

I went to the car after she dropped off the girl, and Alice looked disappointed. "She didn't even say, thanks," was the explanation. Alice was happy to make the sacrifice and she wasn't looking for gas money, but couldn't this girl recognize that someone had gone out of their way just for her? Couldn't she take two seconds to say, "thanks?"

Alice was disappointed, but I was enraged. Later that day I was alone in our apartment fuming over the ungratefulness of this seventh grade girl when a stream of thoughts came unbidden into my mind, "Why are you so angry at her? You do this to Me all the time."

My heart was cut and all my anger was instantly gone. I looked around our apartment and it was as if my eyes were opened. We had almost no money, yet our apartment was fully furnished. There was a story behind everything we owned.

"God, please forgive me," I prayed, and then purposed to make up for all of my ingratitude. "Thank You for this coffee table; thank You for our dining room table and chairs, we don't deserve any of this, yet You have provided them in Your great love." Then I went piece by piece and thanked Him for every item in our apartment. Ever since that time I've tried to count my blessings and cultivate an attitude of thanksgiving. I want to be like the one who came back, don't you?

December 7

Assurance of Salvation

"The testimony is this, that God has given us eternal life, and this life is in His Son. He who has the Son has the life; he who does not have the Son does not have the life. These things I have written to you who believe in the name of the Son of God so that you may know that you have eternal life. 1John 5:11-13

Assurance of salvation begins with the sinner's prayer and the name of Jesus on our lips, and it grows as the nature of Jesus transforms our lives from the inside out. Salvation isn't in a prayer, an altar call, or in a baptismal tank; it's in a Person. "He who has the Son has the life." Jesus said, "I am the way and truth and the life; no one comes to the Father except by Me." (John 14:6)

God doesn't want us to live trying to be accepted by Him. We get to start the Christian life with assurance that salvation is not about our performance, but Jesus' perfect sacrifice on our behalf. We begin being accepted, forgiven, loved, and favored as God's very own children. (1John 3:1-3) To be in God's family and to take His name is a great privilege, and God's will for each of us.

But we must remain in Jesus to be saved. We can't reject the ongoing relationship and expect that an event in our past will save us; that's presumption and produces a false assurance. Jesus said it this way, "If anyone does not remain in Me they are cut off like a branch that withers and is thrown into the fire." (John 15:6)

Jesus is the Friend of sinners and He takes all that come to Him just as they are. (John 6:37) But we must receive Him just as He is, and He is both Savior and Lord. We can't take the benefits of forgiveness and reject the call to follow Him. Here's another way of saying it: We can't just add Jesus to our life and expect to be saved. Jesus must become our life, and following Him must be our primary identity.

December 8

Assurance of Answered Prayer

"Until now you have asked for nothing in My name; ask and you will receive, so that your joy may be made full." John 16:24

There is fullness of joy in partnering with God. To pray in Jesus name is to pray on behalf of His interests, kind of like the ambassador of a country. An ambassador transacts business for the country they represent with the full backing and authority of the place they were sent from. Jesus has sent us into the world (John 17:18), and He wants us to know that all of heaven is behind us as we seek to honor Him.

In the text above, Jesus tells us where assurance in prayer will come from: using His name. When we pray in our own name we base our confidence on how deserving, or undeserving we feel we are, and that's usually based on how we're feeling that day, or on how we have performed recently. This is a recipe for doubt. If I have to achieve a certain spiritual feeling, or live a life that "deserves" God's blessing, I will never have full assurance in prayer.

But if my access has nothing to do with me, but only about how good Jesus is and how complete His sacrifice was for me on the cross, then it becomes easy to believe. Peter said, "I do not possess silver and gold, but what I have I give to you, in Jesus name rise up and walk." (Acts 3:6)

God wants us to possess Jesus' name and our position in this world as His ambassadors. He wants every one of us to know the joy of partnering with Him every day. We're called to nothing less!

December 9

Assurance of Forgiveness

"If we confess our sins He is faithful and just to forgive us our sins and to cleanse us from all unrighteousness." 1John 1:9

When we come to Jesus in simple faith and trust Him for our salvation we become "righteous," or right with God. The gospel isn't about what I can do for God, but about what God did for me on the cross. "He who knew no sin (Jesus), became sin, in order that we (I) might become the righteousness of God in Him." (2Corinthians 5:21)

Yet as Christians we are still broken in many ways and that leads to unplanned sins. God's presence and power are in us and as we walk with Him He is gradually healing us, but it is a process and not an immediate result. Until we're completely healed (which actually won't be until heaven!), we're going to need many new beginnings. God knew this, so He promised to forgive us along the way.

His forgiveness is "just" in His eyes because Jesus already died for those sins. He doesn't arbitrarily forgive sins just because He loves us; He forgives us when we're in Christ because the full punishment for sin has already been paid. Because of Jesus, the only sin that can't be forgiven is the one we are unwilling to confess. (See John 9:41)

Be honest and be humble. Keep short accounts with God and know that He is gradually healing you on the inside, so you won't have to confess the same things over and over forever. As we're healed in one area, however, He will start shining His light on another. All we have to do is keep walking in the light (John 1:7) which is another way of saying we simply need to walk with God.

December 10

Assurance of Guidance

"Trust in the Lord with all your heart and do not lean on your own understanding. In all your ways acknowledge Him and He will make your paths straight." Proverbs 3:5-6

To be assured that God's leading me I must choose to do one thing and choose not to do something else. I must trust God with all my heart. There is no "plan B;" I must be "all in" with God. The most famous poker game today is called, "Texas Hold 'em." Anyone at any time can go "all in," which forces everyone else to decide if their present hand is worth risking the entire game on.

To be assured of God's guidance, we must be "all in" in every circumstance we face. Our lives are His to guide, so we acknowledge Him in all our ways, not just in our religious ways. He is central in our work, our fun, our marriages, our families, our friendships, our vacations, and in our service. Someone said guidance can be broken down this way: The "G" stands for God; the "u and i" stand for you and I, and the "dance" stands for dance. You and I are to live dancing with God and letting Him lead.

But to walk in assurance we must listen to the warning in the text above: "Do not lean on your own understanding." Some have misinterpreted faith by declaring that God doesn't want us to use our minds, but that's false. God gave us minds and wants us to love Him with all our minds. Faith does not contradict our minds but it will transcend them, because God is bigger than our minds can conceive. He calls us beyond what makes "sense" to us. Peter can't walk on water, but Jesus calls him out of the boat – will he trust God or his own common sense? David can't kill Goliath and shouldn't even face him without Saul's armor, but God is speaking something else – which voice is true?

Most people in America, even religious people, are leading their lives by common sense. Living in the "real world" has come to mean making decisions without the possibility of supernatural help. Yet to be assured of God's guidance, we should not be surprised if He calls us to step out beyond what is comfortable for us.

Dance with God. Don't tell Him where it's reasonable and comfortable for you to go – enjoy His leadership and follow!

December 11

The Call to Sexual Purity

"For I am jealous for you with the jealousy of God himself. I promised you as a pure bride to one husband-Christ. But I fear that somehow your pure and undivided devotion to Christ will be corrupted, just as Eve was deceived by the cunning ways of the serpent." 2Corinthians 11:2-3

Why has God given us sexual desire and attraction to the opposite sex and then commanded that we control that desire and attraction to save it only for our present or future spouse? To get to the why of sexual purity we have to go back to why God made sex in the first place. When we understand what it pictures we will more easily be able to accept and even delight in His call to sexual purity.

In the text above, Paul says we are called to be the bride of Christ and have only eyes for Him; pure and undivided in our devotion. In Ephesians 5:31-32 he says: "For this reason a man shall leave his father and mother and shall be joined to his wife, and the two shall become one flesh. This mystery is great; but I am speaking with reference to Christ and the church." So marriage was created to speak of this higher relationship with Christ and human beings.

The two become one not by intercourse but by this "leaving" all others, and this "joining" to only one another. The two becoming one flesh, sexual intercourse, consummates and celebrates that shared devotion to only one another. Why did God make sex fun? Why did he give us desires that are fulfilled in this act of passion? Because it represents the spiritual pleasure available to us in our union with Christ. There is fullness of joy in His presence. But our union to Him is not based on spiritual pleasure, but on His devotion to us and our singular devotion to Him. Spiritual pleasures make it easier to stay devoted to Him, and it strengthens our resolve. It makes our relationship more than a duty; He is our delight.

God created sex within marriage to sweeten our commitment to our spouse, so they wouldn't be our duty, but our delight. Our singular commitment to them pictures for all the world to see our commitment to Christ who left His Father's home, took on flesh, died and rose again, just so we could be His forever.

December 12

Having Godly Sex

"Rejoice in the wife of your youth. She is a loving deer, a graceful doe. Let her breasts satisfy you always. May you always be exhilarated by her love." Proverbs 5:18

As a young husband filled with sexual desire I felt like my sexuality was in opposition to my relationship with God. I often thought that if I was neutered I would be able to serve God better. Then one day I read Proverbs 5:18 and my thinking began to change. This passage is about exciting, passionate sex with no reference to having children. I worshipped Him that day. God is so good He even wants me to have an exhilarating sex life!

How do we have godly sex? First we have to wash our minds of all the ways the enemy has perverted sex and damaged the human race through its abuse. For many, "godly sex," is an oxymoron. "God may allow sex because He wants us to procreate, but He probably looks the other way when we're engaged in it because it's beneath Him." Wrong! God created sexuality and sex, just like He created taste buds. He wanted us to look forward to meals and have our hearts filled with thanksgiving at the pleasure of eating when we are hungry. He is the Author of pleasure.

God created sexuality and sex because He wanted there to be regular celebrations of the intimacy we have in marriage. Intimacy comes by the lifelong commitment of "leaving father and mother" to be joined to one another. It's not easy for two broken, sinful people to be committed for a lifetime to love one another, so God placed a hidden pleasure in the union. Godly sex strengthens the union and makes faithfulness more than our duty; He wants it to be our delight.

December 13

Wake Up!

"You have a reputation of being alive but you are dead. Wake up!... Go back to what you heard and believed at first; hold to it firmly. Repent and turn to Me again. If you don't wake up, I will come to you suddenly, as unexpected as a thief." Revelation 3:1-3

The Christian life is a long journey at night. God has ordained that we would have to choose Him in a world of moral darkness that is opposed to the gospel, so that those who choose Him in the dark will never reject Him in eternity when we see Him in the light. But we have to stay awake!

Presumption put the church at Sardis asleep. They had a reputation of being alive, probably gained by past experiences of life and reflected by a doctrine of life, yet in reality, they had become dead. Like the foolish virgins (See Matthew 25) they presumed that the oil they received at the beginning would be enough, so they didn't bother to keep their relationship with God fresh.

America is one of the most dangerous places in the world spiritually. I've had missionaries tell me that they are glad they don't live here because life is so easy and busy in America that they find it difficult to stay spiritually awake. On the mission field they sense their absolute dependence on God's protection and provision so it's easy to trust Him day by day, but here they find the urgency to seek Him is lacking.

The enemy seeks to put the church to sleep by the cares, worries, and pleasures of this life. (Mark 4:19) Do you have a strategy to stay awake? When I drive at night I make sure there is a passenger to help keep me from dozing off. I believe God has given the church to be that spiritual passenger for each of us. (Hebrews 10:24-25). There's something about gathering together and hearing the word of God that reminds us of who we are, who God is, and of what's truly important. Are you part of a group where someone regularly asks you if you're still awake?

December 14

Receiving God's Love

"For this reason I pray to the Father... that your roots will go down into God's love and keep you strong. And may you have the power to understand... how wide, how long, how high, and how deep His love is."
Ephesians 3:14; 17

A few years ago I had the privilege of doing a youth retreat in another city. During a session I called a young woman out and asked her name, then gave her this word: "When Samuel went to the house of Jesse to anoint one of his sons as king, Jesse had overlooked his son, David. David wasn't even invited to the feast. But God's eye was on David; God saw him and God wants you to know that He sees you." Later that night, after I preached, I invited any who wanted to drink of the Spirit to come up and receive prayer. This young woman came up and when I prayed the Holy Spirit touched her in a dramatic way as He was touching many others.

I didn't know what God was doing in her until the pastor of that church was driving me back to the airport on Monday morning. He told me that she had told her mom on the way to church (we were back from the retreat by then) that she had a new peace and felt different. Her mom shared this with the pastor because to her this was a miracle. She had sent her daughter on this retreat out of desperation.

This girl had grown up in a single parent home and had become wild and agitated all the time. There was nothing the mom who loved her could do to help. Others had tried to help, but it didn't seem to change anything. Yet God saw her. God spoke to her. God touched her and that changed everything.

Maybe you've been overlooked by people and have felt small and rejected. Please know God's loving eye is on you. Why not open up your heart again and ask Him to speak to you and touch you in a new way?

December 15

The Condition of Mercy

"I will have mercy on those I have mercy..." Romans 9:15

There is a tradition of theology that believes there is no condition human beings can meet to receive God's mercy. They believe that before time, God sovereignly chose those who He would have mercy on. These are the elect and believe in Jesus only because God chose them to believe in Jesus. Paul's argument in Romans 9 is key to this theology: "It does not depend on man who runs or wills, but on God who has mercy." (Romans 9:16)

Although I have many friends in this tradition, I disagree with their interpretation of the argument Paul is making in Romans 9. I believe Paul is using dynamite to blow up the present Jewish thinking before laying down God's provision for mercy.

The Jews are certain that God has to give mercy to those who are seeking to follow the law. Paul makes it clear that God doesn't have to give mercy to anyone. He is the Potter and we are the clay, and the clay doesn't have the right to question the Potter about what he's making. Even if God arbitrarily chooses to make some of us objects of His mercy, and others objects of His wrath, we would have no "right" to question Him. God decides who He has mercy on, not us.

So who does He choose? Paul comes to his point: "So the Gentiles who weren't seeking to be right with God, found Him. Why? Because of faith. While the Jews who were seeking to be right with God, didn't find Him. Why? Because they sought Him by works instead of by faith. They stumbled over the great rock in their path. God warned them of this in the Scriptures when He said, 'Behold, I place a stone in Zion that makes people stumble, a rock that makes them fall. But anyone who believes in Him will never be disgraced.'" (Romans 9:30-33)

God is not arbitrary! He sent Jesus to die for the world, and anyone who believes in Him will receive the mercy of God and eternal life. (John 3:16) Those who reject Him will stumble over the One who was sent for them. The whole argument Paul makes doesn't conclude until the end of chapter 11 where He gives God's heart one more time: "For God has imprisoned everyone in disobedience so He could have mercy on everyone." (Romans 11:32)

Jesus didn't just die for the elect; He died for everyone! If we meet His condition for mercy we can be assured that we are one of those He chooses.

December 16

Preparation

"And you, my son, will be called the prophet of the most High, because you will prepare the way for the Lord." Luke 1:76

There had been no prophet in Israel for 400 years. Maybe Zechariah was a picture of all Israel when he refused to believe the angel who said he had come to promise a child in response to his prayers. Maybe he was discouraged and had given up on those prayers from long ago when he and his wife were young?

We don't know, but we do know that the judgment for not believing was silence that lasted the whole nine months of Elizabeth's pregnancy. The text above records some of the first words he spoke when God loosened his tongue at his son's (John the Baptist) birth.

When the silence was broken, Luke tells us, "Awe fell upon the whole neighborhood, and the news of what had happened spread throughout the Judean hills. Everyone who heard about it reflected on these events and asked, 'What will this child turn out to be?'" (Luke 1:65-66)

God uses silence in our lives to produce a longing for Him. Are there prayers you have given up on? Don't interpret delay as God's absence or disinterest; He is planning something bigger that is not just for us, but also for those we influence. John the Baptist's birth was part of preparing hearts for Jesus. "God is doing something," was the feeling in the air. "We may not know what, but He is moving." God is wanting to prepare us in this time for something more than what man is doing or not doing.

Lift your eyes higher than politicians, higher than family, and higher than your own fears and failures. God is alive and He is wanting to pour out His Spirit in this hour if only we will ask and prepare for Him. (Luke 11:13)

Let's plan on having the best Christmas ever because we've asked God to break through the commercialism and cynicism of our day to reveal Jesus afresh to waiting hearts. "Let every heart prepare Him room."

December 17

Redemption!

"But when the set time had fully come, God sent His Son, born of a woman, born under the law, to redeem those under the law, that we might receive adoption to sonship." Galatians 4:4-5

To redeem something means to bring it back from its broken or ruined state by restoring it. After our sin, God could have started over, but He chose instead to redeem.

A few years ago we had our VW Passat fixed from a problem it had with overheating. The first time I drove it after the "fix" was to a place about an hour away where it promptly broke down. We had it towed from there to a local mechanic who told me the engine was destroyed, and said he wouldn't even work on it. We then had it towed back to our mechanic in Madison.

After running tests on it, our mechanic explained what had happened, and owned their mistake. He said that he learned in his analysis that there was a catch underneath this specific engine that collected waste, and at some point it had become too much. When the engine was idling it looked fine, so they thought the problem was solved, but when I drove it away the waste was carried back up into the engine and caused the irreparable damage.

It was a 2003 model, so the book value wasn't much. He said something like this to me: "I could give you a check for $2,000, and you could put that toward a different vehicle, or you could buy a new engine (at a much reduced cost) and I would put it in for free."

It would have been easy to take his check, but I still saw a lot of value in that old car. I chose redemption instead of starting over. So did God, and it wasn't cheap. At just the right time in history, Jesus was born so He could die on a cross and pay for our redemption. The Son became a Savior, so we could become the very children of God.

This is the "good news of great joy!"

December 18

Mary's Faith

"Blessed is she who believed that there would be a fulfillment of what had been spoken to her by the Lord." Luke 1:4

When Elizabeth gives this greeting to Mary I think she is contrasting Mary's faith in the word of the Lord, to her husband's unbelief. Before we look at the example of Mary's faith, I want to look at why sometimes it's hard to believe. Zacharias asked this question to the angel who appeared to him and said he and his wife were going to have a baby: "How will I know this for certain? For I am an old man and my wife is advanced in years." (Luke 1:18) This question led to this response from the angel: "You shall be unable to speak until the day when these things take place, because you did not believe my words, which will be fulfilled in their proper time." (Luke 1:20)

What was behind Zacharias' unbelief? I think he didn't want to become vulnerable again by believing, only to have his and his wife's hopes for a baby go unfulfilled. The great disappointment of their marriage was that they hadn't been able to have children. How many times had they prayed and believed God for a child? When they were young I bet their hopes were high and their anticipation was great. When it didn't happen right away I can imagine they had the local rabbi pray for them, as well as anyone else who was close to them, yet in all their longing and all their praying, there was still no child. Every time they heard a baby cry they were reminded that they couldn't have children. Every time someone else rejoiced over the news that they were pregnant, they were empty inside, even as they offered congratulations. It is easy when our prayers seem to go unanswered to assume they were not heard, and then in an act of self protection from disappointment, harden our hearts.

Let's look at Mary's faith. She was convinced of God's love and mercy toward her. (Luke 1:50) She believed that God's word was true and that it would be fulfilled even if she couldn't understand how God would do it. (Luke 1:34) She refused to believe that God only did things in the past, but was confident He was present, powerful, and active in her day, wanting to extend His mighty arm for the humble and to fill the desperate with good things from His generous heart. (Luke 1:51; 53) She also had a tender heart that was ready to believe whatever the Lord might speak to her.

Where are you at? Have you hardened your heart because life isn't working out the way you hoped? Maybe the Lord wants to do something wonderful for you and is waiting for you to soften your heart again.

December 19

Great Joy

"Do not be afraid; for behold, I bring you good news of great joy; which will be for all the people; for today in the city of David there has been born for you a Savior, who is Christ the Lord." Luke 2:10-11

The angel made a few things clear to the shepherds on that first Christmas evening. One was that the good news he was proclaiming would bring great joy when it was properly received. Two was that the good news was for everyone who would receive it, not just for the Jews, or for a select remnant, but for "all the people." Third, although the good news was comprehensive, it was also personal, because the Savior was born, "for you." They weren't going to the manger to witness something that was for someone else only, but to see the One born for them.

God doesn't really give joy away, He only shares it. "In His Presence is fullness of joy..." (Psalm 16:11) You only get joy when you get near God because the joy you feel is His. Jesus said, "These things I have spoken that My joy may be in you and that your joy may be full." (John 15:11) We share in His joy when we get close enough to Him to experience it. "The joy of the Lord is your strength..." (Nehemiah 8:10) Not "...joy is your strength", but God's joy is your strength. He doesn't give it away, He invites us into it.

These rabbinic shepherds in Bethlehem were watching over the lambs that would be used in the temple for sacrifice. The blood of these lambs would make it possible for God to be in covenant with sinful people, but it was an imperfect covenant because the sacrifices kept having to be made year after year. The good news announced that first Christmas was that another Lamb was born, a human One, who would take away the sins of the world. Great joy comes from recognizing God loves us, Jesus came for us, and died to bring us into the very presence of the joyful God.

Let's believe this Christmas, and let's get close, so that His joy overflows through us to a world that needs to see God's smile.

December 20

Different Genealogies

Matthew 1:16 "... and to Jacob was born Joseph the husband of Mary, by whom was born Jesus, who is called Christ." Matthew 1:6 "... and to David was born Solomon..."

Luke 3:23 "And when He began His ministry, Jesus Himself was about thirty years of age, being supposedly the son of Joseph, the son of Heli..." Luke 3:31 "... the son of Nathan, the son of David..."

Critics of the gospel accounts of Jesus birth have often pointed out the different genealogies given by Matthew and Luke. How do we reconcile two completely different lists that have nothing in common except for David and Joseph? The answer is quite simple if we look at the goals of the two authors.

Matthew is writing to Jews and wants to present Jesus to them as their king. He traces the lineage of Jesus from Abraham through David and then through David's son Solomon all the way to Joseph. Joseph was a direct descendant of the kings which means that Jesus Himself is in that line. Matthew tells Joseph's story – how the angel appeared to him when he was going to divorce Mary; how God spoke to him to flee Bethlehem after the visit of the Magi; and how God spoke to him again when they were in Egypt and it was time to return to Israel. It is only fitting that he gives the genealogy of Joseph which is what he does.

Luke is writing to Greeks and presenting Jesus as the Son of man – the ideal man. He traces the lineage of Jesus from Adam through David and then through David's son Nathan all the way to Joseph: "the son of Heli." Luke says Jesus is "supposedly the son of Joseph." Supposedly, yet he isn't really; he's only the son of Mary. Luke tells Mary's story – how the angel appeared to her and said she would carry the Savior; he tells of her trip to Elizabeth's and about her famous prayer; and then he tells of the visit of the angels at the birth and how Mary, "pondered these things in her heart." It is only fitting that Luke would give the genealogy of Mary who is also a descendant of David and that is what he does.

There is no word in Koine Greek for "son-in-law." If you were describing someone as a son-in-law you would just use the word "son" which is what Luke does here. Joseph's father was Jacob; his father-in-law, Mary's father, was Heli. In the Greek, Joseph could be described as being both the son of Jacob and the son of Heli with no contradiction.

December 21

The Shepherds

"And there were shepherds living out in the fields nearby, keeping watch over their flocks at night. And an angel of the Lord appeared to them, and the glory of the Lord shone around them, and they were terrified. But the angel said to them, 'Do not be afraid. I bring you good news of great joy that will be for all the people. Today in the town of David a Savior has been born to you: He is Christ the Lord.'" Luke 2:8-11

The good news of great joy was not only for "all the people," it was also to be incredibly personal, for the angel said: "a Savior has been born to you." What did this mean to these shepherds?

At that time all Israel was waiting for Messiah because the prophet Daniel had given a timetable of when Messiah should appear on the earth. There is little doubt that the words of the angel would bring to the minds of Jewish shepherds the prophecy Isaiah gave about the Messiah: "For to us a Child is born, to us a Son is given, and the government will be on His shoulders." (Isaiah 9:6) They possibly felt that the joy would be the Messiah defeating Rome, and Israel becoming the governmental head of the nations again.

Yet this Child was born for a different reason than setting up an earthly kingdom at that time, and the joy would be much more than having a good leader running the government.

The fields on the outskirts of Bethlehem were used to raise the lambs used for sacrifices in the temple. The shepherds' job was to watch over lambs whose sacrifice would cover over Israel's sins one year at a time. Little did they know that the angel was calling them to watch over the Lamb who would take away the sins of the whole world; and that all the lambs they had watched over until that time pointed to this One baby, who was Christ the Lord.

Before Messiah rules on this earth, He needed to be a Savior that would die for the sins of all the people, including these shepherds. The great joy would be in the forgiveness of their sins which would allow them to have a personal relationship with God.

I hope you have made Christmas personal by receiving Christ's forgiveness and by embracing a relationship with Him. God wants each of us to hear and believe the good news that brings great joy!

December 22

The Christmas Light

"The people (Galilee of the Gentiles) who walk in darkness will see a great light; those who live in a dark land, the light will shine on them...For a child will be born to us, a son will be given to us; And the government will rest on his shoulders; and his name will be called Wonderful Counselor, Mighty God, Eternal Father, Prince of Peace." Isaiah 9:2; 6

We didn't get the best looking Christmas tree one year. It wasn't exactly a Charlie Brown tree, but it was kind of unshapely and rough looking. Our solution was to put an extra string of lights on it to take attention away from the tree and put it on the lights. It worked! When we turned it on at night it rivaled any tree we ever had.

Our tree is like the human race – we need light. Our text refers to those in Galilee who will see a great light. What is the light? It turns out it will be a child, a son, who will be given to us. Oh, and by the way, this child will be called God in the flesh (Mighty God).

While Isaiah looks forward to the coming Messiah, John looks backward and sees something very similar. "In the beginning was the Word, and the Word was with God, and the Word was God... In Him was life (zoe) and the life (zoe) was the light of men... And the Word became flesh and dwelt among us. (John 1:1, 4; 14)

The Greek word for God's kind of life is zoe. The zoe in Jesus was the light of men. In John 5:26 He says, "Just as the Father has life (zoe) in Himself, even so He gave to the Son also to have life (zoe) in Himself." Then Jesus goes on to say something amazing in John 10:10, "I came that they (us) may have life (zoe)."

Jesus came to light us up. We don't look good or do much good when we're walking in darkness. It's time to forsake the darkness and turn on the great light that first appeared in Bethlehem over 2,000 years ago. It's time to receive the light (John 1:12) and then learn how to live looking up, so the light can draw others who are trapped in darkness.

"Arise, shine; for your light has come, and the glory of the Lord has risen upon you. For behold, darkness will cover the earth and deep darkness the peoples; but the Lord will rise upon you and His glory will appear upon you. Nations will come to your light, and kings to the brightness of your rising." (Isaiah 60:1-3)

December 23

The Gifts of the Magi

"Then they opened their treasures and presented Him with gifts of gold and of incense and of myrrh." Matthew 2:11

As we think about Christmas let us reflect on the gifts given by the magi which speak to the Gift given by the Father to the human race. "Thanks be to God for His indescribable gift." (2Corinthians 9:15)

1. Gold – The gift given to kings. The magi didn't come to worship one who would become king; they came to worship Him who was born king. This caste of wise men from the east were likely in the order of Daniel with access to his prophecies. Daniel gave the time Messiah would appear (see Daniel 9:24-27) and alluded to His Divine nature as well as His universal rule. "One like a son of man...was given power; all the peoples, nations and men of every language worshipped Him." (Daniel 7:13-14)

2. Incense – The gift offered by priests. In the Old Covenant kings were from the tribe of Judah and the family of David; high priests came from the tribe of Levi and the family of Aaron. But God's promised Messiah would be both king and priest as was an obscure person in the Old Testament named Melchizedek. (Genesis 14:18) David prophesied about this new order of priesthood that meant there would have to be a new covenant: "The Lord has sworn and will not change His mind, You are a priest forever according to the order of Melchizedek." (Psalm 110:4)

3. Myrrh – The spice used for burial. Messiah would not only be the priest to offer sacrifice; He Himself would be the sacrifice. "Behold the Lamb of God who takes away the sin of the world." (John 1:29) The shepherds who were called to witness the birth were rabbinic shepherds whose job it was to watch over the lambs that would be sacrificed in the temple. On Christmas, God called them to watch over the Lamb that would replace all other sacrifices. "Jesus sacrificed for our sins once for all when He offered Himself." (Hebrews 7:27) Let's remember the true wonder of Christmas is the One born for us.

December 24

Silent Night

"So Joseph also went up from the town of Nazareth in Galilee to Judea, to Bethlehem the town of David, because he belonged to the house and line of David. He went there to register with Mary, who was pledged to be married to him and was expecting a child. While they were there, the time came for the baby to be born, and she gave birth to her firstborn, a son. She wrapped him in cloths and placed him in a manger, because there was no guest room available for them." Luke 2:3-7

"How silently, how silently the wondrous gift is given…" An engaged couple is found to be pregnant in a religious community. If they try to explain, they receive the silence given to fanatics; if they don't explain, they'd be given the silent shaming of the immoral. As they come to Bethlehem, there is no family to greet them, in fact, there's not even room at the public inn. The Savior comes into the world unattended by a nurse or a midwife, yet in the silence of that night heaven speaks clearly: "Do not be afraid. I bring you good news of great joy that will be for all the people. Today in the town of David a Savior has been born for you; He is Christ the Lord." (Luke 2:11)

Maybe the key to experiencing an increase of joy on Christmas is to turn down all the noise around us and to reflect more on both our need, and God's provision of a Savior. "Silent night, holy night, Son of God, love's pure light; Radiant beams from Thy holy face, bring the dawn of redeeming grace; Jesus, Lord at Thy birth, Jesus, Lord at Thy birth."

December 25

Confidence In God's Provision

"Give, and you will receive. Your gift will return to you in full-pressed down, shaken together to make room for more, running over, and poured into your lap. The amount you give will determine the amount you get back." Luke 6:38

It was November of 2004 in Minnesota when I received the call no homeowner wants to get. It was from my wife.

"Tom, it's raining in the house."

"What does that even mean?" I asked.

"Here's what it means," she replied, "I'm in our bedroom watching water drip through the ceiling onto our bed."

I quickly grasped the problem as fear took hold of my heart. This was not a broken pipe – there were no pipes in our attic – this could only be a leak in our roof. It had been raining for days and apparently enough had leaked into the attic so that it was now coming through the ceiling of our bedroom!

We were a single income family living on a pastor's salary with one child in college and three other children still at home. There was no extra money, no "rainy day fund," though this was what we literally needed at the time.

We received a bid for a newly shingled house (that included removing the old shingles) from a roofing guy at our church for $5,800. Patching was not an option and the work had to be done quickly because winter was coming, so I needed to make a choice.

I had a talk with God. I reminded Him that we were His and that everything we had belonged to Him, and therefore it was His roof that was leaking. I reminded Him that I was a faithful tither and beyond, and that He had promised to open up heaven and pour out resources in my time of need. He said He would rebuke the devourer for my sake. (Malachi 3:10-11) I told Him that I was going to accept this bid unless He showed me a different way, and that His reputation was at stake if I couldn't pay the bill.

In my journal at the time I recorded six different sources of money that came unexpectedly into my hands in the two weeks that followed my prayer. The roof was fixed, the bill was paid, and God's reputation was intact!

December 26

The Point of Choice

"Today if you hear His voice do not harden your hearts." Hebrews 3:15

It was 4:00 a.m. and I was wide awake. We were in Houston, Texas for my son's wedding, and our hotel room was filled with family, so I quietly got up and slipped down to the dining area in the hotel's lobby.

Because of the hour, there was only one light on, so I got a cup of coffee and set up for my quiet time with the Lord in a place where I could read and write. A few minutes later the night manager, Lawrence, came over to talk. With very little prompting he told me he was trying for a new beginning. He was 35 and felt he had made some mistakes so he was buckling down – he was going back to school, working two jobs, and trying to make things right with his girlfriend.

"Lawrence, you'll never really get a new beginning without Jesus," I stated directly. This didn't put him off, in fact, he pulled out the chair across from me and sat down. Lawrence believed in the Bible. He just didn't know what it said or how to respond to God.

After I shared the plan of salvation, I asked him if he was ready to respond to God.

"I don't think I'm ready. I'd have to clean my life up first," was what he said.

"Do you wash up in the sink before taking a shower?" I asked him.

After thinking about this, he smiled and said, "No." The whole point of salvation is that we can't clean ourselves up, only our Savior can wash us, inside and out. But he still wasn't sure he was ready.

"Lawrence, God woke me up at 4:00 a.m. just to talk with you, and you want a new beginning. When will you be more ready than you are right now?"

He assured me that this was what he needed and asked me to write down the prayer he could pray to accept Christ. I prayed for him, shook his hand, and then the lights went on because the woman who prepares the breakfast had arrived.

I don't know if Lawrence went on to make a full response to Jesus but I know God was speaking to him. Whenever God speaks, we must make a decision – not making a decision is a "no" to God, and results in a hardening of our hearts.

When we respond quickly to God's promptings we don't only have the satisfaction of obeying Him, our hearts also become more tender to hear the next time He speaks.

December 27

Stepping Out in Faith

"Go and announce to them that the kingdom of God is near. Heal the sick, raise the dead, cure those with leprosy, and cast out demons. Give as freely as you have received." Matthew 10:7–8

I arrived a little late to my son's football game and couldn't figure out what was going on – the teams were on the field, the crowd was in the stands, but it was completely silent. The school superintendent was standing at the front gate, so I asked him what was going on.

"There was a helmet to helmet collision on the opening kickoff," he explained, "and the player from the visiting team hasn't moved since. We're waiting for the ambulance."

A thought came unbidden into my head: "Pray for him." I knew it wouldn't be obedience to pray for him while sitting safely in the stands. I was supposed to go out onto the field, put my hand on him, and pray for him there.

"But Lord, no one has asked me to pray," I complained. Silence.

I started walking toward the field because I didn't want to disobey. I walked down the sideline and felt I could still turn around without anyone noticing me, but then I came to the point where a decision had to be made. A group of adults, including referees and coaches, were surrounding a young man laid flat on his back in the middle of the field. I could either turn right and go out onto the field, or turn left and join the crowd in the bleachers.

I turned right. When I reached the group, I pretended like this was normal and I belonged there.

"I'm a pastor and I'm here to pray," I said in a calm voice trying to reassure them that this was okay.

No one replied one way or the other but just backed away. I got on my knees, put a hand on the young man, and prayed a short prayer for God's peace and healing to be released.

Just then the ambulance arrived so they put him on a stretcher, and we all followed back through the front gate to load him up. The visiting coach touched my arm on our way out. "Thank you for praying," was all he said. The young man was fine after being examined, but I never knew whether God healed him or whether he even needed healing. What do I know for sure? God wants to meet people at their point of need even if it's awkward for us!

December 28

Assurance of Victory

"No temptation (test) has overtaken you but such as is common to man, and God is faithful, who will not allow you to be tempted (tested) beyond what you are able but with the temptation (test) will provide the way of escape also, so that you will be able to endure it." 1Corinthians 10:13

You and I can win every day, but to do so, we must begin by agreeing with God's definition of what victory as a Christian looks like.

First what it doesn't look like. Winning does not mean having no troubles, struggles, or issues to deal with. Jesus said the wind and the waves will crash against every life (Matthew 7:24-27) and promised His disciples that they would have troubles in this world. (John 16:33) He even warned us ahead of time to not be offended by this. (John 16:1-2)

So what is victory, and how can I walk every day with assurance? Instead of delivering us from life's troubles, God promises to walk with us through them. The same Greek word, "peirasmos," is translated as temptation and test. Which is right? The same set of circumstances can easily be described as both a temptation and a test – Satan tempts to bring us down; God allows tests to purify and strengthen us. God won't always prevent a temptation, but in His faithfulness He will limit them, so that we can walk through our troubles with Him. Tests invite us to draw near, so we will know the way He has provided for our escape even though "escape" may mean strength to endure through instead of a deliverance from.

In school we need to pass tests to advance to the next grade and I think it's the same in the kingdom. God's beloved children don't get an identity of failure when they give into temptation but will just keep retaking the same test until we pass it. We decide how long the process lasts. (Three weeks could end up being 40 years!) He ultimately wants to build in each of us an assurance of victory that is able to say: "I can do all things through Christ who gives me strength." (Philippians 4:13)

December 29

Resting in God

"This is the message from the One who is holy and true... what He opens, no one can close; and what He closes, no one can open." Revelation 3:7

In the spring of 1987, I was excited about a potential transition. For six months I had the impression God was leading me out of the business world (I worked as an Investment Broker), into full time ministry.

You can imagine my excitement when a pastor from Illinois came to interview me. After our meeting, Pastor Braaten felt like this was God's plan for their church, but it wasn't automatic. I needed to come down and "candidate" for the position, he explained.

So we loaded up our young family and went down to Grand de tour, Illinois to spend a weekend at the church, and I preached for them that Sunday. I thought it went well, but Pastor Braaten called the next week, and informed me that I was going to have to return and preach a second time.

I had no idea how churches worked, so I didn't take this as rejection, but just part of the process. Before I preached the second time, Pastor Braaten brought me into his office. "Some of the people didn't like the way you walked back and forth last time. Could you stay behind the pulpit instead of wandering around?" he requested.

No problem. I thought it went well, but once again he called and said I would have to come down a third time to "candidate." Right before I preached the third time, he again pulled me into his office. "Last time you stayed behind the pulpit, but you played with the gooseneck microphone the whole time, and it drove some people crazy. Why don't you go ahead and walk around again."

After that message, the church officially asked me to be their youth pastor, and that was my entrance into full time ministry. Why did it take so long? I think God (and Pastor Braaten) wanted me at that church, and the church didn't want me, but they couldn't close the door no matter how hard they tried.

When we are resting in God, He is able to open doors no man can shut. We don't have to be impressive, we just need to trust in God. And by the way, I've been "wandering around" while preaching ever since!

December 30

Seeking His Face

"My heart has heard You say, 'seek My face.' Your face, oh God, will I seek." Psalm 27:8

A few years ago I went to India to train pastors, but the Sunday before we began, I was asked to preach in a church that met in an orphanage. Kids of all ages joined us and sat up front.

The message was about who God is, His face, verses what He can do for us, His hand. My point was that the higher calling is to seek His face, and that sometimes God calls us, right in the midst of our needs, to seek His face. This Psalm is written while David is being chased by Saul and has a whole army at the door. He desperately needed God's hand, but God spoke to his heart about seeking His face instead.

After I closed with a general prayer for those who wanted to say "yes" to God's invitation, the pastor came up and encouraged people to be prayed for individually. No one came for their needs but only for greater devotion to seek God's face.

At some point while I was praying for people, I told the pastor to invite those who needed healing to come forward. The first lady explained through an interpreter that she had horrible pain throughout her body. I prayed a brief prayer, and she turned around to leave. I called her back. "Tell us how you're feeling?" I asked. She said, "I'm healed; the pain is gone." I said, "Do you mean you're in less pain?" She insisted, "No, I am completely healed!"

It was then I noticed something; my hands were burning. I told the pastor to tell the people my hands were burning, and if they needed healing they should come right now. I prayed for all ages for the next hour, and everyone I prayed for felt the pain immediately leave their bodies. I prayed for the sick the rest of the time in India but never saw the power repeated that was present that Sunday morning.

I think God's heart was touched by the devotion of these orphans. If we would seek His face in the midst of our great needs, He wanted us to know, we would also have His generous hand!

December 31

Made in the USA
Monee, IL
29 June 2020

35269478R10213